Graphic User Interface Programming With C

Robert F. Ladymon

Wordware Publishing, Inc.

Library of Congress Cataloging-in-Publication Data

Ladymon, Robert F.
    Graphic user interface programming with C / by Robert F. Ladymon.
        p.   cm.
    Includes index.
    ISBN 1-55622-188-6
    1. C (Computer program language)   2. Computer graphics.   3. User
interfaces (Computer science)   I. Title.
    QA76.73.C15C32   1991   91-34643
    006.6'762—dc20   CIP

1506 Capital Avenue
Plano, Texas 75074

Printed in the United States of America

ISBN1-55622-188-6

10 9 8 7 6 5 4 3 2 1

9203

All inquiries for volume purchases of this book should be addressed to Wordware Publishing,
Inc., at the above address. Telephone inquiries may be made by calling:

(214) 423-0090

DEDICATION

To my wife Susan, whose love, confidence, and devotion has always been an inspiration to me.

To my daughter Shannon, whose bright eyes and inquisitive mind have a need to know.

ACKNOWLEDGMENTS

I would like to thank to Ralph Goins for his personal input and help in the writing of this book.

A special thanks to Emmett Beam and Russ Stultz for giving me the chance to write down and organize my ideas.

A would like to thank all of the people at AGS Information Services for all of the help and cooperation that they have given me throughout, particularly John Athens and George Hampton.

A personal thanks to James Larsen, Clay McReynolds, and Steve Cummingham for their friendship and our years of programming experience together.

Lastly, I would like to thank the people at the IBM development center at West Lake. Especially, Susan Hoffman, Jon Oelrich, Ron Hubbard, Karen Harrison, Anna Collins, Federico Astristian, and many others for the time we spent on the DisplayWrite project. It was fun working with you.

CONTENTS

CONTENTS (Cont.)

CONTENTS (Cont.)

CONTENTS (Cont.)

CONTENTS (Cont.)

CONTENTS (Cont.)

Chapter 1

INTRODUCTION

USER INTERFACE DESIGN

User interface design has always presented a problem to application programmers. The programmer usually concentrates on making things work instead of worrying about design details of the user interface. So the application, while it may work and be functionally correct, is often not easy to use. This was overlooked when only "computer people" used the programs. However, with the advent of the personal computer, user interface design and dialogue became of vital importance.

Any educated programmer can write a computer program that produces required outputs. But what are these outputs? Are they just calculations and data? What about usability and programming maintenance? The PC has forced programmers to address a whole new set of issues: processing speed, functionality, and usability are much more important today than ever before. The world of PCs now reaches millions of people concerned with the productive use of applications without the need or desire to become involved with the workings of the computer or software. Programmers can no longer concentrate on operating goals alone — they must worry about the user interface as much, if not more, than any other element in the design process.

THE USER INTERFACE DEFINED

What exactly is user interface design? To find the answer, start by finding out who the user is. For the purpose of this book, the *user* is both the person who actually uses the application program to perform a task and the programmer, himself. The programmer is included because he is the one who will have to develop, maintain, and update the application. Throughout this book, the word "user" refers to the person actually using the application program to perform a task. The word *programmer* refers to the person developing the task, although both may actually be users.

Next, the term *user interface* is the use of text, graphics, and sound to communicate information to the user. The interface usually encompasses the screen and keyboard, although the printer and disk drives may also be involved. So when the term user interface is used, think about how the application communicates information to the user and how the programmer programs the application to succinctly communicate that information. For example, a menu on the screen, from the user's point of view, only displays and retrieves information for the user. From the programmer's point of view, many choices have to be made:

- What kind of menu?
- Where should it appear?
- Should it use text, graphics, or both?
- Must it use the mouse?

These and many more questions must be answered.

Finally, the *design* is the overall structure of the application. It must provide for consistency between menus, ease of use, and achieve the program's operational goals. In other words, design is both the external and internal structure of the application. So, to answer the question "What is user interface design?" one might reply that it is the overall concept of application programming.

HARDWARE AND SOFTWARE REQUIREMENTS

This book is written for the application programmer. Its goal is to teach the design of a solid user interface that is menu driven and utilizes the graphics capabilities of the PC from scratch using 'C' and Assembler. Knowledge of both of these languages is assumed and a brief section on 'C' programming standards is outlined in Chapter 2.

To accomplish this task, you begin with a few basic tools:

- An IBM PC-compatible personal computer
- A 'C' compiler
- An object file linker
- A macro assembler
- A 'C' Run-Time Library Utility
- A Make-File Utility

The goal of user interface design is not limited to any one particular computer or group of computers. Its goal is to be as compatible across computer lines as possible. More importantly from a user's standpoint, they must appear to be the same. Although this book uses the PC as the hardware to run the application and the software is coded specifically for the PC, the user interface design of the application is not.

'C' is used as the primary language in this book. It is used to write all of the source code for the functions. Except for screen specific functions, such as display an icon on the screen, Assembler is used. The 'C' compiler is used to compile the 'C' source modules. The Macro Assembler is used to compile the Assembler source modules. The 'C' Run-Time Library Utility is used to link 'C' and Assembler object modules into library modules used by the application. The object file linker is used to link the library modules and the application object modules to make the application executable. The Make-File Utility is used to invoke the 'C' compiler, the Macro-Assembler, the Library Utility, and the object file linker to help the programmer compile and link his source code more efficiently.

This book shows you how to use these tools in a productive and efficient manner.

USER INTERFACE DESIGN PRINCIPLES AND STRUCTURE

This book teaches you how to implement a menu driven graphics user interface design based on the following design concepts:

From the user's point of view

- The application should develop and consistently reinforce the user's concept of how the application works.
- The application should allow the user to control the dialog.
- The application should be usable by novices and experts alike.

From the programmer's point of view

- The use of batch files, the Make-File Utility, and a directory structure to manage the application source files in an efficient and productive manner.
- The use of standard 'C' programming conventions (outlined later in the book) to increase readability and maintainability of the application.
- The use of Libraries to contain common functions that are needed by all applications to increase portability, productivity, and maintainability.
- The use of a Graphics Library to perform all of the screen specific functions needed by the application and menu sections.

- The use of a Menu Library to perform all of the menu specific functions defined and needed by the application.
- The use of a File Library to perform all the data file specific functions needed by the application.

THE APPLICATION

Before any real programming can be done, the programmer needs an application to program. For the purposes of this book I have chosen a Mail List Application. This application will be implemented following the above design principles for both the user and the programmer. From the user's point of view, a Primary Menu appears on the screen upon entry of the application. An Action Bar containing the primary options available to the user is displayed on the Primary Menu. From the Action Bar, the user can select an option that brings up a Pull-Down Menu for his required task. From the Pull-Down Menu, Dialog Boxes are accessed to process the task. From the programmer's point of view, the Application section, the Graphics section, and the Menu section must have already been written even to display this simple menu on the screen.

BUILDING LIBRARIES

The programmer's task is large; it encompasses a wide spectrum of individual problems. How does one go about displaying and accepting information? To do this, begin by building a set of tools called Libraries. The Libraries serve the application programmer like a toolbox. Just as a toolbox with all of the required tools is needed to fix things around the house, you need an application toolbox that can do the things that are common to all applications. For example, every application must be able to display a character on the screen at a given location. This type of function is included in the CGA Graphics Library.

We will build three Libraries to be used by the application: the CGA Graphics Library, the Menu Library, and the Filer Library. These Libraries will be linked in with the application modules to perform the task that every application needs.

CGA Graphics Library

The CGA Graphics Library contains all of the functions needed to display and retrieve information from the screen. It contains such routines as set CRT Mode, display a character to the screen, clear windows, read windows, and line drawing functions. This library is used extensively by the Menu Library to display its menus. This library contains the only assembler functions found in the application because the only time that we need assembler is when processing speed is more important than the readability of the code. An example of where Assembler is used is when a window of screen data needs to be saved or displayed.

Menu Library

The Menu Library contains all the functions needed by the application to display and process the Primary Menu, Action Bar, Dialog Boxes, and Message Boxes. The Menu Library relies heavily on the functions supplied by the CGA Graphics Library to display its menus. The menu definitions are supplied by the application and in this way the programmer can use the Menu Library to display and process the menus specific for that application without having to write new menu drivers for each application.

Filer Library

The Filer library contains all the functions needed by the application to create, update, and maintain the data files used by the application. This library is the most application dependent library because each application has different needs.

SUMMARY

In summary, this book teaches the programmer how to implement an application using a menu driven User Interface Design. The programmer should always keep in mind that the end result of any application is not only to provide the user with a means to manipulate his data but to do it in a consistent and easy-to-learn manner. Also, he must write his application in a manner which helps facilitate the user's goals and at the same time allows the programmer to easily update and change his applications.

Chapter 2
'C' PROGRAMMING STYLE AND STANDARDS

INTRODUCTION

One of the major problems with programming is the readability of code. Code readability does not limit itself to just the difficulty of the application, but also in the coding standards that are used to implement the code. In my experience with several large application projects, I have found that everybody seems to have their own way of doing things. With large applications there are different levels of programming experience between programmers.

This difference in skill leads to differences in the quality of code generated. Coding quality is not only the speed or accuracy of the code, but also the readability, adaptability, and maintainability of the code.

This chapter deals with the application programming standards I apply in this book. Application programming standards encompass the following:

- The use of batch files, the Make-File Utility, and directory structures to increase programming productivity
- The use of Libraries to contain common routines
- The use of 'C' programming standards defined in this book

BATCH FILES, MAKE-FILE UTILITY, DIRECTORY STRUCTURES

Application programming speed does not only pertain to how fast the application runs on the computer, but also how fast the programmer can program it, i.e., programming productivity. This book teaches the programmer how to increase his programming productivity on the PC by the use of batch files. The batch files manage the source, object, and Library files used to make the application.

The batch files are used in conjunction with the Make-File Utility. The Make-File Utility uses the MAKEFILE source file to determine which source modules to recompile and which Libraries to rebuild. The batch files also copy any files that need to be copied.

Before the batch files can run effectively, a directory structure must be created on the disk. From the root directory create the following subdirectories.

Type **CD ** and press **Return**.

Type **MD MAILLIST** and press **Return**.

Type **MD GRAPHICS** and press **Return**.

Type **MD MENU** and press **Return**.

Type **MD FILER** and press **Return**.

These subdirectories contain the source code to the Libraries used by the application. By separating the source code into Libraries, the programmer gains more control over the maintenance of his application. The GRAPHICS subdirectory will contain the source to the Graphics Library, the MENU subdirectory will contain the source to the Menu Library, and the FILE subdirectory will contain the source to the File Library. The source to the Maillist application, i.e., that code pertaining only to the application itself, will be kept in the MAILLIST subdirectory. These Libraries are only a few of the different types of Libraries that might be needed for an application. For example, you might wish to have telecommunications abilities; therefore, you could create a new subdirectory to contain the source for telecommunications.

The use of batch files, the Make-File Utility, and a directory structure to manage the building of the application executable increases programming productivity by taking the burden of responsibility off of the programmer to remember the changes since the last time the executable was built. Many times I have worked on a piece of code only to leave it and go on to something else. When I came back I didn't always remember which source files I had modified since the last time the executable was built. But by using the batch files, I don't have to remember, because they will perform the process for me. Each directory will contain its own set of batch files and will be explained later in the book in each section.

LIBRARIES

As mentioned earlier, the source code of the application needs to be broken down into its individual primary parts called Libraries. The Libraries serve as a toolbox for the application. The application must have several functions available to it for it to be able to run. For example, every application must be able to display information to the user on the screen. But how the application does this depends on the needs of the application.

This book teaches the application programmer how to create a graphical menu driven user-interface design on the PC in four-color graphics (CGA). These Libraries are designed specifically for the PC in four-color graphics mode. But, because they are broken down into separate Libraries, the programmer is able to make new Libraries and link them into the application. For example, consider the use of a Text Library versus the use of the CGA Graphics Library.

The use of Libraries increases the programmer's productivity in the following manner:

- It gives the programmer the ability to use already proven code to perform the basic functions of the application. This ability allows him more time to create new applications more quickly, with less errors, and to have a commonality across all of his applications.

- It gives the programmer the ability to modify the existing functions and to add new functions to the Libraries. All applications that use those Libraries can be relinked and they all contain the changes made. For example, if a bug is found in the CGA Graphics Library and you have seven different applications that use that Library, you only need to change the source in the CGA Graphics Library and relink the applications. This cuts down on the number of errors that could be made modifying each application separately.

- It gives the programmer the ability to replace the Library with a different one without losing the overall structure of the application. For example, you want to upgrade your application to use an EGA Graphics Library, instead of the CGA Graphics Library. Since all of the functions needed for Graphics display are kept in one Library, you need only to change the Library, instead of searching the source code of the application for all of the places that need to be changed.

'C' PROGRAMMING STANDARDS

The unique thing about programming in 'C' is that there are so many different ways things can be done, especially concerning how the code looks on the printed page. It is very important, for readability sake, to use proper levels of indentation and naming conventions. Therefore, I have come up with a list of 'C' programming standard rules. If the programmers always follow these rules, then the readability and maintenance of their code will be much easier.

One of the major problems the industry is facing today is that the application products being produced require so many programmers. With this many programmers, turnover is inevitable, and this is a major problem. Whenever one programmer leaves and another must take his place, the time needed for the new programmer to learn the new code depends on how well that code is written and documented.

The documentation of the code should help the programmer to understand the logic of the function itself. The writing of the code should be consistent in how it looks and reads. The following guidelines are applied throughout this book in regards to how to write clear and readable code in 'C.'

NAMING CONVENTIONS

FUNCTIONS   Function names should always start with a capital letter and should never contain hyphens or underlines. The use of the hyphen in 'C' generates a compile error because the 'C' compiler does not recognize this as being different from a minus sign. The use of underlines, while completely acceptable by 'C,' should not be used for function names. The reason is if function names start only with capital letters and never contain underlines, then the programmer can tell at a glance which words are variables and which ones are functions. Also, the "(" should always be one space after the last character of the function name. This is to aid in readability and in searching for text.

For example:

Correct

```
SampleFunction ();
Sample ();
```

Incorrect

```
sample_function();
Sample_Function ();
sample();
```

VARIABLES   Variable names fall into three basic categories: global and static variables, local variables, and defined data.

Global variables are variables that are used by more than one source file. *Static variables* are variables that are used in one source file, but are used by different functions in the source file. These types of variables always start with a capital letter and always contain an underline. With this naming convention the programmer can tell which variables are used by more than one function.

For example:

Correct

```
Global_Variable;
```

Incorrect

```
globalvariable;
global_variable;
globalVariable;
GlobalVariable;
```

Using global variables should be kept at a minimum, and all of the global variables should be defined in the application source module containing the 'C' required function, main ( ). 'C' is designed to pass information back and forth between functions on the stack. Global variables use real memory, local variables do not. Only data that really needs to be used by functions throughout the application should be defined as global. The reason for placing all of the original definitions for global data in the 'C' source file that contains the required 'C' function, main ( ), is that the programmer can always find this data definition by looking in only one file. This restriction can be modified by creating a source file that is dedicated to contain all of these data definitions.

Local variables are variables defined inside of specific functions or variables that are passed between functions. These variables *never* start with a capital letter and may or may not contain underlines.

For example:
Correct

```
local_variable;
variable;
```

Incorrect

```
Local_Variable;
Variable;
LocalVariable;
```

Defined data is defined to be a certain constant. It will always have this value and it cannot be reassigned a value at run-time. These variables are always in *all* capital letters and may or may not contain underlines.

For example:
Correct

```
DATA_DEFINED;
DATA;
```

Incorrect

```
data_defined;
Data_Defined;
DataDefined;
```

The use of these naming conventions increase the readability and maintenance of the source code. The programmer no longer has to guess the use of certain variables, and the new programmer has an easier time understanding the logic flow and data structure of the application.

One last thing about naming conventions: functions and variables should be named as descriptively as possible. When the microcomputers were first developed, the languages that were available to the programmer did not give the programmer very many characters with which to name the functions or variables in the application source code. This usually led to very cryptic names such as INVTCNTL, for inventory control. When you only had eight characters to work with, it became very difficult, especially on large applications, to come up with unique and descriptive names.

Most of the compilers of today are designed to allow programmers to name the functions and variables with as many characters as they need. This ability should be made use of, as demonstrated throughout this book.

Levels of Indentation, Braces, and Spaces

Problems with writing application programs in 'C' include the levels of indentation, the use of braces, and the use of spaces to separate different parts of code. *Levels of indentation* are designed to give the 'C' code more readability. *Braces* are designed to separate different groups of logic from other groups. *Spaces* separate different 'C' statements, functions, and variables.

In this book, I am using the standards that I have developed for my own applications. These standards have been acquired through my work on large applications that I helped develop for Tandy, Xerox, Siemens, and IBM. 'C' is a great language to develop any application, large or small, and in almost any operating environment. But there are so many different ways of writing code that do the same thing.

One of the major reasons for the development of the 'C' language was to give programmers the ability to write code from a very low level and to interface with assembly code easily. One might call it an Assembly language programmer's language, because there are very few real 'C' statements; the programmer creates most of the functions that are called in the code.

Because 'C' was originally written for experienced programmers, it lets you do about anything you might want to do. This is great for people who know exactly what they are doing. Unfortunately for inexperienced programmers, 'C' will let you shoot your own foot off it you tell it to. It is up to the programmer to maintain memory integrity. If you tell 'C' to write or read from a particular memory address, it will do its best to try.

This is because the 'C' source code is compiled into an object file that is just like an object file created in assembler. In essence it is assembler code. 'C' code is converted to assembler code, which is then compiled into an object file. Assembler and 'C' object files can be linked together to form one library or executable.

As stated before, 'C' lets you do about anything you might want to accomplish with an application. Its code is free form. The use of levels of indentation, braces, and spaces make little difference to the compiler when it comes to the way the code appears on the screen to the programmer or on a listing.

The 'C' compiler does not care what you name your functions or variables. The standards set for the naming conventions are for the programmer's sake. The same thing holds true for the levels of indentation, braces, or spaces. You don't have to put your braces on different lines or keep a constant level of indentation to make the compiler compile your code correctly. This is done so you or someone else will be able to read your code more easily.

The following pieces of code contain the basic elements of how to write more readable 'C' code.

Correct:

```
1. if (local_variable == something)
2.    {
3.    CallAFunction (another_variable);
4.     if (AnotherFunction (somethingelse) != answer) DoFunction2 ();
5.     else
6.     {
7.        if (Global_Variable == DEFINED_DATA &&
8.            local_variable != different_answer)
9.        {
10.          CallAnotherFunction ();
11.          answer += local_variable;
12.        }
13.        else answer += somethingelse;
14.    }
15. }
```

Incorrect:

```
1. if ( local_variable==something ) {
2. Call_A_Function(Another_variable) ;
3.     if ( Another_Function (SomethingElse) !=answer ){
4.        DoFunction2 (); }
```

```
5.   else { if (Global_Variable == DEFINED_DATA && local_variable
6.    != different_answer) {  CallAnotherFunction ();
7.          answer += local_variable;
8.    }
9.       else
10.       {
11.       answer += somethingelse; } }
```

What is wrong with the second example? To the 'C' Compiler, nothing. But the style leaves something to be desired because it does not give the reader an understanding of the logic flow that can be developed in 'C.' I know that this last statement is a matter of opinion, and many qualified people could argue the fine points of my following arguments. My opinion is based on what I have encountered in programming large applications for several major corporations and the programming that I have done for myself.

Let's compare the two pieces of code. Each piece of code will compile to be exactly the same. They will run no faster, take up no more memory, nor act any differently once they have been compiled into their respective object files. So, then what's the big deal? The readability of course. The first example is simply more readable. It follows the standards that I have developed for the writing of the 'C' code in this book.

- The use of standard naming conventions for functions and data types.
- The standard use of levels of indentation. Each new level of logic in the code should be indented 3 spaces.
- The standard use of braces '{ }' is that they should be placed on lines to themselves, directly aligned with the level of indentation they represent.
- The standard use of spaces to separate 'C' statements, functions, and variables.

Now, let's apply these standards to the two pieces of code, starting with statement one.

Correct:

```
1. if (local_variable == something)
2. {
```

Incorrect:

```
1. if ( local_variable==something ) {
```

Both statements say the same thing but the readability is different. There should not be a space separating the variable, local_variable from the '('. There should be spaces separating the '==' from the two variables, local_variable and something.

There should not be a space between the variable, something, and the ').' Also, the '{' should be placed on another line.

Correct:

```
3.   CallAFunction (another_variable);
```

Incorrect:

```
2. Call_A_Function(Another_variable) ;
```

Function names should not contain underlines. A space should separate the '(' from the function name. The ';' should not be separated from the ')' by a space. The incorrect statement does not maintain a proper level of indentation. This type of coding practice, combined with the practice of putting braces at the end of lines, greatly reduces the readability of the 'C' code.

One other problem with the incorrect statement is that the variable, Another_variable, is an incorrect data type. The reader has no idea of what kind of variable this is. The correct statement uses the proper naming standard of naming local variables, that is, in all lowercase letters. The incorrect statement mixes the uppercase and lowercase letters. The reader cannot tell what kind of variable, global or local, the variable really is. By using consistent naming standards, the reader of the code can always tell what kind of data type the variable is.

Correct:

```
4.      if (AnotherFunction (somethingelse) != answer) DoFunction2 ();
```

Incorrect:

```
3.      if ( Another_Function (SomethingElse) !=answer ){
4.         DoFunction2 (); }
```

The problem with the incorrect version is levels of indentation. The function, DoFunction2 ( ), is not aligned with 3 spaces for each level of indentation, and braces are used to separate it. The open brace, "{," and the close brace, "}," should not have been used in these statements. Braces should not be used when there is only ONE statement that is associated with it, such as an 'if' statement. Braces MUST be used to group more than one statement together.

Open braces, "{," should not be placed at the end of a line. They should be placed on lines by themselves, directly under the statement that causes the brace. Close braces, "}," should also be placed on a line by themselves, in the same column as the open brace. In this way the person reading the code can easily scan the code for groups of logic.

Finally, the programmer should try to use one line of code if possible when only one statement is associated with it, such as the function, DoFunction2 ( ), in the correct version.

Correct:

```
 5.    else
 6.    {
 7.        if (Global_Variable == DEFINED_DATA &&
 8.            local_variable != different_answer)
 9.        {
10.          CallAnotherFunction ();
11.          answer += local_variable;
12.        }
```

Incorrect:

```
 5.  else { if (Global_Variable == DEFINED_DATA && local_variable
 6.    != different_answer) {  CallAnotherFunction ();
 7.          answer += local_variable;
 8.    }
```

Again levels of indentation, spaces, and braces are the problems with the incorrect version. The correct version is simply more readable from the programmer's point of view. The 'C' compiler could care less.

The important point about these statements is the breaking up of the "if" statement in the correct version. The two comparisons made are separated on to two lines. Whenever the programmer must break a statement across lines, these statements should be aligned according to the elements in the compare.

Correct:

```
13.        else answer += somethingelse;
14.    }
15. }
```

Incorrect:

```
 9.        else
10.        {
11.        answer += somethingelse; } }
```

These statements conclude both versions of the 'C' code. The problem with this code is the use of extra braces and lines. The "else" statement in the correct version has only one statement associated with it so it is contained on the same line.

SUMMARY

This chapter has dealt with the 'C' programming standards used in this book. These standards are designed to help the programmer write more maintainable code. These standards include function and variable naming, levels of indentation, braces, and spaces used in the writing of 'C' code.

Chapter 3

THE CGA GRAPHICS LIBRARY

INTRODUCTION

The CGA Graphics Library is designed to perform all of the necessary screen Input /Output functions for the application. It uses both the DOS BIOS interface service calls and the Direct Video Access (DVA) method to process these functions. The CGA Graphics Library is written in 'C' and Assembler. Assembler is used to write the functions that actually put data to the screen or read data from the screen, because processing speed is of vital importance when trying to manipulate screen data. 'C' is used to write the functions that do not require the processing speed of Assembler or functions that need to be written in 'C' so that they can be more easily understood by the programmer.

The CGA Graphics Library needs to contain all of the graphic display functions used by the application and Menu Libraries. To start creating the CGA Graphics Library, decisions must be made about which functions need to be placed into the Library. The following list of functions are the CGA Graphics Library functions that are written in 'C.' These functions are kept in the CGAGRAFC.C source file in the GRAPHICS subdirectory.

- GetCrtMode ( ) - This function returns the current screen CRT mode in use at that time. This function is called by the application program when the program is initialized so that the original screen CRT mode can be restored when the program is terminated.

- SelectDisplayPage ( ) - This function activates the requested video display page. This function is called by the application program, when the program is initialized, to activate the video display page being used by the application.

- SetCrtMode ( ) - This function sets the screen CRT mode to one that is requested. This function is called by the application program, when the program is initialized and when the program is terminated, to select the CRT mode used by the application.

- DrawBox ( ) - This function draws a box on the screen starting at the given upper left-hand row and column coordinates, for the given box width and box height, and in the given box color. This function is called whenever a box outline is needed on the screen, such as the outlining of a menu.

- VLine ( ) - This function draws a vertical line on the screen at the given starting row and column coordinates, for the given line length, and in the given line color. This function can be used to separate items on a menu.

- HLine ( ) - This function draws a horizontal line on the screen at the given starting row and column coordinates, for the given line length, and in the given line color. This function can be used to separate items on a menu.

- DisplayDot ( ) - This function displays a dot on the screen at the given row and column coordinates and in the given color. This function is called to display a specific dot on the screen, such as the individual dots in a line.

- DisplayChar ( ) - This function displays the given character on the screen starting at the given upper left-hand row and column coordinates in the given foreground and background colors. This function is called whenever one particular character needs to be displayed on the screen.

- DisplayString ( ) - This function displays a given string of characters, that are terminated with a NULL, on the screen starting at the given upper left-hand row and column coordinates in the given foreground and background colors. This function is called whenever a NULL terminated string needs to be displayed on the screen by the application.

- DisplayStrNum ( ) - This function displays a given string of characters on the screen starting at the given upper left-hand row and column coordinates in the given foreground and background colors, and the given number of characters to display from the string onto the screen. This function is called whenever a string of characters need to be displayed on the screen that are not NULL terminated.

- GetFontNum ( ) - This function returns the font set number to use when displaying a character or string of characters on the screen in the given foreground and background colors. This function is used by the CGA Graphics Library to determine which font set to use to display the given character or string of characters.

- MapFontChar ( ) - This function returns the font set character number associated with the character passed. This function is used by the CGA Graphics Library to determine which font icon represents the given character.

- DisplayCursor ( ) - This function displays an underline under the character passed on the screen starting at the given upper left-hand row and column coordinates in the given foreground and background colors. This function is called whenever the application needs to simulate a cursor on the screen at a given location.

The following functions are written in Assembler and are kept in the CGAGRAFA.ASM source file in the GRAPHICS subdirectory.

- ClearScreen ( ) - This function clears the entire screen in the given color. This function is called when the program is initialized.

- ClearWindow ( ) - This function clears a window on the screen starting at the given upper left-hand row and column coordinates, for the given window width and window height, and in the given window color. This function is called to clear a window on the screen in a particular color, such as when a menu is initialized on the screen.

- DisplayIcon ( ) - This function displays the given icon on the screen starting at the given upper left-hand row and column coordinates, for the given icon width and icon height. This function is called to display an icon on the screen, such as the character 'a.'

- DisplayToBuffer ( ) - This function reads a window of screen data starting at the given upper left-hand row and column coordinates, for the given window width and window height into the given buffer. This function is called to save a window of screen data to be put back to the screen later. An example of this is when a menu is displayed on the screen and the application needs to save what was already on the screen so that it can restore the data when the user is finished with the menu.

- BufferToDisplay ( ) - This function displays the given buffer of screen data to the screen, starting at the given upper left-hand row and column coordinates, for the given window width and window height. This function is called to restore a window of screen data saved by the DisplayToBuffer ( ) function.

- ScrollWindow ( ) - This function scrolls a window of screen data up, down, left, or right, starting at the given source row and column coordinates, and moves it to the given destination row and column coordinates, for the given window width and window height. This function is called whenever a window on the screen needs to be scrolled. An example of this is a list of items that is too long to display at one time on the screen. The list is scrolled up, down, left, or right, depending on the needs of the application.

- ScrollVertical ( ) - This function scrolls a window of screen data up or down, given the source and destination upper left-hand row and column coordinates, for the given window width and window height. This function is called by the CGA Graphics Library whenever a window of screen data needs to be scrolled on the screen either up or down.

- ScrollLeft ( ) - This function scrolls a window of screen data to the left, given the source and destination row and column coordinates, for the given window width and window height. This function is called by the CGA Graphics Library whenever a window of screen data needs to be scrolled to the left.

- ScrollRight ( ) - This function scrolls a window of screen data to the right, given the source and destination row and column coordinates, for the given window width and window height. This function is called by the CGA Graphics Library whenever a window of screen data needs to be scrolled to the right.

CREATING THE CGA GRAPHICS LIBRARY FILES

The above 'C' and Assembler functions are the minimum set of functions needed to be performed by the CGA Graphics Library and are intended to give the programmer enough tools to be able to accomplish his task using four-color graphics. But knowing what we are trying to do and implementing it are two entirely different things.

To begin programming these functions, a batch file is needed to manage the compiling and linking of the CGA Graphics Library. As described in the section on Programming Style and Standards, this batch file is necessary to increase the productivity of the programmer because it makes sure that all new code is included into the CGA Graphics Library whenever a change is made to the CGA Graphics Library code.

Creating the Batch File — BUILD.BAT

First change directories to the CGA Graphics Library directory that was created in the 'C' Programming Style and Standards section. At the DOS command prompt:

Type **CD \GRAPHICS** and press **Return**.

This changes your current directory to the CGA Graphics Library directory. All of the files dealing with the CGA Graphics Library will be stored here for easy accessibility to the programmer. It is important for the programmer to always keep the source for each Library together, because not only can the programmer find the source file he needs much more easily, but any new programmer to the code can also find it.

Using the editor of your choice, create a file called BUILD.BAT. It is used as the main manager of the CGA Graphics Library and allows the programmer to type one statement to recompile and link the CGA Graphics Library. Edit BUILD.BAT, type the following statements, and save the file.

> **copy CGAGRAPH.LIB CGAGRAPH.BAK**
> **del CGAGRAPH.LIB**
> **make MAKEFILE.CGA**

Now when the programmer wishes to recompile and link the CGA Graphics Library, he needs only to do the following at the DOS command prompt:

> Type **BUILD** and press **Return**.

Typing this statement at this time will generate errors because the other files associated with the batch file are not there. Basically the BUILD.BAT file does the following things:

- It copies the current CGA Graphics Library CGAGRAPH.LIB into a backup file called CGAGRAPH.BAK.
- It deletes the CGAGRAPH.LIB file from the GRAPHICS subdirectory.
- It executes the Make-File Utility using the file MAKEFILE.CGA.

Creating the Make-File Utility File — MAKEFILE.CGA

The Make-File Utility uses a file called a makefile to make its decisions on what processes to perform to create the new CGA Graphics Library — CGAGRAPH.LIB. The CGA Graphics Library uses the file MAKEFILE.CGA to contain the information passed to the Make-File Utility. Create the MAKEFILE.CGA file, type the following statements, and save the file.

> **CGAGRAFC.OBJ: CGAGRAFC.C GRAPHICS.H COLORS.H FONTSET.H**
> **msc CGAGRAFC;**
> **CGAGRAFA.OBJ: CGAGRAFA.ASM**
> **masm CGAGRAFA;**
> **CGAGRAPH.LIB: CGAGRAFA.OBJ CGAGRAFA.OBJ**
> **lib @CGAGRAPH.LNK**

MAKEFILE.CGA contains a list of all the files that the Make-File Utility will use to create the CGA Graphics Library. The statements:

> **CGAGRAFC.OBJ: CGAGRAFC.C GRAPHICS.H COLORS.H FONTSET.H**
> **msc CGAGRAFC;**

tell the Make-File Utility to check the time and date of the CGAGRAFC.OBJ file, which is the compiled object file for the CGAGRAFC.C source file, against the time and date of the following files, CGAGRAFC.C, GRAPHICS.H, COLORS.H, and FONTSET.H. If the time and date of the CGAGRAFC.OBJ file is earlier than that of any of the other files, then the statement

msc CGAGRAFC;

is executed, which recompiles the CGAGRAFC.C source file and creates a new CGAGRAFC.OBJ file. By using the Make-File Utility in this way, the programmer can recompile only the source files that need to be recompiled, thereby avoiding recompiling source files that have not been modified.

The statements:

CGAGRAFA.OBJ: CGAGRAFA.ASM
   masm CGAGRAFA;

work in a similar way except that they deal with the Assembler source file CGAGRAFA.ASM and execute the MASM compiler instead of the 'C' compiler.

The statements:

CGAGRAPH.LIB: CGAGRAFA.OBJ CGAGRAFA.OBJ
   lib @CGAGRAPH.LNK

also work in a similar way, except that these statements deal with the creation of CGA Graphics Library file CGAGRAPH.LIB. If either one of the source files has been recompiled, then the 'C' Run-Time Library Utility is executed with the file CGAGRAPH.LNK to create the CGAGRAPH.LIB file.

Creating the Linker File — CGAGRAPH.LNK

The Make-File Utility compares the time and date stamps on files to make its decision on which source files to compile. Whenever new source files are compiled, the new object files generated need to be linked into the new Library file. The 'C' Run-Time Library Utility is executed whenever the Make-File Utility has decided that a new CGA Graphics Library needs to be made.

The file CGAGRAPH.LNK is used to contain all of the information needed by the 'C' Run-Time Library Utility to create the CGA Graphics Library, CGAGRAPH.LIB. This Library is used by the application and is linked, along with other libraries and object files, to create the application executable file. Create the CGAGRAPH.LNK file, type the following statements, and save the file.

```
CGAGRAPH
Y      +CGAGRAFC+CGAGRAFA
CGAGRAPH.MAP
```

The CGAGRAPH.LNK file contains the 'C' Run-Time Library Utility directives. It tells the Library Utility to create a Library called CGAGRAPH.LIB and to use the CGAGRAFC.OBJ and CGAGRAFA.OBJ files to create the library. Also it generates a mapping of the Library containing the functions in the Library called CGAGRAPH.MAP. After the Library Utility is finished, a new CGAGRAPH.LIB file is created.

SUMMARY

In summary, the CGA Graphics Library CGAGRAPH.LIB is built to perform all the graphics functions associated with the four-color graphics adapter on the PC. While these functions are going to be programmed specifically for the PC, this does not mean that other computers do not need the same type of functions. Any application that displays data to the screen needs these types of functions.

The CGA Graphics Library and other Libraries are linked with the application object modules to create the executable. The use of batch files and makefiles and the separation of the graphic functions from the rest of the application gives the programmer an incredible amount of programming flexibility and other benefits, such as the following:

- The building of the CGA Graphics Library becomes a simple process for the programmer; he needs only to type in one command, "BUILD," and the CGAGRAPH.LIB file is generated. This build process increases productivity by decreasing the time needed to build the Library, because no source file is recompiled that does not need to be recompiled. It also decreases programmer errors by not forcing the programmer to remember all of the files that need to be recompiled, especially when the programmer has changed an include file that is used by several different source modules.

- The separation of the graphics functions into the CGA Graphics Library increases programming productivity by allowing the programmer to use this Library for other applications that have similar needs. For example, the Mail List Application that this book is using as a sample application has a particular set of graphic needs, but another application, such as a Check Book Manager, will have the same needs, i.e., they both have to get and set the CRT mode and display data to the screen.

- The creation of the CGA Graphics Library increases the user's ability to learn the application, because it allows consistency across applications. All of the applications that use this Library will look the same, especially when displaying character data to the screen.

- The creation of the CGA Graphics Library increases the maintainability of the applications, because once a function is designed and documented and placed into the Library, the programmer uses them over and over again. He does not have to remember the exact syntax, or where the code can be found, if he needs to use the function.

- The use of the CGA Graphics Library increases the portability of the application because a new graphics library could be used if the application needed to be upgraded to a new display type.

These are only a few of the benefits to be gained by designing your user-interface in this manner. So far only the managing control files have been created. In the next chapter, I deal with the PC video display card and the creation of icons.

Chapter 4

THE COLOR GRAPHICS DISPLAY CARD

Before any code can be written for the CGA Graphics Library, the programmer must know how the PC's video display card is laid out in memory and how to access and manipulate this memory. The video display card is the place in memory where the PC keeps the data that is displayed on the screen. The PC comes with the ability to help the programmer access the video display card. This is accomplished with the DOS BIOS interrupt service calls. There are many different DOS BIOS interrupt service calls, but the only one we are concerned with is the video driver service, which is DOS BIOS call number 16.

'C' uses the DOS BIOS interrupt calls by executing an "int86 ( )" call to DOS. Data definitions are included in the file "dos.h" that is included with the 'C' compiler, that allow you to pass information to DOS and receive information back (more about include files in general in the next chapter). The DOS BIOS interrupt service calls give the programmer the ability to control the screen's environment and data by allowing him to be able to set the screen's CRT mode and display dots to the screen.

Another way of controlling screen data is by the Direct Video Access (DVA) method. DVA allows the programmer to put or retrieve data straight from the video display card, without having to execute a DOS BIOS interrupt service call. This method is a much faster way of displaying large amounts of data to the screen, but it requires the code to be written in Assembler because of the vital urgency of speed needed to display large amounts of data to the screen.

In other words, only functions that are done rarely, or that do not require much processing time, should use the DOS BIOS interrupt service calls, and functions that manipulate the screen data directly should use the Direct Video Access method. For example, the setting of the screen's CRT mode is done usually only once in the application and therefore should be written in 'C' using a DOS BIOS interrupt service call. But the clearing of a window of screen data, which could be thousands of dots, should be written in Assembler using the Direct Video Access method.

For the purposes of this book, I have divided the DOS BIOS interrupt service calls and the DVA methods into separate source files. The file CGAGRAFC.C contains all of the functions that use DOS BIOS interrupt service calls and are written in 'C.' The file CGAGRAFA.ASM contains all of the functions that use the Direct Video Access methods and are written in Assembler. Both of these files are explained in detail in the following chapters.

THE VIDEO DISPLAY FROM THE APPLICATIONS POINT OF VIEW

The CGA Graphics Library is written specifically for the four-color graphics mode of the PC. In this mode the screen is 320 dots wide and 200 dots high making a total of 64,000 individual dots that can be accessed on the screen. The following table shows the coordinate system that is used by the application when making screen requests from the CGA Graphics Library.

Upper Left-hand Corner				*Upper Right-hand Corner*	
(0, 0)	(0, 1)	(0, ...)		(0, 318)	(0, 319)
(1, 0)	(1, 1)	(1, ...)		(1, 318)	(1, 319)
(..., 0)	(...,)	(..., ...)		(..., 318)	(..., 319)
(198, 0)	(198, 1)	(198, ...)		(198, 318)	(198, 319)
(199, 0)	(199, 1)	(199, ,,,)		(199, 318)	(199, 319)
Lower Left-hand Corner				*Lower Right-hand Corner*	

For example, the application needs to display a box on the screen at a given location. The application uses the above grid coordinate system to relay this need to CGA Graphics Library. Let's say that the application wants a red box displayed on the screen starting at row coordinate 50 and column coordinate 100. The box needs to be 135 dots in width and 45 dots in height. The application might issue a statement such as this to the CGA Graphics Library:

DrawBox (50, 100, 135, 45, REDDOT);

It does not matter to the application which way the CGA Graphics Library displays the box on the screen, i.e., DOS BIOS interrupt service calls or Direct Video Access.

Another important thing to know about the PC four-color graphics adapter video card is that it can only display four different colors at the same time. These four colors are black, blue, red, and white. The CGA card also has another palette of colors to choose from, but for the purposes of this book, only these colors will be dealt with because only one palette can be active at any one time.

So far, I have only dealt with how the programmer views things from the application's point of view. The application has several needs that the CGA Graphics Library must perform and most of the time should not care what kind of screen environment the program is running under.

The application interfaces with the CGA Graphics Library by issuing function requests based on the above coordinate system and color layout. The CGA Graphics Library depends on valid data being sent to it because it does not know or care what the application is really trying to do. For example, if the application program issues a function request and does not pass the appropriate data to the CGA Graphics Library, then the Library cannot perform this function correctly.

THE VIDEO DISPLAY LAYOUT — USING THE DIRECT VIDEO ACCESS METHOD

The application makes function requests from the CGA Graphics Library based on the above coordinate system and layout. It expects the CGA Graphics Library to perform this function and return back to it with any information that might be associated with the function. Now comes the tricky part; how does the CGA Graphics Library perform the function?

As explained earlier, each type of graphics function has its own needs and should be written specifically for the task required of it. Some functions are easy, like setting the CRT mode; but other functions, such as displaying an icon to the screen, are much more difficult. To display icons and other screen data intensive tasks, the programmer must go directly to the video display card and manipulate the data there.

To do this, exact knowledge of the video display card being used must be known. The programmer must know where the video display card is kept in memory. For the PC in four-color graphics mode, the card is at segment address 0B800H. This address is the start of video ram memory, and if the programmer changes the bytes located here, he can change what is displayed on the screen almost instantly.

The video ram display card is laid out in the following manner

Upper Left-hand Corner	*Upper Right-hand Corner*
(0, 0) = 0B000H:0000H	(0, 319) = 0B000H:004FH
(1, 0) = 0B000H:2000H	(1, 319) = 0B000H:204FH
(2, 0) = 0B000H:0050H	(2, 319) = 0B000H:009FH
(3, 0) = 0B000H:2050H	(3, 319) = 0B000H:209FH
. . . . .	. . . . .

(198, 0) = 0B000H:1EF0H   (198, 319) = 0B000H:1F39H
(199, 0) = 0B000H:3EF0H   (199, 319) = 0B000H:1F39H

Lower Left-hand Corner   *Lower Right-hand Corner*

The most important thing to remember when dealing with the video display card directly is that the top line of the screen is the first EVEN display scan line, and the second line at the top of the screen is the first ODD display scan line. The first even display scan line starts at offset 0000H and ends at offset 004FH. The next even display scan line, which is the third line on the screen, starts at offset 00050H and ends at offset 009FH. The first odd display scan line, which is the second line on the screen, starts at offset 2000H and ends at offset 204FH. The next odd scan line starts at offset 2050H and ends at offset 209FH.

The reason for the odd way of addressing memory is quite simple; the first 2000H bytes of the display are used when displaying in Black and White mode, the next group of 2000H is used when displaying in the CGA mode. The two groups are combined into the even and odd scan lines to produce four-color images on the screen.

For the purposes of this book, we will deal strictly with the problems of displaying information to the screen in the CGA mode. You have probably already noticed that each display scan line is only 50 hexadecimal (80 decimal) bytes long. That is because in CGA mode, four dots are kept in each byte; therefore, in the first video display byte, offset 0000H, the first four dots on the screen are kept in this byte. So, if the application needs to turn off a dot at location (0, 0), the video display byte that needs to be changed is at offset 0000H.

Each one of the video display scan line bytes contains the bit pattern necessary to display those bytes. Since there are eight bits to a byte and each byte contains four dots, then there are two bits per each dot, making a possible combination of four bit patterns per dot. The following bit patterns are the color patterns used by the PC to represent the color on the screen.

- Black dot - 00
- Blue dot - 01
- Red dot - 10
- White dot - 11

Example - A display scan line byte with a bit pattern of 00011011 would have the first dot black, the second blue, the third red, and the fourth dot white.

In summary, the Direct Video Access method is very fast; it allows the programmer to change the data on the screen almost instantly, but it requires exact knowledge of the display card layout and it requires the programmer to understand bit and byte manipulation that can only be processed fast enough by Assembler.

THE CREATING OF ICONS

Exactly what is an icon? An icon is a group of bytes that contain the dot representation of an object that is to be displayed on the screen by the CGA Graphics Library.

For example, to display the letter 'a' on the screen, an icon representing the letter must be created.

Since we are dealing in graphics, each one of the dots in the letter must be individually displayed on the screen. The CGA Graphics Library contains the functions that will take the icon representation of the character and display it on the screen.

In the above example, displaying the letter 'a' to the screen seems like a simple enough task. It would be if we were in text. But since we are in graphics, the letter 'a' must be represented by an icon, so that the CGA Graphics Library can display it more easily. Not only is the letter 'a' to be represented as an icon, but also the entire alphabet and any characters or pictures that the application might wish to display.

This is one of the primary functions of the CGA Graphics Library. Without this, the application would only be able to draw lines on the screen with any ease. Special routines would have to be built to process each and every individual character or picture that needed to be displayed on the screen.

For this reason, and many others, icons must be used when dealing with the CGA Graphics Library and dealing in graphics in general. This book shows you how to create these icons and the standards established so that any application can create icons and have the CGA Graphics Library display them.

Creating a Sample Icon

'C' gives the programmer the ability to define data that is being used in the application. Special icons used by the application can be defined in the 'C' source modules themselves. Other icons, such as the character set being used by the application, might be read in from disk. The application can also create icons during the running of the application. Basically, an icon is just a group of data representing a particular object.

Example: This example shows the programmer how to go about creating a sample icon that will be displayed on the screen. Later in the book I will deal with how to create the character set icons used as the Font Set for the application. This sample icon will represent a white diamond shape on a black background on the screen. The icon is 11 dots wide and 11 dots high and defined according to 'C.'

To define an icon it needs to be put into an unsigned character array that is large enough to hold the icon. So to define this type of icon the following 'C' code is used:

```
unsigned char Diamond_Icon [11][3] =
{
    {0x00, 0x00, 0x00},
    {0x00, 0x30, 0x00},
    {0x00, 0xCC, 0x00},
    {0x03, 0x03, 0x00},
    {0x0C, 0x00, 0xC0},
    {0x30, 0x00, 0x30},
    {0x0C, 0x00, 0xC0},
    {0x03, 0x03, 0x00},
    {0x00, 0xCC, 0x00},
    {0x00, 0x30, 0x00},
    {0x00, 0x00, 0x00}
};
```

The above code is the final 'C' representation of this icon that represents the shape of a diamond. To generate this data definition, several steps had to be performed. Let's begin with the first statements:

```
unsigned char Diamond_Icon [11][3] =
{
```

These statements declare the unsigned character array of Diamond_Icon and that the array has 11 rows of 3 bytes each. The 11 represents the height of the icon. In the above example, the icon was said to be 11 dots high, so we need to define 11 rows of data. The 3 represents the number of bytes that the icon is wide. In the above example, the icon width was defined as 11 dots. Since there are four dots per video display byte, the number of dots wide needs to be divided by 4 and rounded, thereby making 3 bytes per icon width.

The next statements actually define the icon itself in hexadecimal format. The icon can better be seen in the bit wise format displayed below:

```
00000000000000000000000
00000000000110000000000
00000000011001100000000
00000011000000011000000
00001100000000000110000
00110000000000000001100
```

```
00001100000000000110000
00000011000000011000000
00000000011001100000000
00000000000110000000000
00000000000000000000000
```

This bit pattern can be further defined into its individual byte patterns as shown below:

```
|=============================|
| Byte # 1 Byte # 2 Byte # 3 |
|=============================|
| 00000000 00000000 00000000 |
| 00000000 00110000 00000000 |
| 00000000 11001100 00000000 |
| 00000011 00000011 00000000 |
| 00001100 00000000 11000000 |
| 00110000 00000000 00110000 |
| 00001100 00000000 11000000 |
| 00000011 00000011 00000000 |
| 00000000 11001100 00000000 |
| 00000000 00110000 00000000 |
| 00000000 00000000 00000000 |
|=============================|
```

These bytes are converted into hexadecimal and defined in the above manner in 'C.' For example, the bit pattern 00110011 is equal to 0x33 hexadecimal.

Whenever this icon is to be displayed on the screen, the CGA Graphics Library function DisplayIcon ( ) is called with a pointer to the icon data array along with the icon's width and height. Using the above technique for creating icons will give the programmer complete control over the screen. He can create any design or pattern he chooses and have the CGA Graphics Library display it whenever and wherever the application needs it to be displayed.

SUMMARY

In summary, the Four-Color Graphics Adapter is the graphics adapter being used by the CGA Graphics Library. It gives the programmer 64,000 individual dots to display on the screen. These dots are addressed via a coordinate system where (0, 0) is the upper left-hand corner of the screen and (199, 319) is the bottom right-hand corner. The video display card is located at segment address 0B800H. The even display scan lines start at offset 0000H and the odd scan lines start at offset 2000H. Each video display scan line is made up of 80 bytes, and each byte contains four display dots, and each display dot is two bits long. There are four colors available for the Four-Color Graphics adapter at any one time.

Chapter 4

The creation of icons is essential to the programmer if he wishes to fully utilize the capabilities of the PC's graphics abilities for the following reasons:

- Icons allow the programmer to create a picture of something and display it on the screen.

- The user friendliness of the application increases because the programmer can use pictures instead of words to relay his information to the user.

- The maintainability and changing of the application is easier, thereby increasing productivity because the programmer needs only to create the icon once and every other application can use it. An excellent example of this is the icons used as the font set in the application.

In the next chapter, I begin the programming of the CGA Graphics source code. I show the programmer how to create the 'C' source modules to use in the CGA Graphics Library. The 'C' source code depends heavily on the Assembler source code, and both parts are interrelated, but I have chosen to break it up in this manner for easier learning.

Chapter 5

THE CGA GRAPHICS LIBRARY
INCLUDE SOURCE FILES

The previous two chapters dealt with how to set up the managing control files to compile and link the CGA Graphics Library and how to understand the way the PC displays data to the screen. This chapter teaches you how to create the include source files that make up the CGA Graphics Library.

Since the video display card is being accessed by two methods, the DOS BIOS interrupt service calls and the Direct Video Access method, I have chosen to deal with the two types separately. This chapter deals with the include files that are used by the CGA Graphics Library. The next chapter deals with the DOS BIOS interrupt calls and the 'C' code required by the CGA Graphics Library. The chapter after that deals with the Direct Video Access methods and the Assembler code used by the CGA Graphics Library.

After the creation of the files that manage the CGA Graphics Library build process, you need to create the source files that perform the functions in the CGA Graphics Library. The following source files are used in the CGA Graphics Library.

- CGAGRAFC.C - This source file contains all of the functions that are written in 'C' and use the DOS BIOS interrupt service calls.
- GRAPHICS.H - This include file defines data used by the CGA Graphics Library.
- COLORS.H - This include file defines the color data definitions used by the application and the CGA Graphics Library.
- FONTSET.H - This include file defines the icons used by the CGA Graphics Library for the font set.

- CGAGRAFA.ASM - This file contains the functions that are written in Assembler and use the Direct Video Access method. (This source file is explained in detail in the following chapter.)

Create the GRAPHICS.H Include File

The use of include files is essential to good programming in 'C' because it allows the programmer to group his data definitions. These groups of data definitions can be used by other source modules as well, thereby eliminating the problem of changing something in more than one place when the definition of it changes. The first file to create is the GRAPHICS.H file.

Create the GRAPHICS.H source include file, edit the file, type the following statements, and save the file.

```
/*======================================================================*/
/*                                                                      */
/*   File : GRAPHICS.H                                                  */
/*                                                                      */
/*   Purpose : This include file contains the defined data             */
/*             definitions used by the CGA Graphics Library.           */
/*                                                                      */
/*   Data Defined : DOS_VIDEO_CALL 16 - Defines the DOS_VIDEO_CALL     */
/*                  variable to be 16, which is the DOS BIOS interrupt  */
/*                  call number for dealing with the screen data.      */
/*                                                                      */
/*                  FONTWIDTH 6 - Defines the variable FONTWIDTH to    */
/*                  be 6, which is the width of the character icon      */
/*                  in dots.                                            */
/*                                                                      */
/*                  FONTHEIGHT 10 - Defines the variable FONTHEIGHT to */
/*                  be 10, which is the height of the character icon    */
/*                  in dots.                                            */
/*                                                                      */
/*                  CURSOR 62 - Defines the variable CURSOR to be 62,  */
/*                  which is the font character icon number to use      */
/*                  whenever a DisplayCursor () call is made.          */
/*                                                                      */
/*======================================================================*/

#define DOS_VIDEO_CALL 16
#define FONTWIDTH 6
#define FONTHEIGHT 10
#define CURSOR 62
```

The include file GRAPHICS.H employs the typical style used in this book for documenting code. It uses the 'C' programming style and standards set forth in the chapter on 'C' Programming Style and Standards. The documenting of code starts with a section at the top of the file that describes the following things:

- The name of the source file
- A brief description of the purpose of the source file
- The data definitions defined in the file along with the data's purpose and options
- The functions that are performed by the source file

The GRAPHICS.H include file defines the data definitions needed by the CGAGRAFC.C source file, and it is included into the source file of CGAGRAFC.C.

Create the COLORS.H Include File

The next file to create is the COLORS.H include file. It contains all of the color definitions used by the application and the CGAGRAFC.C source file. Create the COLORS.H file, type the following statements, and save the file.

```
/*=========================================================================*/
/*                                                                         */
/*   File : COLORS.H                                                       */
/*                                                                         */
/*   Purpose : This include file contains the defined data definitions     */
/*             for the colors used by the CGA Graphics Library.            */
/*                                                                         */
/*   Data Defined : BLACK 0x00 - Defines the variable BLACK to be          */
/*                  equal to 0. This variable is used whenever the         */
/*                  color black is to be displayed on the screen as        */
/*                  a foreground or background color.                      */
/*                                                                         */
/*                  BLUE 0x55 - Defines the variable BLUE to be equal      */
/*                  to 55 hexadecimal. This variable is used whenever      */
/*                  the color blue is to be displayed on the screen        */
/*                  as a foreground or background color.                   */
/*                                                                         */
/*                  RED 0xAA - Define the variable RED to be equal         */
/*                  to AA hexadecimal.  This variable is used whenever     */
/*                  the color red is to be displayed on the screen as      */
/*                  a foreground or background color.                      */
/*                                                                         */
/*                  WHITE 0xFF - Defines the variable WHITE to be          */
/*                  equal to FF hexadecimal. This variable is used         */
/*                  whenever the color white is to be displayed on         */
/*                  the screen as a foreground or background color.        */
/*                                                                         */
/*                  BLACKDOT 0x00 - Defines the variable BLACKDOT to       */
/*                  be equal to 0.  This variable is used whenever         */
/*                  the color black is to be displayed on the screen       */
/*                  as a dot or in line drawing functions.                 */
/*                                                                         */
/*                  BLUEDOT 0x01 - Defines the variable BLUEDOT to be      */
/*                  equal to 1.  This variable is used whenever the        */
/*                  color blue is to be displayed on the screen as a       */
```

```
/*                      dot or in line drawing functions.          */
/*                                                                 */
/*                      REDDOT 0x02 - Defines the variable REDDOT to be   */
/*                      equal to 2.  This variable is used whenever the   */
/*                      color red is to be displayed on the screen as a   */
/*                      dot or in line drawing functions.          */
/*                                                                 */
/*                      WHITEDOT 0x03 - Defines the variable WHITEDOT to   */
/*                      be equal to 3.  This variable is used whenever     */
/*                      the color white is to be displayed on the screen   */
/*                      as a dot or in line drawing functions.     */
/*                                                                 */
/*====================================================================*/
```

```
#define BLACK 0x00
#define BLUE   0x55
#define RED    0xAA
#define WHITE 0xFF
#define BLACKDOT 0x00
#define BLUEDOT   0x01
#define REDDOT    0x02
#define WHITEDOT 0x03
```

The data definitions defined in COLORS.H are used throughout the application when dealing with the color attributes. The programmer defines these in this include file and uses these variable names when colors are needed.

Create the FONTSET.H Include File

The FONTSET.H include source file defines the data variable Font_Set. Font_Set contains the data definitions for each displayable character, called icons. Icons were explained earlier in the book and are used to display graphic pictures, in this case, letters, numbers, and other special characters.

The Font_Set variable is used by the CGA Graphics Library in the functions DisplayChar ( ), DisplayString ( ), DisplayStrNum ( ), and DisplayCursor ( ). The CGA Graphics Library function MapFontChar ( ) is used to map the character passed by the calling function into its corresponding character icon.

The Font_Set variable is defined to be of the size [2][95][10][2]. This means that the displayable characters are divided into 2 groups of icons, each group contains 95 different icons, each icon is 10 display lines high and 2 bytes wide. The variables defined in GRAPHICS.H, FONTWIDTH, and FONTHEIGHT are used to get the actual width and height of the character icons.

The first group of icons are all of the displayable character icons shown in a white foreground and black background. The next group shows the same character icons, but they are with a black foreground and a white background.

Create the FONTSET.H source file, edit the file, type the following statements, and save the file.

```
/*======================================================================*/
/*                                                                      */
/*   File : FONTSET.H                                                   */
/*                                                                      */
/*   Purpose : This include file contains the data definitions         */
/*             for the displayable character icons used by the CGA     */
/*             Graphics Library.                                        */
/*                                                                      */
/*   Data Defined : unsigned char Font_Set[2][95][10][2] - Defines the */
/*                  variable Font_Set.  This variable is used to        */
/*                  contain all of the displayable character icon       */
/*                  mappings. There are 2 groups of icons, the first    */
/*                  group is the White on Black icons, the next is the  */
/*                  Black on White icons.  Each icon group contains 95  */
/*                  icons that are 10 display lines high and 2 bytes    */
/*                  wide.                                                */
/*                                                                      */
/*======================================================================*/

unsigned char Font_Set[2][95][10][2] = {
{
    {{0x00, 0x00},      /* 00000000 00000000 */ /* WHITE ON BLACK   'a' */
     {0x00, 0x00},      /* 00000000 00000000 */
     {0x00, 0x00},      /* 00000000 00000000 */
     {0x3C, 0x00},      /* 00111100 00000000 */
     {0x03, 0x00},      /* 00000011 00000000 */
     {0x3F, 0x00},      /* 00111111 00000000 */
     {0xC3, 0x00},      /* 11000011 00000000 */
     {0x3C, 0xC0},      /* 00111100 11000000 */
     {0x00, 0x00},      /* 00000000 00000000 */
     {0x00, 0x00}},     /* 00000000 00000000 */

    {{0x00, 0x00},      /* 00000000 00000000 */ /* WHITE ON BLACK 'b'   */
     {0xF0, 0x00},      /* 11110000 00000000 */
     {0x30, 0x00},      /* 00110000 00000000 */
     {0x30, 0x00},      /* 00110000 00000000 */
     {0x3F, 0x00},      /* 00111111 00000000 */
     {0x30, 0xC0},      /* 00110000 11000000 */
     {0x30, 0xC0},      /* 00110000 11000000 */
     {0xCF, 0x00},      /* 11001111 00000000 */
     {0x00, 0x00},      /* 00000000 00000000 */
     {0x00, 0x00}},     /* 00000000 00000000 */

    {{0x00, 0x00},      /* 00000000 00000000 */ /* WHITE ON BLACK 'c'   */
     {0x00, 0x00},      /* 00000000 00000000 */
     {0x00, 0x00},      /* 00000000 00000000 */
     {0x3F, 0x00},      /* 00111111 00000000 */
     {0xC0, 0xC0},      /* 11000000 11000000 */
     {0xC0, 0x00},      /* 11000000 00000000 */
     {0xC0, 0xC0},      /* 11000000 11000000 */
```

```
{0x3F, 0x00},      /* 00111111 00000000 */
{0x00, 0x00},      /* 00000000 00000000 */
{0x00, 0x00}},     /* 00000000 00000000 */

{{0x00, 0x00},     /* 00000000 00000000 */ /* WHITE ON BLACK 'd'    */
{0x0F, 0x00},      /* 00001111 00000000 */
{0x03, 0x00},      /* 00000011 00000000 */
{0x03, 0x00},      /* 00000011 00000000 */
{0x3F, 0x00},      /* 00111111 00000000 */
{0xC3, 0x00},      /* 11000011 00000000 */
{0xC3, 0x00},      /* 11000011 00000000 */
{0x3C, 0xC0},      /* 00111100 11000000 */
{0x00, 0x00},      /* 00000000 00000000 */
{0x00, 0x00}},     /* 00000000 00000000 */

{{0x00, 0x00},     /* 00000000 00000000 */ /* WHITE ON BLACK 'e'    */
{0x00, 0x00},      /* 00000000 00000000 */
{0x00, 0x00},      /* 00000000 00000000 */
{0x3F, 0x00},      /* 00111111 00000000 */
{0xC0, 0xC0},      /* 11000000 11000000 */
{0xFF, 0xC0},      /* 11111111 11000000 */
{0xC0, 0x00},      /* 11000000 00000000 */
{0x3F, 0x00},      /* 00111111 00000000 */
{0x00, 0x00},      /* 00000000 00000000 */
{0x00, 0x00}},     /* 00000000 00000000 */

{{0x00, 0x00},     /* 00000000 00000000 */ /* WHITE ON BLACK 'f'    */
{0x0F, 0x00},      /* 00001111 00000000 */
{0x30, 0xC0},      /* 00110000 11000000 */
{0x30, 0x00},      /* 00110000 00000000 */
{0xFC, 0x00},      /* 11111100 00000000 */
{0x30, 0x00},      /* 00110000 00000000 */
{0x30, 0x00},      /* 00110000 00000000 */
{0xFC, 0x00},      /* 11111100 00000000 */
{0x00, 0x00},      /* 00000000 00000000 */
{0x00, 0x00}},     /* 00000000 00000000 */

{{0x00, 0x00},     /* 00000000 00000000 */ /* WHITE ON BLACK 'g'    */
{0x00, 0x00},      /* 00000000 00000000 */
{0x00, 0x00},      /* 00000000 00000000 */
{0x3C, 0xC0},      /* 00111100 11000000 */
{0xC3, 0x00},      /* 11000011 00000000 */
{0xC3, 0x00},      /* 11000011 00000000 */
{0x3F, 0x00},      /* 00111111 00000000 */
{0x03, 0x00},      /* 00000011 00000000 */
{0xFC, 0x00},      /* 11111100 00000000 */
{0x00, 0x00}},     /* 00000000 00000000 */

{{0x00, 0x00},     /* 00000000 00000000 */ /* WHITE ON BLACK 'h'    */
{0xF0, 0x00},      /* 11110000 00000000 */
{0x30, 0x00},      /* 00110000 00000000 */
{0x33, 0x00},      /* 00110011 00000000 */
{0x3C, 0xC0},      /* 00111100 11000000 */
```

```
  {0x30, 0xC0},       /* 00110000 11000000 */
  {0x30, 0xC0},       /* 00110000 11000000 */
  {0xF0, 0xC0},       /* 11110000 11000000 */
  {0x00, 0x00},       /* 00000000 00000000 */
  {0x00, 0x00}},      /* 00000000 00000000 */

 {{0x00, 0x00},       /* 00000000 00000000 */ /* WHITE ON BLACK 'i'    */
  {0x0C, 0x00},       /* 00001100 00000000 */
  {0x00, 0x00},       /* 00000000 00000000 */
  {0x3C, 0x00},       /* 00111100 00000000 */
  {0x0C, 0x00},       /* 00001100 00000000 */
  {0x0C, 0x00},       /* 00001100 00000000 */
  {0x0C, 0x00},       /* 00001100 00000000 */
  {0x3F, 0x00},       /* 00111111 00000000 */
  {0x00, 0x00},       /* 00000000 00000000 */
  {0x00, 0x00}},      /* 00000000 00000000 */

 {{0x00, 0x00},       /* 00000000 00000000 */ /* WHITE ON BLACK 'j'    */
  {0x03, 0x00},       /* 00000011 00000000 */
  {0x00, 0x00},       /* 00000000 00000000 */
  {0x03, 0x00},       /* 00000011 00000000 */
  {0x03, 0x00},       /* 00000011 00000000 */
  {0x03, 0x00},       /* 00000011 00000000 */
  {0xC3, 0x00},       /* 11000011 00000000 */
  {0xC3, 0x00},       /* 11000011 00000000 */
  {0x3C, 0x00},       /* 00111100 00000000 */
  {0x00, 0x00}},      /* 00000000 00000000 */

 {{0x00, 0x00},       /* 00000000 00000000 */ /* WHITE ON BLACK 'k'    */
  {0xF0, 0x00},       /* 11110000 00000000 */
  {0x30, 0x00},       /* 00110000 00000000 */
  {0x30, 0xC0},       /* 00110000 11000000 */
  {0x33, 0x00},       /* 00110011 00000000 */
  {0x3C, 0x00},       /* 00111100 00000000 */
  {0x33, 0x00},       /* 00110011 00000000 */
  {0xF0, 0xC0},       /* 11110000 11000000 */
  {0x00, 0x00},       /* 00000000 00000000 */
  {0x00, 0x00}},      /* 00000000 00000000 */

 {{0x00, 0x00},       /* 00000000 00000000 */ /* WHITE ON BLACK 'l'    */
  {0x3C, 0x00},       /* 00111100 00000000 */
  {0x0C, 0x00},       /* 00001100 00000000 */
  {0x0C, 0x00},       /* 00001100 00000000 */
  {0x0C, 0x00},       /* 00001100 00000000 */
  {0x0C, 0x00},       /* 00001100 00000000 */
  {0x0C, 0x00},       /* 00001100 00000000 */
  {0x3F, 0x00},       /* 00111111 00000000 */
  {0x00, 0x00},       /* 00000000 00000000 */
  {0x00, 0x00}},      /* 00000000 00000000 */

 {{0x00, 0x00},       /* 00000000 00000000 */ /* WHITE ON BLACK 'm'    */
  {0x00, 0x00},       /* 00000000 00000000 */
  {0x00, 0x00},       /* 00000000 00000000 */
```

```
        {0xC0, 0xC0},        /* 11000000 11000000 */
        {0xF3, 0xC0},        /* 11110011 11000000 */
        {0xFF, 0xC0},        /* 11111111 11000000 */
        {0xCC, 0xC0},        /* 11001100 11000000 */
        {0xC0, 0xC0},        /* 11000000 11000000 */
        {0x00, 0x00},        /* 00000000 00000000 */
        {0x00, 0x00}},       /* 00000000 00000000 */

     {{0x00, 0x00},          /* 00000000 00000000 */ /* WHITE ON BLACK 'n'    */
        {0x00, 0x00},        /* 00000000 00000000 */
        {0x00, 0x00},        /* 00000000 00000000 */
        {0xCF, 0x00},        /* 11001111 00000000 */
        {0xF0, 0xC0},        /* 11110000 11000000 */
        {0xC0, 0xC0},        /* 11000000 11000000 */
        {0xC0, 0xC0},        /* 11000000 11000000 */
        {0xC0, 0xC0},        /* 11000000 11000000 */
        {0x00, 0x00},        /* 00000000 00000000 */
        {0x00, 0x00}},       /* 00000000 00000000 */

     {{0x00, 0x00},          /* 00000000 00000000 */ /* WHITE ON BLACK 'o'    */
        {0x00, 0x00},        /* 00000000 00000000 */
        {0x00, 0x00},        /* 00000000 00000000 */
        {0x3F, 0x00},        /* 00111111 00000000 */
        {0xC0, 0xC0},        /* 11000000 11000000 */
        {0xC0, 0xC0},        /* 11000000 11000000 */
        {0xC0, 0xC0},        /* 11000000 11000000 */
        {0x3F, 0x00},        /* 00111111 00000000 */
        {0x00, 0x00},        /* 00000000 00000000 */
        {0x00, 0x00}},       /* 00000000 00000000 */

     {{0x00, 0x00},          /* 00000000 00000000 */ /* WHITE ON BLACK 'p'    */
        {0x00, 0x00},        /* 00000000 00000000 */
        {0x00, 0x00},        /* 00000000 00000000 */
        {0xCF, 0x00},        /* 11001111 00000000 */
        {0x30, 0xC0},        /* 00110000 11000000 */
        {0x30, 0xC0},        /* 00110000 11000000 */
        {0x3F, 0x00},        /* 00111111 00000000 */
        {0x30, 0x00},        /* 00110000 00000000 */
        {0xFC, 0x00},        /* 11111100 00000000 */
        {0x00, 0x00}},       /* 00000000 00000000 */

     {{0x00, 0x00},          /* 00000000 00000000 */ /* WHITE ON BLACK 'q'    */
        {0x00, 0x00},        /* 00000000 00000000 */
        {0x00, 0x00},        /* 00000000 00000000 */
        {0x3C, 0xC0},        /* 00111100 11000000 */
        {0xC3, 0x00},        /* 11000011 00000000 */
        {0xC3, 0x00},        /* 11000011 00000000 */
        {0x3F, 0x00},        /* 00111111 00000000 */
        {0x03, 0x00},        /* 00000011 00000000 */
        {0x0F, 0xC0},        /* 00001111 11000000 */
        {0x00, 0x00}},       /* 00000000 00000000 */

     {{0x00, 0x00},          /* 00000000 00000000 */ /* WHITE ON BLACK 'r'    */
```

```
    {0x00, 0x00},      /* 00000000 00000000 */
    {0x00, 0x00},      /* 00000000 00000000 */
    {0xCF, 0x00},      /* 11001111 00000000 */
    {0x30, 0xC0},      /* 00110000 11000000 */
    {0x30, 0x00},      /* 00110000 00000000 */
    {0x30, 0x00},      /* 00110000 00000000 */
    {0xFC, 0x00},      /* 11111100 00000000 */
    {0x00, 0x00},      /* 00000000 00000000 */
    {0x00, 0x00}},     /* 00000000 00000000 */

   {{0x00, 0x00},      /* 00000000 00000000 */ /* WHITE ON BLACK 's'    */
    {0x00, 0x00},      /* 00000000 00000000 */
    {0x00, 0x00},      /* 00000000 00000000 */
    {0x3F, 0xC0},      /* 00111111 11000000 */
    {0xC0, 0x00},      /* 11000000 00000000 */
    {0x3F, 0x00},      /* 00111111 00000000 */
    {0x00, 0xC0},      /* 00000000 11000000 */
    {0xFF, 0x00},      /* 11111111 00000000 */
    {0x00, 0x00},      /* 00000000 00000000 */
    {0x00, 0x00}},     /* 00000000 00000000 */

   {{0x00, 0x00},      /* 00000000 00000000 */ /* WHITE ON BLACK 't'    */
    {0x30, 0x00},      /* 00110000 00000000 */
    {0x30, 0x00},      /* 00110000 00000000 */
    {0xFC, 0x00},      /* 11111100 00000000 */
    {0x30, 0x00},      /* 00110000 00000000 */
    {0x30, 0xC0},      /* 00110000 11000000 */
    {0x30, 0xC0},      /* 00110000 11000000 */
    {0x0F, 0x00},      /* 00001111 00000000 */
    {0x00, 0x00},      /* 00000000 00000000 */
    {0x00, 0x00}},     /* 00000000 00000000 */

   {{0x00, 0x00},      /* 00000000 00000000 */ /* WHITE ON BLACK 'u'    */
    {0x00, 0x00},      /* 00000000 00000000 */
    {0x00, 0x00},      /* 00000000 00000000 */
    {0xC3, 0x00},      /* 11000011 00000000 */
    {0xC3, 0x00},      /* 11000011 00000000 */
    {0xC3, 0x00},      /* 11000011 00000000 */
    {0xC3, 0x00},      /* 11000011 00000000 */
    {0x3C, 0xC0},      /* 00111100 11000000 */
    {0x00, 0x00},      /* 00000000 00000000 */
    {0x00, 0x00}},     /* 00000000 00000000 */

   {{0x00, 0x00},      /* 00000000 00000000 */ /* WHITE ON BLACK 'v'    */
    {0x00, 0x00},      /* 00000000 00000000 */
    {0x00, 0x00},      /* 00000000 00000000 */
    {0xC0, 0xC0},      /* 11000000 11000000 */
    {0xC0, 0xC0},      /* 11000000 11000000 */
    {0xC0, 0xC0},      /* 11000000 11000000 */
    {0x33, 0x00},      /* 00110011 00000000 */
    {0x0C, 0x00},      /* 00001100 00000000 */
    {0x00, 0x00},      /* 00000000 00000000 */
    {0x00, 0x00}},     /* 00000000 00000000 */
```

```
{{0x00, 0x00},      /* 00000000 00000000 */ /* WHITE ON BLACK 'w'    */
 {0x00, 0x00},      /* 00000000 00000000 */
 {0x00, 0x00},      /* 00000000 00000000 */
 {0xC0, 0xC0},      /* 11000000 11000000 */
 {0xC0, 0xC0},      /* 11000000 11000000 */
 {0xCC, 0xC0},      /* 11001100 11000000 */
 {0xCC, 0xC0},      /* 11001100 11000000 */
 {0x3F, 0x00},      /* 00111111 00000000 */
 {0x00, 0x00},      /* 00000000 00000000 */
 {0x00, 0x00}},     /* 00000000 00000000 */

{{0x00, 0x00},      /* 00000000 00000000 */ /* WHITE ON BLACK 'x'    */
 {0x00, 0x00},      /* 00000000 00000000 */
 {0x00, 0x00},      /* 00000000 00000000 */
 {0xC0, 0xC0},      /* 11000000 11000000 */
 {0x33, 0x00},      /* 00110011 00000000 */
 {0x0C, 0x00},      /* 00001100 00000000 */
 {0x33, 0x00},      /* 00110011 00000000 */
 {0xC0, 0xC0},      /* 11000000 11000000 */
 {0x00, 0x00},      /* 00000000 00000000 */
 {0x00, 0x00}},     /* 00000000 00000000 */

{{0x00, 0x00},      /* 00000000 00000000 */ /* WHITE ON BLACK 'y'    */
 {0x00, 0x00},      /* 00000000 00000000 */
 {0x00, 0x00},      /* 00000000 00000000 */
 {0xC0, 0xC0},      /* 11000000 11000000 */
 {0xC0, 0xC0},      /* 11000000 11000000 */
 {0xC0, 0xC0},      /* 11000000 11000000 */
 {0x3F, 0xC0},      /* 00111111 11000000 */
 {0x00, 0xC0},      /* 00000000 11000000 */
 {0x3F, 0x00},      /* 00111111 00000000 */
 {0x00, 0x00}},     /* 00000000 00000000 */

{{0x00, 0x00},      /* 00000000 00000000 */ /* WHITE ON BLACK 'z'    */
 {0x00, 0x00},      /* 00000000 00000000 */
 {0x00, 0x00},      /* 00000000 00000000 */
 {0xFF, 0xC0},      /* 11111111 11000000 */
 {0x03, 0x00},      /* 00000011 00000000 */
 {0x0C, 0x00},      /* 00001100 00000000 */
 {0x30, 0x00},      /* 00110000 00000000 */
 {0xFF, 0xC0},      /* 11111111 11000000 */
 {0x00, 0x00},      /* 00000000 00000000 */
 {0x00, 0x00}},     /* 00000000 00000000 */

{{0x00, 0x00},      /* 00000000 00000000 */ /* WHITE ON BLACK 'A'    */
 {0x0C, 0x00},      /* 00001100 00000000 */
 {0x33, 0x00},      /* 00110011 00000000 */
 {0xC0, 0xC0},      /* 11000000 11000000 */
 {0xC0, 0xC0},      /* 11000000 11000000 */
 {0xFF, 0xC0},      /* 11111111 11000000 */
 {0xC0, 0xC0},      /* 11000000 11000000 */
 {0xC0, 0xC0},      /* 11000000 11000000 */
```

```
    {0x00, 0x00},        /* 00000000 00000000 */
    {0x00, 0x00}},       /* 00000000 00000000 */

   {{0x00, 0x00},        /* 00000000 00000000 */ /* WHITE ON BLACK 'B'     */
    {0xFF, 0x00},        /* 11111111 00000000 */
    {0x30, 0xC0},        /* 00110000 11000000 */
    {0x30, 0xC0},        /* 00110000 11000000 */
    {0x3F, 0x00},        /* 00111111 00000000 */
    {0x30, 0xC0},        /* 00110000 11000000 */
    {0x30, 0xC0},        /* 00110000 11000000 */
    {0xFF, 0x00},        /* 11111111 00000000 */
    {0x00, 0x00},        /* 00000000 00000000 */
    {0x00, 0x00}},       /* 00000000 00000000 */

   {{0x00, 0x00},        /* 00000000 00000000 */ /* WHITE ON BLACK 'C'     */
    {0x3F, 0x00},        /* 00111111 00000000 */
    {0xC0, 0xC0},        /* 11000000 11000000 */
    {0xC0, 0x00},        /* 11000000 00000000 */
    {0xC0, 0x00},        /* 11000000 00000000 */
    {0xC0, 0x00},        /* 11000000 00000000 */
    {0xC0, 0xC0},        /* 11000000 11000000 */
    {0x3F, 0x00},        /* 00111111 00000000 */
    {0x00, 0x00},        /* 00000000 00000000 */
    {0x00, 0x00}},       /* 00000000 00000000 */

   {{0x00, 0x00},        /* 00000000 00000000 */ /* WHITE ON BLACK 'D'     */
    {0xFF, 0x00},        /* 11111111 00000000 */
    {0x30, 0xC0},        /* 00110000 11000000 */
    {0x30, 0xC0},        /* 00110000 11000000 */
    {0x30, 0xC0},        /* 00110000 11000000 */
    {0x30, 0xC0},        /* 00110000 11000000 */
    {0x30, 0xC0},        /* 00110000 11000000 */
    {0xFF, 0x00},        /* 11111111 00000000 */
    {0x00, 0x00},        /* 00000000 00000000 */
    {0x00, 0x00}},       /* 00000000 00000000 */

   {{0x00, 0x00},        /* 00000000 00000000 */ /* WHITE ON BLACK 'E'     */
    {0xFF, 0xC0},        /* 11111111 11000000 */
    {0x30, 0xC0},        /* 00110000 11000000 */
    {0x30, 0x00},        /* 00110000 00000000 */
    {0x3F, 0x00},        /* 00111111 00000000 */
    {0x30, 0x00},        /* 00110000 00000000 */
    {0x30, 0xC0},        /* 00110000 11000000 */
    {0xFF, 0xC0},        /* 11111111 11000000 */
    {0x00, 0x00},        /* 00000000 00000000 */
    {0x00, 0x00}},       /* 00000000 00000000 */

   {{0x00, 0x00},        /* 00000000 00000000 */ /* WHITE ON BLACK 'F'     */
    {0xFF, 0xC0},        /* 11111111 11000000 */
    {0x30, 0xC0},        /* 00110000 11000000 */
    {0x30, 0x00},        /* 00110000 00000000 */
    {0x3C, 0x00},        /* 00111100 00000000 */
    {0x30, 0x00},        /* 00110000 00000000 */
```

```
{0x30, 0x00},        /* 00110000 00000000 */
{0xFC, 0x00},        /* 11111100 00000000 */
{0x00, 0x00},        /* 00000000 00000000 */
{0x00, 0x00}},       /* 00000000 00000000 */

{{0x00, 0x00},       /* 00000000 00000000 */ /* WHITE ON BLACK 'G'    */
{0x3F, 0x00},        /* 00111111 00000000 */
{0xC0, 0xC0},        /* 11000000 11000000 */
{0xC0, 0x00},        /* 11000000 00000000 */
{0xCF, 0xC0},        /* 11001111 11000000 */
{0xC0, 0xC0},        /* 11000000 11000000 */
{0xC0, 0xC0},        /* 11000000 11000000 */
{0x3F, 0x00},        /* 00111111 00000000 */
{0x00, 0x00},        /* 00000000 00000000 */
{0x00, 0x00}},       /* 00000000 00000000 */

{{0x00, 0x00},       /* 00000000 00000000 */ /* WHITE ON BLACK 'H'    */
{0xC0, 0xC0},        /* 11000000 11000000 */
{0xC0, 0xC0},        /* 11000000 11000000 */
{0xC0, 0xC0},        /* 11000000 11000000 */
{0xFF, 0xC0},        /* 11111111 11000000 */
{0xC0, 0xC0},        /* 11000000 11000000 */
{0xC0, 0xC0},        /* 11000000 11000000 */
{0xC0, 0xC0},        /* 11000000 11000000 */
{0x00, 0x00},        /* 00000000 00000000 */
{0x00, 0x00}},       /* 00000000 00000000 */

{{0x00, 0x00},       /* 00000000 00000000 */ /* WHITE ON BLACK 'I'    */
{0x3F, 0x00},        /* 00111111 00000000 */
{0x0C, 0x00},        /* 00001100 00000000 */
{0x0C, 0x00},        /* 00001100 00000000 */
{0x0C, 0x00},        /* 00001100 00000000 */
{0x0C, 0x00},        /* 00001100 00000000 */
{0x0C, 0x00},        /* 00001100 00000000 */
{0x3F, 0x00},        /* 00111111 00000000 */
{0x00, 0x00},        /* 00000000 00000000 */
{0x00, 0x00}},       /* 00000000 00000000 */

{{0x00, 0x00},       /* 00000000 00000000 */ /* WHITE ON BLACK 'J'    */
{0x0F, 0xC0},        /* 00001111 11000000 */
{0x03, 0x00},        /* 00000011 00000000 */
{0x03, 0x00},        /* 00000011 00000000 */
{0x03, 0x00},        /* 00000011 00000000 */
{0x03, 0x00},        /* 00000011 00000000 */
{0x03, 0x00},        /* 00000011 00000000 */
{0xC3, 0x00},        /* 11000011 00000000 */
{0x3C, 0x00},        /* 00111100 00000000 */
{0x00, 0x00}},       /* 00000000 00000000 */

{{0x00, 0x00},       /* 00000000 00000000 */ /* WHITE ON BLACK 'K'    */
{0xF0, 0xC0},        /* 11110000 11000000 */
{0x30, 0xC0},        /* 00110000 11000000 */
{0x33, 0x00},        /* 00110011 00000000 */
```

```
    {0x3C, 0x00},      /* 00111100 00000000 */
    {0x33, 0x00},      /* 00110011 00000000 */
    {0x30, 0xC0},      /* 00110000 11000000 */
    {0xF0, 0xC0},      /* 11110000 11000000 */
    {0x00, 0x00},      /* 00000000 00000000 */
    {0x00, 0x00}},     /* 00000000 00000000 */

    {{0x00, 0x00},     /* 00000000 00000000 */ /* WHITE ON BLACK 'L'    */
    {0xF0, 0x00},      /* 11110000 00000000 */
    {0x30, 0x00},      /* 00110000 00000000 */
    {0x30, 0x00},      /* 00110000 00000000 */
    {0x30, 0x00},      /* 00110000 00000000 */
    {0x30, 0x00},      /* 00110000 00000000 */
    {0x30, 0xC0},      /* 00110000 11000000 */
    {0xFF, 0xC0},      /* 11111111 11000000 */
    {0x00, 0x00},      /* 00000000 00000000 */
    {0x00, 0x00}},     /* 00000000 00000000 */

    {{0x00, 0x00},     /* 00000000 00000000 */ /* WHITE ON BLACK 'M'    */
    {0xC0, 0xC0},      /* 11000000 11000000 */
    {0xF3, 0xC0},      /* 11110011 11000000 */
    {0xCC, 0xC0},      /* 11001100 11000000 */
    {0xCC, 0xC0},      /* 11001100 11000000 */
    {0xC0, 0xC0},      /* 11000000 11000000 */
    {0xC0, 0xC0},      /* 11000000 11000000 */
    {0xC0, 0xC0},      /* 11000000 11000000 */
    {0x00, 0x00},      /* 00000000 00000000 */
    {0x00, 0x00}},     /* 00000000 00000000 */

    {{0x00, 0x00},     /* 00000000 00000000 */ /* WHITE ON BLACK 'N'    */
    {0xC0, 0xC0},      /* 11000000 11000000 */
    {0xF0, 0xC0},      /* 11110000 11000000 */
    {0xCC, 0xC0},      /* 11001100 11000000 */
    {0xC3, 0xC0},      /* 11000011 11000000 */
    {0xC0, 0xC0},      /* 11000000 11000000 */
    {0xC0, 0xC0},      /* 11000000 11000000 */
    {0xC0, 0xC0},      /* 11000000 11000000 */
    {0x00, 0x00},      /* 00000000 00000000 */
    {0x00, 0x00}},     /* 00000000 00000000 */

    {{0x00, 0x00},     /* 00000000 00000000 */ /* WHITE ON BLACK 'O'    */
    {0x3F, 0x00},      /* 00111111 00000000 */
    {0xC0, 0xC0},      /* 11000000 11000000 */
    {0xC0, 0xC0},      /* 11000000 11000000 */
    {0xC0, 0xC0},      /* 11000000 11000000 */
    {0xC0, 0xC0},      /* 11000000 11000000 */
    {0xC0, 0xC0},      /* 11000000 11000000 */
    {0x3F, 0x00},      /* 00111111 00000000 */
    {0x00, 0x00},      /* 00000000 00000000 */
    {0x00, 0x00}},     /* 00000000 00000000 */

    {{0x00, 0x00},     /* 00000000 00000000 */ /* WHITE ON BLACK 'P'    */
    {0xFF, 0x00},      /* 11111111 00000000 */
```

```
{0x30, 0xC0},        /* 00110000 11000000 */
{0x30, 0xC0},        /* 00110000 11000000 */
{0x3F, 0x00},        /* 00111111 00000000 */
{0x30, 0x00},        /* 00110000 00000000 */
{0x30, 0x00},        /* 00110000 00000000 */
{0xFC, 0x00},        /* 11111100 00000000 */
{0x00, 0x00},        /* 00000000 00000000 */
{0x00, 0x00}},       /* 00000000 00000000 */

{{0x00, 0x00},       /* 00000000 00000000 */ /* WHITE ON BLACK 'Q'    */
{0x3F, 0x00},        /* 00111111 00000000 */
{0xC0, 0xC0},        /* 11000000 11000000 */
{0xC0, 0xC0},        /* 11000000 11000000 */
{0xC0, 0xC0},        /* 11000000 11000000 */
{0xC0, 0xC0},        /* 11000000 11000000 */
{0xCC, 0xC0},        /* 11001100 11000000 */
{0x3F, 0x00},        /* 00111111 00000000 */
{0x00, 0xC0},        /* 00000000 11000000 */
{0x00, 0x00}},       /* 00000000 00000000 */

{{0x00, 0x00},       /* 00000000 00000000 */ /* WHITE ON BLACK 'R'    */
{0xFF, 0x00},        /* 11111111 00000000 */
{0x30, 0xC0},        /* 00110000 11000000 */
{0x30, 0xC0},        /* 00110000 11000000 */
{0x3F, 0x00},        /* 00111111 00000000 */
{0x33, 0x00},        /* 00110011 00000000 */
{0x30, 0xC0},        /* 00110000 11000000 */
{0xF0, 0xC0},        /* 11110000 11000000 */
{0x00, 0x00},        /* 00000000 00000000 */
{0x00, 0x00}},       /* 00000000 00000000 */

{{0x00, 0x00},       /* 00000000 00000000 */ /* WHITE ON BLACK 'S'    */
{0x3F, 0xC0},        /* 00111111 11000000 */
{0xC0, 0x00},        /* 11000000 00000000 */
{0xC0, 0x00},        /* 11000000 00000000 */
{0x3F, 0x00},        /* 00111111 00000000 */
{0x00, 0xC0},        /* 00000000 11000000 */
{0x00, 0xC0},        /* 00000000 11000000 */
{0xFF, 0x00},        /* 11111111 00000000 */
{0x00, 0x00},        /* 00000000 00000000 */
{0x00, 0x00}},       /* 00000000 00000000 */

{{0x00, 0x00},       /* 00000000 00000000 */ /* WHITE ON BLACK 'T'    */
{0xFF, 0xC0},        /* 11111111 11000000 */
{0xCC, 0xC0},        /* 11001100 11000000 */
{0x0C, 0x00},        /* 00001100 00000000 */
{0x0C, 0x00},        /* 00001100 00000000 */
{0x0C, 0x00},        /* 00001100 00000000 */
{0x0C, 0x00},        /* 00001100 00000000 */
{0x0C, 0x00},        /* 00001100 00000000 */
{0x00, 0x00},        /* 00000000 00000000 */
{0x00, 0x00}},       /* 00000000 00000000 */
```

```
{{0x00, 0x00},      /* 00000000 00000000 */ /* WHITE ON BLACK 'U'    */
 {0xC0, 0xC0},      /* 11000000 11000000 */
 {0xC0, 0xC0},      /* 11000000 11000000 */
 {0xC0, 0xC0},      /* 11000000 11000000 */
 {0xC0, 0xC0},      /* 11000000 11000000 */
 {0xC0, 0xC0},      /* 11000000 11000000 */
 {0xC0, 0xC0},      /* 11000000 11000000 */
 {0x3F, 0x00},      /* 00111111 00000000 */
 {0x00, 0x00},      /* 00000000 00000000 */
 {0x00, 0x00}},     /* 00000000 00000000 */

{{0x00, 0x00},      /* 00000000 00000000 */ /* WHITE ON BLACK 'V'    */
 {0xC0, 0xC0},      /* 11000000 11000000 */
 {0xC0, 0xC0},      /* 11000000 11000000 */
 {0xC0, 0xC0},      /* 11000000 11000000 */
 {0xC0, 0xC0},      /* 11000000 11000000 */
 {0xC0, 0xC0},      /* 11000000 11000000 */
 {0x33, 0x00},      /* 00110011 00000000 */
 {0x0C, 0x00},      /* 00001100 00000000 */
 {0x00, 0x00},      /* 00000000 00000000 */
 {0x00, 0x00}},     /* 00000000 00000000 */

{{0x00, 0x00},      /* 00000000 00000000 */ /* WHITE ON BLACK 'W'    */
 {0xC0, 0xC0},      /* 11000000 11000000 */
 {0xC0, 0xC0},      /* 11000000 11000000 */
 {0xC0, 0xC0},      /* 11000000 11000000 */
 {0xCC, 0xC0},      /* 11001100 11000000 */
 {0xCC, 0xC0},      /* 11001100 11000000 */
 {0xCC, 0xC0},      /* 11001100 11000000 */
 {0x33, 0x00},      /* 00110011 00000000 */
 {0x00, 0x00},      /* 00000000 00000000 */
 {0x00, 0x00}},     /* 00000000 00000000 */

{{0x00, 0x00},      /* 00000000 00000000 */ /* WHITE ON BLACK 'X'    */
 {0xC0, 0xC0},      /* 11000000 11000000 */
 {0xC0, 0xC0},      /* 11000000 11000000 */
 {0x33, 0x00},      /* 00110011 00000000 */
 {0x0C, 0x00},      /* 00001100 00000000 */
 {0x0C, 0x00},      /* 00001100 00000000 */
 {0x33, 0x00},      /* 00110011 00000000 */
 {0xC0, 0xC0},      /* 11000000 11000000 */
 {0x00, 0x00},      /* 00000000 00000000 */
 {0x00, 0x00}},     /* 00000000 00000000 */

{{0x00, 0x00},      /* 00000000 00000000 */ /* WHITE ON BLACK 'Y'    */
 {0xC0, 0xC0},      /* 11000000 11000000 */
 {0xC0, 0xC0},      /* 11000000 11000000 */
 {0xC0, 0xC0},      /* 11000000 11000000 */
 {0x33, 0x00},      /* 00110011 00000000 */
 {0x0C, 0x00},      /* 00001100 00000000 */
 {0x0C, 0x00},      /* 00001100 00000000 */
 {0x3F, 0x00},      /* 00111111 00000000 */
 {0x00, 0x00},      /* 00000000 00000000 */
```

```
    {0x00, 0x00}},       /* 00000000 00000000 */

   {{0x00, 0x00},        /* 00000000 00000000 */ /* WHITE ON BLACK 'Z'    */
    {0xFF, 0xC0},        /* 11111111 11000000 */
    {0xC0, 0xC0},        /* 11000000 11000000 */
    {0x03, 0x00},        /* 00000011 00000000 */
    {0x0C, 0x00},        /* 00001100 00000000 */
    {0x30, 0x00},        /* 00110000 00000000 */
    {0xC0, 0xC0},        /* 11000000 11000000 */
    {0xFF, 0xC0},        /* 11111111 11000000 */
    {0x00, 0x00},        /* 00000000 00000000 */
    {0x00, 0x00}},       /* 00000000 00000000 */

   {{0x00, 0x00},        /* 00000000 00000000 */ /* WHITE ON BLACK '!'    */
    {0x0C, 0x00},        /* 00001100 00000000 */
    {0x0C, 0x00},        /* 00001100 00000000 */
    {0x0C, 0x00},        /* 00001100 00000000 */
    {0x0C, 0x00},        /* 00001100 00000000 */
    {0x0C, 0x00},        /* 00001100 00000000 */
    {0x00, 0x00},        /* 00000000 00000000 */
    {0x0C, 0x00},        /* 00001100 00000000 */
    {0x00, 0x00},        /* 00000000 00000000 */
    {0x00, 0x00}},       /* 00000000 00000000 */

   {{0x00, 0x00},        /* 00000000 00000000 */ /* WHITE ON BLACK '@'    */
    {0x3C, 0x00},        /* 00111100 00000000 */
    {0xC3, 0x00},        /* 11000011 00000000 */
    {0xCF, 0x00},        /* 11001111 00000000 */
    {0xCF, 0x00},        /* 11001111 00000000 */
    {0xCF, 0x00},        /* 11001111 00000000 */
    {0xC0, 0x00},        /* 11000000 00000000 */
    {0x3C, 0x00},        /* 00111100 00000000 */
    {0x00, 0x00},        /* 00000000 00000000 */
    {0x00, 0x00}},       /* 00000000 00000000 */

   {{0x00, 0x00},        /* 00000000 00000000 */ /* WHITE ON BLACK '#'    */
    {0x33, 0x00},        /* 00110011 00000000 */
    {0x33, 0x00},        /* 00110011 00000000 */
    {0xFF, 0xC0},        /* 11111111 11000000 */
    {0x33, 0x00},        /* 00110011 00000000 */
    {0xFF, 0xC0},        /* 11111111 11000000 */
    {0x33, 0x00},        /* 00110011 00000000 */
    {0x33, 0x00},        /* 00110011 00000000 */
    {0x00, 0x00},        /* 00000000 00000000 */
    {0x00, 0x00}},       /* 00000000 00000000 */

   {{0x00, 0x00},        /* 00000000 00000000 */ /* WHITE ON BLACK '$'    */
    {0x0C, 0x00},        /* 00001100 00000000 */
    {0x3F, 0xC0},        /* 00111111 11000000 */
    {0xC0, 0x00},        /* 11000000 00000000 */
    {0x3F, 0x00},        /* 00111111 00000000 */
    {0x00, 0xC0},        /* 00000000 11000000 */
    {0xFF, 0x00},        /* 11111111 00000000 */
```

```
      {0x0C, 0x00},      /* 00001100 00000000 */
      {0x00, 0x00},      /* 00000000 00000000 */
      {0x00, 0x00}},     /* 00000000 00000000 */

     {{0x00, 0x00},      /* 00000000 00000000 */ /* WHITE ON BLACK '%'    */
      {0x00, 0x00},      /* 00000000 00000000 */
      {0xC0, 0xC0},      /* 11000000 11000000 */
      {0xC3, 0x00},      /* 11000011 00000000 */
      {0x0C, 0x00},      /* 00001100 00000000 */
      {0x30, 0xC0},      /* 00110000 11000000 */
      {0xC0, 0xC0},      /* 11000000 11000000 */
      {0x00, 0x00},      /* 00000000 00000000 */
      {0x00, 0x00},      /* 00000000 00000000 */
      {0x00, 0x00}},     /* 00000000 00000000 */

     {{0x00, 0x00},      /* 00000000 00000000 */ /* WHITE ON BLACK '^'    */
      {0x0C, 0x00},      /* 00001100 00000000 */
      {0x33, 0x00},      /* 00110011 00000000 */
      {0xC0, 0xC0},      /* 11000000 11000000 */
      {0x00, 0x00},      /* 00000000 00000000 */
      {0x00, 0x00},      /* 00000000 00000000 */
      {0x00, 0x00},      /* 00000000 00000000 */
      {0x00, 0x00},      /* 00000000 00000000 */
      {0x00, 0x00}},     /* 00000000 00000000 */

     {{0x00, 0x00},      /* 00000000 00000000 */ /* WHITE ON BLACK '&'    */
      {0x0C, 0x00},      /* 00001100 00000000 */
      {0x33, 0x00},      /* 00110011 00000000 */
      {0x33, 0x00},      /* 00110011 00000000 */
      {0x3C, 0x00},      /* 00111100 00000000 */
      {0xCC, 0xC0},      /* 11001100 11000000 */
      {0xC3, 0x00},      /* 11000011 00000000 */
      {0x3C, 0xC0},      /* 00111100 11000000 */
      {0x00, 0x00},      /* 00000000 00000000 */
      {0x00, 0x00}},     /* 00000000 00000000 */

     {{0x00, 0x00},      /* 00000000 00000000 */ /* WHITE ON BLACK '*'    */
      {0x0C, 0x00},      /* 00001100 00000000 */
      {0xCC, 0xC0},      /* 11001100 11000000 */
      {0x3F, 0x00},      /* 00111111 00000000 */
      {0x0C, 0x00},      /* 00001100 00000000 */
      {0x3F, 0x00},      /* 00111111 00000000 */
      {0xCC, 0xC0},      /* 11001100 11000000 */
      {0x0C, 0x00},      /* 00001100 00000000 */
      {0x00, 0x00},      /* 00000000 00000000 */
      {0x00, 0x00}},     /* 00000000 00000000 */

     {{0x00, 0x00},      /* 00000000 00000000 */ /* WHITE ON BLACK '('    */
      {0x03, 0x00},      /* 00000011 00000000 */
      {0x0C, 0x00},      /* 00001100 00000000 */
      {0x30, 0x00},      /* 00110000 00000000 */
      {0x30, 0x00},      /* 00110000 00000000 */
```

```
    {0x30, 0x00},       /* 00110000 00000000 */
    {0x0C, 0x00},       /* 00001100 00000000 */
    {0x03, 0x00},       /* 00000011 00000000 */
    {0x00, 0x00},       /* 00000000 00000000 */
    {0x00, 0x00}},      /* 00000000 00000000 */

   {{0x00, 0x00},       /* 00000000 00000000 */ /* WHITE ON BLACK ')'    */
    {0x30, 0x00},       /* 00110000 00000000 */
    {0x0C, 0x00},       /* 00001100 00000000 */
    {0x03, 0x00},       /* 00000011 00000000 */
    {0x03, 0x00},       /* 00000011 00000000 */
    {0x03, 0x00},       /* 00000011 00000000 */
    {0x0C, 0x00},       /* 00001100 00000000 */
    {0x30, 0x00},       /* 00110000 00000000 */
    {0x00, 0x00},       /* 00000000 00000000 */
    {0x00, 0x00}},      /* 00000000 00000000 */

   {{0x00, 0x00},       /* 00000000 00000000 */ /* WHITE ON BLACK '_'    */
    {0x00, 0x00},       /* 00000000 00000000 */
    {0x00, 0x00},       /* 00000000 00000000 */
    {0x00, 0x00},       /* 00000000 00000000 */
    {0x00, 0x00},       /* 00000000 00000000 */
    {0x00, 0x00},       /* 00000000 00000000 */
    {0x00, 0x00},       /* 00000000 00000000 */
    {0x00, 0x00},       /* 00000000 00000000 */
    {0x00, 0x00},       /* 00000000 00000000 */
    {0xFF, 0xF0}},      /* 11111111 11110000 */

   {{0x00, 0x00},       /* 00000000 00000000 */ /* WHITE ON BLACK '-'    */
    {0x00, 0x00},       /* 00000000 00000000 */
    {0x00, 0x00},       /* 00000000 00000000 */
    {0x00, 0x00},       /* 00000000 00000000 */
    {0xFF, 0xC0},       /* 11111111 11000000 */
    {0x00, 0x00},       /* 00000000 00000000 */
    {0x00, 0x00},       /* 00000000 00000000 */
    {0x00, 0x00},       /* 00000000 00000000 */
    {0x00, 0x00},       /* 00000000 00000000 */
    {0x00, 0x00}},      /* 00000000 00000000 */

   {{0x00, 0x00},       /* 00000000 00000000 */ /* WHITE ON BLACK '+'    */
    {0x0C, 0x00},       /* 00001100 00000000 */
    {0x0C, 0x00},       /* 00001100 00000000 */
    {0x0C, 0x00},       /* 00001100 00000000 */
    {0xFF, 0xC0},       /* 11111111 11000000 */
    {0x0C, 0x00},       /* 00001100 00000000 */
    {0x0C, 0x00},       /* 00001100 00000000 */
    {0x0C, 0x00},       /* 00001100 00000000 */
    {0x00, 0x00},       /* 00000000 00000000 */
    {0x00, 0x00}},      /* 00000000 00000000 */

   {{0x00, 0x00},       /* 00000000 00000000 */ /* WHITE ON BLACK '='    */
    {0x00, 0x00},       /* 00000000 00000000 */
    {0x00, 0x00},       /* 00000000 00000000 */
```

```
    {0xFF, 0xC0},     /* 11111111 11000000 */
    {0x00, 0x00},     /* 00000000 00000000 */
    {0x00, 0x00},     /* 00000000 00000000 */
    {0xFF, 0xC0},     /* 11111111 11000000 */
    {0x00, 0x00},     /* 00000000 00000000 */
    {0x00, 0x00},     /* 00000000 00000000 */
    {0x00, 0x00}},    /* 00000000 00000000 */

  {{0x00, 0x00},      /* 00000000 00000000 */ /* WHITE ON BLACK '{'    */
    {0x0F, 0x00},     /* 00001111 00000000 */
    {0x30, 0x00},     /* 00110000 00000000 */
    {0x30, 0x00},     /* 00110000 00000000 */
    {0xC0, 0x00},     /* 11000000 00000000 */
    {0x30, 0x00},     /* 00110000 00000000 */
    {0x30, 0x00},     /* 00110000 00000000 */
    {0x0F, 0x00},     /* 00001111 00000000 */
    {0x00, 0x00},     /* 00000000 00000000 */
    {0x00, 0x00}},    /* 00000000 00000000 */

  {{0x00, 0x00},      /* 00000000 00000000 */ /* WHITE ON BLACK '}'    */
    {0xF0, 0x00},     /* 11110000 00000000 */
    {0x0C, 0x00},     /* 00001100 00000000 */
    {0x0C, 0x00},     /* 00001100 00000000 */
    {0x03, 0x00},     /* 00000011 00000000 */
    {0x0C, 0x00},     /* 00001100 00000000 */
    {0x0C, 0x00},     /* 00001100 00000000 */
    {0xF0, 0x00},     /* 11110000 00000000 */
    {0x00, 0x00},     /* 00000000 00000000 */
    {0x00, 0x00}},    /* 00000000 00000000 */

  {{0x00, 0x00},      /* 00000000 00000000 */ /* WHITE ON BLACK '['    */
    {0x3F, 0x00},     /* 00111111 00000000 */
    {0x30, 0x00},     /* 00110000 00000000 */
    {0x30, 0x00},     /* 00110000 00000000 */
    {0x30, 0x00},     /* 00110000 00000000 */
    {0x30, 0x00},     /* 00110000 00000000 */
    {0x30, 0x00},     /* 00110000 00000000 */
    {0x3F, 0x00},     /* 00111111 00000000 */
    {0x00, 0x00},     /* 00000000 00000000 */
    {0x00, 0x00}},    /* 00000000 00000000 */

  {{0x00, 0x00},      /* 00000000 00000000 */ /* WHITE ON BLACK ']'    */
    {0x3F, 0x00},     /* 00111111 00000000 */
    {0x03, 0x00},     /* 00000011 00000000 */
    {0x03, 0x00},     /* 00000011 00000000 */
    {0x03, 0x00},     /* 00000011 00000000 */
    {0x03, 0x00},     /* 00000011 00000000 */
    {0x03, 0x00},     /* 00000011 00000000 */
    {0x3F, 0x00},     /* 00111111 00000000 */
    {0x00, 0x00},     /* 00000000 00000000 */
    {0x00, 0x00}},    /* 00000000 00000000 */

  {{0x00, 0x00},      /* 00000000 00000000 */ /* WHITE ON BLACK '~'    */
```

```
       {0x33, 0x00},      /* 00110011 00000000 */
       {0xCC, 0x00},      /* 11001100 00000000 */
       {0x00, 0x00},      /* 00000000 00000000 */
       {0x00, 0x00},      /* 00000000 00000000 */
       {0x00, 0x00},      /* 00000000 00000000 */
       {0x00, 0x00},      /* 00000000 00000000 */
       {0x00, 0x00},      /* 00000000 00000000 */
       {0x00, 0x00},      /* 00000000 00000000 */
       {0x00, 0x00}},     /* 00000000 00000000 */

      {{0x00, 0x00},      /* 00000000 00000000 */ /* WHITE ON BLACK ''' */
       {0x30, 0x00},      /* 00110000 00000000 */
       {0x30, 0x00},      /* 00110000 00000000 */
       {0x0C, 0x00},      /* 00001100 00000000 */
       {0x00, 0x00},      /* 00000000 00000000 */
       {0x00, 0x00},      /* 00000000 00000000 */
       {0x00, 0x00},      /* 00000000 00000000 */
       {0x00, 0x00},      /* 00000000 00000000 */
       {0x00, 0x00}},     /* 00000000 00000000 */

      {{0x00, 0x00},      /* 00000000 00000000 */ /* WHITE ON BLACK ':' */
       {0x00, 0x00},      /* 00000000 00000000 */
       {0x0C, 0x00},      /* 00001100 00000000 */
       {0x0C, 0x00},      /* 00001100 00000000 */
       {0x00, 0x00},      /* 00000000 00000000 */
       {0x00, 0x00},      /* 00000000 00000000 */
       {0x0C, 0x00},      /* 00001100 00000000 */
       {0x0C, 0x00},      /* 00001100 00000000 */
       {0x00, 0x00},      /* 00000000 00000000 */
       {0x00, 0x00}},     /* 00000000 00000000 */

      {{0x00, 0x00},      /* 00000000 00000000 */ /* WHITE ON BLACK ';' */
       {0x00, 0x00},      /* 00000000 00000000 */
       {0x0C, 0x00},      /* 00001100 00000000 */
       {0x0C, 0x00},      /* 00001100 00000000 */
       {0x00, 0x00},      /* 00000000 00000000 */
       {0x00, 0x00},      /* 00000000 00000000 */
       {0x0C, 0x00},      /* 00001100 00000000 */
       {0x0C, 0x00},      /* 00001100 00000000 */
       {0x30, 0x00},      /* 00110000 00000000 */
       {0x00, 0x00}},     /* 00000000 00000000 */

      {{0x00, 0x00},      /* 00000000 00000000 */ /* WHITE ON BLACK '"' */
       {0x33, 0x00},      /* 00110011 00000000 */
       {0x33, 0x00},      /* 00110011 00000000 */
       {0x33, 0x00},      /* 00110011 00000000 */
       {0x00, 0x00},      /* 00000000 00000000 */
       {0x00, 0x00},      /* 00000000 00000000 */
       {0x00, 0x00},      /* 00000000 00000000 */
       {0x00, 0x00},      /* 00000000 00000000 */
       {0x00, 0x00},      /* 00000000 00000000 */
       {0x00, 0x00}},     /* 00000000 00000000 */
```

```
{{0x00, 0x00},      /* 00000000 00000000 */ /* WHITE ON BLACK ''   */
 {0x0C, 0x00},      /* 00001100 00000000 */
 {0x0C, 0x00},      /* 00001100 00000000 */
 {0x30, 0x00},      /* 00110000 00000000 */
 {0x00, 0x00},      /* 00000000 00000000 */
 {0x00, 0x00},      /* 00000000 00000000 */
 {0x00, 0x00},      /* 00000000 00000000 */
 {0x00, 0x00},      /* 00000000 00000000 */
 {0x00, 0x00},      /* 00000000 00000000 */
 {0x00, 0x00}},     /* 00000000 00000000 */

{{0x00, 0x00},      /* 00000000 00000000 */ /* WHITE ON BLACK '|'   */
 {0x0C, 0x00},      /* 00001100 00000000 */
 {0x0C, 0x00},      /* 00001100 00000000 */
 {0x0C, 0x00},      /* 00001100 00000000 */
 {0x00, 0x00},      /* 00000000 00000000 */
 {0x0C, 0x00},      /* 00001100 00000000 */
 {0x0C, 0x00},      /* 00001100 00000000 */
 {0x0C, 0x00},      /* 00001100 00000000 */
 {0x00, 0x00},      /* 00000000 00000000 */
 {0x00, 0x00}},     /* 00000000 00000000 */

{{0x00, 0x00},      /* 00000000 00000000 */ /* WHITE ON BLACK '\'   */
 {0x00, 0x00},      /* 00000000 00000000 */
 {0xC0, 0x00},      /* 11000000 00000000 */
 {0x30, 0x00},      /* 00110000 00000000 */
 {0x0C, 0x00},      /* 00001100 00000000 */
 {0x03, 0x00},      /* 00000011 00000000 */
 {0x00, 0xC0},      /* 00000000 11000000 */
 {0x00, 0x00},      /* 00000000 00000000 */
 {0x00, 0x00},      /* 00000000 00000000 */
 {0x00, 0x00}},     /* 00000000 00000000 */

{{0x00, 0x00},      /* 00000000 00000000 */ /* WHITE ON BLACK '<'   */
 {0x03, 0x00},      /* 00000011 00000000 */
 {0x0C, 0x00},      /* 00001100 00000000 */
 {0x30, 0x00},      /* 00110000 00000000 */
 {0xC0, 0x00},      /* 11000000 00000000 */
 {0x30, 0x00},      /* 00110000 00000000 */
 {0x0C, 0x00},      /* 00001100 00000000 */
 {0x03, 0x00},      /* 00000011 00000000 */
 {0x00, 0x00},      /* 00000000 00000000 */
 {0x00, 0x00}},     /* 00000000 00000000 */

{{0x00, 0x00},      /* 00000000 00000000 */ /* WHITE ON BLACK ','   */
 {0x00, 0x00},      /* 00000000 00000000 */
 {0x00, 0x00},      /* 00000000 00000000 */
 {0x00, 0x00},      /* 00000000 00000000 */
 {0x00, 0x00},      /* 00000000 00000000 */
 {0x00, 0x00},      /* 00000000 00000000 */
 {0x0C, 0x00},      /* 00001100 00000000 */
 {0x0C, 0x00},      /* 00001100 00000000 */
```

```
    {0x30, 0x00},      /* 00110000 00000000 */
    {0x00, 0x00}},     /* 00000000 00000000 */

  {{0x00, 0x00},       /* 00000000 00000000 */ /* WHITE ON BLACK '>'    */
    {0xC0, 0x00},      /* 11000000 00000000 */
    {0x30, 0x00},      /* 00110000 00000000 */
    {0x0C, 0x00},      /* 00001100 00000000 */
    {0x03, 0x00},      /* 00000011 00000000 */
    {0x0C, 0x00},      /* 00001100 00000000 */
    {0x30, 0x00},      /* 00110000 00000000 */
    {0xC0, 0x00},      /* 11000000 00000000 */
    {0x00, 0x00},      /* 00000000 00000000 */
    {0x00, 0x00}},     /* 00000000 00000000 */

  {{0x00, 0x00},       /* 00000000 00000000 */ /* WHITE ON BLACK '.'    */
    {0x00, 0x00},      /* 00000000 00000000 */
    {0x00, 0x00},      /* 00000000 00000000 */
    {0x00, 0x00},      /* 00000000 00000000 */
    {0x00, 0x00},      /* 00000000 00000000 */
    {0x00, 0x00},      /* 00000000 00000000 */
    {0x0C, 0x00},      /* 00001100 00000000 */
    {0x0C, 0x00},      /* 00001100 00000000 */
    {0x00, 0x00},      /* 00000000 00000000 */
    {0x00, 0x00}},     /* 00000000 00000000 */

  {{0x00, 0x00},       /* 00000000 00000000 */ /* WHITE ON BLACK '?'    */
    {0x3F, 0x00},      /* 00111111 00000000 */
    {0xC0, 0xC0},      /* 11000000 11000000 */
    {0x03, 0x00},      /* 00000011 00000000 */
    {0x0C, 0x00},      /* 00001100 00000000 */
    {0x0C, 0x00},      /* 00001100 00000000 */
    {0x00, 0x00},      /* 00000000 00000000 */
    {0x0C, 0x00},      /* 00001100 00000000 */
    {0x00, 0x00},      /* 00000000 00000000 */
    {0x00, 0x00}},     /* 00000000 00000000 */

  {{0x00, 0x00},       /* 00000000 00000000 */ /* WHITE ON BLACK '/'    */
    {0x00, 0x00},      /* 00000000 00000000 */
    {0x00, 0xC0},      /* 00000000 11000000 */
    {0x03, 0x00},      /* 00000011 00000000 */
    {0x0C, 0x00},      /* 00001100 00000000 */
    {0x30, 0x00},      /* 00110000 00000000 */
    {0xC0, 0x00},      /* 11000000 00000000 */
    {0x00, 0x00},      /* 00000000 00000000 */
    {0x00, 0x00},      /* 00000000 00000000 */
    {0x00, 0x00}},     /* 00000000 00000000 */

  {{0x00, 0x00},       /* 00000000 00000000 */ /* WHITE ON BLACK ' '    */
    {0x00, 0x00},      /* 00000000 00000000 */
    {0x00, 0x00},      /* 00000000 00000000 */
    {0x00, 0x00},      /* 00000000 00000000 */
    {0x00, 0x00},      /* 00000000 00000000 */
    {0x00, 0x00},      /* 00000000 00000000 */
```

```
    {0x00, 0x00},      /* 00000000 00000000 */
    {0x00, 0x00},      /* 00000000 00000000 */
    {0x00, 0x00},      /* 00000000 00000000 */
    {0x00, 0x00}},     /* 00000000 00000000 */

  {{0x00, 0x00},       /* 00000000 00000000 */ /* WHITE ON BLACK '0'    */
    {0x3F, 0x00},      /* 00111111 00000000 */
    {0xC0, 0xC0},      /* 11000000 11000000 */
    {0xC3, 0xC0},      /* 11000011 11000000 */
    {0xCC, 0xC0},      /* 11001100 11000000 */
    {0xF0, 0xC0},      /* 11110000 11000000 */
    {0xC0, 0xC0},      /* 11000000 11000000 */
    {0x3F, 0x00},      /* 00111111 00000000 */
    {0x00, 0x00},      /* 00000000 00000000 */
    {0x00, 0x00}},     /* 00000000 00000000 */

  {{0x00, 0x00},       /* 00000000 00000000 */ /* WHITE ON BLACK '1'    */
    {0x0C, 0x00},      /* 00001100 00000000 */
    {0x3C, 0x00},      /* 00111100 00000000 */
    {0x0C, 0x00},      /* 00001100 00000000 */
    {0x0C, 0x00},      /* 00001100 00000000 */
    {0x0C, 0x00},      /* 00001100 00000000 */
    {0x0C, 0x00},      /* 00001100 00000000 */
    {0xFF, 0xC0},      /* 11111111 11000000 */
    {0x00, 0x00},      /* 00000000 00000000 */
    {0x00, 0x00}},     /* 00000000 00000000 */

  {{0x00, 0x00},       /* 00000000 00000000 */ /* WHITE ON BLACK '2'    */
    {0x3F, 0x00},      /* 00111111 00000000 */
    {0xC0, 0xC0},      /* 11000000 11000000 */
    {0x00, 0xC0},      /* 00000000 11000000 */
    {0x0F, 0x00},      /* 00001111 00000000 */
    {0x30, 0x00},      /* 00110000 00000000 */
    {0xC0, 0xC0},      /* 11000000 11000000 */
    {0xFF, 0xC0},      /* 11111111 11000000 */
    {0x00, 0x00},      /* 00000000 00000000 */
    {0x00, 0x00}},     /* 00000000 00000000 */

  {{0x00, 0x00},       /* 00000000 00000000 */ /* WHITE ON BLACK '3'    */
    {0x3F, 0x00},      /* 00111111 00000000 */
    {0xC0, 0xC0},      /* 11000000 11000000 */
    {0x00, 0xC0},      /* 00000000 11000000 */
    {0x0F, 0x00},      /* 00001111 00000000 */
    {0x00, 0xC0},      /* 00000000 11000000 */
    {0xC0, 0xC0},      /* 11000000 11000000 */
    {0x3F, 0x00},      /* 00111111 00000000 */
    {0x00, 0x00},      /* 00000000 00000000 */
    {0x00, 0x00}},     /* 00000000 00000000 */

  {{0x00, 0x00},       /* 00000000 00000000 */ /* WHITE ON BLACK '4'    */
    {0x0F, 0x00},      /* 00001111 00000000 */
    {0x33, 0x00},      /* 00110011 00000000 */
    {0xC3, 0x00},      /* 11000011 00000000 */
```

```
   {0xFF, 0xC0},        /* 11111111 11000000 */
   {0x03, 0x00},        /* 00000011 00000000 */
   {0x03, 0x00},        /* 00000011 00000000 */
   {0x0F, 0xC0},        /* 00001111 11000000 */
   {0x00, 0x00},        /* 00000000 00000000 */
   {0x00, 0x00}},       /* 00000000 00000000 */

  {{0x00, 0x00},        /* 00000000 00000000 */ /* WHITE ON BLACK '5'   */
   {0xFF, 0xC0},        /* 11111111 11000000 */
   {0xC0, 0x00},        /* 11000000 00000000 */
   {0xFF, 0x00},        /* 11111111 00000000 */
   {0x00, 0xC0},        /* 00000000 11000000 */
   {0x00, 0xC0},        /* 00000000 11000000 */
   {0xC0, 0xC0},        /* 11000000 11000000 */
   {0x3F, 0x00},        /* 00111111 00000000 */
   {0x00, 0x00},        /* 00000000 00000000 */
   {0x00, 0x00}},       /* 00000000 00000000 */

  {{0x00, 0x00},        /* 00000000 00000000 */ /* WHITE ON BLACK '6'   */
   {0x0F, 0x00},        /* 00001111 00000000 */
   {0x30, 0x00},        /* 00110000 00000000 */
   {0xC0, 0x00},        /* 11000000 00000000 */
   {0xFF, 0x00},        /* 11111111 00000000 */
   {0xC0, 0xC0},        /* 11000000 11000000 */
   {0xC0, 0xC0},        /* 11000000 11000000 */
   {0x3F, 0x00},        /* 00111111 00000000 */
   {0x00, 0x00},        /* 00000000 00000000 */
   {0x00, 0x00}},       /* 00000000 00000000 */

  {{0x00, 0x00},        /* 00000000 00000000 */ /* WHITE ON BLACK '7'   */
   {0xFF, 0xC0},        /* 11111111 11000000 */
   {0xC0, 0xC0},        /* 11000000 11000000 */
   {0x00, 0xC0},        /* 00000000 11000000 */
   {0x03, 0x00},        /* 00000011 00000000 */
   {0x0C, 0x00},        /* 00001100 00000000 */
   {0x0C, 0x00},        /* 00001100 00000000 */
   {0x0C, 0x00},        /* 00001100 00000000 */
   {0x00, 0x00},        /* 00000000 00000000 */
   {0x00, 0x00}},       /* 00000000 00000000 */

  {{0x00, 0x00},        /* 00000000 00000000 */ /* WHITE ON BLACK '8'   */
   {0x3F, 0x00},        /* 00111111 00000000 */
   {0xC0, 0xC0},        /* 11000000 11000000 */
   {0xC0, 0xC0},        /* 11000000 11000000 */
   {0x3F, 0x00},        /* 00111111 00000000 */
   {0xC0, 0xC0},        /* 11000000 11000000 */
   {0xC0, 0xC0},        /* 11000000 11000000 */
   {0x3F, 0x00},        /* 00111111 00000000 */
   {0x00, 0x00},        /* 00000000 00000000 */
   {0x00, 0x00}},       /* 00000000 00000000 */

  {{0x00, 0x00},        /* 00000000 00000000 */ /* WHITE ON BLACK '9'   */
   {0x3F, 0x00},        /* 00111111 00000000 */
```

```
      {0xC0, 0xC0},      /* 11000000 11000000 */
      {0xC0, 0xC0},      /* 11000000 11000000 */
      {0x3F, 0xC0},      /* 00111111 11000000 */
      {0x00, 0xC0},      /* 00000000 11000000 */
      {0x03, 0x00},      /* 00000011 00000000 */
      {0x3C, 0x00},      /* 00111100 00000000 */
      {0x00, 0x00},      /* 00000000 00000000 */
      {0x00, 0x00}},     /* 00000000 00000000 */
  },
  {
    {{0xFF, 0xFF},       /* 11111111 11111111 */ /* BLACK ON WHITE   'a'  */
      {0xFF, 0xFF},      /* 11111111 11111111 */
      {0xFF, 0xFF},      /* 11111111 11111111 */
      {0xC3, 0xFF},      /* 11000011 11111111 */
      {0xFC, 0xFF},      /* 11111100 11111111 */
      {0xC0, 0xFF},      /* 11000000 11111111 */
      {0x3C, 0xFF},      /* 00111100 11111111 */
      {0xC3, 0x3F},      /* 11000011 00111111 */
      {0xFF, 0xFF},      /* 11111111 11111111 */
      {0xFF, 0xFF}},     /* 11111111 11111111 */

    {{0xFF, 0xFF},       /* 11111111 11111111 */ /* BLACK ON WHITE   'b'  */
      {0x0F, 0xFF},      /* 00001111 11111111 */
      {0xCF, 0xFF},      /* 11001111 11111111 */
      {0xCF, 0xFF},      /* 11001111 11111111 */
      {0xC0, 0xFF},      /* 11000000 11111111 */
      {0xCF, 0x3F},      /* 11001111 00111111 */
      {0xCF, 0x3F},      /* 11001111 00111111 */
      {0x30, 0xFF},      /* 00110000 11111111 */
      {0xFF, 0xFF},      /* 11111111 11111111 */
      {0xFF, 0xFF}},     /* 11111111 11111111 */

    {{0xFF, 0xFF},       /* 11111111 11111111 */ /* BLACK ON WHITE   'c'  */
      {0xFF, 0xFF},      /* 11111111 11111111 */
      {0xFF, 0xFF},      /* 11111111 11111111 */
      {0xC0, 0xFF},      /* 11000000 11111111 */
      {0x3F, 0x3F},      /* 00111111 00111111 */
      {0x3F, 0xFF},      /* 00111111 11111111 */
      {0x3F, 0x3F},      /* 00111111 00111111 */
      {0xC0, 0xFF},      /* 11000000 11111111 */
      {0xFF, 0xFF},      /* 11111111 11111111 */
      {0xFF, 0xFF}},     /* 11111111 11111111 */

    {{0xFF, 0xFF},       /* 11111111 11111111 */ /* BLACK ON WHITE   'd'  */
      {0xF0, 0xFF},      /* 11110000 11111111 */
      {0xFC, 0xFF},      /* 11111100 11111111 */
      {0xFC, 0xFF},      /* 11111100 11111111 */
      {0xC0, 0xFF},      /* 11000000 11111111 */
      {0x3C, 0xFF},      /* 00111100 11111111 */
      {0x3C, 0xFF},      /* 00111100 11111111 */
      {0xC3, 0x3F},      /* 11000011 00111111 */
      {0xFF, 0xFF},      /* 11111111 11111111 */
      {0xFF, 0xFF}},     /* 11111111 11111111 */
```

```
{{0xFF, 0xFF},       /* 11111111 11111111 */ /* BLACK ON WHITE    'e'   */
 {0xFF, 0xFF},       /* 11111111 11111111 */
 {0xFF, 0xFF},       /* 11111111 11111111 */
 {0xC0, 0xFF},       /* 11000000 11111111 */
 {0x3F, 0x3F},       /* 00111111 00111111 */
 {0x00, 0x3F},       /* 00000000 00111111 */
 {0x3F, 0xFF},       /* 00111111 11111111 */
 {0xC0, 0xFF},       /* 11000000 11111111 */
 {0xFF, 0xFF},       /* 11111111 11111111 */
 {0xFF, 0xFF}},      /* 11111111 11111111 */

{{0xFF, 0xFF},       /* 11111111 11111111 */ /* BLACK ON WHITE    'f'   */
 {0xF0, 0xFF},       /* 11110000 11111111 */
 {0xCF, 0x3F},       /* 11001111 00111111 */
 {0xCF, 0xFF},       /* 11001111 11111111 */
 {0x03, 0xFF},       /* 00000011 11111111 */
 {0xCF, 0xFF},       /* 11001111 11111111 */
 {0xCF, 0xFF},       /* 11001111 11111111 */
 {0x03, 0xFF},       /* 00000011 11111111 */
 {0xFF, 0xFF},       /* 11111111 11111111 */
 {0xFF, 0xFF}},      /* 11111111 11111111 */

{{0xFF, 0xFF},       /* 11111111 11111111 */ /* BLACK ON WHITE    'g'   */
 {0xFF, 0xFF},       /* 11111111 11111111 */
 {0xFF, 0xFF},       /* 11111111 11111111 */
 {0xC3, 0x3F},       /* 11000011 00111111 */
 {0x3C, 0xFF},       /* 00111100 11111111 */
 {0x3C, 0xFF},       /* 00111100 11111111 */
 {0xC0, 0xFF},       /* 11000000 11111111 */
 {0xFC, 0xFF},       /* 11111100 11111111 */
 {0x03, 0xFF},       /* 00000011 11111111 */
 {0xFF, 0xFF}},      /* 11111111 11111111 */

{{0xFF, 0xFF},       /* 11111111 11111111 */ /* BLACK ON WHITE    'h'   */
 {0x0F, 0xFF},       /* 00001111 11111111 */
 {0xCF, 0xFF},       /* 11001111 11111111 */
 {0xCC, 0xFF},       /* 11001100 11111111 */
 {0xC3, 0x3F},       /* 11000011 00111111 */
 {0xCF, 0x3F},       /* 11001111 00111111 */
 {0xCF, 0x3F},       /* 11001111 00111111 */
 {0x0F, 0x3F},       /* 00001111 00111111 */
 {0xFF, 0xFF},       /* 11111111 11111111 */
 {0xFF, 0xFF}},      /* 11111111 11111111 */

{{0xFF, 0xFF},       /* 11111111 11111111 */ /* BLACK ON WHITE    'i'   */
 {0xF3, 0xFF},       /* 11110011 11111111 */
 {0xFF, 0xFF},       /* 11111111 11111111 */
 {0xC3, 0xFF},       /* 11000011 11111111 */
 {0xF3, 0xFF},       /* 11110011 11111111 */
 {0xF3, 0xFF},       /* 11110011 11111111 */
 {0xF3, 0xFF},       /* 11110011 11111111 */
 {0xC0, 0xFF},       /* 11000000 11111111 */
```

```
    {0xFF, 0xFF},       /* 11111111 11111111 */
    {0xFF, 0xFF}},      /* 11111111 11111111 */

   {{0xFF, 0xFF},       /* 11111111 11111111 */ /* BLACK ON WHITE   'j'  */
    {0xFC, 0xFF},       /* 11111100 11111111 */
    {0xFF, 0xFF},       /* 11111111 11111111 */
    {0xFC, 0xFF},       /* 11111100 11111111 */
    {0xFC, 0xFF},       /* 11111100 11111111 */
    {0xFC, 0xFF},       /* 11111100 11111111 */
    {0x3C, 0xFF},       /* 00111100 11111111 */
    {0x3C, 0xFF},       /* 00111100 11111111 */
    {0xC3, 0xFF},       /* 11000011 11111111 */
    {0xFF, 0xFF}},      /* 11111111 11111111 */

   {{0xFF, 0xFF},       /* 11111111 11111111 */ /* BLACK ON WHITE   'k'  */
    {0x0F, 0xFF},       /* 00001111 11111111 */
    {0xCF, 0xFF},       /* 11001111 11111111 */
    {0xCF, 0x3F},       /* 11001111 00111111 */
    {0xCC, 0xFF},       /* 11001100 11111111 */
    {0xC3, 0xFF},       /* 11000011 11111111 */
    {0xCC, 0xFF},       /* 11001100 11111111 */
    {0x0F, 0x3F},       /* 00001111 00111111 */
    {0xFF, 0xFF},       /* 11111111 11111111 */
    {0xFF, 0xFF}},      /* 11111111 11111111 */

   {{0xFF, 0xFF},       /* 11111111 11111111 */ /* BLACK ON WHITE   'l'  */
    {0xC3, 0xFF},       /* 11000011 11111111 */
    {0xF3, 0xFF},       /* 11110011 11111111 */
    {0xF3, 0xFF},       /* 11110011 11111111 */
    {0xF3, 0xFF},       /* 11110011 11111111 */
    {0xF3, 0xFF},       /* 11110011 11111111 */
    {0xF3, 0xFF},       /* 11110011 11111111 */
    {0xC0, 0xFF},       /* 11000000 11111111 */
    {0xFF, 0xFF},       /* 11111111 11111111 */
    {0xFF, 0xFF}},      /* 11111111 11111111 */

   {{0xFF, 0xFF},       /* 11111111 11111111 */ /* BLACK ON WHITE   'm'  */
    {0xFF, 0xFF},       /* 11111111 11111111 */
    {0xFF, 0xFF},       /* 11111111 11111111 */
    {0x3F, 0x3F},       /* 00111111 00111111 */
    {0x0C, 0x3F},       /* 00001100 00111111 */
    {0x33, 0x3F},       /* 00110011 00111111 */
    {0x3F, 0x3F},       /* 00111111 00111111 */
    {0x3F, 0x3F},       /* 00111111 00111111 */
    {0xFF, 0xFF},       /* 11111111 11111111 */
    {0xFF, 0xFF}},      /* 11111111 11111111 */

   {{0xFF, 0xFF},       /* 11111111 11111111 */ /* BLACK ON WHITE   'n'  */
    {0xFF, 0xFF},       /* 11111111 11111111 */
    {0xFF, 0xFF},       /* 11111111 11111111 */
    {0x30, 0xFF},       /* 00110000 11111111 */
    {0x0F, 0x3F},       /* 00001111 00111111 */
    {0x3F, 0x3F},       /* 00111111 00111111 */
```

```
    {0x3F, 0x3F},      /* 00111111 00111111 */
    {0x3F, 0x3F},      /* 00111111 00111111 */
    {0xFF, 0xFF},      /* 11111111 11111111 */
    {0xFF, 0xFF}},     /* 11111111 11111111 */

   {{0xFF, 0xFF},      /* 11111111 11111111 */ /* BLACK ON WHITE    'o'  */
    {0xFF, 0xFF},      /* 11111111 11111111 */
    {0xFF, 0xFF},      /* 11111111 11111111 */
    {0xC0, 0xFF},      /* 11000000 11111111 */
    {0x3F, 0x3F},      /* 00111111 00111111 */
    {0x3F, 0x3F},      /* 00111111 00111111 */
    {0x3F, 0x3F},      /* 00111111 00111111 */
    {0xC0, 0xFF},      /* 11000000 11111111 */
    {0xFF, 0xFF},      /* 11111111 11111111 */
    {0xFF, 0xFF}},     /* 11111111 11111111 */

   {{0xFF, 0xFF},      /* 11111111 11111111 */ /* BLACK ON WHITE    'p'  */
    {0xFF, 0xFF},      /* 11111111 11111111 */
    {0xFF, 0xFF},      /* 11111111 11111111 */
    {0x30, 0xFF},      /* 00110000 11111111 */
    {0xCF, 0x3F},      /* 11001111 00111111 */
    {0xCF, 0x3F},      /* 11001111 00111111 */
    {0xC0, 0xFF},      /* 11000000 11111111 */
    {0xCF, 0xFF},      /* 11001111 11111111 */
    {0x03, 0xFF},      /* 00000011 11111111 */
    {0xFF, 0xFF}},     /* 11111111 11111111 */

   {{0xFF, 0xFF},      /* 11111111 11111111 */ /* BLACK ON WHITE    'q'  */
    {0xFF, 0xFF},      /* 11111111 11111111 */
    {0xFF, 0xFF},      /* 11111111 11111111 */
    {0xC3, 0x3F},      /* 11000011 00111111 */
    {0x3C, 0xFF},      /* 00111100 11111111 */
    {0x3C, 0xFF},      /* 00111100 11111111 */
    {0xC0, 0xFF},      /* 11000000 11111111 */
    {0xFC, 0xFF},      /* 11111100 11111111 */
    {0xF0, 0x3F},      /* 11110000 00111111 */
    {0xFF, 0xFF}},     /* 11111111 11111111 */

   {{0xFF, 0xFF},      /* 11111111 11111111 */ /* BLACK ON WHITE    'r'  */
    {0xFF, 0xFF},      /* 11111111 11111111 */
    {0xFF, 0xFF},      /* 11111111 11111111 */
    {0x30, 0xFF},      /* 00110000 11111111 */
    {0xCF, 0x3F},      /* 11001111 00111111 */
    {0xCF, 0xFF},      /* 11001111 11111111 */
    {0xCF, 0xFF},      /* 11001111 11111111 */
    {0x03, 0xFF},      /* 00000011 11111111 */
    {0xFF, 0xFF},      /* 11111111 11111111 */
    {0xFF, 0xFF}},     /* 11111111 11111111 */

   {{0xFF, 0xFF},      /* 11111111 11111111 */ /* BLACK ON WHITE    's'  */
    {0xFF, 0xFF},      /* 11111111 11111111 */
    {0xFF, 0xFF},      /* 11111111 11111111 */
    {0xC0, 0x3F},      /* 11000000 00111111 */
```

```
    {0x3F, 0xFF},       /* 00111111 11111111 */
    {0xC0, 0xFF},       /* 11000000 11111111 */
    {0xFF, 0x3F},       /* 11111111 00111111 */
    {0x00, 0xFF},       /* 00000000 11111111 */
    {0xFF, 0xFF},       /* 11111111 11111111 */
    {0xFF, 0xFF}},      /* 11111111 11111111 */

   {{0xFF, 0xFF},       /* 11111111 11111111 */ /* BLACK ON WHITE   't'   */
    {0xCF, 0xFF},       /* 11001111 11111111 */
    {0xCF, 0xFF},       /* 11001111 11111111 */
    {0x03, 0xFF},       /* 00000011 11111111 */
    {0xCF, 0xFF},       /* 11001111 11111111 */
    {0xCF, 0x3F},       /* 11001111 00111111 */
    {0xCF, 0x3F},       /* 11001111 00111111 */
    {0xF0, 0xFF},       /* 11110000 11111111 */
    {0xFF, 0xFF},       /* 11111111 11111111 */
    {0xFF, 0xFF}},      /* 11111111 11111111 */

   {{0xFF, 0xFF},       /* 11111111 11111111 */ /* BLACK ON WHITE   'u'   */
    {0xFF, 0xFF},       /* 11111111 11111111 */
    {0xFF, 0xFF},       /* 11111111 11111111 */
    {0x3C, 0xFF},       /* 00111100 11111111 */
    {0x3C, 0xFF},       /* 00111100 11111111 */
    {0x3C, 0xFF},       /* 00111100 11111111 */
    {0x3C, 0xFF},       /* 00111100 11111111 */
    {0xC3, 0x3F},       /* 11000011 00111111 */
    {0xFF, 0xFF},       /* 11111111 11111111 */
    {0xFF, 0xFF}},      /* 11111111 11111111 */

   {{0xFF, 0xFF},       /* 11111111 11111111 */ /* BLACK ON WHITE   'v'   */
    {0xFF, 0xFF},       /* 11111111 11111111 */
    {0xFF, 0xFF},       /* 11111111 11111111 */
    {0x3F, 0x3F},       /* 00111111 00111111 */
    {0x3F, 0x3F},       /* 00111111 00111111 */
    {0x3F, 0x3F},       /* 00111111 00111111 */
    {0xCC, 0xFF},       /* 11001100 11111111 */
    {0xF3, 0xFF},       /* 11110011 11111111 */
    {0xFF, 0xFF},       /* 11111111 11111111 */
    {0xFF, 0xFF}},      /* 11111111 11111111 */

   {{0xFF, 0xFF},       /* 11111111 11111111 */ /* BLACK ON WHITE   'w'   */
    {0xFF, 0xFF},       /* 11111111 11111111 */
    {0xFF, 0xFF},       /* 11111111 11111111 */
    {0x3F, 0x3F},       /* 00111111 00111111 */
    {0x3F, 0x3F},       /* 00111111 00111111 */
    {0x33, 0x3F},       /* 00110011 00111111 */
    {0x33, 0x3F},       /* 00110011 00111111 */
    {0xCC, 0xFF},       /* 11001100 11111111 */
    {0xFF, 0xFF},       /* 11111111 11111111 */
    {0xFF, 0xFF}},      /* 11111111 11111111 */

   {{0xFF, 0xFF},       /* 11111111 11111111 */ /* BLACK ON WHITE   'x'   */
    {0xFF, 0xFF},       /* 11111111 11111111 */
```

```
    {0xFF, 0xFF},      /* 11111111 11111111 */
    {0x3F, 0x3F},      /* 00111111 00111111 */
    {0xCC, 0xFF},      /* 11001100 11111111 */
    {0xF3, 0xFF},      /* 11110011 11111111 */
    {0xCC, 0xFF},      /* 11001100 11111111 */
    {0x3F, 0x3F},      /* 00111111 00111111 */
    {0xFF, 0xFF},      /* 11111111 11111111 */
    {0xFF, 0xFF}},     /* 11111111 11111111 */

   {{0xFF, 0xFF},      /* 11111111 11111111 */ /* BLACK ON WHITE    'y'  */
    {0xFF, 0xFF},      /* 11111111 11111111 */
    {0xFF, 0xFF},      /* 11111111 11111111 */
    {0x3F, 0x3F},      /* 00111111 00111111 */
    {0x3F, 0x3F},      /* 00111111 00111111 */
    {0x3F, 0x3F},      /* 00111111 00111111 */
    {0xC0, 0x3F},      /* 11000000 00111111 */
    {0xFF, 0x3F},      /* 11111111 00111111 */
    {0xC0, 0xFF},      /* 11000000 11111111 */
    {0xFF, 0xFF}},     /* 11111111 11111111 */

   {{0xFF, 0xFF},      /* 11111111 11111111 */ /* BLACK ON WHITE    'z'  */
    {0xFF, 0xFF},      /* 11111111 11111111 */
    {0xFF, 0xFF},      /* 11111111 11111111 */
    {0x00, 0x3F},      /* 00000000 00111111 */
    {0xFC, 0xFF},      /* 11111100 11111111 */
    {0xF3, 0xFF},      /* 11110011 11111111 */
    {0xCF, 0xFF},      /* 11001111 11111111 */
    {0x00, 0x3F},      /* 00000000 00111111 */
    {0xFF, 0xFF},      /* 11111111 11111111 */
    {0xFF, 0xFF}},     /* 11111111 11111111 */

   {{0xFF, 0xFF},      /* 11111111 11111111 */ /* BLACK ON WHITE    'A'  */
    {0xF3, 0xFF},      /* 11110011 11111111 */
    {0xCC, 0xFF},      /* 11001100 11111111 */
    {0x3F, 0x3F},      /* 00111111 00111111 */
    {0x3F, 0x3F},      /* 00111111 00111111 */
    {0x00, 0x3F},      /* 00000000 00111111 */
    {0x3F, 0x3F},      /* 00111111 00111111 */
    {0x3F, 0x3F},      /* 00111111 00111111 */
    {0xFF, 0xFF},      /* 11111111 11111111 */
    {0xFF, 0xFF}},     /* 11111111 11111111 */

   {{0xFF, 0xFF},      /* 11111111 11111111 */ /* BLACK ON WHITE    'B'  */
    {0x00, 0xFF},      /* 00000000 11111111 */
    {0xCF, 0x3F},      /* 11001111 00111111 */
    {0xCF, 0x3F},      /* 11001111 00111111 */
    {0xC0, 0xFF},      /* 11000000 11111111 */
    {0xCF, 0x3F},      /* 11001111 00111111 */
    {0xCF, 0x3F},      /* 11001111 00111111 */
    {0x00, 0xFF},      /* 00000000 11111111 */
    {0xFF, 0xFF},      /* 11111111 11111111 */
    {0xFF, 0xFF}},     /* 11111111 11111111 */
```

```
{{0xFF, 0xFF},      /* 11111111 11111111 */ /* BLACK ON WHITE   'C'   */
 {0xC0, 0xFF},      /* 11000000 11111111 */
 {0x3F, 0x3F},      /* 00111111 00111111 */
 {0x3F, 0xFF},      /* 00111111 11111111 */
 {0x3F, 0xFF},      /* 00111111 11111111 */
 {0x3F, 0xFF},      /* 00111111 11111111 */
 {0x3F, 0x3F},      /* 00111111 00111111 */
 {0xC0, 0xFF},      /* 11000000 11111111 */
 {0xFF, 0xFF},      /* 11111111 11111111 */
 {0xFF, 0xFF}},     /* 11111111 11111111 */

{{0xFF, 0xFF},      /* 11111111 11111111 */ /* BLACK ON WHITE   'D'   */
 {0x00, 0xFF},      /* 00000000 11111111 */
 {0xCF, 0x3F},      /* 11001111 00111111 */
 {0xCF, 0x3F},      /* 11001111 00111111 */
 {0xCF, 0x3F},      /* 11001111 00111111 */
 {0xCF, 0x3F},      /* 11001111 00111111 */
 {0xCF, 0x3F},      /* 11001111 00111111 */
 {0x00, 0xFF},      /* 00000000 11111111 */
 {0xFF, 0xFF},      /* 11111111 11111111 */
 {0xFF, 0xFF}},     /* 11111111 11111111 */

{{0xFF, 0xFF},      /* 11111111 11111111 */ /* BLACK ON WHITE   'E'   */
 {0x00, 0x3F},      /* 00000000 00111111 */
 {0xCF, 0x3F},      /* 11001111 00111111 */
 {0xCF, 0xFF},      /* 11001111 11111111 */
 {0xC0, 0xFF},      /* 11000000 11111111 */
 {0xCF, 0xFF},      /* 11001111 11111111 */
 {0xCF, 0x3F},      /* 11001111 00111111 */
 {0x00, 0x3F},      /* 00000000 00111111 */
 {0xFF, 0xFF},      /* 11111111 11111111 */
 {0xFF, 0xFF}},     /* 11111111 11111111 */

{{0xFF, 0xFF},      /* 11111111 11111111 */ /* BLACK ON WHITE   'F'   */
 {0x00, 0x3F},      /* 00000000 00111111 */
 {0xCF, 0x3F},      /* 11001111 00111111 */
 {0xCF, 0xFF},      /* 11001111 11111111 */
 {0xC3, 0xFF},      /* 11000011 11111111 */
 {0xCF, 0xFF},      /* 11001111 11111111 */
 {0xCF, 0xFF},      /* 11001111 11111111 */
 {0x03, 0xFF},      /* 00000011 11111111 */
 {0xFF, 0xFF},      /* 11111111 11111111 */
 {0xFF, 0xFF}},     /* 11111111 11111111 */

{{0xFF, 0xFF},      /* 11111111 11111111 */ /* BLACK ON WHITE   'G'   */
 {0xC0, 0xFF},      /* 11000000 11111111 */
 {0x3F, 0x3F},      /* 00111111 00111111 */
 {0x3F, 0xFF},      /* 00111111 11111111 */
 {0x30, 0x3F},      /* 00110000 00111111 */
 {0x3F, 0x3F},      /* 00111111 00111111 */
 {0x3F, 0x3F},      /* 00111111 00111111 */
 {0xC0, 0xFF},      /* 11000000 11111111 */
 {0xFF, 0xFF},      /* 11111111 11111111 */
```

```
        {0xFF, 0xFF}},      /* 11111111 11111111 */

       {{0xFF, 0xFF},       /* 11111111 11111111 */ /* BLACK ON WHITE    'H'   */
        {0x3F, 0x3F},       /* 00111111 00111111 */
        {0x3F, 0x3F},       /* 00111111 00111111 */
        {0x3F, 0x3F},       /* 00111111 00111111 */
        {0x00, 0x3F},       /* 00000000 00111111 */
        {0x3F, 0x3F},       /* 00111111 00111111 */
        {0x3F, 0x3F},       /* 00111111 00111111 */
        {0x3F, 0x3F},       /* 00111111 00111111 */
        {0xFF, 0xFF},       /* 11111111 11111111 */
        {0xFF, 0xFF}},      /* 11111111 11111111 */

       {{0xFF, 0xFF},       /* 11111111 11111111 */ /* BLACK ON WHITE    'I'   */
        {0xC0, 0xFF},       /* 11000000 11111111 */
        {0xF3, 0xFF},       /* 11110011 11111111 */
        {0xF3, 0xFF},       /* 11110011 11111111 */
        {0xF3, 0xFF},       /* 11110011 11111111 */
        {0xF3, 0xFF},       /* 11110011 11111111 */
        {0xF3, 0xFF},       /* 11110011 11111111 */
        {0xC0, 0xFF},       /* 11000000 11111111 */
        {0xFF, 0xFF},       /* 11111111 11111111 */
        {0xFF, 0xFF}},      /* 11111111 11111111 */

       {{0xFF, 0xFF},       /* 11111111 11111111 */ /* BLACK ON WHITE    'J'   */
        {0xF0, 0x3F},       /* 11110000 00111111 */
        {0xFC, 0xFF},       /* 11111100 11111111 */
        {0xFC, 0xFF},       /* 11111100 11111111 */
        {0xFC, 0xFF},       /* 11111100 11111111 */
        {0xFC, 0xFF},       /* 11111100 11111111 */
        {0xFC, 0xFF},       /* 11111100 11111111 */
        {0x3C, 0xFF},       /* 00111100 11111111 */
        {0xC3, 0xFF},       /* 11000011 11111111 */
        {0xFF, 0xFF}},      /* 11111111 11111111 */

       {{0xFF, 0xFF},       /* 11111111 11111111 */ /* BLACK ON WHITE    'K'   */
        {0x0F, 0x3F},       /* 00001111 00111111 */
        {0xCF, 0x3F},       /* 11001111 00111111 */
        {0xCC, 0xFF},       /* 11001100 11111111 */
        {0xC3, 0xFF},       /* 11000011 11111111 */
        {0xCC, 0xFF},       /* 11001100 11111111 */
        {0xCF, 0x3F},       /* 11001111 00111111 */
        {0x0F, 0x3F},       /* 00001111 00111111 */
        {0xFF, 0xFF},       /* 11111111 11111111 */
        {0xFF, 0xFF}},      /* 11111111 11111111 */

       {{0xFF, 0xFF},       /* 11111111 11111111 */ /* BLACK ON WHITE    'L'   */
        {0x0F, 0xFF},       /* 00001111 11111111 */
        {0xCF, 0xFF},       /* 11001111 11111111 */
        {0xCF, 0xFF},       /* 11001111 11111111 */
        {0xCF, 0xFF},       /* 11001111 11111111 */
        {0xCF, 0xFF},       /* 11001111 11111111 */
        {0xCF, 0x3F},       /* 11001111 00111111 */
```

```
     {0x00, 0x3F},        /* 00000000 00111111 */
     {0xFF, 0xFF},        /* 11111111 11111111 */
     {0xFF, 0xFF}},       /* 11111111 11111111 */

    {{0xFF, 0xFF},        /* 11111111 11111111 */ /* BLACK ON WHITE   'M'  */
     {0x3F, 0x3F},        /* 00111111 00111111 */
     {0x0C, 0x3F},        /* 00001100 00111111 */
     {0x33, 0x3F},        /* 00110011 00111111 */
     {0x33, 0x3F},        /* 00110011 00111111 */
     {0x3F, 0x3F},        /* 00111111 00111111 */
     {0x3F, 0x3F},        /* 00111111 00111111 */
     {0x3F, 0x3F},        /* 00111111 00111111 */
     {0xFF, 0xFF},        /* 11111111 11111111 */
     {0xFF, 0xFF}},       /* 11111111 11111111 */

    {{0xFF, 0xFF},        /* 11111111 11111111 */ /* BLACK ON WHITE   'N'  */
     {0x3F, 0x3F},        /* 00111111 00111111 */
     {0x0F, 0x3F},        /* 00001111 00111111 */
     {0x33, 0x3F},        /* 00110011 00111111 */
     {0x3C, 0x3F},        /* 00111100 00111111 */
     {0x3F, 0x3F},        /* 00111111 00111111 */
     {0x3F, 0x3F},        /* 00111111 00111111 */
     {0xFF, 0xFF},        /* 11111111 11111111 */
     {0xFF, 0xFF}},       /* 11111111 11111111 */

    {{0xFF, 0xFF},        /* 11111111 11111111 */ /* BLACK ON WHITE   'O'  */
     {0xC0, 0xFF},        /* 11000000 11111111 */
     {0x3F, 0x3F},        /* 00111111 00111111 */
     {0x3F, 0x3F},        /* 00111111 00111111 */
     {0x3F, 0x3F},        /* 00111111 00111111 */
     {0x3F, 0x3F},        /* 00111111 00111111 */
     {0xC0, 0xFF},        /* 11000000 11111111 */
     {0xFF, 0xFF},        /* 11111111 11111111 */
     {0xFF, 0xFF}},       /* 11111111 11111111 */

    {{0xFF, 0xFF},        /* 11111111 11111111 */ /* BLACK ON WHITE   'P'  */
     {0x00, 0xFF},        /* 00000000 11111111 */
     {0xCF, 0x3F},        /* 11001111 00111111 */
     {0xCF, 0x3F},        /* 11001111 00111111 */
     {0xC0, 0xFF},        /* 11000000 11111111 */
     {0xCF, 0xFF},        /* 11001111 11111111 */
     {0xCF, 0xFF},        /* 11001111 11111111 */
     {0x03, 0xFF},        /* 00000011 11111111 */
     {0xFF, 0xFF},        /* 11111111 11111111 */
     {0xFF, 0xFF}},       /* 11111111 11111111 */

    {{0xFF, 0xFF},        /* 11111111 11111111 */ /* BLACK ON WHITE   'Q'  */
     {0xC0, 0xFF},        /* 11000000 11111111 */
     {0x3F, 0x3F},        /* 00111111 00111111 */
     {0x3F, 0x3F},        /* 00111111 00111111 */
     {0x3F, 0x3F},        /* 00111111 00111111 */
```

```
  {0x3F, 0x3F},      /* 00111111 00111111 */
  {0x33, 0x3F},      /* 00110011 00111111 */
  {0xC0, 0xFF},      /* 11000000 11111111 */
  {0xFF, 0x3F},      /* 11111111 00111111 */
  {0xFF, 0xFF}},     /* 11111111 11111111 */

 {{0xFF, 0xFF},      /* 11111111 11111111 */ /* BLACK ON WHITE   'R'  */
  {0x00, 0xFF},      /* 00000000 11111111 */
  {0xCF, 0x3F},      /* 11001111 00111111 */
  {0xCF, 0x3F},      /* 11001111 00111111 */
  {0xC0, 0xFF},      /* 11000000 11111111 */
  {0xCC, 0xFF},      /* 11001100 11111111 */
  {0xCF, 0x3F},      /* 11001111 00111111 */
  {0x0F, 0x3F},      /* 00001111 00111111 */
  {0xFF, 0xFF},      /* 11111111 11111111 */
  {0xFF, 0xFF}},     /* 11111111 11111111 */

 {{0xFF, 0xFF},      /* 11111111 11111111 */ /* BLACK ON WHITE   'S'  */
  {0xC0, 0x3F},      /* 11000000 00111111 */
  {0x3F, 0xFF},      /* 00111111 11111111 */
  {0x3F, 0xFF},      /* 00111111 11111111 */
  {0xC0, 0xFF},      /* 11000000 11111111 */
  {0xFF, 0x3F},      /* 11111111 00111111 */
  {0xFF, 0x3F},      /* 11111111 00111111 */
  {0x00, 0xFF},      /* 00000000 11111111 */
  {0xFF, 0xFF},      /* 11111111 11111111 */
  {0xFF, 0xFF}},     /* 11111111 11111111 */

 {{0xFF, 0xFF},      /* 11111111 11111111 */ /* BLACK ON WHITE   'T'  */
  {0x00, 0x3F},      /* 00000000 00111111 */
  {0x33, 0x3F},      /* 00110011 00111111 */
  {0xF3, 0xFF},      /* 11110011 11111111 */
  {0xF3, 0xFF},      /* 11110011 11111111 */
  {0xF3, 0xFF},      /* 11110011 11111111 */
  {0xF3, 0xFF},      /* 11110011 11111111 */
  {0xC0, 0xFF},      /* 11000000 11111111 */
  {0xFF, 0xFF},      /* 11111111 11111111 */
  {0xFF, 0xFF}},     /* 11111111 11111111 */

 {{0xFF, 0xFF},      /* 11111111 11111111 */ /* BLACK ON WHITE   'U'  */
  {0x3F, 0x3F},      /* 00111111 00111111 */
  {0x3F, 0x3F},      /* 00111111 00111111 */
  {0x3F, 0x3F},      /* 00111111 00111111 */
  {0x3F, 0x3F},      /* 00111111 00111111 */
  {0x3F, 0x3F},      /* 00111111 00111111 */
  {0x3F, 0x3F},      /* 00111111 00111111 */
  {0xC0, 0xFF},      /* 11000000 11111111 */
  {0xFF, 0xFF},      /* 11111111 11111111 */
  {0xFF, 0xFF}},     /* 11111111 11111111 */

 {{0xFF, 0xFF},      /* 11111111 11111111 */ /* BLACK ON WHITE   'V'  */
  {0x3F, 0x3F},      /* 00111111 00111111 */
  {0x3F, 0x3F},      /* 00111111 00111111 */
```

```
    {0x3F, 0x3F},      /* 00111111 00111111 */
    {0x3F, 0x3F},      /* 00111111 00111111 */
    {0x3F, 0x3F},      /* 00111111 00111111 */
    {0xCC, 0xFF},      /* 11001100 11111111 */
    {0xF3, 0xFF},      /* 11110011 11111111 */
    {0xFF, 0xFF},      /* 11111111 11111111 */
    {0xFF, 0xFF}},     /* 11111111 11111111 */

  {{0xFF, 0xFF},       /* 11111111 11111111 */ /* BLACK ON WHITE   'W'  */
    {0x3F, 0x3F},      /* 00111111 00111111 */
    {0x3F, 0x3F},      /* 00111111 00111111 */
    {0x3F, 0x3F},      /* 00111111 00111111 */
    {0x33, 0x3F},      /* 00110011 00111111 */
    {0x33, 0x3F},      /* 00110011 00111111 */
    {0x33, 0x3F},      /* 00110011 00111111 */
    {0xCC, 0xFF},      /* 11001100 11111111 */
    {0xFF, 0xFF},      /* 11111111 11111111 */
    {0xFF, 0xFF}},     /* 11111111 11111111 */

  {{0xFF, 0xFF},       /* 11111111 11111111 */ /* BLACK ON WHITE   'X'  */
    {0x3F, 0x3F},      /* 00111111 00111111 */
    {0x3F, 0x3F},      /* 00111111 00111111 */
    {0xCC, 0xFF},      /* 11001100 11111111 */
    {0xF3, 0xFF},      /* 11110011 11111111 */
    {0xF3, 0xFF},      /* 11110011 11111111 */
    {0xCC, 0xFF},      /* 11001100 11111111 */
    {0x3F, 0x3F},      /* 00111111 00111111 */
    {0xFF, 0xFF},      /* 11111111 11111111 */
    {0xFF, 0xFF}},     /* 11111111 11111111 */

  {{0xFF, 0xFF},       /* 11111111 11111111 */ /* BLACK ON WHITE   'Y'  */
    {0x3F, 0x3F},      /* 00111111 00111111 */
    {0x3F, 0x3F},      /* 00111111 00111111 */
    {0x3F, 0x3F},      /* 00111111 00111111 */
    {0xCC, 0xFF},      /* 11001100 11111111 */
    {0xF3, 0xFF},      /* 11110011 11111111 */
    {0xF3, 0xFF},      /* 11110011 11111111 */
    {0xF3, 0xFF},      /* 11110011 11111111 */
    {0xFF, 0xFF},      /* 11111111 11111111 */
    {0xFF, 0xFF}},     /* 11111111 11111111 */

  {{0xFF, 0xFF},       /* 11111111 11111111 */ /* BLACK ON WHITE   'Z'  */
    {0x00, 0x3F},      /* 00000000 00111111 */
    {0x3F, 0x3F},      /* 00111111 00111111 */
    {0xFC, 0xFF},      /* 11111100 11111111 */
    {0xF3, 0xFF},      /* 11110011 11111111 */
    {0xCF, 0xFF},      /* 11001111 11111111 */
    {0x3F, 0x3F},      /* 00111111 00111111 */
    {0x00, 0x3F},      /* 00000000 00111111 */
    {0xFF, 0xFF},      /* 11111111 11111111 */
    {0xFF, 0xFF}},     /* 11111111 11111111 */

  {{0xFF, 0xFF},       /* 11111111 11111111 */ /* BLACK ON WHITE   '!'  */
```

```
    {0xF3, 0xFF},       /* 11110011 11111111 */
    {0xF3, 0xFF},       /* 11110011 11111111 */
    {0xF3, 0xFF},       /* 11110011 11111111 */
    {0xF3, 0xFF},       /* 11110011 11111111 */
    {0xF3, 0xFF},       /* 11110011 11111111 */
    {0xFF, 0xFF},       /* 11111111 11111111 */
    {0xF3, 0xFF},       /* 11110011 11111111 */
    {0xFF, 0xFF},       /* 11111111 11111111 */
    {0xFF, 0xFF}},      /* 11111111 11111111 */

  {{0xFF, 0xFF},       /* 11111111 11111111 */ /* BLACK ON WHITE   '@' */
    {0xC0, 0xFF},       /* 11000000 11111111 */
    {0x3F, 0x3F},       /* 00111111 00111111 */
    {0x30, 0x3F},       /* 00110000 00111111 */
    {0x30, 0x3F},       /* 00110000 00111111 */
    {0x30, 0x3F},       /* 00110000 00111111 */
    {0x3F, 0xFF},       /* 00111111 11111111 */
    {0xC0, 0xFF},       /* 11000000 11111111 */
    {0xFF, 0xFF},       /* 11111111 11111111 */
    {0xFF, 0xFF}},      /* 11111111 11111111 */

  {{0xFF, 0xFF},       /* 11111111 11111111 */ /* BLACK ON WHITE   '#' */
    {0xCC, 0xFF},       /* 11001100 11111111 */
    {0xCC, 0xFF},       /* 11001100 11111111 */
    {0x00, 0x3F},       /* 00000000 00111111 */
    {0xCC, 0xFF},       /* 11001100 11111111 */
    {0x00, 0x3F},       /* 00000000 00111111 */
    {0xCC, 0xFF},       /* 11001100 11111111 */
    {0xCC, 0xFF},       /* 11001100 11111111 */
    {0xFF, 0xFF},       /* 11111111 11111111 */
    {0xFF, 0xFF}},      /* 11111111 11111111 */

  {{0xFF, 0xFF},       /* 11111111 11111111 */ /* BLACK ON WHITE   '$' */
    {0xF3, 0xFF},       /* 11110011 11111111 */
    {0xC0, 0x3F},       /* 11000000 00111111 */
    {0x3F, 0xFF},       /* 00111111 11111111 */
    {0xC0, 0xFF},       /* 11000000 11111111 */
    {0xFF, 0x3F},       /* 11111111 00111111 */
    {0x00, 0xFF},       /* 00000000 11111111 */
    {0xF3, 0xFF},       /* 11110011 11111111 */
    {0xFF, 0xFF},       /* 11111111 11111111 */
    {0xFF, 0xFF}},      /* 11111111 11111111 */

  {{0xFF, 0xFF},       /* 11111111 11111111 */ /* BLACK ON WHITE   '%' */
    {0xFF, 0xFF},       /* 11111111 11111111 */
    {0x3F, 0x3F},       /* 00111111 00111111 */
    {0x3C, 0xFF},       /* 00111100 11111111 */
    {0xF3, 0xFF},       /* 11110011 11111111 */
    {0xCF, 0x3F},       /* 11001111 00111111 */
    {0x3F, 0x3F},       /* 00111111 00111111 */
    {0xFF, 0xFF},       /* 11111111 11111111 */
    {0xFF, 0xFF},       /* 11111111 11111111 */
    {0xFF, 0xFF}},      /* 11111111 11111111 */
```

```
    {{0xFF, 0xFF},      /* 11111111 11111111 */ /* BLACK ON WHITE    '^'   */
     {0xF3, 0xFF},      /* 11110011 11111111 */
     {0xCC, 0xFF},      /* 11001100 11111111 */
     {0x3F, 0x3F},      /* 00111111 00111111 */
     {0xFF, 0xFF},      /* 11111111 11111111 */
     {0xFF, 0xFF},      /* 11111111 11111111 */
     {0xFF, 0xFF},      /* 11111111 11111111 */
     {0xFF, 0xFF},      /* 11111111 11111111 */
     {0xFF, 0xFF},      /* 11111111 11111111 */
     {0xFF, 0xFF}},     /* 11111111 11111111 */

    {{0xFF, 0xFF},      /* 11111111 11111111 */ /* BLACK ON WHITE    '&'   */
     {0xF3, 0xFF},      /* 11110011 11111111 */
     {0xCC, 0xFF},      /* 11001100 11111111 */
     {0xCC, 0xFF},      /* 11001100 11111111 */
     {0xC3, 0xFF},      /* 11000011 11111111 */
     {0x33, 0x3F},      /* 00110011 00111111 */
     {0x3C, 0xFF},      /* 00111100 11111111 */
     {0xC3, 0x3F},      /* 11000011 00111111 */
     {0xFF, 0xFF},      /* 11111111 11111111 */
     {0xFF, 0xFF}},     /* 11111111 11111111 */

    {{0xFF, 0xFF},      /* 11111111 11111111 */ /* BLACK ON WHITE    '*'   */
     {0xF3, 0xFF},      /* 11110011 11111111 */
     {0x33, 0x3F},      /* 00110011 00111111 */
     {0xC0, 0xFF},      /* 11000000 11111111 */
     {0xF3, 0xFF},      /* 11110011 11111111 */
     {0xC0, 0xFF},      /* 11000000 11111111 */
     {0x33, 0x3F},      /* 00110011 00111111 */
     {0xFF, 0xFF},      /* 11111111 11111111 */
     {0xFF, 0xFF},      /* 11111111 11111111 */
     {0xFF, 0xFF}},     /* 11111111 11111111 */

    {{0xFF, 0xFF},      /* 11111111 11111111 */ /* BLACK ON WHITE    '('   */
     {0xF3, 0xFF},      /* 11110011 11111111 */
     {0xCF, 0xFF},      /* 11001111 11111111 */
     {0x3F, 0xFF},      /* 00111111 11111111 */
     {0x3F, 0xFF},      /* 00111111 11111111 */
     {0x3F, 0xFF},      /* 00111111 11111111 */
     {0xCF, 0xFF},      /* 11001111 11111111 */
     {0xF3, 0xFF},      /* 11110011 11111111 */
     {0xFF, 0xFF},      /* 11111111 11111111 */
     {0xFF, 0xFF}},     /* 11111111 11111111 */

    {{0xFF, 0xFF},      /* 11111111 11111111 */ /* BLACK ON WHITE    ')'   */
     {0x3F, 0xFF},      /* 00111111 11111111 */
     {0xCF, 0xFF},      /* 11001111 11111111 */
     {0xF3, 0xFF},      /* 11110011 11111111 */
     {0xF3, 0xFF},      /* 11110011 11111111 */
     {0xF3, 0xFF},      /* 11110011 11111111 */
     {0xCF, 0xFF},      /* 11001111 11111111 */
     {0x3F, 0xFF},      /* 00111111 11111111 */
```

```
      {0xFF, 0xFF},      /* 11111111 11111111 */
      {0xFF, 0xFF}},     /* 11111111 11111111 */

     {{0xFF, 0xFF},      /* 11111111 11111111 */ /* BLACK ON WHITE   '_'   */
      {0xFF, 0xFF},      /* 11111111 11111111 */
      {0xFF, 0xFF},      /* 11111111 11111111 */
      {0xFF, 0xFF},      /* 11111111 11111111 */
      {0xFF, 0xFF},      /* 11111111 11111111 */
      {0xFF, 0xFF},      /* 11111111 11111111 */
      {0xFF, 0xFF},      /* 11111111 11111111 */
      {0xFF, 0xFF},      /* 11111111 11111111 */
      {0xFF, 0xFF},      /* 11111111 11111111 */
      {0x00, 0x0F}},     /* 00000000 00001111 */

     {{0xFF, 0xFF},      /* 11111111 11111111 */ /* BLACK ON WHITE   '-'   */
      {0xFF, 0xFF},      /* 11111111 11111111 */
      {0xFF, 0xFF},      /* 11111111 11111111 */
      {0xFF, 0xFF},      /* 11111111 11111111 */
      {0x00, 0x3F},      /* 00000000 00111111 */
      {0xFF, 0xFF},      /* 11111111 11111111 */
      {0xFF, 0xFF},      /* 11111111 11111111 */
      {0xFF, 0xFF},      /* 11111111 11111111 */
      {0xFF, 0xFF}},     /* 11111111 11111111 */

     {{0xFF, 0xFF},      /* 11111111 11111111 */ /* BLACK ON WHITE   '+'   */
      {0xF3, 0xFF},      /* 11110011 11111111 */
      {0xF3, 0xFF},      /* 11110011 11111111 */
      {0xF3, 0xFF},      /* 11110011 11111111 */
      {0x00, 0x3F},      /* 00000000 00111111 */
      {0xF3, 0xFF},      /* 11110011 11111111 */
      {0xF3, 0xFF},      /* 11110011 11111111 */
      {0xF3, 0xFF},      /* 11110011 11111111 */
      {0xFF, 0xFF},      /* 11111111 11111111 */
      {0xFF, 0xFF}},     /* 11111111 11111111 */

     {{0xFF, 0xFF},      /* 11111111 11111111 */ /* BLACK ON WHITE   '='   */
      {0xFF, 0xFF},      /* 11111111 11111111 */
      {0xFF, 0xFF},      /* 11111111 11111111 */
      {0x00, 0x3F},      /* 00000000 00111111 */
      {0xFF, 0xFF},      /* 11111111 11111111 */
      {0xFF, 0xFF},      /* 11111111 11111111 */
      {0x00, 0x3F},      /* 00000000 00111111 */
      {0xFF, 0xFF},      /* 11111111 11111111 */
      {0xFF, 0xFF},      /* 11111111 11111111 */
      {0xFF, 0xFF}},     /* 11111111 11111111 */

     {{0xFF, 0xFF},      /* 11111111 11111111 */ /* BLACK ON WHITE   '{'   */
      {0xF0, 0xFF},      /* 11110000 11111111 */
      {0xCF, 0xFF},      /* 11001111 11111111 */
      {0xCF, 0xFF},      /* 11001111 11111111 */
      {0x3F, 0xFF},      /* 00111111 11111111 */
      {0xCF, 0xFF},      /* 11001111 11111111 */
```

```
    {0xCF, 0xFF},       /* 11001111 11111111 */
    {0xF0, 0xFF},       /* 11110000 11111111 */
    {0xFF, 0xFF},       /* 11111111 11111111 */
    {0xFF, 0xFF}},      /* 11111111 11111111 */

   {{0xFF, 0xFF},       /* 11111111 11111111 */ /* BLACK ON WHITE    '}'   */
    {0x0F, 0xFF},       /* 00001111 11111111 */
    {0xF3, 0xFF},       /* 11110011 11111111 */
    {0xF3, 0xFF},       /* 11110011 11111111 */
    {0xFC, 0xFF},       /* 11111100 11111111 */
    {0xF3, 0xFF},       /* 11110011 11111111 */
    {0xF3, 0xFF},       /* 11110011 11111111 */
    {0x0F, 0xFF},       /* 00001111 11111111 */
    {0xFF, 0xFF},       /* 11111111 11111111 */
    {0xFF, 0xFF}},      /* 11111111 11111111 */

   {{0xFF, 0xFF},       /* 11111111 11111111 */ /* BLACK ON WHITE    '['   */
    {0xC0, 0xFF},       /* 11000000 11111111 */
    {0xCF, 0xFF},       /* 11001111 11111111 */
    {0xCF, 0xFF},       /* 11001111 11111111 */
    {0xCF, 0xFF},       /* 11001111 11111111 */
    {0xCF, 0xFF},       /* 11001111 11111111 */
    {0xCF, 0xFF},       /* 11001111 11111111 */
    {0xC0, 0xFF},       /* 11000000 11111111 */
    {0xFF, 0xFF},       /* 11111111 11111111 */
    {0xFF, 0xFF}},      /* 11111111 11111111 */

   {{0xFF, 0xFF},       /* 11111111 11111111 */ /* BLACK ON WHITE    ']'   */
    {0xC0, 0xFF},       /* 11000000 11111111 */
    {0xFC, 0xFF},       /* 11111100 11111111 */
    {0xFC, 0xFF},       /* 11111100 11111111 */
    {0xFC, 0xFF},       /* 11111100 11111111 */
    {0xFC, 0xFF},       /* 11111100 11111111 */
    {0xC0, 0xFF},       /* 11000000 11111111 */
    {0xFF, 0xFF},       /* 11111111 11111111 */
    {0xFF, 0xFF}},      /* 11111111 11111111 */

   {{0xFF, 0xFF},       /* 11111111 11111111 */ /* BLACK ON WHITE    '~'   */
    {0xCC, 0xFF},       /* 11001100 11111111 */
    {0x33, 0xFF},       /* 00110011 11111111 */
    {0xFF, 0xFF},       /* 11111111 11111111 */
    {0xFF, 0xFF},       /* 11111111 11111111 */
    {0xFF, 0xFF},       /* 11111111 11111111 */
    {0xFF, 0xFF},       /* 11111111 11111111 */
    {0xFF, 0xFF},       /* 11111111 11111111 */
    {0xFF, 0xFF}},      /* 11111111 11111111 */

   {{0xFF, 0xFF},       /* 11111111 11111111 */ /* BLACK ON WHITE    '`'   */
    {0xCF, 0xFF},       /* 11001111 11111111 */
    {0xCF, 0xFF},       /* 11001111 11111111 */
    {0xF3, 0xFF},       /* 11110011 11111111 */
```

```
      {0xFF, 0xFF},      /* 11111111 11111111 */
      {0xFF, 0xFF},      /* 11111111 11111111 */
      {0xFF, 0xFF},      /* 11111111 11111111 */
      {0xFF, 0xFF},      /* 11111111 11111111 */
      {0xFF, 0xFF},      /* 11111111 11111111 */
      {0xFF, 0xFF}},     /* 11111111 11111111 */

     {{0xFF, 0xFF},      /* 11111111 11111111 */ /* BLACK ON WHITE    ':'   */
      {0xFF, 0xFF},      /* 11111111 11111111 */
      {0xF3, 0xFF},      /* 11110011 11111111 */
      {0xF3, 0xFF},      /* 11110011 11111111 */
      {0xFF, 0xFF},      /* 11111111 11111111 */
      {0xF3, 0xFF},      /* 11110011 11111111 */
      {0xF3, 0xFF},      /* 11110011 11111111 */
      {0xFF, 0xFF},      /* 11111111 11111111 */
      {0xFF, 0xFF},      /* 11111111 11111111 */
      {0xFF, 0xFF}},     /* 11111111 11111111 */

     {{0xFF, 0xFF},      /* 11111111 11111111 */ /* BLACK ON WHITE    ';'   */
      {0xFF, 0xFF},      /* 11111111 11111111 */
      {0xF3, 0xFF},      /* 11110011 11111111 */
      {0xF3, 0xFF},      /* 11110011 11111111 */
      {0xFF, 0xFF},      /* 11111111 11111111 */
      {0xF3, 0xFF},      /* 11110011 11111111 */
      {0xF3, 0xFF},      /* 11110011 11111111 */
      {0xCF, 0xFF},      /* 11001111 11111111 */
      {0xFF, 0xFF},      /* 11111111 11111111 */
      {0xFF, 0xFF}},     /* 11111111 11111111 */

     {{0xFF, 0xFF},      /* 11111111 11111111 */ /* BLACK ON WHITE    '"'   */
      {0xCC, 0xFF},      /* 11001100 11111111 */
      {0xCC, 0xFF},      /* 11001100 11111111 */
      {0xCC, 0xFF},      /* 11001100 11111111 */
      {0xFF, 0xFF},      /* 11111111 11111111 */
      {0xFF, 0xFF},      /* 11111111 11111111 */
      {0xFF, 0xFF},      /* 11111111 11111111 */
      {0xFF, 0xFF},      /* 11111111 11111111 */
      {0xFF, 0xFF},      /* 11111111 11111111 */
      {0xFF, 0xFF}},     /* 11111111 11111111 */

     {{0xFF, 0xFF},      /* 11111111 11111111 */ /* BLACK ON WHITE    '''   */
      {0xF3, 0xFF},      /* 11110011 11111111 */
      {0xF3, 0xFF},      /* 11110011 11111111 */
      {0xCF, 0xFF},      /* 11001111 11111111 */
      {0xFF, 0xFF},      /* 11111111 11111111 */
      {0xFF, 0xFF},      /* 11111111 11111111 */
      {0xFF, 0xFF},      /* 11111111 11111111 */
      {0xFF, 0xFF},      /* 11111111 11111111 */
      {0xFF, 0xFF}},     /* 11111111 11111111 */

     {{0xFF, 0xFF},      /* 11111111 11111111 */ /* BLACK ON WHITE    '|'   */
      {0xF3, 0xFF},      /* 11110011 11111111 */
```

```
  {0xF3, 0xFF},      /* 11110011 11111111 */
  {0xF3, 0xFF},      /* 11110011 11111111 */
  {0xFF, 0xFF},      /* 11111111 11111111 */
  {0xF3, 0xFF},      /* 11110011 11111111 */
  {0xF3, 0xFF},      /* 11110011 11111111 */
  {0xF3, 0xFF},      /* 11110011 11111111 */
  {0xFF, 0xFF},      /* 11111111 11111111 */
  {0xFF, 0xFF}},     /* 11111111 11111111 */

 {{0xFF, 0xFF},      /* 11111111 11111111 */ /* BLACK ON WHITE    '\'   */
  {0xFF, 0xFF},      /* 11111111 11111111 */
  {0x3F, 0xFF},      /* 00111111 11111111 */
  {0xCF, 0xFF},      /* 11001111 11111111 */
  {0xF3, 0xFF},      /* 11110011 11111111 */
  {0xFC, 0xFF},      /* 11111100 11111111 */
  {0xFF, 0x3F},      /* 11111111 00111111 */
  {0xFF, 0xFF},      /* 11111111 11111111 */
  {0xFF, 0xFF},      /* 11111111 11111111 */
  {0xFF, 0xFF}},     /* 11111111 11111111 */

 {{0xFF, 0xFF},      /* 11111111 11111111 */ /* BLACK ON WHITE    '<'   */
  {0xFC, 0xFF},      /* 11111100 11111111 */
  {0xF3, 0xFF},      /* 11110011 11111111 */
  {0xCF, 0xFF},      /* 11001111 11111111 */
  {0x3F, 0xFF},      /* 00111111 11111111 */
  {0xCF, 0xFF},      /* 11001111 11111111 */
  {0xF3, 0xFF},      /* 11110011 11111111 */
  {0xFC, 0xFF},      /* 11111100 11111111 */
  {0xFF, 0xFF},      /* 11111111 11111111 */
  {0xFF, 0xFF}},     /* 11111111 11111111 */

 {{0xFF, 0xFF},      /* 11111111 11111111 */ /* BLACK ON WHITE    ','   */
  {0xFF, 0xFF},      /* 11111111 11111111 */
  {0xFF, 0xFF},      /* 11111111 11111111 */
  {0xFF, 0xFF},      /* 11111111 11111111 */
  {0xFF, 0xFF},      /* 11111111 11111111 */
  {0xFF, 0xFF},      /* 11111111 11111111 */
  {0xF3, 0xFF},      /* 11110011 11111111 */
  {0xF3, 0xFF},      /* 11110011 11111111 */
  {0xCF, 0xFF},      /* 11001111 11111111 */
  {0xFF, 0xFF}},     /* 11111111 11111111 */

 {{0xFF, 0xFF},      /* 11111111 11111111 */ /* BLACK ON WHITE    '>'   */
  {0x3F, 0xFF},      /* 00111111 11111111 */
  {0xCF, 0xFF},      /* 11001111 11111111 */
  {0xF3, 0xFF},      /* 11110011 11111111 */
  {0xFC, 0xFF},      /* 11111100 11111111 */
  {0xF3, 0xFF},      /* 11110011 11111111 */
  {0xCF, 0xFF},      /* 11001111 11111111 */
  {0x3F, 0xFF},      /* 00111111 11111111 */
  {0xFF, 0xFF},      /* 11111111 11111111 */
  {0xFF, 0xFF}},     /* 11111111 11111111 */
```

```
{{0xFF, 0xFF},      /* 11111111 11111111 */ /* BLACK ON WHITE    '.'   */
 {0xFF, 0xFF},      /* 11111111 11111111 */
 {0xFF, 0xFF},      /* 11111111 11111111 */
 {0xFF, 0xFF},      /* 11111111 11111111 */
 {0xFF, 0xFF},      /* 11111111 11111111 */
 {0xFF, 0xFF},      /* 11111111 11111111 */
 {0xF3, 0xFF},      /* 11110011 11111111 */
 {0xF3, 0xFF},      /* 11110011 11111111 */
 {0xFF, 0xFF},      /* 11111111 11111111 */
 {0xFF, 0xFF}},     /* 11111111 11111111 */

{{0xFF, 0xFF},      /* 11111111 11111111 */ /* BLACK ON WHITE    '?'   */
 {0xC0, 0xFF},      /* 11000000 11111111 */
 {0x3F, 0x3F},      /* 00111111 00111111 */
 {0xFC, 0xFF},      /* 11111100 11111111 */
 {0xF3, 0xFF},      /* 11110011 11111111 */
 {0xF3, 0xFF},      /* 11110011 11111111 */
 {0xFF, 0xFF},      /* 11111111 11111111 */
 {0xF3, 0xFF},      /* 11110011 11111111 */
 {0xFF, 0xFF},      /* 11111111 11111111 */
 {0xFF, 0xFF}},     /* 11111111 11111111 */

{{0xFF, 0xFF},      /* 11111111 11111111 */ /* BLACK ON WHITE    '/'   */
 {0xFF, 0xFF},      /* 11111111 11111111 */
 {0xFF, 0xCF},      /* 11111111 11001111 */
 {0xFF, 0x3F},      /* 11111111 00111111 */
 {0xFC, 0xFF},      /* 11111100 11111111 */
 {0xF3, 0xFF},      /* 11110011 11111111 */
 {0xCF, 0xFF},      /* 11001111 11111111 */
 {0xFF, 0xFF},      /* 11111111 11111111 */
 {0xFF, 0xFF},      /* 11111111 11111111 */
 {0xFF, 0xFF}},     /* 11111111 11111111 */

{{0xFF, 0xFF},      /* 11111111 11111111 */ /* BLACK ON WHITE    ' '   */
 {0xFF, 0xFF},      /* 11111111 11111111 */
 {0xFF, 0xFF},      /* 11111111 11111111 */
 {0xFF, 0xFF},      /* 11111111 11111111 */
 {0xFF, 0xFF},      /* 11111111 11111111 */
 {0xFF, 0xFF},      /* 11111111 11111111 */
 {0xFF, 0xFF},      /* 11111111 11111111 */
 {0xFF, 0xFF},      /* 11111111 11111111 */
 {0xFF, 0xFF},      /* 11111111 11111111 */
 {0xFF, 0xFF}},     /* 11111111 11111111 */

{{0xFF, 0xFF},      /* 11111111 11111111 */ /* BLACK ON WHITE    '0'   */
 {0xC0, 0xFF},      /* 11000000 11111111 */
 {0x3F, 0x3F},      /* 00111111 00111111 */
 {0x3C, 0x3F},      /* 00111100 00111111 */
 {0x33, 0x3F},      /* 00110011 00111111 */
 {0x0F, 0x3F},      /* 00001111 00111111 */
 {0x3F, 0x3F},      /* 00111111 00111111 */
 {0xC0, 0xFF},      /* 11000000 11111111 */
 {0xFF, 0xFF},      /* 11111111 11111111 */
```

```
        {0xFF, 0xFF}},    /* 11111111 11111111 */

       {{0xFF, 0xFF},     /* 11111111 11111111 */ /* BLACK ON WHITE   '1'   */
        {0xF3, 0xFF},     /* 11110011 11111111 */
        {0xC3, 0xFF},     /* 11000011 11111111 */
        {0xF3, 0xFF},     /* 11110011 11111111 */
        {0xF3, 0xFF},     /* 11110011 11111111 */
        {0xF3, 0xFF},     /* 11110011 11111111 */
        {0xF3, 0xFF},     /* 11110011 11111111 */
        {0x00, 0x3F},     /* 00000000 00111111 */
        {0xFF, 0xFF},     /* 11111111 11111111 */
        {0xFF, 0xFF}},    /* 11111111 11111111 */

       {{0xFF, 0xFF},     /* 11111111 11111111 */ /* BLACK ON WHITE   '2'   */
        {0xC0, 0xFF},     /* 11000000 11111111 */
        {0x3F, 0x3F},     /* 00111111 00111111 */
        {0xFF, 0x3F},     /* 11111111 00111111 */
        {0xF0, 0xFF},     /* 11110000 11111111 */
        {0xCF, 0xFF},     /* 11001111 11111111 */
        {0x3F, 0x3F},     /* 00111111 00111111 */
        {0x00, 0x3F},     /* 00000000 00111111 */
        {0xFF, 0xFF},     /* 11111111 11111111 */
        {0xFF, 0xFF}},    /* 11111111 11111111 */

       {{0xFF, 0xFF},     /* 11111111 11111111 */ /* BLACK ON WHITE   '3'   */
        {0xC0, 0xFF},     /* 11000000 11111111 */
        {0x3F, 0x3F},     /* 00111111 00111111 */
        {0xFF, 0x3F},     /* 11111111 00111111 */
        {0xF0, 0xFF},     /* 11110000 11111111 */
        {0xFF, 0x3F},     /* 11111111 00111111 */
        {0x3F, 0x3F},     /* 00111111 00111111 */
        {0xC0, 0xFF},     /* 11000000 11111111 */
        {0xFF, 0xFF},     /* 11111111 11111111 */
        {0xFF, 0xFF}},    /* 11111111 11111111 */

       {{0xFF, 0xFF},     /* 11111111 11111111 */ /* BLACK ON WHITE   '4'   */
        {0xF0, 0xFF},     /* 11110000 11111111 */
        {0xCC, 0xFF},     /* 11001100 11111111 */
        {0x3C, 0xFF},     /* 00111100 11111111 */
        {0x00, 0x3F},     /* 00000000 00111111 */
        {0xFC, 0xFF},     /* 11111100 11111111 */
        {0xFC, 0xFF},     /* 11111100 11111111 */
        {0xF0, 0x3F},     /* 11110000 00111111 */
        {0xFF, 0xFF},     /* 11111111 11111111 */
        {0xFF, 0xFF}},    /* 11111111 11111111 */

       {{0xFF, 0xFF},     /* 11111111 11111111 */ /* BLACK ON WHITE   '5'   */
        {0x00, 0x3F},     /* 00000000 00111111 */
        {0x3F, 0xFF},     /* 00111111 11111111 */
        {0x00, 0xFF},     /* 00000000 11111111 */
        {0xFF, 0x3F},     /* 11111111 00111111 */
        {0xFF, 0x3F},     /* 11111111 00111111 */
        {0x3F, 0x3F},     /* 00111111 00111111 */
```

```
    {0xC0, 0xFF},      /* 11000000 11111111 */
    {0xFF, 0xFF},      /* 11111111 11111111 */
    {0xFF, 0xFF}},     /* 11111111 11111111 */

    {{0xFF, 0xFF},     /* 11111111 11111111 */ /* BLACK ON WHITE    '6'  */
    {0xF0, 0xFF},      /* 11110000 11111111 */
    {0xCF, 0xFF},      /* 11001111 11111111 */
    {0x3F, 0xFF},      /* 00111111 11111111 */
    {0x00, 0xFF},      /* 00000000 11111111 */
    {0x3F, 0x3F},      /* 00111111 00111111 */
    {0x3F, 0x3F},      /* 00111111 00111111 */
    {0xC0, 0xFF},      /* 11000000 11111111 */
    {0xFF, 0xFF},      /* 11111111 11111111 */
    {0xFF, 0xFF}},     /* 11111111 11111111 */

    {{0xFF, 0xFF},     /* 11111111 11111111 */ /* BLACK ON WHITE    '7'  */
    {0x00, 0x3F},      /* 00000000 00111111 */
    {0x3F, 0x3F},      /* 00111111 00111111 */
    {0xFF, 0x3F},      /* 11111111 00111111 */
    {0xFC, 0xFF},      /* 11111100 11111111 */
    {0xF3, 0xFF},      /* 11110011 11111111 */
    {0xF3, 0xFF},      /* 11110011 11111111 */
    {0xF3, 0xFF},      /* 11110011 11111111 */
    {0xFF, 0xFF},      /* 11111111 11111111 */
    {0xFF, 0xFF}},     /* 11111111 11111111 */

    {{0xFF, 0xFF},     /* 11111111 11111111 */ /* BLACK ON WHITE    '8'  */
    {0xC0, 0xFF},      /* 11000000 11111111 */
    {0x3F, 0x3F},      /* 00111111 00111111 */
    {0x3F, 0x3F},      /* 00111111 00111111 */
    {0xC0, 0xFF},      /* 11000000 11111111 */
    {0x3F, 0x3F},      /* 00111111 00111111 */
    {0x3F, 0x3F},      /* 00111111 00111111 */
    {0xC0, 0xFF},      /* 11000000 11111111 */
    {0xFF, 0xFF},      /* 11111111 11111111 */
    {0xFF, 0xFF}},     /* 11111111 11111111 */

    {{0xFF, 0xFF},     /* 11111111 11111111 */ /* BLACK ON WHITE    '9'  */
    {0xC0, 0xFF},      /* 11000000 11111111 */
    {0x3F, 0x3F},      /* 00111111 00111111 */
    {0x3F, 0x3F},      /* 00111111 00111111 */
    {0xC0, 0x3F},      /* 11000000 00111111 */
    {0xFF, 0x3F},      /* 11111111 00111111 */
    {0xFC, 0xFF},      /* 11111100 11111111 */
    {0xC3, 0xFF},      /* 11000011 11111111 */
    {0xFF, 0xFF},      /* 11111111 11111111 */
    {0xFF, 0xFF}}      /* 11111111 11111111 */
}
};
```

SUMMARY

The CGA Graphics Library uses three include source files: GRAPHICS.H, COLORS.H, and FONTSET.H. Each one of these files contains information used by the CGA Graphics Library source file CGAGRAFC.C. Include files are used to contain information that might be needed by other source modules and to keep information separated into related groups.

The GRAPHICS.H include source file defines the defined data, DOS_VIDEO_ CALL, FONTWIDTH, FONTHEIGHT, and CURSOR. These defined variables are used throughout the CGA Graphics Library to make DOS BIOS interrupt service calls and to pass information to the DisplayIcon ( ) function in the source file CGAGRAFA.ASM.

The COLORS.H include file defines the defined data variables BLACK, BLUE, RED, WHITE, BLACKDOT, BLUEDOT, REDDOT, and WHITEDOT. These defined variables are used by the CGA Graphics Library and the application to display different colors on the screen.

The FONTSET.H include file defines the data variable Font_Set. This variable is used to contain the definitions of all of the displayable character icons available to the CGA Graphics Library. It contains two groups of icons, one defining the character white on black and the other defining the character black on white.

The next chapter in the book shows you how to build the 'C' source file CGAGRAFC.C. This source file contains all of the functions used by the CGA Graphics Library that are written in 'C' and use the DOS BIOS interrupt service calls.

Chapter 6

THE CGA GRAPHICS LIBRARY
'C' SOURCE FILES

INTRODUCTION

The CGAGRAFC.C is the only 'C' file in the CGA Graphics Library. It makes use of the include files GRAPHICS.H, COLORS.H, and FONTSET.H that are also part of the CGA Graphics Library source code. It also makes use of certain include files that are supplied with your 'C' compiler. The CGAGRAFC.C source file will contain all of the source code needed to perform those functions in the CGA Graphics Library that use the DOS BIOS interrupt service calls and are written in 'C.'

Create the CGAGRAFC.C, edit the file, type the following statements, and save the file.

```
/*======================================================================*/
/*                                                                      */
/* File : CGAGRAFC.C                                                    */
/*                                                                      */
/* Purpose : This 'C' source file contains the CGA Graphics Library     */
/*           functions that use the DOS BIOS interrupt service calls.   */
/*                                                                      */
/* Include Files : GRAPHICS.H - This include file contains the data     */
/*                 definitions for the DOS BIOS interface service       */
/*                 calls and other data specific for the CGA Graphics   */
/*                 Library.                                             */
/*                                                                      */
/*                 COLORS.H - This include file contains the data       */
/*                 definitions used to define the colors used by the    */
/*                 application and CGA Graphics Library.                */
/*                                                                      */
/*                 FONTSET.H - This include file contains the data      */
```

```
/*                 definitions used to define the displayable        */
/*                 character icons used by the CGA Graphics Library.  */
/*                                                                    */
/*                 <dos.h> - This include file is supplied by the 'C' */
/*                 compiler and it is used to define variables that   */
/*                 are needed to use the DOS BIOS interface service   */
/*                 calls.                                              */
/*                                                                    */
/* Static Data Definitions : static union REGS In_Regs - This static  */
/*                 data definition is defined to pass information     */
/*                 to the DOS BIOS interrupt service calls.           */
/*                                                                    */
/*                 static union REGS Out_Regs - This static data      */
/*                 definition is defined to receive information from  */
/*                 the DOS BIOS interrupt service calls.              */
/*                                                                    */
/*                 static int Current_Foreground - This static data   */
/*                 definition is used by the GetFontNum () function    */
/*                 to facilitate the mapping of the font set color    */
/*                 combinations.                                      */
/*                                                                    */
/*                 static int Current_Background = 0; This data       */
/*                 definition is used by the GetFontNum () function    */
/*                 to facilitate the mapping of the font set color    */
/*                 combinations.                                      */
/*                                                                    */
/*                 static Temp_Font_Set[95][10][2]; This data         */
/*                 definition is used to contain a mapping of the     */
/*                 Font_Set variable into different colors.           */
/*                                                                    */
/*                 static unsigned char Special[33] =                 */
/*                   {"!@#$%^&*()_-+={[}]~':;\"\'|\\<,>.?/ "};         */
/*                 This data definition defines all of the special    */
/*                 display characters, i.e., all of those characters  */
/*                 that are not alphabetic or numeric.  It is used    */
/*                 by the MapFontChar () function to map the special  */
/*                 characters in the font set.                        */
/*                                                                    */
/* Functions : GetCrtMode () - This function returns the current      */
/*             screen CRT mode in use at the time the call is made.   */
/*                                                                    */
/*             SelectDisplayPage () - This function activates the     */
/*             requested video display page.                         */
/*                                                                    */
/*             SetCrtMode () - This function sets the screen CRT      */
/*             mode to the one that is requested.                     */
/*                                                                    */
/*             DrawBox () - This function draws a box on the screen   */
/*             starting at the given upper left-hand row and column   */
/*             coordinates, for the given box width and box height,   */
/*             and in the given box color.                           */
/*                                                                    */
/*             VLine () - This function draws a vertical line on      */
```

```
/*          the screen at the given starting row and column       */
/*          coordinates, for the given line length, and in the    */
/*          given line color.                                      */
/*                                                                 */
/*          HLine () - This function draws a horizontal line on    */
/*          the screen at the given starting row and column        */
/*          coordinates, for the given line length, and in the     */
/*          given line color.                                      */
/*                                                                 */
/*          DisplayDot () - This function displays a dot on        */
/*          the screen at the given row and column coordinates     */
/*          and in the given color.                                */
/*                                                                 */
/*          DisplayChar () - This function displays the given      */
/*          character icon on the screen, starting at the given    */
/*          upper left-hand row and column coordinates, and in the */
/*          given foreground and background colors.                */
/*                                                                 */
/*          DisplayString () - This function displays a given      */
/*          string of characters that are terminated with a NULL,  */
/*          on the screen, starting at the given upper left-hand   */
/*          row and column coordinates and in the given foreground */
/*          and background colors.                                 */
/*                                                                 */
/*          DisplayStrNum () - This function displays a given      */
/*          string of characters on the screen, starting at the    */
/*          given upper left-hand row and column coordinates, in   */
/*          the given foreground and background  colors, and the   */
/*          given number of characters to display from the string  */
/*          onto the screen.                                       */
/*                                                                 */
/*          GetFontNum () - This function returns the font set     */
/*          number to use when displaying a character or string    */
/*          of characters on the screen in the given foreground    */
/*          and background colors.                                 */
/*                                                                 */
/*          MapFontChar () - This function returns the font set    */
/*          number associated with the character passed.           */
/*                                                                 */
/*          DisplayCursor () - This function displays an underline */
/*          under the character passed, on the screen starting at  */
/*          the given upper left-hand row and column coordinates,  */
/*          in the given foreground and background colors.         */
/*                                                                 */
/*=================================================================*/

#include <dos.h>
#include "graphics.h"
#include "colors.h"
#include "fontset.h"

static union REGS In_Regs;
static union REGS Out_Regs;
```

```
static int Current_Foreground = 0;
static int Current_Background = 0;
static int Temp_Font_Set[95][10][2];
static unsigned char Special[33] =
   {"!@#$%^&*()_-+={[}]~':;\"\'|\\<,>.?/ "};
```

The above code is mostly documentation; it defines only the include files and data definitions used by the CGAGRAFC.C source file. But it is necessary that I take the time to restate that it is important for the application programmer to document his code. By using the above technique for coding documentation, the programmer helps others to more easily understand his code.

Following is the code for the functions used in the CGA Graphics Library. Each function contains a documentation section which contains the following information:

- The function name along with the names of any parameters passed to the function.
- A brief description of the purpose of the function.
- An explanation of all the parameters passed to the function.
- An explanation of all variables used and/or defined by the function.
- A brief description of the logic flow of the function.
- An explanation of all values returned from the function.

Create the GetCrtMode ( ) Function

The GetCrtMode ( ) function returns to the calling function the value of the current CRT mode. The value is needed by the application program so that it can restore the CRT mode back to its original mode when terminating. This routine is an example of writing user friendly code. Frequently, especially when the application uses graphics, the user wants the CRT mode set back to its original state.

Using the above outline for code documentation, edit the CGAGRAFC.C source file, type the following statements, and save the file.

```
/*========================================================================*/
/*                                                                        */
/* Function : GetCrtMode ()                                               */
/*                                                                        */
/* Purpose  : This function returns the current Crt mode to the           */
/*            calling process.                                            */
/*                                                                        */
/* Functions Called : int86 () - This function is called to execute       */
/*            a DOS BIOS interrupt service routine.                       */
/*                                                                        */
/* Logic Flow : The GetCrtMode () is called to return the current CRT */
/*            mode being used.  The variable In_Regs.h.ah is set to       */
```

```
/*              15 to set the DOS BIOS interrupt service number for  */
/*              getting the current CRT Mode.  The function int86 () */
/*              is called to perform the service request.  The variable */
/*              Out_Regs.h.al contains the value of the current CRT mode */
/*              and this value is returned to the calling function. */
/*                                                                  */
/* Exit : The value of the current CRT mode is returned.           */
/*                                                                  */
/*================================================================*/

GetCrtMode ()
{
   In_Regs.h.ah = 15;
   int86 (DOS_VIDEO_CALL, &In_Regs, &Out_Regs);
   return (Out_Regs.h.al);
}
```

Create the SelectDisplayPage ( ) Function

The SelectDisplayPage ( ) function allows the application to be able to select which display page to use. For the purposes of this book, we only deal with display page 0.

Edit the CGAGRAFC.C source file, type the following statements, and save the file.

```
/*================================================================*/
/*                                                                  */
/* Function : SelectDisplayPage (page);                            */
/*                                                                  */
/* Purpose  : This function selects a video page to activate.      */
/*                                                                  */
/* Entry Parameters : int page  - The video page to activate.      */
/*                                                                  */
/* Functions Called : int86 () - This function is called to execute */
/*              a DOS BIOS interrupt service routine.              */
/*                                                                  */
/* Logic Flow : The SetCrtMode () function is called with the CRT  */
/*              mode to set.  The variable In_Regs.h.al is set to   */
/*              the CRT mode passed.  The variable In_Regs.h.ah is  */
/*              set to 5 to set the DOS BIOS interrupt service number */
/*              to set the current video display page.  The int86 () */
/*              function is called to perform the interrupt service */
/*              request.                                           */
/*                                                                  */
/* Exit : The video display page is set to the one requested.      */
/*                                                                  */
/*================================================================*/

SelectDisplayPage (page)
int    page;
{
   In_Regs.h.al = page;
```

```
   In_Regs.h.ah = 5;
   int86 (DOS_VIDEO_CALL, &In_Regs, &Out_Regs);
}
```

Create the SetCrtMode ( ) Function

The SetCrtMode ( ) function allows the application to be able to set which CRT mode is active. This book is designed for the Four-Color Graphics Adapter card so the application must call this function at least once to set up the video display card for graphics.

Edit the CGAGRAFC.C file, type the following statements, and save the file.

```
/*====================================================================*/
/*                                                                    */
/* Function : SetCrtMode (mode);                                      */
/*                                                                    */
/* Purpose  : Activates a screen CRT mode.                            */
/*                                                                    */
/* Entry Parameters : unsigned char mode  - The CRT mode to activate. */
/*                                                                    */
/* Functions Called : int86 () - This function is called to execute   */
/*            a DOS BIOS interrupt service routine.                   */
/*                                                                    */
/* Logic Flow : The SetCrtMode () function is called with the CRT     */
/*            mode to set.  The variable In_Regs.h.al is set to       */
/*            the CRT mode passed.  The variable In_Regs.h.ah is      */
/*            set to 0 to set the DOS BIOS interrupt service number   */
/*            to set the current CRT mode.  The int86 () function     */
/*            is called to perform the interrupt service request.     */
/*                                                                    */
/* Exit : The CRT mode is set to the one requested.                   */
/*                                                                    */
/*====================================================================*/

SetCrtMode (mode)
unsigned char mode;
{
   In_Regs.h.ah = 0;
   In_Regs.h.al = mode;
   int86 (DOS_VIDEO_CALL, &In_Regs, &Out_Regs);
}
```

Create the DrawBox ( ) Function

The DrawBox ( ) function is designed to draw a box on the screen at a given location. The function is called by the application whenever a box needs to be drawn on the screen, such as the outline of a menu. The application calls the function with the starting upper left-hand row and column coordinates, the width and the height of the box, and the color to display the box in.

This function is written using the DOS BIOS interrupt service routines; it could be written using DVA if the programmer needs more speed. It is written here using the DOS BIOS calls to show how these calls are implemented.

Edit the CGAGRAFC.C file, type the following statements, and save the file.

```
/*===================================================================*/
/*                                                                   */
/* Function : DrawBox (row, column, width, height, color);           */
/*                                                                   */
/* Purpose  : Draws a box on the screen at the given location, width,*/
/*            height, and color.                                     */
/*                                                                   */
/* Entry Parameters : int row - The row coordinate of the upper left-*/
/*            hand corner of the box to display.                     */
/*                                                                   */
/*            int column - The column coordinate of the upper left-  */
/*            hand corner of the box to display.                     */
/*                                                                   */
/*            int width  - The width of the box to display.          */
/*                                                                   */
/*            int height - The height of the box to display.         */
/*                                                                   */
/*            int color  - The color in which to display the box.    */
/*                                                                   */
/* Local Data Definitions : int i - This variable is used as a       */
/*            counter to display the width and the height of the box.*/
/*                                                                   */
/* Functions Called : DisplayDot (); - This function is called to    */
/*            display the individual dots of the box on the screen.  */
/*                                                                   */
/* Logic Flow : The DrawBox () function is called with the row and   */
/*            column coordinates of the upper left-hand corner of the*/
/*            box, the box width and height, and the box color.  The */
/*            top and bottom lines of the box are displayed using the*/
/*            DisplayDot () function for the width of the box.  Then  */
/*            the left and right lines of the box are displayed using*/
/*            the DisplayDot () function for the height of the box.   */
/*                                                                   */
/* Exit : The box is displayed on the screen                         */
/*                                                                   */
/*===================================================================*/

DrawBox (row, column, width, height, color)
int row, column, width, height, color;
{
    int i;

    height--;
```

```
    for (i = 0; i < width; i++)
    {
        DisplayDot (row          , column + i, color);
        DisplayDot (row + height, column + i, color);
    }
    width--;
    for (i = 1; i < height; i++)
    {
        DisplayDot (row + i, column          , color);
        DisplayDot (row + i, column + width, color);
    }
}
```

Create the VLine ( ) Function

The VLine ( ) function is designed to draw a vertical line on the screen at a given location. This function is called by the application whenever a vertical line needs to be displayed on the screen, such as when items on a menu need to be separated or for general cosmetic reasons. The function is called with the starting row and column coordinates, the line length, and line color.

This function could also be written in Assembler using DVA. If the programmer has only one line to draw, then the DOS BIOS version is acceptable. But if many lines need to be drawn, then Assembler should be used.

Edit the CGAGRAFC.C file, type the following statements, and save the file.

```
/*=========================================================================*/
/*                                                                         */
/* Function : VLine (row, column, length, color);                         */
/*                                                                         */
/* Purpose  : This function draws a vertical line on the screen            */
/*            starting at the given row and column coordinates, for        */
/*            the given length, and in the given color.                    */
/*                                                                         */
/* Entry Parameters : int row - Starting row coordinate of the line.       */
/*                                                                         */
/*            int column - The starting column coordinate of the line.     */
/*                                                                         */
/*            int length - The length of the line.                         */
/*                                                                         */
/*            int color  - The color of the line.                          */
/*                                                                         */
/* Local Data Definitions : int i - This variable is used as a             */
/*            counter for the line length.                                 */
/*                                                                         */
/* Functions Called : DisplayDot (); - This function is called to          */
/*            display the individual dots of the line on the screen.       */
/*                                                                         */
/* Logic Flow : The VLine () function is called to display a vertical      */
/*            line on the screen and is called with the starting row       */
```

```
/*          and column coordinates, the length of the line, and the  */
/*          color of the line.  The DisplayDot () function is called  */
/*          to display each individual dot on the line.               */
/*                                                                    */
/* Exit : A vertical line is displayed on the screen.                 */
/*                                                                    */
/*==================================================================*/

VLine (row, column, length, color)
int row, column, length, color;
{
   int i;

   for (i = 0; i < length; i++) DisplayDot (row + i, column, color);
}
```

Create the HLine ( ) Function

The HLine ( ) function is designed to display a horizontal line on the screen at a given location. The application calls this function whenever a horizontal line needs to be drawn on the screen, such as to separate items on a menu or for general cosmetic reasons. The function is called with the starting row and column coordinates, the line length, and line color.

Edit the CGAGRAFC.C file, type the following statements, and save the file.

```
/*==================================================================*/
/*                                                                    */
/* Function : HLine (row, column, length, color);                     */
/*                                                                    */
/* Purpose  : This function draws a horizontal line on the screen     */
/*            at the given starting row and column coordinates, for   */
/*            the given length and in the given color.                */
/*                                                                    */
/* Entry Parameters : int row - The starting row coordinate of the    */
/*            horizontal line.                                        */
/*                                                                    */
/*            int column - The starting column coordinate of the line.*/
/*                                                                    */
/*            int length - The length of the line.                    */
/*                                                                    */
/*            int color  - The color of the line.                     */
/*                                                                    */
/* Local Data Definitions : int i - This variable is used as a        */
/*            counter for the line length.                            */
/*                                                                    */
/* Functions Called : DisplayDot (); - This function is called to     */
/*            display the individual dots of the box on the screen.   */
/*                                                                    */
/* Logic Flow : The HLine () function is called to display a          */
/*            horizontal line on the screen and is called with the    */
```

```
/*          starting row and column coordinates, the line length and */
/*          line color.  The DisplayDot () function is called to     */
/*          display the individual dots of the line.                  */
/*                                                                    */
/* Exit : A horizontal line is displayed on the screen.              */
/*                                                                    */
/*==================================================================*/

HLine (row, column, length, color)
int row, column, length, color;
{
   int i;

   for (i = 0; i < length; i++) DisplayDot (row, column + i, color);
}
```

Create the DisplayDot ( ) Function

The DisplayDot ( ) function is designed to display one dot of a given color on the screen at a given location. This function is called by the application or CGA Graphics Library whenever a dot needs to be displayed on the screen. The function is called with the row and column coordinates at which to display the dot, and the color of the dot.

Edit the CGAGRAFC.C file, type the following statements, and save the file.

```
/*==================================================================*/
/*                                                                    */
/* Function : DisplayDot (row, column, color);                        */
/*                                                                    */
/* Purpose  : This function displays a dot on the screen at the given */
/*            row and column coordinates.                             */
/*                                                                    */
/* Entry Parameters : int row - The row coordinate of the dot.        */
/*                                                                    */
/*            int column - The column coordinate of the dot.          */
/*                                                                    */
/*            int color  - The color of the dot.                      */
/*                                                                    */
/* Functions Called : int86 () - This function executes a DOS BIOS    */
/*            interrupt service routine.                              */
/*                                                                    */
/* Logic Flow : The DisplayDot () function is called to display one   */
/*            dot on the screen at the given row and column and in    */
/*            the given color.  The variable In_Regs.h.al is          */
/*            assigned to the dot color.  In_Regs.h.ah is set to 12   */
/*            for the DOS BIOS service number to display a dot on the */
/*            screen.  In_Regs.x.cx is set to the column coordinate.  */
/*            In_Regs.x.dx is set to the row coordinate.  The         */
/*            int86 () function is called to display the dot on the   */
/*            screen.                                                 */
```

```
/*                                                                      */
/* Exit : A dot is displayed on the screen.                            */
/*                                                                      */
/*=====================================================================*/

DisplayDot (row, column, color)
int row, column, color;
{
    In_Regs.h.al = color;
    In_Regs.h.ah = 12;
    In_Regs.x.cx = column;
    In_Regs.x.dx = row;
    int86 (DOS_VIDEO_CALL, &In_Regs, &Out_Regs);
}
```

THE FONT SET AND CHARACTER DISPLAY FUNCTIONS

The character display functions DisplayChar ( ), DisplayString ( ), DisplayStrNum ( ) make use of the same font set. The font set is nothing more than an array of icons that represent each individual displayable character. The creation of the font set was explained in Chapter 5.

The variable Font_Set is used to define all of the display character icons. Font_Set [0] contains the icon representation of the characters with a white foreground and a black background. The variable Font_Set [1] contains the icon representation of the characters with a black foreground and white background. The variable Temp_Font_Set is used whenever a different color combination, such as a red character on a blue background, is needed.

Create the DisplayChar ( ) Function

The DisplayChar ( ) function is designed to display one character on the screen at a given location in the given foreground and background colors. The application calls this routine whenever a single character needs to be displayed on the screen. The function is called with the upper left-hand row and column coordinates to start the display of the character icon, the character to display, and the foreground and background colors in which to display the icon.

Edit the CGAGRAFC.C file, type the following statements, and save the file.

```
/*=====================================================================*/
/*                                                                      */
/* Function : DisplayChar (row, column, c, foreground, background);    */
/*                                                                      */
/* Purpose  : This function displays a character on the screen at the  */
/*            given upper left-hand row and column coordinates, the     */
/*            ASCII character to display, and the foreground and        */
/*            background colors of the character.                       */
```

```
/*                                                                    */
/* Entry Parameters : int row - The upper left-hand corner row        */
/*            coordinate at which display the character.              */
/*                                                                    */
/*             int column - The upper left-hand column coordinate at  */
/*             which to display the character.                        */
/*                                                                    */
/*             char c - The character to display, such as 'a.'        */
/*                                                                    */
/*             int foreground - The foreground color of the character. */
/*                                                                    */
/*             int background - The background color of the character. */
/*                                                                    */
/* Local Data Definitions : int i - This variable is used to contain  */
/*             the icon number to use to display the displayable      */
/*             character icon.                                        */
/*                                                                    */
/* Functions Called : DisplayIcon (); - This function is called to    */
/*             display the individual icon on the screen.             */
/*                                                                    */
/*             GetFontNum (); - This function is called to get which  */
/*             font number to use when displaying the icon.           */
/*                                                                    */
/*             MapFontChar (); - This function is called to select    */
/*             which displayable character icon to use.               */
/*                                                                    */
/* Logic Flow : The DisplayChar () function is called to display a    */
/*             character on the screen at the given upper left-hand row */
/*             and column coordinates, the ASCII character to display, */
/*             and the foreground and background colors of the        */
/*             character.  The GetFontNum () function is called to     */
/*             determine which font set will be used to display the   */
/*             character. The font set will be either Font_Set[0],    */
/*             Font_Set[1], or Temp_Font_Set.  If the font set is not  */
/*             equal to 2, then the font set being used is Font_Set[i]; */
/*             otherwise, the Temp_Font_Set is used.  In either case,  */
/*             DisplayIcon () function is called to display the icon   */
/*             representing that character.  The MapFontChar () function*/
/*             is called to map the ASCII character into the correct  */
/*             icon array.                                            */
/*                                                                    */
/* Exit    : The character is displayed on the screen at the given    */
/*             location and in the given color.                       */
/*                                                                    */
/*====================================================================*/

DisplayChar (row, column, c, foreground, background)
int row, column;
char c;
int foreground, background;
{
   int i;
```

```
    if ((i = GetFontNum (foreground, background)) != 2)
       DisplayIcon (Font_Set[i][MapFontChar (c)], row, column,
                    FONTWIDTH, FONTHEIGHT);
    else DisplayIcon (Temp_Font_Set[MapFontChar (c)], row, column,
                    FONTWIDTH, FONTHEIGHT);
}
```

Create the DisplayString ( ) Function

The DisplayString ( ) function is designed to display a string of character icons on the screen at a given location and color. The application calls this function whenever it needs to display a string of characters on the screen, instead of just one character. The function is called with the starting row and column, a pointer to the display string, and the foreground and background colors in which to display the string. The function starts displaying the characters on the screen, advancing to the next character until a NULL is encountered.

Edit the CGAGRAFC.C file, type the following statements, and save the file.

```
/*======================================================================*/
/*                                                                      */
/* Function : DisplayString (row, column, string, foreground,           */
/*                           background);                               */
/*                                                                      */
/* Purpose  : This function displays a string of characters on the      */
/*            screen at a given location and given foreground and        */
/*            background colors.                                         */
/*                                                                      */
/* Entry Parameters : int row - The upper left-hand corner row          */
/*            coordinate at which to start the display of the            */
/*            character string.                                          */
/*                                                                      */
/*            int column - The upper left-hand column coordinate at      */
/*            which to start the display of the character string.        */
/*                                                                      */
/*            char *string - The character string to display, such       */
/*            as "Mail List."                                            */
/*                                                                      */
/*            int foreground - The foreground color of the string.       */
/*                                                                      */
/*            int background - The background color of the string.       */
/*                                                                      */
/* Local Data Definitions : int fontset - This variable is used to       */
/*            contain the font set number used.                          */
/*                                                                      */
/* Functions Called : DisplayIcon (); - This function is called to       */
/*            display the individual icon on the screen.                 */
/*                                                                      */
/*            GetFontNum (); - This function is called to get which      */
/*            font number to use when displaying the icon.               */
/*                                                                      */
```

```
/*          MapFontChar (); - This function is called to select      */
/*          which displayable character icon to use.                 */
/*                                                                    */
/* Logic Flow : The DisplayString () function is called to display a */
/*          NULL terminated string of characters on the screen. It   */
/*          is passed the row and column coordinates of the upper    */
/*          left-hand corner of where to display the first character,*/
/*          a pointer to the string to display, and the foreground   */
/*          and background colors in which to display the string.    */
/*          The GetFontNum () function is called to get the font     */
/*          set to use to display the string.  If the font set is    */
/*          not equal to 2, then the font set is Font_Set, else it   */
/*          is Temp_Font_Set.  The DisplayIcon () function is called */
/*          to display each character in the string.  The column     */
/*          coordinates are adjusted for each character.             */
/*                                                                    */
/* Exit    : The character string is displayed on the screen at the  */
/*          given location and in the given color.                   */
/*                                                                    */
/*==================================================================*/

DisplayString (row, column, string, foreground, background)
int    row, column;
char   *string;
int    foreground, background;
{
   int fontset;

   if ((fontset = GetFontNum (foreground, background)) != 2)
   {
      while (*string)
      {
         DisplayIcon (Font_Set[fontset][MapFontChar (*string++)],
                   row, column, FONTWIDTH, FONTHEIGHT);
         column += FONTWIDTH;
      }
   }
   else
   {
      while (*string)
      {
         DisplayIcon (Temp_Font_Set[MapFontChar (*string++)],
                   row, column, FONTWIDTH, FONTHEIGHT);
         column += FONTWIDTH;
      }
   }
}
```

Create the DisplayStrNum ( ) Function

The DisplayStrNum ( ) function is to display a string of character icons on the screen at a given location and color, that is NOT NULL terminated. The application calls this function to display a string on the screen, but it tells the function how many characters to process from the string before returning. The function is called with the starting row and column coordinates, a pointer to the character string to display, the number of characters to display from the string, and the foreground and background colors in which to display the string.

Edit the CGAGRAFC.C file, type the following statements, and save the file.

```
/*=====================================================================*/
/*                                                                     */
/* Function : DisplayStrNum (row, column, string, number, foreground,  */
/*                           background);                              */
/*                                                                     */
/* Purpose  : This function displays a string of characters on the     */
/*            screen at a given location and given foreground and       */
/*            background colors, for the given number of characters     */
/*            to display.                                              */
/*                                                                     */
/* Entry Parameters : int row - The upper left-hand corner row         */
/*            coordinate at which to display the character string.      */
/*                                                                     */
/*            int column - The upper left-hand column coordinate at     */
/*            which to display the character string.                    */
/*                                                                     */
/*            char *string - The character string to display, such      */
/*            as "Mail List."                                          */
/*                                                                     */
/*            int number - The number of characters to display from     */
/*            the given string.                                         */
/*                                                                     */
/*            int foreground - The foreground color of the string.      */
/*                                                                     */
/*            int background - The background color of the string.      */
/*                                                                     */
/* Local Data Definitions : int fontset - This variable is used to      */
/*            contain the font set number to use to display the          */
/*            character.                                               */
/*                                                                     */
/*            int i - This variable is used as a counter to count the   */
/*            number of characters displayed from the given string.      */
/*                                                                     */
/* Functions Called : DisplayIcon () - This function is called to       */
/*            display an individual character icon on the screen.        */
/*                                                                     */
/*            GetFontNum () - This function is called to get which       */
/*            font number to use when displaying the icon.               */
/*                                                                     */
```

```
/*          MapFontChar () - This function is called to select       */
/*          which displayable character icon to use.                 */
/*                                                                    */
/* Logic Flow : The DisplayStrNum () function is called to display a  */
/*          certain number of characters from a string of characters  */
/*          on the screen at a given location in the given            */
/*          foreground and background colors.  The GetFontNum ()      */
/*          function is called to get the font set to use.  If the    */
/*          font set is not equal to 2, then Font_Set is used, else   */
/*          Temp_Font_Set is used.  For each character in the string, */
/*          until the number of characters given are displayed or a   */
/*          NULL is encountered, the DisplayIcon () function is       */
/*          called to display the character. The MapFontChar ()       */
/*          function is called to return the icon number of the       */
/*          character to display.  The DisplayIcon () function is     */
/*          also passed the row and column coordinates at which to    */
/*          display the icon and the width and the height of the      */
/*          icon.                                                     */
/*                                                                    */
/* Exit    : The character string is displayed on the screen at the   */
/*          given location, in the given color, the given number      */
/*          of characters to display.                                 */
/*                                                                    */
/*==================================================================*/

DisplayStrNum (row, column, string, number, foreground, background)
int    row, column;
char   *string;
int    number, foreground, background;
{
   int fontset, i;

   if ((fontset = GetFontNum (foreground, background)) != 2)
   {
      for (i = 0; i < number; i++)
      {
         if (*string == 0) return;
         DisplayIcon (Font_Set[fontset][MapFontChar (*string++)],
                   row, column, FONTWIDTH, FONTHEIGHT);
         column += FONTWIDTH;
      }
   }
   else
   {
      for (i = 0; i < number; i++)
      {
         if (*string == 0) return;
         DisplayIcon (Temp_Font_Set[MapFontChar (*string++)],
                   row, column, FONTWIDTH, FONTHEIGHT);
         column += FONTWIDTH;
      }
   }
}
```

Create the GetFontNum ( ) Function

The GetFontNum ( ) function is designed to return the font set number to use to display a character with the given foreground and background colors. The functions DisplayChar ( ), DisplayString ( ), DisplayStrNum ( ), and DisplayCursor ( ) use this function to determine which font set to use. The font set used by the CGA Graphics Library is the variable Font_Set. This variable is defined in the file FONTSET.H to hold two different font sets. The static variable Temp_Font_Set is used to contain any special mapping to produce the different foreground and background colors.

Based on the foreground and background colors passed, the function will do the following things:

- If the foreground color is White and the background color is Black, the function returns a 0, telling the calling function to use Font_Set[0] to display the string.

- If the foreground color is Black and the background color is White, the function returns a 1, telling the calling function to use Font_set [1] to display the string.

- If the foreground and background colors are anything else, the function returns a 2, telling the calling function to use Temp_Font_Set to display the string. The function also does a mapping of the font set to get the right color combination to display.

Before we begin the coding of this function, let me describe this function's purpose. This function is used by the CGA Graphics Library ONLY. The application does not call this function directly. The CGA Graphics Library uses this function, along with the MapFontChar ( ) function, to determine which font set to use as the displayable character icons. As explained above, the Temp_Font_Set is used whenever a character needs to be displayed that is not WHITE on BLACK or BLACK on WHITE. It is for this purpose that the GetFontNum ( ) function is used.

The logic flow of the GetFontNum ( ) function is designed for speed. If the foreground color is WHITE and the background color is BLACK, then Font_Set[0] is used and a 0 is returned so indicating. If the foreground color is BLACK and the background color is WHITE, the Font_Set[1] is used and a 1 is returned. On any other color combination, the Temp_Font_Set is used.

At this point, we already know that the Temp_Font_Set needs to be mapped and we need to determine how to map it. The Font_Set[0] and Font_Set[1] variables will be used and they will be OR'ed, AND'ed, and XOR'ed with the colors needed. First a switch is performed to determine the foreground color passed.

If the foreground color passed is WHITE, then Font_Set[0] is OR'ed with the background color passed, either BLUE or RED. For example, the function is called with the foreground color being WHITE and the background color being RED. As explained in an earlier chapter, the two-bit dot color pattern for WHITE is 11, and the two-bit dot color pattern for RED is 10. Font_Set[0] contains all of the icons that are in a WHITE foreground and a BLACK background; by OR'ing a RED byte pattern to this, we can get the WHITE foreground on a RED background.

To explain further:

We have the icon for the letter 'a' in a WHITE foreground and a BLACK background. This is Font_Set[0][0], the first icon in the Font_Set.

```
00000000 00000000
00000000 00000000
00000000 00000000
00111100 00000000
00000011 00000000
00111111 00000000
11000011 00000000
00111100 11000000
00000000 00000000
00000000 00000000
```

If we need to display this character with a WHITE foreground and a RED background, each byte of the icon must be masked with a RED byte pattern, 10101010. This byte pattern is OR'ed with the icon byte and the new byte pattern is saved in Temp_Font_Set.

When the byte pattern 00111100 is OR with the byte pattern 10101010, the byte pattern generated is 10111110. When all of the bytes have been OR with the RED byte pattern, the following icon display is made:

```
10101010 10101010
10101010 10101010
10101010 00101010
10111110 10101010
10101011 10101010
10111111 10101010
11101011 10101010
10111110 11101010
10101010 10101010
10101010 10101010
```

Although it is difficult to see the 'a' in the byte patterns above, this icon will display a WHITE 'a' on a RED background. This process is performed on each of the other characters in the font set and are saved in the variable Temp_Font_Set.

Each color combination available to the CGA Graphics Library is mapped in this function using the byte patterns defined in the COLORS.H include file. The reader should take extra time analyzing the way each color combination is generated. The particular function could be written in Assembler to make it execute faster, but it is written in 'C' because of the readability factor.

Edit the CGAGRAFC.C source file, type the following statements, and save the file.

```
/*=====================================================================*/
/*                                                                     */
/* Function : GetFontNum (foreground, background);                     */
/*                                                                     */
/* Purpose  : This function returns the font set to use with the       */
/*            given foreground and background colors.                  */
/*                                                                     */
/* Entry Parameters : int foreground - The foreground color of the     */
/*            character to display.                                    */
/*                                                                     */
/*            int background - The background color of the character   */
/*            to display.                                              */
/*                                                                     */
/* Local Data Definition : int i,j,k; - These variables are used as    */
/*            counters when Font_Set needs to be mapped into the       */
/*            Temp_Font_Set.                                           */
/*                                                                     */
/* Logic Flow : The GetFontNum () is called by the CGA Graphics        */
/*            Library function to return which font set to use when    */
/*            displaying a character icon to the screen.  The function */
/*            is passed the foreground and background colors of the    */
/*            character to display.  If the foreground color passed is */
/*            WHITE and the background color is BLACK then the         */
/*            function returns a 0 indicating that Font_Set[0] is used */
/*            to display characters of the color. If the foreground    */
/*            color passed is BLACK and the background color is        */
/*            WHITE, then the function returns 1 indicating that       */
/*            Font_Set[1] is used.  If the Current_Foreground and      */
/*            Current_Background variables are different than the ones */
/*            passed, then a mapping needs to be done to represent the */
/*            character icons in this color.  First, a switch is done  */
/*            on the foreground color passed.  If it is WHITE, then the*/
/*            variables i, j, and k are used to map each icon in the   */
/*            fontset (95).  Font_Set [0] is used because it contains  */
/*            the WHITE on BLACK icons. If the foreground color passed */
/*            is BLACK, then Font_Set[1] is used.  If the foreground   */
/*            color is not WHITE or BLACK, then a switch is made on    */
/*            the background color passed.  If the background color is */
/*            WHITE then Font_Set[0] is used as the map.  This is      */
/*            continued for each color combination possible.           */
/*                                                                     */
/* Exit       : Return 0 - Font_Set[0] = WHITE on BLACK                */
/*              Return 1 - Font_Set[1] = BLACK on WHITE                */
/*              Return 2 - Temp_Font_Set = Special map of any other    */
```

```
/*                          color combinations                         */
/*                                                                      */
/*====================================================================*/

GetFontNum (foreground, background)
int foreground, background;
{
   int i,j,k;

   if (foreground == WHITE && background == BLACK) return (0);
   else if (foreground == BLACK && background ==  WHITE) return (1);
   if (foreground != Current_Foreground ||
       background != Current_Background)
   {
      switch (foreground)
      {
         case WHITE:
            for (i = 0; i < 95; i++)
               for (j = 0; j < 10; j++)
                  for (k = 0; k < 2; k++)
                     Temp_Font_Set[i][j][k] = Font_Set[0][i][j][k] |
                                              background;
            break;

         case BLACK:
            for (i = 0; i < 95; i++)
               for (j = 0; j < 10; j++)
                  for (k = 0; k < 2; k++)
                     Temp_Font_Set[i][j][k] = Font_Set[1][i][j][k] &
                                              background;
            break;

         default:
            switch (background)
            {
               case WHITE:
                  for (i = 0; i < 95; i++)
                     for (j = 0; j < 10; j++)
                        for (k = 0; k < 2; k++)
                           Temp_Font_Set[i][j][k] =
                              Font_Set[1][i][j][k] | foreground;
                  break;

               case BLACK:
                  for (i = 0; i < 95; i++)
                     for (j = 0; j < 10; j++)
                        for (k = 0; k < 2; k++)
                           Temp_Font_Set[i][j][k] =
                              Font_Set[0][i][j][k] & foreground;
                  break;

               default:
                  for (i = 0; i < 95; i++)
```

```
                    for (j = 0; j < 10; j++)
                        for (k = 0; k < 2; k++)
                            Temp_Font_Set[i][j][k] =
                                Font_Set[0][i][j][k] ^ background;
                    break;
            }
            break;
    }
    Current_Foreground = foreground;
    Current_Background = background;
    }
    return (2);
}
```

Create the MapFontChar ( ) Function

The MapFontChar ( ) function is designed to take a given character and return the icon number to use to display the character. The Font_Set variable contains the icons for 95 different displayable characters. The first icons are the letters of the alphabet, first in lowercase, then in uppercase. Next are the numeric digits 0 - 9, and finally, all of the special displayable characters. The functions DisplayChar ( ), DisplayString ( ), DisplayStrNum ( ), and DisplayCursor ( ) use this function when displaying a character icon on the screen.

Edit the CGAGRAFC.C file, type the following statements, and save the file.

```
/*=====================================================================*/
/*                                                                     */
/* Function : MapFontChar (c)                                          */
/*                                                                     */
/* Purpose  : This function maps the given character into its          */
/*            corresponding character icon number.                     */
/*                                                                     */
/* Entry Parameters : char c - The character to map.                   */
/*                                                                     */
/* Local Data Definitions : int i - This variable is used to search    */
/*            the special character list.                              */
/*                                                                     */
/* Logic Flow : The MapFontChar () function is called by the CGA       */
/*            Graphics Library to return the icon array number that     */
/*            represents the character passed to the function.         */
/*            First, the character is checked to see if it is a lower- */
/*            case alphabetic character.  Then it is checked to see if */
/*            it is an uppercase alphabetic character.  Then it is     */
/*            checked to see if it is a number.  Then the special      */
/*            displayable characters are checked.  If there is no      */
/*            match, then a negative one is returned.                  */
/*                                                                     */
/* Exit     : Return = -1 - Invalid character                          */
/*            Return >= 0 - Character is mapped                        */
/*                                                                     */
```

```
/*========================================================================*/

MapFontChar (c)
char c;
{
    int i;

    if (c >= 'a' && c <= 'z') return (c - 'a');
    else if (c >= 'A' && c <= 'Z') return (c - 'A' + 26);
    else if (c >= '0' && c <= '9') return (c - '0' + 85);
    else for (i = 0; i < 33; i++) if (Special[i] == c) return (i + 52);
    return (-1);
}
```

Create the DisplayCursor ( ) Function

The DisplayCursor ( ) function is designed to simulate a cursor on the screen. It does this by placing an underline beneath the character passed. The row and column coordinates, the character to display the cursor under, and the foreground and background colors are passed to the function. The function uses the defined data variable CURSOR as the mapping of the character icon to use as the cursor.

Edit the CGAGRAFC.C file, type the following statements, and save the file.

```
/*========================================================================*/
/*                                                                        */
/* Function : DisplayCursor (row, column, c, foreground,background);      */
/*                                                                        */
/* Purpose  : This function displays the given character with an          */
/*            underline on the screen at the given location in the        */
/*            given foreground and background colors.                     */
/*                                                                        */
/* Entry Parameters : int row - The row coordinate at which to            */
/*            display the cursor.                                         */
/*                                                                        */
/*            int column - The column coordinate at which to display      */
/*            the cursor.                                                 */
/*                                                                        */
/*            char c - The character to display with underline.          */
/*                                                                        */
/*            int foreground - The foreground color of the character.    */
/*                                                                        */
/*            int background - The background color of the character.    */
/*                                                                        */
/* Exit : The character is displayed with an underline.                  */
/*                                                                        */
/*========================================================================*/

DisplayCursor (row, column, c, foreground, background)
int row, column;
char c;
```

```
int foreground, background;
{
    int    i,j;
    int    fontset, fontchar;
    unsigned char tempfont[10][2];

    fontset  = GetFontNum (foreground, background);
    fontchar = MapFontChar (c);
    for (i = 0; i < 10; i++)
        for (j = 0; j < 2; j++)
            tempfont[i][j] = Font_Set[fontset][fontchar][i][j] &
                             Font_Set[fontset][CURSOR][i][j];
    DisplayIcon (tempfont[0], row, column, FONTWIDTH, FONTHEIGHT);
}
```

SUMMARY

The CGAGRAFC.C source file contains the functions that are written in 'C' and use the DOS BIOS interrupt service routines. The functions that are defined in this source file are just some of the many graphic functions that the programmer may need to have in the graphics library. Some of the functions written in this source file could be rewritten in Assembler and use Direct Video Access, but they were written here in 'C' because of the readability and for the examples that need to be shown for each type of video access.

In the next chapter we create the source file CGAGRAFA.ASM. This source file contains the functions that are written in Assembler and make use of the Direct Video Access method of screen data manipulation. Some of these function are called from the functions written in this chapter, some are called from the application, and others are called from within the CGAGRAFA.ASM source file. These functions deal with large amounts of screen data.

Chapter 7

THE CGA GRAPHICS LIBRARY
ASSEMBLER SOURCE FILES

INTRODUCTION

In the previous chapters, we dealt with the creation of the CGA Graphics Library include source files and 'C' source files. In this chapter we create the CGAGRAFA.ASM source file. This file contains the source code for all of the functions written in Assembler that use Direct Video Access.

The following functions are included in the source file:

- ClearScreen ( ) - This function clears the screen in a given color.
- ClearWindow ( ) - This function clears a window on the screen at the given upper left-hand row and column coordinates, the window width and height, and the color to clear the window in.
- DisplayIcon ( ) - This function displays an icon on the screen at the given upper left-hand row and column coordinates, the icon width and height, and a pointer to the icon to display.
- DisplayToBuffer ( ) - This function copies a window of display information into a buffer so that the window display information can be restored back to the screen. The function is called with a pointer to the buffer, the upper left-hand row and column coordinates, and the window width and height.
- BufferToDisplay ( ) - This function displays a buffer of display information on the screen at the given upper left-hand row and column coordinates, the window width and height, and a pointer to the display buffer.
- ScrollWindow ( ) - This function is called by the application whenever a window of screen data needs to be scrolled up, down, left, or right. The

function is called with the destination row and column coordinates, the source row and column coordinates, the window width and height, and the direction to scroll.

- ScrollVertical ( ) - This function is used by the CGA Graphics Library to scroll a window of screen data up or down.

- ScrollLeft ( ) - This function is used by the CGA Graphics Library to scroll a window of screen data to the left.

- ScrollRight ( ) - This function is used by the CGA Graphics Library to scroll a window of screen data to the right.

Create the CGAGRAFA.ASM source file, type the following statements, and save the file.

```
;*=========================================================================*/
;*                                                                         */
;* File : CGAGRAFA.ASM                                                     */
;*                                                                         */
;* Purpose : This Assembler source file contains the CGA Graphics          */
;*           Library functions that use Direct Video Access.               */
;*                                                                         */
;* Functions : ClearScreen () - This function clears the screen in         */
;*             the given color.                                            */
;*                                                                         */
;*             ClearWindow () - This function clears a window on the        */
;*             screen, given the upper left-hand row and column            */
;*             coordinates, the window width and height, and the           */
;*             color in which to clear the window.                         */
;*                                                                         */
;*             DisplayIcon () - This function displays an icon on          */
;*             the screen at the given upper left-hand row and column      */
;*             coordinates, the icon width and height, and a pointer       */
;*             to the icon to display.                                     */
;*                                                                         */
;*             DisplayToBuffer () - This function copies a window of        */
;*             display information into a buffer so that the window         */
;*             display information can be restored back to the screen.      */
;*             The function is called with a pointer to the buffer,         */
;*             the upper left-hand row and column coordinates, and          */
;*             the window width and height.                                 */
;*                                                                         */
;*             BufferToDisplay () - This function displays a buffer         */
;*             of display information on the screen at the given upper      */
;*             left-hand row and column coordinates, the window width       */
;*             and height, and a pointer to the display buffer.             */
;*                                                                         */
;*             ScrollWindow () - This function is called by the             */
;*             application whenever a window of screen data needs to         */
;*             be scrolled up, down, left, or right.  The function is       */
;*             called with the destination row and column coordinates,      */
;*             the source row and column coordinates, the window width      */
```

```
;*              and height, and the direction to scroll.            */
;*                                                                  */
;*              ScrollVertical () - This function is used by the CGA */
;*              Graphics Library to scroll a window of screen data up */
;*              or down.                                            */
;*                                                                  */
;*              ScrollLeft () - This function is used by the CGA    */
;*              Graphics Library to scroll a window of screen data   */
;*              to the left.                                        */
;*                                                                  */
;*              ScrollRight () - This function is used by the CGA   */
;*              Graphics Library to scroll a window of screen data   */
;*              to the right.                                       */
;*                                                                  */
;*================================================================*/

_TEXT    SEGMENT  BYTE PUBLIC 'CODE'
_TEXT    ENDS

CONST    SEGMENT  WORD PUBLIC 'CONST'
CONST    ENDS

_BSS     SEGMENT  WORD PUBLIC 'BSS'
_BSS     ENDS

_DATA    SEGMENT  WORD PUBLIC 'DATA'
_DATA    ENDS

DGROUP   GROUP    CONST, _BSS,  _DATA
         ASSUME   CS: _TEXT, DS: DGROUP, SS: DGROUP, ES: DGROUP
_DATA    SEGMENT
_DATA    ENDS

_TEXT    SEGMENT
```

The above code defines the statements needed by the MASM compiler to be able to compile the CGAGRAFA.ASM source file. The following code also contains comments next to the source code. This style of commenting is used in Assembler because the code sometimes becomes so complicated that extra comments are needed.

Create the ClearScreen ( ) Function

The ClearScreen ( ) function is designed to clear the entire screen in a given color. This function is called by the application whenever it needs the entire screen cleared in a particular color, such as during initialization of the program.

Edit the CGAGRAFA.ASM file, type the following statements, and save the file.

```
;*=====================================================================*/
;*                                                                     */
;* Function : ClearScreen (color);                                     */
;*                                                                     */
;* Purpose  : This function clears the screen in the given color.      */
;*                                                                     */
;* Entry Parameters : char color - Byte color to clear the screen.     */
;*                                                                     */
;* Logic Flow : The ClearScreen () function is called to clear the     */
;*              entire screen in the given color pattern passed.  The   */
;*              segment registers es and ds are assigned to point to   */
;*              video display address in memory (B800H).  The si and di */
;*              registers are pointed at the first video display byte.  */
;*              The cx register contains the number of bytes to move,   */
;*              2000H.  The al and ah registers contain the color byte  */
;*              passed on the stack.  The first word is moved into memory*/
;*              and the repeat word instruction is used to repeat until */
;*              all of the words have been moved.                       */
;*                                                                     */
;* Exit : Screen is cleared in the given byte color pattern.           */
;*                                                                     */
;*=====================================================================*/

        PUBLIC  _ClearScreen

_ClearScreen PROC        NEAR
        push    bp                      ; save the registers being used
        mov     bp,sp                   ; on the stack, using the base
        push    ds                      ; pointer as a pointer to the
        push    es                      ; parameters passed on the stack
        push    si
        push    di
        mov     ax,0b800h               ; set ds and es to point to the
        mov     ds,ax                   ; video ram buffer
        mov     es,ax
        mov     si,0                    ; set si and di to point at the
        mov     di,0                    ; first byte of the video buffer
        mov     cx,2000h                ; cx = number of bytes to move
        mov     al,[bp + 4]             ; ax = get the color attribute
        mov     ah,al
        mov     [di],ax                 ; store the color attribute
        inc     di                      ; advance to the next word
        inc     di
        rep     movsw                   ; use repeat instruction to move
        pop     di                      ; restore the stack
        pop     si
        pop     es
        pop     ds
        pop     bp
        ret                             ; return to the calling process

_ClearScreen    ENDP
```

Create the ClearWindow ( ) Function

The ClearWindow ( ) function is designed to clear a window on the screen in a given color. The application calls this function whenever it needs to clear a window on the screen at a given location, size, and color. The function is called with the upper left-hand row and column coordinates, the window width and height and the window color.

Edit the CGAGRAFA.ASM file, type the following statements, and save the file.

```
;*=====================================================================*/
;*                                                                     */
;* Function : ClearWindow (row, column, width, height, color);         */
;*                                                                     */
;* Purpose  : This function clears a window on the screen at the       */
;*            given upper left-hand corner, width, height, and color.  */
;*                                                                     */
;* Entry Parameters : int row - The upper left-hand row coordinate     */
;*            of the window to clear.                                  */
;*                                                                     */
;*            int column - The upper left-hand column coordinate of    */
;*            the window to clear.                                     */
;*                                                                     */
;*            int width - The width of the window to clear.            */
;*                                                                     */
;*            int height - The height of the window to clear.          */
;*                                                                     */
;*            int color - The color in which to clear the window.      */
;*                                                                     */
;* Logic Flow : The ClearWindow () function is called to clear a       */
;*            window on the screen at a given location, width, height  */
;*            and color.  The es and ds segment registers are set to   */
;*            point at the video ram segment address (B800H).  Next,   */
;*            the starting video ram address is calculated.  First,    */
;*            the row coordinate is divided by two because the video   */
;*            plains are separated between even and odd scan lines.    */
;*            This value is then multiplied by eighty because there    */
;*            are eighty bytes per video scan line.  The starting row  */
;*            coordinate is checked to see if the window starts on an  */
;*            even row or an odd row.  The column coordinate is then   */
;*            multiplied by two to get the actual number of bits to    */
;*            clear.  This number is then divided by eight to get the  */
;*            number of bytes into the scan line to start clearing the */
;*            screen.  The di register is used to contain the byte     */
;*            address of where to begin the clearing of the window.    */
;*            The starting column is then used to determine how many   */
;*            bits in the first byte will be cleared by ANDing a bit   */
;*            mask to it.  First a seven is ANDed to it, leaving a     */
;*            number from zero to seven.  This number is then          */
;*            subtracted from eight to get the actual number of bits   */
;*            to clear in the first byte of each scan line.  The width */
;*            of the window is multiplied by two to get the actual     */
```

```
;*              number of bits the window is wide.  A comparison is made*/
;*              to determine if there are any more lines to clear on      */
;*              the screen.  If there are, then decrement the height       */
;*              counter and do the following.  Save the registers used    */
;*              that contain the information about the scan line to        */
;*              clear.  Get the color pattern and shift off the bits       */
;*              that are not to be cleared and put the byte to screen.     */
;*              Subtract from the width the number of actual bits moved    */
;*              onto the screen.  Next, check to see if there are more     */
;*              than eight more bits left to move to the screen.  If       */
;*              there are, then do the following.  Move the color byte     */
;*              pattern onto the screen until there are less than eight    */
;*              bits to move.  When there are less than eight bits and     */
;*              at least 1 bit, then move the last bits of this scan       */
;*              to the screen.  If there are more scan lines left, then    */
;*              clear the next scan line.                                  */
;*                                                                         */
;* Exit      : A window is cleared at the given location, width,           */
;*              height, and color.                                         */
;*                                                                         */
;*=========================================================================*/

           PUBLIC _ClearWindow

_ClearWindow    PROC    NEAR
           push    bp                          ; save the registers used
           mov     bp,sp
           push    ds
           push    es
           push    si
           push    di
           mov     ax,0b800h
           mov     ds,ax
           mov     es,ax                       ; es and ds point at video ram
           mov     al,[bp + 4]                 ; get starting row coordinate
           shr     al,1                        ; calculate starting video row
           mov     dl,80                       ; by taking the starting row (al)
           mul     dl                          ; multiply it by 80 to get the
           mov     dx,ax                       ; video scan line address
           mov     al,[bp + 4]                 ; check to see if the starting row
           test    al,1                        ; started on an even or odd line
           jz      ClearWindow0                ; jump if it started on even line
           or      dx,2000h                    ; advance to odd scan line

ClearWindow0:
           and     word ptr [bp + 4],1         ; set row to even or odd status
           shl     word ptr [bp + 6],1         ; multiply column by 2
           mov     ax,[bp + 6]                 ; starting column coordinate
           shr     ax,1                        ; divide starting column by 8 to get
           shr     ax,1                        ; the byte offset in to the video
           shr     ax,1                        ; ram buffer starting row
           add     ax,dx                       ; add in the starting row offset
           mov     di,ax                       ; di = starting video ram location
```

```
        mov     cx,[bp + 6]          ; cx = the number of first byte
        and     cx,7                 ; bits NOT cleared on each line
        mov     bx,8                 ; bx = the number of first byte
        sub     bx,cx                ; bits that ARE cleared
        shl     word ptr [bp + 8],1  ; multiply the window width by two
        mov     dx,[bp + 8]          ; dx = number of bits per scan line

ClearWindow1:
        cmp     word ptr [bp + 10],0 ; check the window height counter
        jz      ClearWindowExit      ; exit if there are no more lines
        dec     word ptr [bp + 10]   ; decrement the height counter
        push    dx                   ; push the window width
        push    di                   ; push the video ram address
        push    cx                   ; push 1st byte bits NOT cleared
        push    bx                   ; push 1st byte bits cleared
        mov     al,[bp + 12]         ; get the color byte pattern
        shr     al,cl                ; shift off the bits NOT cleared
        mov     ah,0FFh              ; ah = the bit mask being used
        xchg    cx,bx                ; get the 1st byte bits to clear
        shl     ah,cl                ; ah = the byte with cleared bits
        xchg    bx,cx                ; restore register integrity
        and     ah,es:[di]           ; mask cleared byte with current
        or      al,ah                ; video byte and NOT cleared byte
        stosb                        ; move in the byte to the screen
        sub     dx,bx                ; subtract number of bits cleared
        mov     al,[bp + 12]         ; get the color byte pattern

ClearWindow2:
        cmp     dx,8                 ; less than 8 bits left on line
        jl      ClearWindow3         ; process the last byte if there is
        stosb                        ; move the color byte to the screen
        sub     dx,8                 ; subtract the number of bits moved
        jmp     ClearWindow2         ; process the next byte on the line

ClearWindow3:
        or      dx,dx                ; if there are no more bits to move
        jz      ClearWindow4         ; then start on the next scan line
        xchg    dx,cx                ; set cl to number of bits left to
        mov     bx,8                 ; put in the last byte of the line
        sub     bx,cx
        xchg    bx,cx
        shl     al,cl                ; al = number of bits NOT cleared
        mov     cx,bx
        mov     ah,0FFh
        shr     ah,cl                ; ah = number of bits cleared
        and     ah,es:[di]           ; mask the current video byte with
        or      al,ah                ; the cleared and not cleared byte
        stosb                        ; patterns and put it to the screen

ClearWindow4:
        pop     bx                   ; pop 1st byte bits cleared
        pop     cx                   ; pop 1st byte bits NOT cleared
        pop     di                   ; pop the video ram address
```

```
        pop     dx                  ; pop the window width
        xor     di,2000h            ; advance to the next scan line
        xor     word ptr [bp + 4],1 ; check even/odd status
        jnz     ClearWindow1        ; advance to the next line if odd
        add     di,80               ; advance to the next even scan
        jmp     ClearWindow1        ; process the next scan line

ClearWindowExit:
        pop     di                  ; restore the registers used
        pop     si
        pop     es
        pop     ds
        pop     bp
        ret                         ; return to the calling process

_ClearWindow    ENDP
```

Create the DisplayIcon ( ) Function

The DisplayIcon ( ) function is designed to display an icon on the screen at a given location. The application calls the function whenever it wishes to display an icon on the screen, such as an arrow or character. The function is called with a pointer to the icon to display, the upper left-hand row and column coordinates, and the width and height of the icon.

Edit the CGAGRAFA.ASM file, type the following statements, and save the file.

```
;*=====================================================================*/
;*                                                                     */
;* Function : DisplayIcon (icon, row, column, width, height);          */
;*                                                                     */
;* Purpose  : This function displays a video icon on the screen at     */
;*            the given upper left-hand row and column coordinates     */
;*            and the given width and height of the icon.              */
;*                                                                     */
;* Entry Parameters : char *icon - The icon to display.                */
;*                                                                     */
;*            int row   - The upper left-hand row coordinate.          */
;*                                                                     */
;*            int column - The upper left-hand column coordinate.      */
;*                                                                     */
;*            int width  - The width of the icon.                      */
;*                                                                     */
;*            int height - The height of the icon.                     */
;*                                                                     */
;* Logic Flow : The DisplayIcon () function is called to display icons*/
;*            on the screen at a given location.  The function is      */
;*            called with a pointer to the icon, the upper left-hand   */
;*            row and column coordinates, and the icon width and       */
;*            height.  The es:di register pair is used to point at     */
;*            the video display ram buffer. The ds:si register pair    */
```

```
;*              points at the icon source buffer to display. The first  */
;*              byte of the icon is displayed, the next bytes on the     */
;*              line are displayed, and the last byte. Each line of the  */
;*              icon is displayed until the last line is displayed.      */
;*                                                                       */
;* Exit : The icon is displayed on the screen.                          */
;*                                                                       */
;*=====================================================================*/

        PUBLIC  _DisplayIcon

_DisplayIcon    PROC  NEAR
        push    bp                  ; save base pointer
        mov     bp,sp               ; move current stack pointer to bp
        push    es                  ; save es
        push    di                  ; save di
        push    si                  ; save si
        mov     ax,0B800h           ; point to video ram
        mov     es,ax               ; es = points to video ram
        mov     si,[bp + 4]         ; si = point to Icon source buffer
        mov     al,[bp + 6]         ; al = start row
        shr     al,1                ; divide starting row by 2
        mov     dl,80               ; multiply starting row by the
        mul     dl                  ; number of bytes in a video row
        mov     dx,ax               ; dx = starting row offset
        mov     al,[bp + 6]         ; get starting row
        test    al,1                ; check for even/odd status
        jz      DisplayIcon0        ; Icon starts on an even row
        or      dx,2000h            ; Icon starts on an odd row

DisplayIcon0:
        shl     word ptr [bp + 8],1 ; Column * 2 = total column bits
        mov     ax,[bp + 8]         ; starting column bit offset
        shr     ax,1                ; divide by 8 to get byte offset
        shr     ax,1                ; in the video display buffer
        shr     ax,1
        add     ax,dx               ; add to the row address
        mov     di,ax               ; di = destination address
        mov     cx,[bp + 8]         ; get starting column bit number
        nd      cx,7                ; cl = 1st byte bits NOT changed
        ov      bx,8
        ub      bx,cx               ; bl = 1st byte bits used by icon
        shl     word ptr [bp + 10],1 ; width = width * 2 - total bits
        mov     dx,[bp + 10]        ; dx = width of icon in bits
        and     word ptr [bp + 6],1 ; set row status to even or odd

DisplayIcon1:
        cmp     word ptr [bp + 12],0 ; check the height
        jz      DisplayIconExit     ; jump to end if finished
        dec     word ptr [bp + 12]  ; decrement the height
        push    dx                  ; dx = save icon width
        push    di                  ; di = save starting video address
        mov     al,[si]             ; get source byte
```

113

```
        shr     al,cl               ; shift source by start shift bytes
        mov     ah,0FFh             ; set up for mask
        xchg    cx,bx
        shl     ah,cl               ; shift off the bits not used
        xchg    cx,bx
        and     ah,es:[di]          ; bring in video byte
        or      al,ah               ; al = byte to put first
        stosb                       ; put al to video
        sub     dx,bx               ; subtract out number of bits moved

DisplayIcon2:
        cmp     dx,8                ; if < than one byte to move left
        jl      displayIcon3        ; then move last byte
        lodsb                       ; get source byte
        mov     ah,[si]             ; get next byte
        xchg    al,ah
        shr     ax,cl               ; shift to get right byte
        stosb                       ; store byte to video
        sub     dx,8                ; subtract number of bits moved
        jmp     DisplayIcon2        ; do next byte

DisplayIcon3:
        or      dx,dx              ; have all the bits been moved
        jz      DisplayIcon4        ; process the next line if true
        lodsb                       ; al = read video byte
        mov     ah,[si]             ; ah = last icon byte
        xchg    al,ah
        shr     ax,cl               ; shift in the last icon byte
        push    cx                  ; push start byte bit counter
        mov     cx,8                ; set up mask based on the number
        sub     cx,dx               ; of bits left to move
        mov     ah,0FFh
        shl     ah,cl
        pop     cx                  ; pop start byte but counter
        and     al,ah
        not     ah
        and     ah,es:[di]
        or      al,ah
        mov     es:[di],al

DisplayIcon4:
        mov     ax,[bp + 10]        ; get the icon width
        push    cx                  ; push start byte bits
        mov     cx,8
        div     cl                  ; check if width divisible by 8
        pop     cx                  ; pop start byte bits
        cmp     ah,0                ; if width is divisible by 8
        jz      DisplayIcon5
        cmp     cx,6                ; else if start bits = 6
        jz      DisplayIcon6
        inc     si                  ; increment the icon source buffer
        jmp     DisplayIcon6
```

```
DisplayIcon5:
        or      cx,cx                   ; if start bits are not zero
        jnz     DisplayIcon6
        inc     si                      ; increment the icon source buffer

DisplayIcon6:
        pop     di                      ; pop the video ram address
        pop     dx                      ; pop the number ofwidth bits
        xor     di,2000h                ; advance to next video scan line
        xor     word ptr [bp + 6],1     ; check to see if row is odd/even
        jnz     DisplayIcon1            ; process the next line of the icon
        add     di,80                   ; add in 80 bytes if last scan line
        jmp     DisplayIcon1            ; was odd, then process next line

DisplayIconExit:
        pop     si                      ; pop off the original register
        pop     di                      ; values
        pop     es
        pop     bp
        ret

_DisplayIcon    ENDP
```

Create the DisplayToBuffer ( ) Function

The DisplayToBuffer ( ) function is designed to read the video display and save it to a buffer. The application calls this function whenever it needs to save a part of the screen, such as when a menu needs to be displayed, so that it can restore the screen back when the menu is finished. The function is called with the upper left-hand row and column coordinates, the window width and height, and the buffer to save the data into.

The programmer should be aware that this function basically clips an area of video memory and copies it to another area in memory. This function does not bit align the video image in the buffer. This means that if the window area being saved is not aligned on a byte boundary or it has a width not evenly divisible by four, that the buffer cannot be used as a real icon. The BufferToDisplay ( ) function is called to restore the buffer to the screen.

Edit the CGAGRAFA.ASM source file, type the following statements, and save the file.

```
;*========================================================================*/
;*                                                                        */
;* Function : DisplayToBuffer (row, column, width, height, buffer);       */
;*                                                                        */
;* Purpose  : This function copies the video display at the given         */
;*            upper left-hand row and column coordinates, width and       */
;*            height into the given buffer.                               */
```

```
;*                                                                    */
;* Entry Parameters : int row - The upper left-hand row coordinate.   */
;*                                                                    */
;*            int column - The upper left-hand column coordinate.     */
;*                                                                    */
;*            int width - The width of the window.                    */
;*                                                                    */
;*            int height - The height of the window.                  */
;*                                                                    */
;*            char *buffer - The destination buffer to copy the       */
;*            display screen into.                                    */
;*                                                                    */
;* Logic Flow :  The DisplayToBuffer () function is called to save a  */
;*            window of screen memory.  The function is called with   */
;*            the upper left-hand row and column coordinates, the     */
;*            window width and height, and a pointer to the buffer to */
;*            save the screen.  The ds segment register is pointed at */
;*            video ram.  The starting row and column coordinates are */
;*            used to point at the starting scan line.  For each line,*/
;*            save the first byte of each line, then each byte in the */
;*            line until the last byte has been saved in the line.    */
;*                                                                    */
;* Exit : The display window is copied into the buffer.               */
;*                                                                    */
;*==================================================================*/

        PUBLIC    _DisplayToBuffer

_DisplayToBuffer  PROC    NEAR
        push    bp                  ; save the registers used
        mov     bp,sp
        push    ds
        push    es
        push    si
        push    di
        push    ds
        pop     es
        mov     di,[bp + 12]        ; es:[di] = destination buffer
        mov     ax,0b800h
        mov     ds,ax               ; ds points at the video display
        mov     al,[bp + 4]         ; get starting row coordinate
        shr     al,1                ; calculate starting video row
        mov     dl,80               ; by taking the starting row (al)
        mul     dl                  ; multiply by the number of bytes
        mov     dx,ax               ; video scan line, dx = video addr
        mov     al,[bp + 4]         ; check to see if the starting row
        test    al,1                ; started on an even or odd line
        jz      DisplayToBuffer0    ; jump if it started on an even one
        or      dx,2000h            ; advance to odd scan line

DisplayToBuffer0:
        and     word ptr [bp + 4],1 ; set row to even or odd status
        shl     word ptr [bp + 6],1 ; multiply column by 2
```

116

```
        mov     ax,[bp + 6]          ; starting column coordinate
        shr     ax,1                 ; divide starting column by 8 for
        shr     ax,1                 ; the byte offset in the video
        shr     ax,1                 ; ram buffer starting row
        add     ax,dx                ; add in the starting row offset
        mov     si,ax                ; si = starting video ram location
        mov     cx,[bp + 6]          ; get starting column
        and     cx,7                 ; cl = 1st byte bits not saved
        mov     bx,8
        sub     bx,cx                ; bl = 1st byte bits saved
        shl     word ptr [bp + 8],1  ; multiply width * 2
        mov     dx,[bp + 8]          ; dx = number of bits to move

DisplayToBuffer1:
        cmp     word ptr [bp + 10],0 ; check the height
        jz      DisplayToBufferExit  ; jump to exit
        dec     word ptr [bp + 10]   ; decrement the height
        push    dx                   ; push the window width
        push    si                   ; push video ram address
        push    cx                   ; push 1st byte bits NOT saved
        push    bx                   ; push 1st byte bits saved
        mov     ah,0FFh              ; set up to mask video byte
        shr     ah,cl
        mov     al,ds:[si]           ; get the video byte
        and     al,ah                ; mask out the unwanted bits
        mov     es:[di],al           ; move it to the buffer
        inc     si                   ; advance to the next video byte
        inc     di                   ; advance to the next buffer byte
        sub     dx,bx                ; subtract the number of bits moved

DisplayToBuffer2:
        cmp     dx,8                 ; see if less than one byte to move
        jl      DisplayToBuffer3     ; then move in the remaining byte
        lodsb                        ; move in the rest of the display
        stosb                        ; line into the buffer
        sub     dx,8                 ; subtract the number of bits moved
        jmp     DisplayToBuffer2     ; move the next byte

DisplayToBuffer3:
        or      dx,dx                ; if there are no more bits to move
        jz      DisplayToBuffer4     ; then advance to next scan line
        mov     al,ds:[si]           ; get last video scan line byte
        mov     cx,8                 ; set up to mask out bits not saved
        sub     cx,dx                ; cl = number of unwanted bits
        shr     al,cl                ; shift off the unwanted bits
        shl     al,cl
        mov     es:[di],al           ; save it in the buffer
        inc     di                   ; increment to the next buffer byte

DisplayToBuffer4:
        pop     bx                   ; pop 1st byte bits saved
        pop     cx                   ; pop 1st byte bits NOT saved
        pop     si                   ; pop video ram address
```

```
        pop     dx                      ; pop the window width
        xor     si,2000h                ; change to even/odd scan line
        xor     word ptr [bp + 4],1     ; check even/odd odd scan line
        jnz     DisplayToBuffer1        ; if odd then get the next line
        add     si,80                   ; advance to the next even line
        jmp     DisplayToBuffer1        ; process the next scan line

DisplayToBufferExit:
        pop     di                      ; pop off the saved registers
        pop     si
        pop     es
        pop     ds
        pop     bp
        ret

_DisplayToBuffer  ENDP
```

Create the BufferToDisplay ( ) Function

The BufferToDisplay ( ) function is designed to restore a buffer of screen data that was saved by the DisplayToBuffer ( ) function. The application calls this function to restore screen data that had previously been saved so that it can restore the screen back to its original condition. The function is called with the upper left-hand row and column coordinates, the display width and the display height, and a pointer to the buffer containing the screen data.

Edit the CGAGRAFA.ASM file, type the following statements, and save the file.

```
;*=====================================================================*/
;*                                                                     */
;* Function : BufferToDisplay (row, column, width, height, buffer);    */
;*                                                                     */
;* Purpose  : This function displays the given buffer at the given     */
;*            upper left-hand row and column coordinates, width and     */
;*            height on the screen.                                     */
;*                                                                     */
;* Entry Parameters : int row - The upper left-hand row coordinate.    */
;*                                                                     */
;*            int column - The upper left-hand column coordinate.      */
;*                                                                     */
;*            int width - The width of the window.                     */
;*                                                                     */
;*            int height - The height of the window.                   */
;*                                                                     */
;*            char *buffer - The source buffer to display on the       */
;*            screen.                                                   */
;*                                                                     */
;* Logic Flow : This BufferToDisplay () function is called to restore  */
;*            a window of screen data that had previously been saved   */
;*            by the DisplayToBuffer () function.  The function is      */
;*            called with the upper left-hand row and column           */
```

```
;*              coordinates, the window width and height, and a pointer */
;*              to the buffer to display.  The ds:si register pair is     */
;*              used to point at the display buffer.  The es:di pair      */
;*              is used to point at the video display.  The starting      */
;*              row and column coordinates are used to determine the      */
;*              starting video scan line.  For each line, the first       */
;*              byte of the line is moved to the screen, then the next    */
;*              bytes until the last byte is moved to the screen.         */
;*                                                                        */
;* Exit     : The source buffer is displayed on the screen               */
;*                                                                        */
;*=======================================================================*/

            PUBLIC   _BufferToDisplay

_BufferToDisplay   PROC    NEAR
            push    bp                      ; save the registers used
            mov     bp,sp
            push    ds
            push    es
            push    si
            push    di
            mov     si,[bp + 12]            ; ds:[si] = source buffer address
            mov     ax,0b800h               ; es:[di] = point at video buffer
            mov     es,ax
            mov     al,[bp + 4]             ; get starting row coordinate
            shr     al,1                    ; calculate starting video row
            mov     dl,80                   ; by taking the starting row (al)
            mul     dl                      ; multiply by the number of bytes
            mov     dx,ax                   ; video scan line, dx = video addr
            mov     al,[bp + 4]             ; check to see if the starting row
            test    al,1                    ; started on an even or odd line
            jz      BufferToDisplay0        ; jump if it started on an even
            or      dx,2000h                ; advance to odd scan line

BufferToDisplay0:
            and     word ptr [bp + 4],1     ; set row to even or odd status
            shl     word ptr [bp + 6],1     ; multiply column by 2
            mov     ax,[bp + 6]             ; starting column coordinate
            shr     ax,1                    ; divide starting column by 8 for
            shr     ax,1                    ; the byte offset in the video
            shr     ax,1                    ; ram buffer starting row
            add     ax,dx                   ; add in the starting row offset
            mov     di,ax                   ; di = starting video ram location
            mov     cx,[bp + 6]             ; get starting column
            and     cx,7                    ; cl = 1st byte bits NOT copied
            mov     bx,8
            sub     bx,cx                   ; bl = 1st byte bits copied
            shl     word ptr [bp + 8],1     ; multiply width * two
            mov     dx,[bp + 8]             ; dx = window width

BufferToDisplay1:
            cmp     word ptr [bp + 10],0 ; check the height
```

```
        jz      BufferToDisplayExit  ; exit if no more line left
        dec     word ptr [bp + 10]   ; decrement the height
        push    dx                   ; push window width
        push    di                   ; push video ram address
        push    cx                   ; push 1st byte bits NOT copied
        push    bx                   ; push 1st byte bits copied
        mov     al,es:[di]           ; get first video byte on the line
        xchg    bx,cx                ; shift bits that will be copied
        shr     al,cl
        shl     al,cl
        xchg    cx,bx
        mov     ah,ds:[si]           ; get the source byte
        or      al,ah                ; mask in the video byte
        mov     es:[di],al           ; put the byte to the screen
        inc     si                   ; advance to the next source byte
        inc     di                   ; advance to the next video byte
        sub     dx,bx                ; subtract the number of bits moved

BufferToDisplay2:
        cmp     dx,8                 ; if we have less than one byte
        jl      BufferToDisplay3     ; then display the last byte
        lodsb                        ; get the next source byte
        stosb                        ; move it to the screen
        sub     dx,8                 ; subtract the number of bits moved
        jmp     BufferToDisplay2     ; go to the next byte

BufferToDisplay3:
        or      dx,dx                ; if we have moved all of the bits
        jz      BufferToDisplay4     ; then advance to the next line
        mov     al,es:[di]           ; get the last video byte
        mov     cx,dx                ; shift to leave only the bits not
        shl     al,cl                ; used by the last byte
        shr     al,cl
        mov     ah,ds:[si]           ; get the last source byte
        or      al,ah                ; mask it to the video byte
        mov     es:[di],al           ; save the byte to video
        inc     si                   ; advance to the next source byte

BufferToDisplay4:
        pop     bx                   ; pop 1st byte bits copied
        pop     cx                   ; pop 1st byte bits NOT copied
        pop     di                   ; pop video ram address
        pop     dx                   ; pop window width
        xor     di,2000h             ; advance to the next scan line
        xor     word ptr [bp + 4],1  ; check even/odd status
        jnz     BufferToDisplay1     ; process the next line if odd
        add     di,80                ; advance to the next even line
        jmp     BufferToDisplay1     ; process the next line

BufferToDisplayExit:
        pop     di                   ; restore the registers used
        pop     si
        pop     es
```

```
        pop     ds
        pop     bp
        ret

_BufferToDisplay  ENDP
```

Create the ScrollWindow ( ) Function

The ScrollWindow ( ) function is designed to scroll a window of screen data on the screen. The application calls this function whenever it needs to scroll the display window on the screen, such as a list box that needs to be scrolled up or down. The function is called with the destination row and column coordinates, the source row and column coordinates, the width and height of the window to scroll, and the type of scroll to do, up, down, left, or right.

Edit the CGAGRAFA.ASM file, type the following statements, and save the file.

```
;*=======================================================================*/
;*                                                                       */
;* Function : ScrollWindow (d_row, d_column, s_row, s_column,            */
;*                           width, height, type);                       */
;*                                                                       */
;* Purpose  : This function scrolls a window on the screen up, down,     */
;*            left, or right depending on the variables passed.          */
;*                                                                       */
;* Entry Parameters : int d_row  - The destination upper left-hand       */
;*            row coordinate.                                            */
;*                                                                       */
;*            int d_column - The destination upper left-hand column      */
;*            coordinate.                                                 */
;*                                                                       */
;*            int s_row - The source upper left-hand row coordinate.     */
;*                                                                       */
;*            int s_column - The source upper left-hand column           */
;*            coordinate.                                                 */
;*                                                                       */
;*            int width - The width of the window to scroll.             */
;*                                                                       */
;*            int height - The height of the window to scroll.           */
;*                                                                       */
;*            int type  - The type of scroll to be performed.            */
;*            0 - Up, 1 - Down, 2 - Left, 3 - Right.                     */
;*                                                                       */
;* Logic Flow : The ScrollWindow () function is called to scroll a       */
;*            window on the screen.  The function is passed the          */
;*            destination row and column coordinates, the source row     */
;*            and column coordinates, the width of the window, the       */
;*            height of the window, and the type of scroll to perform.*/
;*            The ds and es segment registers point at video ram. The    */
;*            destination row and column coordinates are used to         */
;*            calculate the destination video ram address. The source    */
```

```
;*              row and column coordinates are used to calculate the   */
;*              source video ram address.  If the scroll is either up  */
;*              or down, then the function ScrollVertical () is called  */
;*              to scroll the screen vertically.  If the scroll is to   */
;*              the left, then the ScrollLeft () function is called.    */
;*              If the scroll is to the right, then the ScrollRight ()  */
;*              function is called.                                     */
;*                                                                      */
;* Exit : The screen display is scrolled in the given direction.        */
;*                                                                      */
;*====================================================================*/

        PUBLIC  _ScrollWindow

_ScrollWindow   PROC    NEAR
        push    bp                      ; save the registers used
        mov     bp,sp
        push    ds
        push    es
        push    si
        push    di
        mov     ax,0B800H               ; ds and es point at video ram
        mov     ds,ax
        mov     es,ax
        mov     ax,[bp + 16]            ; get the type of scroll
        cmp     al,1                    ; check scroll type
        ja      ScrollWindowHorz        ; Scroll requested left or right
        mov     al,[bp + 4]             ; get destination starting row
        shr     al,1                    ; divide starting row by 2
        mov     dl,80                   ; multiply starting row by the
        mul     dl                      ; number of bytes in a video row
        mov     dx,ax                   ; dx = starting row offset
        mov     al,[bp + 4]             ; get starting row
        test    al,1                    ; check for even/odd status
        jz      ScrollWindow0           ; starts on an even row
        or      dx,2000h                ; starts on an odd row

ScrollWindow0:
        and     word ptr [bp + 4],1     ; set dest. row to even/odd
        mov     ax,[bp + 6]             ; starting column bit offset
        shr     ax,1                    ; divide by 4 to get number of
        shr     ax,1                    ; byte offset
        add     ax,dx                   ; add to the row address to get
        mov     di,ax                   ; di = destination address
        mov     al,[bp + 8]             ; get source start row
        shr     al,1                    ; divide starting row by 2
        mov     dl,80                   ; multiply starting row by the
        mul     dl                      ; number of bytes in a video row
        mov     dx,ax                   ; dx = starting row offset
        mov     al,[bp + 8]             ; get starting row
        test    al,1                    ; check for even/odd status
        jz      ScrollWindow1           ; starts on an even row
        or      dx,2000h                ; starts on an odd row
```

```
ScrollWindow1:
        and     word ptr [bp + 8],1     ; set source row to even/odd
        mov     ax,[bp + 10]            ; starting column bit offset
        shr     ax,1                    ; divide by 4 to get the byte
        shr     ax,1                    ; in the video display buffer
        add     ax,dx                   ; add to the row address
        mov     si,ax                   ; si = source address
        shl     word ptr [bp + 6],1
        mov     cx,[bp + 6]             ; get the starting column bit
        and     cx,7                    ; cl = 1st byte bits NOT moved
        mov     bx,8
        sub     bx,cx                   ; bx = 1st byte bits cleared
        shl     word ptr [bp + 12],1    ; width = width * 2
        mov     dx,[bp + 12]            ; dx = total width bits to move
        call    ScrollVertical          ; Scroll the window vertically
        jmp     ScrollWindowExit

ScrollWindowHorz:
        cmp     al,2
        jnz     ScrollWindowHorz1
        call    ScrollLeft              ; Scroll the window left
        jmp     ScrollWindowExit

ScrollWindowHorz1:
        call    ScrollRight             ; Scroll the window right
ScrollWindowExit:
        pop     di                      ; restore the registers saved on
        pop     si                      ; stack
        pop     es
        pop     ds
        pop     bp
        ret

_ScrollWindow   ENDP
```

Create the ScrollVertical ( ) Function

The ScrollVertical ( ) function is designed to scroll a window of screen data vertically. This function is called by the ScrollWindow ( ) function only. Several registers have already been calculated before this function is called.

Edit the CGAGRAFA.ASM file, type the following statements, and save the file.

```
;*=========================================================================*/
;*                                                                         */
;* Function : ScrollVertical ();                                           */
;*                                                                         */
;* Purpose  : This function scrolls the screen vertically either up        */
;*            or down depending on the variables passed.                   */
;*                                                                         */
;* Logic Flow : The ScrollVertical () function is called by the            */
```

```
;*              ScrollWindow () function to scroll a window of screen    */
;*              data vertically, either up or down.  The ds:si register  */
;*              pair points at the source address in video ram.  The     */
;*              es:di register pair points at the destination address in */
;*              video ram.  For each line to scroll, get the first byte  */
;*              in the line and move it to the destination first byte.    */
;*              Then move in the rest of the bytes in the line.          */
;*                                                                        */
;* Exit : The screen display is scrolled vertically.                     */
;*                                                                        */
;*====================================================================*/

ScrollVertical  PROC    NEAR

ScrollVertical0:
        cmp     word ptr [bp + 14],0    ; check the height
        jnz     ScrollVertical1         ; process the line
        ret                             ; return to ScrollWindow ()

ScrollVertical1:
        dec     word ptr [bp + 14]      ; decrement the height
        push    dx                      ; push window width
        push    di                      ; push destination address
        push    si                      ; push source address
        push    cx                      ; push 1st byte bits to keep
        mov     al,ds:[si]              ; get source byte
        shl     al,cl                   ; shift off the bits NOT
        shr     al,cl                   ; to be scrolled
        mov     ah,es:[di]              ; get 1st destination byte
        xchg    bx,cx                   ; shift the destination byte
        shr     ah,cl                   ; get the byte mask
        shl     ah,cl
        xchg    bx,cx
        or      al,ah                   ; put masked byte to destination
        mov     es:[di],al
        inc     di                      ; advance to next destination
        inc     si                      ; advance to next source byte
        sub     dx,bx                   ; subtract number of bits moved

ScrollVertical2:
        cmp     dx,8                    ; if < than one byte to move
        jl      ScrollVertical3         ; then move last byte
        lodsb                           ; load source byte ds:[si], inc
        stosb                           ; st or e source byte
        sub     dx,8                    ; subtract number of bits moved
        jmp     ScrollVertical2         ; do next byte

ScrollVertical6:
        jmp     ScrollVertical0         ; process the next scan line

ScrollVertical3:
        or      dx,dx                   ; check to see if all bits moved
        jz      ScrollVertical4         ; jump if we have moved all
```

```
        mov     cx,8                    ; set up last byte on the line
        sub     cx,dx                   ; move in the last bits
        mov     ah,ds:[si]              ; ah - last byte to move
        shr     ah,cl                   ; mask out the unwanted bits
        shl     ah,cl
        mov     cx,dx                   ; mask the destination byte
        mov     al,es:[di]              ; the number of bits moved
        shl     al,cl
        shr     al,cl
        or      al,ah                   ; put bytes together
        mov     es:[di],al              ; put last byte on the line

ScrollVertical4:
        pop     cx                      ; pop 1st byte bits NOT moved
        pop     si                      ; pop source video ram address
        pop     di                      ; pop destination video ram addr
        pop     dx                      ; pop number of width bits
        xor     di,2000h                ; advance destination scan line
        xor     si,2000h                ; advance source scan line
        xor     word ptr [bp + 4],1     ; check if row is odd/even
        jnz     ScrollVertical5         ; check source, if odd
        add     di,80                   ; advance to next even scan line
        cmp     word ptr [bp + 16],0    ; check for scroll up or down
        jz      ScrollVertical5         ; check source, if scroll up
        sub     di,160                  ; advance to the next scan line

ScrollVertical5:
        xor     word ptr [bp + 8],1     ; check if source row is odd
        jnz     ScrollVertical6         ; process the next line if odd
        add     si,80                   ; advance to next even scan line
        cmp     word ptr [bp + 16],0    ; check if scrolling up or down
        jz      ScrollVertical6         ; process the next line
        sub     si,160                  ; advance to next scan line
        jmp     ScrollVertical6         ; process the next line

ScrollVertical    ENDP
```

Create the ScrollLeft ( ) Function

The ScrollLeft ( ) function is designed to scroll a window of screen data to the left. This function is called by the ScrollWindow ( ) function only. The scrolling of screen data to the left or right is much more difficult than scrolling data up or down. This is because when data is scrolled left or right, the bit alignment may be off, so there is much more bit manipulation to be done.

For example, if the application wanted to scroll a window of screen data at row 40, column 50, with a width of 90, and a height of 60, to the left 5 dots, then several different calculations need to be done. Let's break this example into its different parts.

First, the starting column coordinate (50) is not evenly divisible by four. This means that only the last two dots of the first byte on each scan line is to be moved. The first two dots of this byte are not to be moved. Next, when the length of the move is subtracted from the starting column coordinate, the destination coordinate becomes 45. This is also not evenly divisible by 4, meaning that the first dot moved will be placed at the second dot of the destination byte. Since only the first two dots where contained in the first source byte, then the next dot from the next source byte must be shifted into the first before it can be moved. This type of shifting must occur for each byte until the ending byte of the line is reached.

As the reader can tell, it requires much more calculations to be able to scroll nonbyte-aligned windows, left or right. Whenever, possible, the programmer should use aligned windows that are to be scrolled left or right on bit-aligned boundaries because they will scroll faster.

Edit the CGAGRAFA.ASM file, type the following statements, and save the file.

```
;*=======================================================================*/
;*                                                                       */
;* Function : ScrollLeft ();                                             */
;*                                                                       */
;* Purpose  : This function scrolls the screen to the left.             */
;*                                                                       */
;* Logic Flow : The ScrollLeft () function is called to scroll a        */
;*              window of screen data to the left.  It is called by the */
;*              ScrollWindow () function.  The starting row coordinate   */
;*              is used to calculate the starting row offset of the      */
;*              first video scan line.  Then the column coordinates      */
;*              are used to determine the scan line byte for the         */
;*              destination and the source.  The ds:si register pair     */
;*              point at the first source byte.  The es:di register      */
;*              pair point at the destination byte.  For each line to    */
;*              be scrolled, the first byte is moved in and shifted      */
;*              if it needs to be.  Then the rest of the line is moved.  */
;*              Then the last byte of the line is moved in.              */
;*                                                                       */
;* Exit : The screen display is scrolled to the left.                   */
;*                                                                       */
;*=======================================================================*/

ScrollLeft      PROC    NEAR
        mov     ax,[bp + 4]             ; get row coordinate
        mov     bx,ax
        mov     cx,40
        shr     bx,1
        jc      ScrollLeft0
        mul     cx
        mov     cx,0                    ; set to even status
        jmp     ScrollLeft1
```

```
ScrollLeft0:
        dec     ax
        mul     cx
        add     ax,2000h
        mov     cx,1                    ; set to odd status

ScrollLeft1:
        push    cx                      ; save row even/odd status
        mov     di,ax                   ; di = destination row offset
        mov     si,ax                   ; si = source row offset
        mov     ax,[bp + 6]             ; destination starting column
        mov     cl,4
        div     cl                      ; al = number of bytes
        push    ax                      ; ah = extra dots
        mov     ah,0
        add     di,ax                   ; di = destination offset
        mov     ax,[bp + 10]            ; source starting column
        div     cl
        push    ax                      ; al = number source bytes
        mov     ah,0
        add     si,ax                   ; si = source starting offset
        pop     dx                      ; dh = source byte extra bits
        pop     ax
        mov     al,dh                   ; al = source bytes extra bits
        push    ax
        mov     ax,[bp + 12]            ; ax = width of the move
        div     cl                      ; al = bytes, ah = extra bits
        mov     bx,ax                   ; bx = width of move
        pop     ax
        pop     cx
        cmp     bh,bh
        jnz     ScrollLeft2
        inc     bl

ScrollLeft2:
        mov     dx,[bp + 14]            ; dl = height of the window
        mov     dh,cl                   ; dh = even/odd row status
        shl     al,1
        shl     ah,1
        shl     bh,1

ScrollLeft3:
        push    di
        push    si
        push    dx                      ; save window height/row status
        push    bx                      ; save window width
        push    ax                      ; save byte shift amount
        mov     cl,ah                   ; get destination shift dots
        mov     al,es:[di]              ; al = starting destination byte
        mov     ch,8                    ; calculate bits to shift off
        sub     ch,cl
        mov     cl,ch
        shr     al,cl
```

```
        shl     al,cl                   ; al = destination byte mask
        pop     cx
        push    cx                      ; cl = source mask bit number
        mov     ah,ds:[si]              ; ah = get source byte
        shl     ah,cl
        shr     ah,cl                   ; ah = source start byte shifted
        cmp     cl,ch                   ; source and destination shift
        jnz     ScrollLeft5             ; bits are not the same
        or      al,ah                   ; al = first byte to move

ScrollLeft4:
        mov     es:[di],al              ; move byte to destination
        dec     bl                      ; decrement byte counter
        jz      ScrollLeft9             ; if no more whole bytes left
        inc     di                      ; move to next destination byte
        inc     si                      ; move to next source byte
        mov     al,ds:[si]              ; get next source byte
        jmp     ScrollLeft4             ; process the next byte

ScrollLeft5:
        jb      ScrollLeft7             ; source less than destination
        sub     cl,ch                   ; calculate extra bits to move
        shl     ah,cl                   ; move over source byte
        mov     ch,8
        sub     ch,cl
        push    cx
        mov     cl,ch
        mov     dl,ds:[si + 1]          ; get next source byte
        shr     dl,cl                   ; shift only bits wanted
        pop     cx
        or      ah,dl                   ; ah = new source byte
        or      al,ah

ScrollLeft6:
        mov     es:[di],al              ; move byte to destination
        dec     bl                      ; decrement byte counter
        jz      ScrollLeft9             ; do last byte on line
        inc     si                      ; advance to next source byte
        inc     di                      ; advance to destination byte
        mov     al,ds:[si]              ; get next source byte
        shl     al,cl                   ; used bits shifted off
        push    cx
        mov     cl,ch
        mov     dl,ds:[si + 1]          ; get source next byte
        shr     dl,cl                   ; dl = extra bits from next byte
        pop     cx
        or      al,dl                   ; al = next byte to move
        jmp     ScrollLeft6             ; process the next byte

ScrollLeft7:
        sub     ch,cl                   ; calculate extra bits to move
        mov     cl,ch                   ; cl = shift off bits
        mov     ch,8
```

```
        sub     ch,cl               ; ch = shift on bits
        shr     ah,cl               ; shift source byte over
        or      al,ah

ScrollLeft8:
        mov     es:[di],al          ; move byte to destination
        dec     bl                  ; decrement byte counter
        jz      ScrollLeft9         ; do last byte if needed
        inc     di                  ; advance to next destination
        mov     al,ds:[si]          ; get source byte
        push    cx
        mov     cl,ch
        shl     al,cl               ; first byte mask
        pop     cx
        inc     si
        mov     ah,ds:[si]          ; get next source byte
        shr     ah,cl               ; shift off needed bits
        or      al,ah               ; al = byte mask
        jmp     ScrollLeft8         ; process the next byte

ScrollLeft9:
        pop     ax                  ; pop byte shift amount
        pop     bx                  ; pop window width
        pop     dx                  ; pop window height / row status
        pop     si                  ; pop source offset
        pop     di                  ; pop destination offset
        dec     dl                  ; decrement the line counter
        jz      ScrollLeftExit      ; have finished scrolling window
        or      dh,dh               ; check to see if it was odd
        jnz     ScrollLeft10        ; jump if it is odd
        add     si,2000h            ; adjust source offset
        add     di,2000h            ; adjust destination offset
        mov     dh,1                ; set scan line to odd row
        jmp     ScrollLeft3         ; go do the next line

ScrollLeft10:
        sub     si,2000h            ; adjust source offset
        add     si,50h
        sub     di,2000h            ; adjust destination offset
        add     di,50h
        mov     dh,0                ; set scan line to even
        jmp     ScrollLeft3         ; go do the next line

ScrollLeftExit:
        RET

ScrollLeft     ENDP
```

Create the ScrollRight ( ) Function

The ScrollRight ( ) function is designed to scroll a window of screen data horizontally to the right. This function is called by the ScrollWindow ( ) function only. The scrolling of a window to the right is very similar to scrolling to the left, except that the scan line data must be done in reverse order. All other screen functions have started from the left-hand side of the screen as the first byte in the scan line. But to move something to the right, the first byte in the scan line must be the LEFTmost byte.

Edit the CGAGRAFA.ASM file, type the following statements, and save the file.

```
;*=====================================================================*/
;*                                                                     */
;* Function : ScrollRight ();                                          */
;*                                                                     */
;* Purpose  : This function scrolls a window of screen data to the     */
;*            right.                                                    */
;*                                                                     */
;* Logic Flow : The ScrollRight () function is called by the           */
;*              ScrollWindow () function to scroll a window of screen   */
;*              data to the right.  The starting row coordinate is used */
;*              to calculate the starting video scan line address. The  */
;*              source column coordinate and destination column         */
;*              coordinate are used to calculate the source and         */
;*              destination starting video byte offset.  For each line  */
;*              to scroll, the first byte of the line is moved in, then  */
;*              the rest of the bytes in the line are moved until the   */
;*              last byte of the line has been moved.                   */
;*                                                                     */
;* Exit : The screen display is scrolled to the right.                 */
;*                                                                     */
;*=====================================================================*/

ScrollRight     PROC    NEAR
        mov     ax,[bp + 4]             ; get row coordinate
        mov     bx,ax
        mov     cx,40
        shr     bx,1
        jc      ScrollRight0           ; starting row is on odd
        mul     cx
        mov     cx,0                    ; set to even status
        jmp     ScrollRight1

ScrollRight0:
        dec     ax
        mul     cx
        add     ax,2000h
        mov     cx,1                    ; set to odd status

ScrollRight1:
```

```
        push    cx              ; save row even/odd status
        mov     di,ax           ; di = destination row offset
        mov     si,ax           ; si = source row offset
        mov     ax,[bp + 6]     ; destination column coordinate
        mov     cl,4
        div     cl              ; al = number of bytes
        push    ax              ; ah = extra dots
        mov     ah,0
        add     di,ax           ; di = destination row offset
        mov     ax,[bp + 10]    ; get source start column
        div     cl
        push    ax              ; al = source extra bytes
        mov     ah,0
        add     si,ax           ; si = source starting offset
        pop     dx
        pop     ax
        mov     al,dh           ; al = source bytes extra dots
        push    ax
        mov     ax,[bp + 12]    ; get width of the move
        div     cl              ; al = number of whole bytes
        mov     bx,ax           ; bx = width of move
        pop     ax
        pop     cx
        cmp     bh,bh
        jnz     ScrollRight2
        inc     bl

ScrollRight2:
        mov     dx,[bp + 14]    ; dl = height of the window
        mov     dh,cl           ; dh = even/odd row status
        shl     al,1
        shl     ah,1
        shl     bh,1

ScrollRight3:
        push    di              ; push destination address
        push    si              ; push source address
        push    dx              ; push window height/row status
        push    bx              ; push window width
        push    ax              ; push byte shift amount
        cmp     al,ah           ; source and destination bytes
        jnz     ScrollRight5    ; not bit aligned
        mov     cx,ax
        inc     cl
        inc     cl
        mov     dl,ds:[si]      ; get source byte
        mov     dh,es:[di]      ; get destination byte
        cmp     cl,8
        jz      ScrollRight4    ; if no need to shift
        shl     dh,cl
        shr     dh,cl
        mov     ch,8
        sub     ch,cl
```

```
        mov     cl,ch
        shl     dl,cl
        shr     dl,cl
        or      dl,dh

ScrollRight4:
        mov     es:[di],dl          ; move byte to destination
        dec     bl                  ; decrement width byte counter
        jz      ScrollRight9        ; do last byte
        dec     di                  ; move to next destination byte
        dec     si                  ; move to next source byte
        mov     dl,ds:[si]          ; get next source byte
        jmp     ScrollRight4        ; process the next byte

ScrollRight5:
        mov     cl,ah
        inc     cl
        inc     cl
        mov     dl,ds:[si]          ; get next source byte
        cmp     cl,8
        jz      ScrollRight6        ; no need to shift
        mov     dh,es:[di]          ; get next destination byte
        shr     dh,cl
        shl     dh,cl
        jmp     ScrollRight7

ScrollRight6:
        mov     dh,15

ScrollRight7:
        mov     cl,6
        sub     cl,al
        shl     dl,cl
        shr     dl,cl               ; dl = masked source byte

ScrollRight8:
        push    ax
        sub     ah,al
        mov     cl,ah
        shr     dl,cl               ; adjust over to correct mask
        mov     al,ds:[si - 1]      ; get next source byte
        mov     ch,8                ; and get the extra bits needed
        sub     ch,cl
        mov     cl,ch
        shl     al,cl
        or      dl,al
        or      dl,dh
        pop     ax
        mov     es:[di],dl          ; move the byte to destination
        dec     bl                  ; decrement byte counter
        jz      ScrollRight9        ; do last byte
        dec     di                  ; move to next destination byte
        dec     si                  ; move to next source byte
```

```
        mov     dl,ds:[si]              ; get next source byte
        mov     dh,0
        jmp     ScrollRight8            ; process next byte

ScrollRight9:
        pop     ax                      ; pop byte shift amount
        pop     bx                      ; pop window width
        pop     dx                      ; pop window height / row status
        pop     si                      ; pop source offset
        pop     di                      ; pop destination offset
        dec     dl                      ; decrement the line counter
        jz      ScrollRightExit         ; have finished scrolling window
        or      dh,dh                   ; check last scan line
        jnz     ScrollRight10           ; jump if it is odd
        add     si,2000h                ; adjust starting offset
        add     di,2000h                ; adjust destination offset
        mov     dh,1                    ; set scan line to odd row
        jmp     ScrollRight3            ; go do the next line

ScrollRight10:
        sub     si,2000h                ; adjust starting offset
        add     si,50h
        sub     di,2000h                ; adjust destination offset
        add     di,50h
        mov     dh,0                    ; set scan line to even
        jmp     ScrollRight3            ; go do the next line

ScrollRightExit:
        RET

ScrollRight      ENDP
```

The next section of code ends the CGAGRAFA.ASM source file.

Edit the CGAGRAFA.ASM source file, type the following statements, and save the file.

```
_TEXT   ENDS

END
```

SUMMARY

The CGA Graphics Library source file CGAGRAFA.ASM contains all of the functions that are written in Assembler and use the Direct Video Access method of display. All of the functions are needed to be able to manipulate the video display. These functions are very data intensive and because of this, they are written in Assembler using the Direct Video Access method. The reader should analyze these functions in detail to really understand the video display techniques involved. The bit manipulation used throughout these functions is very difficult to understand and should be studied.

This chapter concludes the section on the CGA Graphics Library. In the next chapters I deal with the creation of the Menu Library. The functions in the Menu Library rely heavily on the functions written in the CGA Graphics Library to do the screen displaying for it.

Chapter 8

THE MENU LIBRARY

INTRODUCTION

The Menu Library is designed to perform all of the menu functions needed by the application. It relies heavily on the functions written for the CGA Graphics Library to perform all of the necessary screen Input/Output functions. All of the functions in the Menu Library are written in 'C' and use the standards described in the previous chapters.

To start programming the Menu library, a list of the basic functions needed by the application needs to be decided upon. The Menu Library functions provided in this book do not contain all of the different types of menus that are possible, only a small subset. This subset however, contains most of the primary types of menus used in the industry today. The following is a list of the types of menus the Menu Library supports.

- Primary Menus - Primary menus drive the application from the beginning to the end. A primary menu must have a header and an action bar. The action bar is used to allow the user quick and easy reference to the application. In general, there should be only one primary menu to an application.

- Dialog Boxes - Dialog boxes aid the user in accessing the necessary functions performed by the application. Dialog boxes are composed of entry fields, push buttons, radio buttons, check boxes, and list boxes. The primary menu contains at least one dialog box, and dialog boxes can be called from the action bar or from pull-down menus. Sometimes dialog boxes are called pop-up menus because of the way they appear on the screen, but a dialog box is much more than that, because it allows the user to have a *dialogue* with the computer. This is a major part of user interface design because the computer seems to interact with the user.

- Pull-Down Menus - Pull-down menus are menus that appear to pull down from the selected item. A good example of this is when the user selects an item from the action bar list, a pull-down menu appears on the screen giving the user more items to select from. Usually, selecting one of the items from a pull-down menu activates a dialog box allowing the user to perform the function selected.

- Message Boxes - A message box is a type of dialog box but it does not allow much user interaction. Usually, a message box is displayed when an error occurs, such as a file not found message.

The application uses these menus to perform the functions needed by the application. The following is an explanation that shows the logic flow of designing interactive menus.

- Start with a primary menu. The primary menu is defined to contain a heading such as 'MAIL LIST.' It also defines an action bar with several options on it, such as 'File,' 'Edit,' 'Options,' 'Help.' Lastly, the primary menu defines a dialog box that displays the primary information to the user, such as a list box containing a list of the names in the Mail List file being edited.

- Next, define the action bar of the primary menu. The action bar is used to display a list of commands that are available to the user from the primary menu. Each one of the action bar selections contains information relating to the pull-down menu that is displayed when the user selects that item. For example, the user selects 'File' from the action bar; a pull-down menu containing a list of options, such as 'Create,' 'Save,' 'Load,' 'Delete,' is displayed.

- Next, define the dialog boxes associated with each selection available from the pull-down menus. The dialog boxes use entry fields, push buttons, check boxes, radio buttons, and list boxes to convey and retrieve information to the user. From the previous example, if the user selects 'Load' from the pull-down menu, a dialog box containing an entry field for the filename and push buttons will be processed.

- Next, define the message boxes associated with the menus that have been defined. For example, if the file to load cannot be found, a message box might be displayed conveying that information to the user.

The programmer can mix and match the use of the menus to achieve the type of user interface that he needs for any application.

DEFINING THE INCLUDE AND 'C' SOURCE FILES

The Menu Library is divided up into eight include source files and ten 'C' source files. The following is a list of the files needed by the Menu Library to perform all of the functions described above.

The Menu Library Include Source Files

- DEFINES.H - This include file contains the data definitions needed by the Menu Library in general.
- MENU.H - This include file contains the data definitions needed to define a primary menu.
- DIALOG.H - This include file contains the data definitions needed to define a dialog box.
- KEYBOARD.H - This include file contains all of the data definitions needed to process keyboard input for the Menu Library.
- MESSAGE.H - This include file contains the data definitions needed by the message handler to know which error message to display.
- ARROWS.H - This include file contains the data definitions used by the list box functions to display the arrow icons.
- RADIO.H - This include file contains the data definitions needed to display a radio button icon.
- CHECKBOX.H - This include file contains the data definitions needed to display a check box icon.

The Menu Library 'C' Source Files

- MENU.C - This 'C' source file contains the functions needed to process a primary menu.
- KEYBOARD.C - This 'C' source file contains the function to return a keystroke from the keyboard.
- ACTION.C - This 'C' source file contains the function needed to process the action bar of the primary menu.
- PULLDOWN.C - This 'C' source file contains the functions needed to process the pull-down menus.
- DIALOG.C - This 'C' source file contains the functions needed to process a dialog box.
- PUSHBUTN.C - This 'C' source file contains the functions needed to process the push buttons for dialog boxes and message boxes.

- ENTRY.C - This 'C' source file contains the functions needed to process an entry field.
- GROUPS.C - This 'C' source file contains the functions needed to process the check box and radio button groups.
- LISTBOX.C - This 'C' source file contains the functions needed to process a list box.
- MESSAGE.C - This 'C' source file contains the functions needed to process the message boxes.

CREATING THE MENU LIBRARY FILES

The Menu Library batch files are designed in the same manner as the CGA Graphics Library, except that these manage the Menu Library. The batch file and makefile allow the application programmer to better manage the creation of the Menu Library.

Creating the Batch File — BUILD.BAT

This BUILD.BAT file is very similar to the one created in the CGA Graphics Library section. First, at the DOS command prompt:

Type **CD \MENU** and press **Return**.

This will change directories to the Menu Library directory created earlier.

NOTE
Since the BUILD.BAT file was created in another directory, the programmer must make sure that he is in the right directory before creating the file.

Edit the BUILD.BAT file, type the following statements, and save the file.

```
copy MENU.LIB MENU.BAK
del MENU.LIB
make MAKEFILE.MNU
```

Now when the programmer needs to recompile and test the Menu Library he only needs to do the following at the DOS command prompt:

Type **BUILD** and press **Return**.

Typing this statement at this time will generate errors because the other files associated with the batch file have not been created. Basically, the BUILD.BAT file does the following things:

- It copies the current Menu Library, MENU.LIB, into a backup file called MENU.BAK.
- It deletes the current Menu Library.
- It executes the Make-File Utility using the makefile MAKEFILE.MNU.

Creating the Make-File Utility File — MAKEFILE.MNU

The Make-File Utility uses the file MAKEFILE.MNU to make the necessary decisions needed to create the new Menu Library called MENU.LIB.

Create the MAKEFILE.MNU file, type the following statements, and save the file.

```
menu.obj: menu.c \graphics\colors.h menu.h defines.h
 msc menu;

keyboard.obj: keyboard.c
 msc keyboard;

action.obj: action.c \graphics\colors.h defines.h keyboard.h
 msc action;

pulldown.obj: pulldown.c \graphics\colors.h defines.h menu.h \
            keyboard.h
 msc pulldown;

dialog.obj: dialog.c \graphics\colors.h defines.h keyboard.h \
            dialog.h
 msc dialog;

pushbutn.obj: pushbutn.c \graphics\colors.h defines.h dialog.h \
            keyboard.h
 msc pushbutn;

entry.obj: entry.c \graphics\colors.h defines.h dialog.h keyboard.h
 msc entry;

groups.obj: groups.c \graphics\colors.h defines.h dialog.h \
            checkbox.h radio.h
 msc groups;

listbox.obj: listbox.c \graphics\colors.h defines.h menu.h \
            keyboard.h arrows.h
 msc listbox;

message.obj: message.c \graphics\colors.h defines.h message.h
 msc message;

menu.lib: menu.obj keyboard.obj action.obj pulldown.obj dialog.obj \
            pushbutn.obj entry.obj groups.obj listbox.obj message.obj
 lib @menu.lnk
```

The Menu Library makefile, MAKEFILE.MNU, contains all of the information that the Make-File Utility needs to make its determination of which files to recompile. Several files need to be checked, especially the include files associated with that particular 'C' file. In this way, the programmer does not have to remember which 'C' files need to be recompiled if an include file changes.

Creating the Menu Library Linker File — MENU.LNK

The last thing the Make-File Utility does is check to see if the Menu Library needs to be relinked. If it does, then the file MENU.LNK is used to tell the 'C' Run-Time Library Utility how to create the MENU.LIB Library file.

Create the MENU.LNK file, type the following statements, and save the file.

```
menu
Y
menu+keyboard+action+pulldown+dialog+
pushbutn+entry+groups+listbox+message
menu.map
```

After the build process is complete, the programmer will have a new Menu Library called MENU.LIB in the MENU subdirectory. This Library is linked in with the application when the application is linked into its executable form.

SUMMARY

The Menu Library contains all of the functions the application needs to perform all menu requests by the application. It uses the CGA Graphics Library to process its screen Input/Output. The Menu Library is made up of eight include source files and ten 'C' source files. A batch file, makefile, and linker file are used to compile and link the Menu Library into the MENU.LIB file that is included into the application.

The primary purpose for creating the Menu Library is to allow the programmer to create and maintain his menus more easily. By separating the menu functions into a library, the programmer can use these functions in more than one application. It also helps the programmer distinguish between what is really application specific functions, and those functions that are menu functions.

The following chapters show the programmer how to create the include and 'C' source files needed to perform the Menu Library functions.

Chapter 9

THE MENU LIBRARY
INCLUDE SOURCE FILES

INTRODUCTION

The Menu Library uses eight different include files specially designed for the Menu Library. These include files define the menu structures associated with each different kind of menu that the application might need to define. The application uses these include files whenever it has a need to define a particular kind of menu.

Create the DEFINES.H Include Source File

The first file to create is the DEFINES.H include source file. This file contains the data definitions needed by the Menu Library to perform the menu functions requested, and by the application to direct the menu functions.

Create the DEFINES.H file, type the following statements, and save the file.

```
/*======================================================================*/
/*                                                                      */
/* File : DEFINES.H                                                     */
/*                                                                      */
/* Purpose : This include file contains the defined data definitions    */
/*           used by the Menu Library functions.                        */
/*                                                                      */
/* Data Defined : FONTWIDTH 6 - Defines FONTWIDTH to be 6; it is the    */
/*           width of a character icon.                                 */
/*                                                                      */
/*           FONTHEIGHT 10 - Defines FONTHEIGHT to be 10; it is the     */
/*           height of a character icon.                                */
/*                                                                      */
/*           RADIO_BUTTON 0 - Defines RADIO_BUTTON to be 0; it is       */
/*           used to define a radio button group type in a dialog box.*/
/*                                                                      */
```

```
/*           CHECK_BOX 1 - Defines CHECK_BOX to be 1; it is used to    */
/*           define a check box group type in a dialog box.            */
/*                                                                     */
/*           OFF 0 - Defines OFF to be 0; it is used to define a       */
/*           radio button or a check box to be off.                    */
/*                                                                     */
/*           ON 1 - Defines ON to be 0; it is used to define a radio   */
/*           button or a check box to be on.                           */
/*                                                                     */
/*           ENTRY 1 - Defines ENTRY to be 1; it is used by the        */
/*           dialog box function to indicate that the entry fields     */
/*           are being processed.                                      */
/*                                                                     */
/*           BUTTONS 2 - Defines BUTTONS to be 2; it is used by the    */
/*           dialog box function to indicate that the radio buttons    */
/*           are being processed.                                      */
/*                                                                     */
/*           NO_HIGHLIGHT 0 - Defines NO_HIGHLIGHT to be 0; it is      */
/*           used to indicate a list box display string as being       */
/*           not highlighted.                                          */
/*                                                                     */
/*           HIGHLIGHT 1 - Defines HIGHLIGHT to be 1; it is used to    */
/*           indicate a list box display string as being highlighted. */
/*                                                                     */
/*           SCROLL_UP 0 - Defines SCROLL_UP to be 0; it is used       */
/*           by the list box functions to scroll the list box UP.      */
/*                                                                     */
/*           SCROLL_DOWN 1 - Defines SCROLL_DOWN to be 1; it is        */
/*           used by the list box functions to scroll the list box     */
/*           DOWN.                                                      */
/*                                                                     */
/*           SCROLL_LEFT 2 - Defines SCROLL_LEFT to be 2; it is        */
/*           used by the list box functions to scroll the list box     */
/*           to the LEFT.                                              */
/*                                                                     */
/*           SCROLL_RIGHT 3 - Defines SCROLL_RIGHT to be 3; it is      */
/*           used by the list box functions to scroll the list box     */
/*           to the RIGHT.                                             */
/*                                                                     */
/*           UPARROW 4 - Defines UPARROW to be 4; it is used by the    */
/*           list box functions to move the highlight one line up.     */
/*                                                                     */
/*           DOWNARROW 5 - Defines DOWNARROW to be 5; it is used by    */
/*           the list box functions to move the highlight down one     */
/*           line.                                                     */
/*                                                                     */
/*           REFRESH 6 - Defines REFRESH to be 6; it is used by the    */
/*           list box functions to refresh to scroll box window.       */
/*                                                                     */
/*=====================================================================*/

#define FONTWIDTH    6
#define FONTHEIGHT  10
```

```
#define RADIO_BUTTON  0
#define CHECK_BOX     1
#define OFF           0
#define ON            1
#define ENTRY         1
#define BUTTONS       2
#define RADIOS        3
#define BOXES         4
#define NO_HIGHLIGHT  0
#define HIGHLIGHT     1
#define SCROLL_UP     0
#define SCROLL_DOWN   1
#define SCROLL_LEFT   2
#define SCROLL_RIGHT  3
#define UPARROW       4
#define DOWNARROW     5
#define REFRESH       6
```

The DEFINES.H include source file in the subdirectory \MENU is used only by the Menu Library. It defines actions to be taken or directions given to the Menu Library functions.

Create the MENU.H Include Source File

The MENU.H include source file contains the data structure definitions needed to define a Primary Menu. This include file is used by the application and the Menu Library whenever a Primary Menu needs to be defined. The application includes this include file when it defines a menu structure. The Menu Library uses this include file as the mapping structure to process a given Primary Menu.

The defining of a Primary Menu is explained in detail in the section dealing with the application itself.

Create the MENU.H include source file, type the following statements, and save the file.

```
/*====================================================================*/
/*                                                                    */
/* File : MENU.H                                                      */
/*                                                                    */
/* Purpose : This include file contains the data structure           */
/*           definitions of a Primary Menu that is processed by      */
/*           the Menu Library functions.                             */
/*                                                                    */
/* Include Files : DIALOG.H - This include file contains the data    */
/*           structure definitions used to define a dialog box       */
/*           to be used by the Menu Library functions.               */
/*                                                                    */
/* Data Structures - typedef struct ACTION_BAR, PULL_DOWN defines a  */
/*           structure that is used to define action bar menus and   */
/*           also pull-down menus.  Each action bar menu or pull-down */
```

```
/*           menu has the following characteristics.  Where : int r    */
/*           is the row coordinate and int c is the column coordinate */
/*           of where to print the char *str.  The int hot_key        */
/*           variable defines the ALT+key that brings up the pull-    */
/*           down menu automatically.  The int hot_loc is the letter  */
/*           number to underline in the char *str. ITEM_PTR *item_list*/
/*           points at a list of selectable strings to display. The   */
/*           int num_items variable defines how many items are in     */
/*           the list of strings. The variable int start is the       */
/*           starting selectable string. The variable int exit is     */
/*           return code from the action bar or pull-down menu.       */
/*                                                                     */
/*           typedef struct MENU_FORM is the data structure           */
/*           definition of a primary menu.  The variables int r,      */
/*           int c, int w, int h are used to define how large the     */
/*           menu is and its display location.  The variable          */
/*           char *hdr is a character pointer to the header string of */
/*           the menu.  ACTION_BAR *action_bar is a pointer to a      */
/*           group of action bar menus to be displayed on the screen. */
/*           WORK_AREA *workarea is a group of work areas defined in  */
/*           the DIALOG.H include file and it defines the working     */
/*           area of the primary menu.  The variable int (*function)  */
/*           is the name of the function to call after the primary    */
/*           menu has been initialized and displayed.                 */
/*                                                                     */
/*====================================================================*/

#include "\menu\dialog.h"

typedef struct ACTION_STRUCT
{
    int r;
    int c;
    char *str;
    int hot_key;
    int hot_loc;
    ITEM_PTR *item_list;
    int num_items;
    int (*function) ();
    int  start;
    int  exit;
} ACTION_BAR, PULL_DOWN;

typedef struct
{
    int r;
    int c;
    int w;
    int h;
    char *hdr;
    ACTION_BAR *action_bar;
    WORK_AREA  *workarea;
    int  (*function) ();
```

```
} MENU_FORM;
```

It is important to note that several 'C' specific coding techniques where used in defining the primary menu structure, MENU_FORM. The include file DIALOG.H must be included before the rest of the data structure is defined because of the way the compiler works. It cannot resolve references to data structures that have not been defined. The WORK_AREA data structure is defined in DIALOG.H and had to be defined before MENU_FORM referenced it.

Another interesting point about 'C' is the int (*function) ( ) declaration. This is the way that you can assign a data structure to contain a pointer to a function in your application. More is explained about this in the chapter on the main menu of the application.

Create the DIALOG.H Include Source File

The DIALOG.H include source file contains the data structure definitions needed by the Menu Library and application to define the dialog boxes needed to be processed by the application.

As described earlier, a dialog box is the way that the computer and the user interacts. Dialog boxes can stand alone or can be part of a primary menu. The most common use of a dialog box is that it is called from a pull-down menu.

The DIALOG.H source include file is included already into the primary menu structure definition, but it is broken out into its own include file because it can also be used by itself.

Create the DIALOG.H source file, type the following statements, and save the file.

```
/*=========================================================================*/
/*                                                                         */
/* File : DIALOG.H                                                         */
/*                                                                         */
/* Purpose : This include file contains the dialog box data structure */
/*           definitions used by the Menu Library functions.            */
/*                                                                         */
/* Data Defined : HORZ_SCROLL 0 - Defines HORZ_SCROLL for the           */
/*           horizontal scroll bar data definitions.                    */
/*                                                                         */
/*           VERT_SCROLL 1 - Defines VERT_SCROLL for the vertical       */
/*           scroll bar data definitions.                               */
/*                                                                         */
/* Data Structures - typedef struct ENTRY_FIELD is used to define      */
/*           an entry field in a dialog box.  The variable             */
/*           int field_num is used to define the logical field number */
/*           of the entry field. The variables int label_row and       */
/*           label_col are used to define where the entry field        */
/*           label string, char *label, is to be displayed. The        */
```

```
/*          variables int box_row, box_col, box_width, and          */
/*          box_height are used to draw a box around the entry       */
/*          field.  The variable int line_length defines how many    */
/*          characters of the string are displayed at one time.  The */
/*          variable int buffer_length is the actual length of the   */
/*          entry field buffer.  The variable char *buffer is a      */
/*          character pointer to the buffer string to edit in the    */
/*          entry field.                                             */
/*                                                                   */
/*          The typedef struct PUSH_BUTTON is used to define a       */
/*          push button. The variable int field_num is used to       */
/*          define the logical field number within the work area.    */
/*          The variable char *label is the string to display        */
/*          inside of the push button.  The variables int row and    */
/*          int col define where to display the push button string.  */
/*                                                                   */
/*          The typedef struct GROUP_FIELD is used to define a       */
/*          check box or a radio button. The variable int field_num  */
/*          is used to define the logical field number of the work   */
/*          area.  The variable char *label is the string to display */
/*          next to the check box or radio button.  The variables    */
/*          int r and int c define where to display the string.      */
/*          The variable int status is used to define the check box  */
/*          or radio button in an OFF or ON state.                   */
/*                                                                   */
/*          The typedef struct WORK_GROUP defines a GROUP of radio   */
/*          buttons or check boxes.  The variable char *group_str    */
/*          is the string that defines the group. The variables      */
/*          int r, int c, int w, and int h define the box outline    */
/*          to display around the group.  GROUP_FIELD *fields is     */
/*          a pointer to a list of check boxes or radio buttons.     */
/*          The variable int number is defined to the number of      */
/*          check boxes or radio buttons defined in the group. The   */
/*          variable type is used to define a type of group, a       */
/*          group of check boxes, or a group of radio buttons.       */
/*                                                                   */
/*          The typedef struct SCROLL_BAR defines a scroll bar. The  */
/*          variable int type defines the type of scroll bar,        */
/*          horizontal or vertical.  The variables int r, int c, and */
/*          int l, define the starting row and column coordinates    */
/*          of the scroll bar and its length.  The variable int bl   */
/*          is used as the current location of the scroll bar box.   */
/*                                                                   */
/*          The typedef struct LIST_BOX defines a list box structure.*/
/*          The variable int r and int c are used to define the      */
/*          upper left-hand column coordinates of the list box. The  */
/*          variable int length is the number of displayable         */
/*          characters the list box contains in width. The variable  */
/*          int index is used to define the current item in the list.*/
/*          The variable char **items is a pointer to a list of      */
/*          strings to be displayed in the list box.  The variable   */
/*          int num_items is used to define the number of strings    */
/*          that can be displayed at one time.  SCROLL_BAR           */
```

```
/*            *v_scroll_bar and SCROLL_BAR *h_scroll_bar are pointers  */
/*            to the scroll bars to maintain for the list box. The     */
/*            variable int (*initialize_function) () is used to define */
/*            the application specific function to call to initialize  */
/*            the list box strings to display.  The variable           */
/*            int (*update_function) () is used to define the          */
/*            application specific function to update the list of      */
/*            strings to display.                                      */
/*                                                                     */
/*            The typedef struct WORK_AREA defines the work area of a  */
/*            DIALOG_BOX.  ENTRY_FIELD *entry is a pointer to a group  */
/*            of entry fields.  The variable int entry_num defines     */
/*            how many entry fields there are.  PUSH_BUTTON *buttons   */
/*            is a pointer to a group of push buttons.  The variable   */
/*            int button_num defines how many push buttons there are.  */
/*            The variable int current_button is used to define which  */
/*            push button is active.  WORK_GROUP *groups is a pointer  */
/*            to groups of check boxes and/or radio buttons. The       */
/*            variable int group_num is used to define how many groups */
/*            there are.  LIST_BOX *listbox is a pointer to a group    */
/*            of list boxes.  The variable int box_num is used to      */
/*            define the number of list boxes there are.               */
/*                                                                     */
/*            The typedef struct DIALOG_BOX is used to define a dialog */
/*            box. The variables int r, int c, int w, and int h are    */
/*            used to define the window area of the dialog box.  The   */
/*            variable char *hdr is the header string to display.      */
/*            WORK_AREA *workarea is a pointer to a group of work      */
/*            areas. The variable int (*function) () is used to define */
/*            the application specific function to call to process the */
/*            information from the dialog box.                         */
/*                                                                     */
/*=====================================================================*/

#define HORZ_SCROLL 0
#define VERT_SCROLL 1
typedef char *ITEM_PTR;

typedef struct
{
    int field_num;
    int label_row;
    int label_col;
    char *label;
    int  box_row;
    int  box_col;
    int  box_width;
    int  box_height;
    int  line_length;
    int  buffer_length;
    char *buffer;
} ENTRY_FIELD;
```

```
typedef struct
{
    int field_num;
    char *label;
    int  r;
    int  c;
} PUSH_BUTTON;

typedef struct
{
    int field_num;
    char *label;
    int r;
    int c;
    int status;
} GROUP_FIELD;

typedef struct
{
    char *group_str;
    int r;
    int c;
    int w;
    int h;
    GROUP_FIELD *fields;
    int number;
    int type;
} WORK_GROUP;

typedef struct
{
    int type;
    int r;
    int c;
    int l;
    int bl;
} SCROLL_BAR;

typedef struct
{
    int r;
    int c;
    int length;
    int index;
    char **items;
    int num_items;
    SCROLL_BAR *v_scroll_bar;
    SCROLL_BAR *h_scroll_bar;
    int (*initialize_function) ();
    int (*update_function) ();
} LIST_BOX;

typedef  struct
```

```
{
   ENTRY_FIELD  *entry;
   int entry_num;
   PUSH_BUTTON  *buttons;
   int button_num;
   int current_button;
   WORK_GROUP *groups;
   int group_num;
   LIST_BOX *listbox;
   int box_num;
} WORK_AREA;

typedef struct
{
   int r;
   int c;
   int w;
   int h;
   char *hdr;
   WORK_AREA  *workarea;
   int (*function) ();
} DIALOG_BOX;
```

The DIALOG.H include source file defines a dialog box that can have any number of entry fields, push buttons, list boxes, check boxes, or radio buttons. The application can create almost any type of menu with this type of structure. Any combination can be included that is necessary to achieve the user interface that is desired.

Create the KEYBOARD.H Include Source File

The KEYBOARD.H source include file contains the keyboard definitions needed by the application and the Menu Libraries to be able to process keyboard input.

Create the KEYBOARD.H source file, type the following statements, and save the file.

```
/*====================================================================*/
/*                                                                    */
/* File : KEYBOARD.H                                                  */
/*                                                                    */
/* Purpose : This include file contains the keyboard data definitions */
/*           used by the Menu Library functions.                      */
/*                                                                    */
/* Data Defined - The data definitions defined in KEYBOARD.H define   */
/*           the special keystrokes that are to be interpreted by     */
/*           the Menu Library functions and the application.          */
/*                                                                    */
/*====================================================================*/

#define F1          0x3b00
```

```
#define F2              0x3c00
#define F3              0x3d00
#define F4              0x3e00
#define F5              0x3f00
#define F6              0x4000
#define F7              0x4100
#define F8              0x4200
#define F9              0x4300
#define F10             0x4400

#define LEFT_ARROW   0x4b00
#define RIGHT_ARROW  0x4d00
#define UP_ARROW     0x4800
#define DOWN_ARROW   0x5000
#define HOME         0x4700
#define PGUP         0x4900
#define END          0x4f00
#define PGDN         0x5100
#define ENTER        0x000D
#define ESC          0x001B
#define BACKSPACE    0x0008
#define TAB          0x0009
#define SHIFT_TAB    0x0F00
#define INSERT       0x5200
#define DELETE       0x5300
#define CTRL_HOME    0x7700
#define CTRL_END     0x7500
#define CTRL_PGUP    0x8400
#define CTRL_PGDN    0x7600
#define CTRL_LEFT_ARROW   0x7300
#define CTRL_RIGHT_ARROW  0x7400
#define CTRL_UP_ARROW        0x8d00
#define CTRL_DOWN_ARROW      0x9100
#define ALT_A 0x1e00
#define ALT_B 0x3000
#define ALT_C 0x2e00
#define ALT_D 0x2000
#define ALT_E 0x1200
#define ALT_F 0x2100
#define ALT_G 0x2200
#define ALT_H 0x2300
#define ALT_I 0x1700
#define ALT_J 0x2400
#define ALT_K 0x2500
#define ALT_L 0x2600
#define ALT_M 0x3200
#define ALT_N 0x3100
#define ALT_O 0x1800
#define ALT_P 0x1900
#define ALT_Q 0x1000
#define ALT_R 0x1300
#define ALT_S 0x1f00
#define ALT_T 0x1400
```

```
#define ALT_U 0x1600
#define ALT_V 0x2f00
#define ALT_W 0x1100
#define ALT_X 0x2d00
#define ALT_Y 0x1500
#define ALT_Z 0x2c00
```

Create the ARROWS.H Include Source File

The ARROWS.H include source file contains the icon array descriptions of the arrows displayed on the list box scroll bars.

Create the ARROWS.H source file, type the following statements, and save the file.

```
/*====================================================================*/
/*                                                                    */
/* File : ARROWS.H                                                    */
/*                                                                    */
/* Purpose : This include file contains the arrow icon definitions    */
/*           used by the Menu Library List Box functions.             */
/*                                                                    */
/* Icons Defined : Up_Arrow_Icon[8][2] - The array Up_Arrow_Icon is   */
/*           used to contain the icon definition needed to display    */
/*           the up arrow of the List Box Vertical Scroll Bar.        */
/*                                                                    */
/*           Down_Arrow_Icon[8][2] - The array Down_Arrow_Icon is     */
/*           used to contain the icon definition needed to display    */
/*           the down arrow of the List Box Vertical Scroll Bar.      */
/*                                                                    */
/*           Left_Arrow_Icon[8][2] - The array Left_Arrow_Icon is     */
/*           used to contain the icon definition needed to display    */
/*           the left arrow of the List Box Horizontal Scroll Bar.    */
/*                                                                    */
/*           Right_Arrow_Icon[8][2] - The array Right_Arrow_Icon is   */
/*           used to contain the icon definition needed to display    */
/*           the right arrow of the List Box Horizontal Scroll Bar.   */
/*                                                                    */
/*====================================================================*/

unsigned char Up_Arrow_Icon[8][2] =
{
    {0xFC, 0xFF },    /* {11111100 11111111} */
    {0xF0, 0x3F },    /* {11110000 00111111} */
    {0xC0, 0x0F },    /* {11000000 00001111} */
    {0x00, 0x03 },    /* {00000000 00000011} */
    {0xF0, 0x3F },    /* {11110000 00111111} */
    {0xF0, 0x3F },    /* {11110000 00111111} */
    {0xF0, 0x3F },    /* {11110000 00111111} */
    {0xF0, 0x3F }     /* {11110000 00111111} */
};

unsigned char Down_Arrow_Icon[8][2] =
```

```
{
    {0xF0, 0x3F },    /* {11110000 00111111}, */
    {0xF0, 0x3F },    /* {11110000 00111111}, */
    {0xF0, 0x3F },    /* {11110000 00111111}, */
    {0xF0, 0x3F },    /* {11110000 00111111}, */
    {0x00, 0x03 },    /* {00000000 00000011}, */
    {0xC0, 0x0F },    /* {11000000 00001111}, */
    {0xF0, 0x3F },    /* {11110000 00111111}, */
    {0xFC, 0xFF }     /* {11111100 11111111}  */
};

unsigned char Left_Arrow_Icon[8][2] =
{
    {0xFC, 0xFF },    /* {11111100 11111111}, */
    {0xF0, 0xFF },    /* {11110000 11111111}, */
    {0xC0, 0x00 },    /* {11000000 00000000}, */
    {0x00, 0x00 },    /* {00000000 00000000}, */
    {0xC0, 0x00 },    /* {11000000 00000000}, */
    {0xF0, 0xFF },    /* {11110000 11111111}, */
    {0xFC, 0xFF },    /* {11111100 11111111}, */
    {0xFF, 0xFF }     /* {11111111 11111111}  */
};

unsigned char Right_Arrow_Icon[8][2] =
{
    {0xFF, 0x3F },    /* {11111111 00111111}, */
    {0xFF, 0x0F },    /* {11111111 00001111}, */
    {0x00, 0x03 },    /* {00000000 00000011}, */
    {0x00, 0x00 },    /* {00000000 00000000}, */
    {0x00, 0x03 },    /* {00000000 00000011}, */
    {0xFF, 0x0F },    /* {11111111 00001111}, */
    {0xFF, 0x3F },    /* {11111111 00111111}, */
    {0xFF, 0xFF }     /* {11111111 11111111}  */
};
```

Create the RADIO.H Include Source File

The RADIO.H include source file contains the icon array descriptions of the radio buttons to display for radio button groups.

Create the RADIO.H source file, type the following statements, and save the file.

```
/*========================================================================*/
/*                                                                        */
/* File : RADIO.H                                                         */
/*                                                                        */
/* Purpose : This include file contains the Radio Button icon            */
/*           definitions used by the Menu Library functions.             */
/*                                                                        */
/* Icons Defined : On_Radio_Button[8][2] - The array On_Radio_Button     */
/*           is used to contain the icon definition needed to display     */
/*           a Radio Button that is ON.                                  */
```

```
/*                                                                      */
/*              Off_Radio_Button[8][2] - The array Off_Radio_Button is  */
/*              used to contain the icon definition needed to display   */
/*              a Radio Button box that is OFF.                         */
/*                                                                      */
/*======================================================================*/

unsigned char On_Radio_Button[8][2] =
{
    {0xFF, 0xFF },      /* {1111 1111 1111 1111 }, */
    {0xF0, 0x0F },      /* {1111 0000 0000 1111 }, */
    {0xCF, 0xF3 },      /* {1100 1111 1111 0011 }, */
    {0x30, 0x0C },      /* {0011 0000 0000 1100 }, */
    {0x30, 0x0C },      /* {0011 0000 0000 1100 }, */
    {0x30, 0x0C },      /* {0011 0000 0000 1100 }, */
    {0xCF, 0xF3 },      /* {1100 1111 1111 0011 }, */
    {0xF0, 0x0F }       /* {1111 0000 0000 1111 }  */
};

unsigned char Off_Radio_Button[8][2] =
{
    {0xFF, 0xFF },      /* {1111 1111 1111 1111 }, */
    {0xF0, 0x0F },      /* {1111 0000 0000 1111 }, */
    {0xCF, 0xF3 },      /* {1100 1111 1111 0011 }, */
    {0x3F, 0xFC },      /* {0011 1111 1111 1100 }, */
    {0x3F, 0xFC },      /* {0011 1111 1111 1100 }, */
    {0x3F, 0xFC },      /* {0011 1111 1111 1100 }, */
    {0xCF, 0xF3 },      /* {1100 1111 1111 0011 }, */
    {0xF0, 0x0F }       /* {1111 0000 0000 1111 }  */
};
```

Create the CHECKBOX.H Include Source File

The CHECKBOX.H include source file contains the icon array descriptions of the check boxes used by the Menu Library functions.

Create the CHECKBOX.H source file, type the following statements, and save the file.

```
/*======================================================================*/
/*                                                                      */
/* File : CHECKBOX.H                                                     */
/*                                                                      */
/* Purpose : This include file contains the Check Box icon              */
/*           definitions used by the Menu Library functions.            */
/*                                                                      */
/* Icons Defined : On_Check_Box [8][2] - The array On_Check_Box is      */
/*           used to contain the icon definition needed to display a    */
/*           Check Box that is ON.                                      */
/*                                                                      */
/*           Off_Check_Box [8][2] - The array Off_Check_Box is used     */
/*           to contain the icon definition needed to display a         */
```

```
/*              Check Box that is OFF.                                    */
/*                                                                        */
/*=======================================================================*/

unsigned char On_Check_Box[8][2] =
{
    {0x00, 0x00 },    /* {0000 0000 0000 0000 }, */
    {0x0F, 0xF0 },    /* {0000 1111 1111 0000 }, */
    {0x33, 0xCC },    /* {0011 0011 1100 1100 }, */
    {0x3C, 0x3C },    /* {0011 1100 0011 1100 }, */
    {0x3C, 0x3C },    /* {0011 1100 0011 1100 }, */
    {0x33, 0xCC },    /* {0011 0011 1100 1100 }, */
    {0x0F, 0xF0 },    /* {0000 1111 1111 0000 }, */
    {0x00, 0x00 }     /* {0000 0000 0000 0000 }  */
};

unsigned char Off_Check_Box[8][2] =
{
    {0x00, 0x00 },    /* {0000 0000 0000 0000 }, */
    {0x3F, 0xFC },    /* {0011 1111 1111 1100 }, */
    {0x3F, 0xFC },    /* {0011 1111 1111 1100 }, */
    {0x3F, 0xFC },    /* {0011 1111 1111 1100 }, */
    {0x3F, 0xFC },    /* {0011 1111 1111 1100 }, */
    {0x3F, 0xFC },    /* {0011 1111 1111 1100 }, */
    {0x3F, 0xFC },    /* {0011 1111 1111 1100 }, */
    {0x00, 0x00 }     /* {0000 0000 0000 0000 }  */
};
```

Create the MESSAGE.H Include Source File

The MESSAGE.H include source file contains the data structure definitions needed to display the message boxes. A message box is a special type of dialog box that is used to display information to the user.

Create the MESSAGE.H source file, type the following statements, and save the file.

```
/*=======================================================================*/
/*                                                                        */
/* File : MESSAGE.H                                                        */
/*                                                                        */
/* Purpose : This include file contains the message box definitions       */
/*           used by the Menu Library functions.                          */
/*                                                                        */
/* Include Files - DIALOG.H - This include contains the data structure*/
/*           definitions needed to define a message box.                  */
/*                                                                        */
/* Data Structures - The typedef MSG_AREA defines the message box         */
/*           work area.  The variable ITEM_PTR *strs is a pointer to      */
/*           a group of strings to display in the message box. The        */
/*           variable int strs_num defines how many strings there         */
/*           are to display.  PUSH_BUTTON *buttons is a pointer to a       */
/*           group of push buttons.  The variable int button_num is       */
```

```
/*          defined as the number of push buttons there are. The     */
/*          variable int current button defines the active push      */
/*          button.                                                   */
/*                                                                    */
/*          The typedef struct MESSAGE_BOX defines a message box.     */
/*          The variable int r, int c, int w, and int h define the    */
/*          window size of the message box.  The variable char *hdr   */
/*          is the message box header string.  MSG_AREA *msgarea is   */
/*          a pointer to the message box work area.  The variable     */
/*          int (*function) () is the application specific function   */
/*          to call after an answer is received from the message      */
/*          box.                                                      */
/*                                                                    */
/*================================================================*/

#include "\menu\dialog.h"

typedef  struct
{
   ITEM_PTR   *strs;
   int strs_num;
   PUSH_BUTTON   *buttons;
   int button_num;
   int current_button;
} MSG_AREA;

typedef struct
{
   int r;
   int c;
   int w;
   int h;
   char *hdr;
   MSG_AREA *msgarea;
   int (*function) ();
} MESSAGE_BOX;
```

SUMMARY

The Menu Library makes use of include files to define the data definitions and structures that it will process. The Menu Library structures are flexible enough to allow the application programmer to build any type of menu he desires.

Also, the structures are designed in such a way that the programmer can add new attributes to them without affecting the overall Menu Library functions. The programmer might want to add color attributes to each one of the strings defined or to the colors used to display the menu. These extras were not added in this book because we are working with only four colors. If you wish to go to EGA or VGA, then the menu structures should be modified to contain color attributes.

Chapter 10

THE MENU LIBRARY 'C' SOURCE FILES

INTRODUCTION

The Menu Library uses the ten different 'C' source files to process the menu function requests made by the application. These source files rely heavily on the include files described in Chapter 9. These source files are combined into the one library file called MENU.LIB. The application links this library, along with other libraries, into its executable to be able to process the menu functions.

In this chapter, I deal with the functions needed to process and display the primary menu and action bar menus. The source files MENU.C, KEYBOARD.C, ACTION.C, and PULLDOWN.C contain the functions needed to do this.

Create the MENU.C Source File

The MENU.C source file contains the functions needed to display and process a primary menu. This function is called once from the application and is passed a pointer to the primary menu to process. The Menu ( ) function takes the information in the primary menu structure and initializes and displays the primary menu on the screen. After this has been done, it then calls an application specific function in the primary menu structure that takes over the processing of the primary menu.

The MENU.C source file contains the functions MENU ( ) and DrawMenuOutline ( ).

Create the MENU.C source file, type the following statements, and save the file.

```
/*******************************************************************/
/*                                                                 */
/* File : MENU.C                                                   */
/*                                                                 */
/* Purpose : This 'C' source file contains the functions needed to */
```

```
/*            display and process a primary menu.              */
/*                                                             */
/* Include Files : \graphics\COLORS.H - This include file contains  */
/*          the color definitions used by the Menu Library.    */
/*                                                             */
/*          MENU.H - This include file contains the menu data  */
/*          structures needed to define a primary menu.        */
/*                                                             */
/*          DEFINES.H - This include file contains the data    */
/*          definitions specific for the Menu Library functions. */
/*                                                             */
/* Functions : Menu () - This function is called by the application  */
/*          whenever a primary menu needs to be processed.     */
/*                                                             */
/*          DrawMenuOutline () - This function is called by Menu ()*/
/*          to initialize the primary menu on the screen.      */
/*                                                             */
/***************************************************************/

#include "\graphics\colors.h"
#include "menu.h"
#include "defines.h"
```

Create the MENU.C Function — Menu ( )

The first function in MENU.C is Menu ( ). This function is called by the application to initialize and display the primary menu of the application. The application passes a data structure of the type MENU_FORM that contains the description of the primary menu.

Edit the MENU.C source file, type the following statements, and save the file.

```
/*===========================================================*/
/*                                                             */
/* Function : Menu (md);                                       */
/*                                                             */
/* Purpose : This function initializes and displays a primary menu on */
/*           the screen for the application.                   */
/*                                                             */
/* Entry Parameters : MENU_FORM *md - A pointer to the primary menu  */
/*           structure to initialize and display.             */
/*                                                             */
/* Local Data Definitions : int i - This variable is used as a  */
/*           temporary variable to calculate the display location of  */
/*           the header string of the primary menu.           */
/*                                                             */
/* Functions Called : DrawMenuOutline () - This function is called  */
/*           to draw the outline boarder of the primary menu. */
/*                                                             */
/*           DisplayString () - This function is called to display  */
/*           strings of data on the screen.                   */
```

```
/*                                                                    */
/*          ClearWindow () - This function is called to clear a       */
/*          window of a given size on the screen in a given color.    */
/*                                                                    */
/*          InitializeActionBar () - This function is called to       */
/*          initialize the primary menu's action bar on the screen.   */
/*                                                                    */
/*          HLine () - This function is called to draw a horizontal   */
/*          line on the screen to separate the action bar from the    */
/*          rest of the primary menu.                                 */
/*                                                                    */
/*          InitializeWorkGroups () - This function is called to      */
/*          initialize the work groups of the primary menu.           */
/*                                                                    */
/*          InitializePushButtons () - This function is called to     */
/*          initialize the push buttons of the primary menu.          */
/*                                                                    */
/*          InitializeEntryFields () - This function is called to     */
/*          initialize the entry fields of the primary menu.          */
/*                                                                    */
/*          InitializeListBox () - This function is called to         */
/*          initialize the list box of the primary menu.              */
/*                                                                    */
/* Logic Flow : The Menu () function is called with a pointer to the  */
/*          primary menu to initialize, display, and process. The     */
/*          function DrawMenuOutline () is called to draw the primary */
/*          menu's outline on the screen.  The variable int i is      */
/*          then used to calculate the starting column location to    */
/*          center the header in the primary menu.  The location is   */
/*          based on the primary menu width and the length of the     */
/*          header string.  The function DisplayString () is then     */
/*          called to display the header on the screen.  The function */
/*          ClearWindow () is then called to clear the rest of the    */
/*          primary menu on the screen.  The InitializeActionBar ()   */
/*          function is then called to display the primary menu's     */
/*          action bar selections.  The function HLine () is called   */
/*          to display a horizontal line to separate the action bar   */
/*          selections from the rest of the primary menu.  If the     */
/*          primary menu contains work groups, then the function      */
/*          InitializeWorkGroups () is called to display the work     */
/*          groups on the screen.  If the primary menu contains       */
/*          push buttons, then the function InitializePushButtons ()  */
/*          is called to display the push buttons on the screen.  If  */
/*          the primary menu contains entry fields, then the function */
/*          InitializeEntryFields () is displayed on the screen. If   */
/*          the primary menu contains list boxes, then the function   */
/*          InitializeListBox () is called to display the list box    */
/*          on the screen.  The last thing the Menu () function does  */
/*          is call an application specific function that takes        */
/*          control of the primary menu.  When the application        */
/*          function returns, the primary menu processing has been    */
/*          completed.                                                */
/*                                                                    */
```

```
/* Exit : The primary menu has been processed.                          */
/*                                                                      */
/*======================================================================*/

Menu(md)
MENU_FORM *md;
{
    int i;

    DrawMenuOutline (md->r, md->c, md->w, md->h);
    i = ((md->w - 3) / 2) - ((strlen (md->hdr) * FONTWIDTH) / 2);
    DisplayString (md->r +  4, md->c + i, md->hdr, WHITE, BLACK);
    ClearWindow (md->r + 16, md->c + 4, md->w - 8, md->h - 19, WHITE);
    InitializeActionBar (md);
    HLine (md->r + (FONTHEIGHT * 2) + (FONTHEIGHT / 2) + 2,
           md->c + (FONTWIDTH / 2) + 1, md->w - FONTWIDTH + 2, BLACK);
    if (md->workarea[0].group_num)
        InitializeWorkGroups (&md->workarea[0]);
    if (md->workarea[0].button_num)
        InitializePushButtons (&md->workarea[0]);
    if (md->workarea[0].entry_num)
        InitializeEntryFields (&md->workarea[0]);
    if (md->workarea[0].box_num)
        InitializeListBox (&md- >workarea[0].listbox[0]);
    (*md->function) (md);
}
```

Create the MENU.C Function — DrawMenuOutline ( )

The DrawMenuOutline ( ) function is called by the Menu ( ) function. It draws the primary menu's outline on the screen based on the row, column, width, and height parameters passed. This is one area of the code that the programmer can change that can have a big effect on the look of the application menus. This book draws a double line around the menu. Other menu types use a shading effect around the menu to make it appear to be on top of the other menus. Personally, I like the double line menus because they take up less room on the screen.

Edit the MENU.C source file, type the following statements, and save the file.

```
/*======================================================================*/
/*                                                                      */
/* Function : DrawMenuOutline (row, column, width, height);             */
/*                                                                      */
/* Purpose : This function draws an outline on the screen for a menu    */
/*           based on the row, column, width, and height values given.  */
/*                                                                      */
/* Entry Parameters : int row - The upper left-hand row coordinate of   */
/*             the primary menu.                                        */
/*                                                                      */
/*             int column - The upper left-hand column coordinate of    */
/*             the primary menu.                                        */
```

```
/*                                                                  */
/*          int width  - The width of the primary menu.             */
/*                                                                  */
/*          int height - The height of the primary menu.            */
/*                                                                  */
/* Functions Called : DrawBox () - This function is called to display */
/*          a box on the screen in a given color.                   */
/*                                                                  */
/*          VLine () - This function is called to display a         */
/*          vertical line on the screen at a given location.        */
/*                                                                  */
/*          ClearWindow () - This function is called to clear a     */
/*          window of screen data in a given color.                 */
/*                                                                  */
/*          HLine () - This function is called to display a         */
/*          horizontal line on the screen at a given location.      */
/*                                                                  */
/* Logic Flow : The DrawMenuOutline () function is called by Menu (). */
/*          It is passed the primary menu's upper left-hand row and */
/*          column coordinates, the menu's width and height. The    */
/*          function DrawBox () is called to display a box on the   */
/*          screen of this size.  The function VLine () is called   */
/*          to display vertical lines on the side of the menu to    */
/*          add depth to the menu outline.  The DrawBox () function */
/*          is called again to display a box in WHITE, then it      */
/*          is called again to display a box in BLACK. At this      */
/*          point the primary menu's border has been displayed.     */
/*          The function ClearWindow () is called to clear the area */
/*          used by the header string.  The function HLine () is    */
/*          then called to separate the header section of the       */
/*          primary menu from the action bar section.               */
/*                                                                  */
/* Exit : The primary menu outline is drawn on the screen.          */
/*                                                                  */
/*================================================================*/

DrawMenuOutline (row, column, width, height)
int   row, column, width, height;
{
   DrawBox (row, column, width, height, BLACKDOT);
   VLine (row, column + 1, height, BLACKDOT);
   VLine (row, column + width - 2, height, BLACKDOT);
   DrawBox (row + 1, column + 2, width - 4, height - 2, WHITEDOT);
   DrawBox (row + 2, column + 3, width - 6, height - 4, BLACKDOT);
   ClearWindow (row + 3, column + 4, width - 8, FONTHEIGHT + 2, BLUE);
   HLine (row + 5 + FONTHEIGHT, column + 4, width - 8, BLACK);
}
```

The MENU.C source file contains the function Menu ( ). Menu ( ) is called by the application whenever a primary menu needs to be displayed on the screen. As stated earlier, there should be only one call per application to this function. The Menu ( ) function is designed to process the primary menu structure passed. To do this, it must first initialize the primary menu and display it on the screen. Once the primary menu has been initialized and displayed, an application specific function is called to process the primary menu.

Create the KEYBOARD.C Source File

The KEYBOARD.C source file contains the function GetKey ( ). This function is used by the Menu Library and the application to return a keystroke from the keyboard. The keystroke definitions are defined in the KEYBOARD.H source file.

This is only one of many types of keyboard input that the application might wish to have. Some applications need functions that return a signal that a key has been pressed. They would call this function to see if a key was there; if one is not, then the application is free to perform some other function. Also, if the application includes a mouse, then the applications keyboard functions must be tied in with the mouse interrupts.

Create the KEYBOARD.C source file, type the following statements, and save the file.

```
/**********************************************************************/
/* File : KEYBOARD.C                                                  */
/*                                                                    */
/* Purpose : This 'C' source file contains the functions needed to   */
/*           get input from the keyboard.                            */
/*                                                                    */
/* Functions : GetKey () - This function is called by the application */
/*           to return a keystroke from the keyboard.  This function  */
/*           waits until a keystroke has been pressed and does not    */
/*           trap out the CTRL-C interrupt.                          */
/*                                                                    */
/**********************************************************************/

#include <dos.h>
static union REGS In_Regs;
static union REGS Out_Regs;
```

Create the KEYBOARD.C Function — GetKey ( )

The GeyKey ( ) function is the only function included in the KEYBOARD.C source file. It is called to return a keystroke from the keyboard. It will not return until a keystroke has been pressed and does not trap out the CTRL-C break interrupt. The programmer can change this function to keep the user from terminating the program, but it is written this way in the book to allow the programmer to break out of the application at any time.

Edit the KEYBOARD.C source file, type the following statements, and save the file.

```
/*=====================================================================*/
/*                                                                     */
/* Function : GetKey ();                                               */
/*                                                                     */
/* Purpose : This function gets a key from the keyboard.               */
/*                                                                     */
/* Functions Called : int86 () - This function is called to perform    */
/*            a DOS BIOS service call to return a keystroke from the    */
/*            keyboard.                                                 */
/*                                                                     */
/* Logic Flow : The GetKey () function is called to return a keystroke */
/*            from the keyboard.  This function makes use of the        */
/*            global variables In_Regs and Out_Regs to send and return */
/*            information from the DOS BIOS service call 0x21.  The     */
/*            In_Regs.h.ah is set to eight which is the keyboard        */
/*            service routine number.  The int86 () function is called  */
/*            to perform the keyboard request.  When the function       */
/*            returns, the variable Out_Regs.h.al is checked to see if  */
/*            it contains a zero.  If it does not, then a normal key    */
/*            has been pressed and it is returned to the caller.  If    */
/*            it was zero, then a special keystroke has been received,  */
/*            such as an arrow key.  The int86 () function is called    */
/*            again and the key is put into the high order byte and     */
/*            returned to the caller.                                  */
/*                                                                     */
/* Exit : A keystroke is returned from the keyboard.                   */
/*                                                                     */
/*=====================================================================*/

GetKey ()
{
   In_Regs.h.ah = 8;
   int86 (0x21, &In_Regs, &Out_Regs);
   Out_Regs.h.ah = 0;
   if (Out_Regs.h.al != 0) return (Out_Regs.x.ax);
   int86 (0x21, &In_Regs, &Out_Regs);
   Out_Regs.h.ah = Out_Regs.h.al;
   Out_Regs.h.al = 0;
   return (Out_Regs.x.ax);
}
```

Create the ACTION.C Source File

The ACTION.C source file contains the functions needed to initialize, display, and process the action bar. The Menu ( ) function calls the InitializeActionBar ( ) function whenever a primary menu is being initialized for the first time. The function ProcessActionBar ( ) is called whenever the user activates the action bar.

Create the ACTION.C source file, type the following statements, and save the file.

```
/*======================================================================*/
/*                                                                      */
/* File : ACTION.C                                                      */
/*                                                                      */
/* Purpose : This 'C' source file contains the functions needed to     */
/*           initialize, display, and process the action bar of a      */
/*           primary menu.                                              */
/*                                                                      */
/* Include Files : \graphics\COLORS.H - This include file contains     */
/*           the color definitions used by the Menu Library functions. */
/*                                                                      */
/*           MENU.H - This include file contains the data structure    */
/*           definitions that define a primary menu.                   */
/*                                                                      */
/*           DEFINES.H - This include file contains the defined data   */
/*           definitions used by the Menu Library functions.           */
/*                                                                      */
/*           KEYBOARD.H - This include file contains the defined data  */
/*           definitions used to determine keyboard input.             */
/*                                                                      */
/* Static Data Definitions : int Number_ActionBar_Menus - This static  */
/*           variable is used to count the number of action bar menus  */
/*           there are available to the user.                          */
/*                                                                      */
/* Functions : InitializeActionBar () - This function is called by     */
/*           Menu () to initialize the action bar of a primary menu.   */
/*                                                                      */
/*           ProcessActionBar () - This function is called to process  */
/*           the action bar whenever the application needs to do so.   */
/*                                                                      */
/*======================================================================*/

#include "\graphics\colors.h"
#include "menu.h"
#include "defines.h"
#include "keyboard.h"

extern int Number_ActionBar_Menus;
extern int ActionBar_Hot_Keys[10];
```

Create the ACTION.C Function — InitializeActionBar ( )

The InitializeActionBar ( ) function is called by the Menu ( ) function whenever a primary menu is being initialized. This function should be called only once because the application should have only one primary menu. This function displays the primary menu's action bar on the screen and counts the number of available selections from the action bar.

Edit the ACTION.C source file, type the following statements, and save the file.

```
/*=======================================================================*/
/*                                                                       */
/* Function : InitializeActionBar (md);                                  */
/*                                                                       */
/* Purpose  : This function initializes the action bar of the primary    */
/*            menu. It displays the action bar selections, assigns        */
/*            the row and column coordinates of the selections, and       */
/*            counts the number of action bar selections.                 */
/*                                                                       */
/* Entry Parameters : MENU_FORM *md - A pointer to the primary menu       */
/*            structure containing the action bar structure to            */
/*            initialize.                                                 */
/*                                                                       */
/* Local Data Definitions - int row - This variable is used to assign     */
/*            each of the action bar menus with the row coordinate        */
/*            of the action bar menu on the screen.                       */
/*                                                                       */
/*            int column - This variable is used to assign each of        */
/*            the action bar menus with the column coordinate of the      */
/*            action bar menu on the screen.                              */
/*                                                                       */
/* Functions Called : DisplayString () - This function is called to       */
/*            display the action bar menu header string.                  */
/*                                                                       */
/* Logic Flow : The InitializeActionBar () function is called with a      */
/*            pointer to the primary menu structure being processed.      */
/*            The variable int row is set to the row coordinate that      */
/*            the action bar menu header strings will be displayed.       */
/*            The row coordinate calculated is based on the way the       */
/*            primary menu is displayed.  The variable int column is      */
/*            set to the column coordinate of the first action bar        */
/*            menu header string to be displayed.  The variable           */
/*            Number_ActionBar_Menus is set to 0.  While there are        */
/*            still action bar menu header strings to display, the        */
/*            DisplayString () function is called to display the          */
/*            header string at the calculated row and column              */
/*            coordinates.  The action bar menu header string's           */
/*            row and column coordinates are saved in the action bar      */
/*            menu structure.  Then a new column coordinate is            */
/*            calculated based on the length of the action bar menu       */
/*            header string just displayed.  When all of the action       */
/*            bar headers have been displayed the variable                */
/*            Number_ActionBar_Menus is decremented so that the           */
/*            first action bar menu is indexed by zero.                   */
/*                                                                       */
/* Exit : The action bar selections are initialized and displayed on      */
/*        the screen.                                                    */
/*                                                                       */
/*=======================================================================*/

InitializeActionBar (md)
MENU_FORM *md;
{
```

```
   int row, column, length, index;

   row = md->r + FONTHEIGHT + (FONTHEIGHT / 2) + 1;
   column = md->c + FONTWIDTH;
   Number_ActionBar_Menus = 0;
   while (md->action_bar[Number_ActionBar_Menus].str)
   {
      DisplayString (row, column,
                     md->action_bar[Number_ActionBar_Menus].str,
                     BLACK, WHITE);
      index = md->action_bar[Number_ActionBar_Menus].hot_loc;
      DisplayCursor (row, column + (index * FONTWIDTH),
                     md->action_bar[Number_ActionBar_Menus].str[index],
                     BLACK, WHITE);
      ActionBar_Hot_Keys[Number_ActionBar_Menus] =
         md->action_bar[Number_ActionBar_Menus].hot_key;
      md->action_bar[Number_ActionBar_Menus].r = row;
      md->action_bar[Number_ActionBar_Menus].c = column;
      column += (strlen (md->action_bar[Number_ActionBar_Menus].str)
            * FONTWIDTH);
      Number_ActionBar_Menus++;
   }
   Number_ActionBar_Menus--;
}
```

Create the ACTION.C Function — ProcessActionBar ( )

The ProcessActionBar ( ) function is called by the application whenever there is a need to select an option from the action bar. The function is passed a pointer to the primary menu structure containing the action bar structure to process. It is also passed the current selection number index.

This function displays the action bar menu based on the index passed by calling the function ProcessPullDownMenu ( ). The action bar menu exit variable is checked to see if another action bar menu needs to be displayed.

Edit the ACTION.C source file, type the following statements, and save the file.

```
/*======================================================================*/
/*                                                                      */
/* Function : ProcessActionBar (md, index);                             */
/*                                                                      */
/* Purpose  : This function processes the menus for the action bar      */
/*            selections starting with the given menu index.  This      */
/*            function calls the ProcessPullDownMenu () function with    */
/*            the current action bar menu to process.                   */
/*                                                                      */
/* Entry Parameters : MENU_FORM *md - A pointer to the primary menu     */
/*            structure containing the action bar structure to process*/
/*                                                                      */
/*            int index - The current action bar selection to process   */
```

```
/*              first from the action bar selections.                  */
/*                                                                     */
/* Functions Called : ProcessPullDownMenu () - This function is called*/
/*            to initialize, display, and process the action bar       */
/*            selection's pull-down menus.                             */
/*                                                                     */
/* Logic Flow : The ProcessActionBar () function is called by the      */
/*            application to process the action bar of the primary     */
/*            menu.  The function is passed a pointer to the primary    */
/*            menu structure containing the action bar menu structure */
/*            to process.  The variable int index is also passed to    */
/*            the function and it is used to determine which action    */
/*            bar menu to process first.  Until the user exits the     */
/*            action bar, the ProcessActionBar () function will call    */
/*            the ProcessPullDownMenu () function with a pointer to     */
/*            the action bar menu structure to process.  The action    */
/*            bar menu structure variable md->action_bar[index].exit   */
/*            contains the return code from the ProcessPullDownMenu ()*/
/*            function.  If the return code is a LEFT_ARROW, then the  */
/*            action bar menu to the left of the current menu is        */
/*            processed.  If there are no more menus to the left,      */
/*            then the rightmost action bar menu is processed.  If     */
/*            the return code is a RIGHT_ARROW, then the action bar    */
/*            menu to the right is processed. If there are no more     */
/*            menus to the right, then the leftmost menu is            */
/*            processed.  If any other return code is returned, then   */
/*            the ProcessActionBar () function returns this code to    */
/*            the calling function.                                    */
/*                                                                     */
/* Exit : The action bar has been processed.                          */
/*                                                                     */
/*===================================================================*/

ProcessActionBar (md, index)
MENU_FORM *md;
int index;
{
    int key,i;

    for (;;)
    {
        ProcessPullDownMenu (&md->action_bar[index]);
        switch ((key = md->action_bar[index].exit))
        {
            case LEFT_ARROW:
                if (index > 0) index--;
                else index = Number_ActionBar_Menus;
                break;

            case RIGHT_ARROW:
                if (index < Number_ActionBar_Menus) index++;
                else index = 0;
                break;
```

```
    default:
        for (i = 0; i <= Number_ActionBar_Menus; i++)
        {
            if (key == ActionBar_Hot_Keys[i])
            {
                index = i;
                break;
            }
        }
        if (i != index) return (index);
    }
  }
}
```

The ACTION.C source file contains two distinctly different functions. The InitializeActionBar ( ) function is called when the primary menu is being initialized. It displays and calculates information that is used by the ProcessActionBar ( ) function.

The ProcessActionBar ( ) function is called when the user presses a key to activate the action bar select line. The application calls this function, passing it a pointer to the primary menu structure to use along with the current action bar menu to process. The ProcessPullDownMenu ( ) function is called to initialize, display, and process the pull-down menu associated with the current action bar selection.

Create the PULLDOWN.C Source File

The PULLDOWN.C source file contains the functions needed to initialize, display, and process a pull-down menu. This function is called with a pointer to a pull-down menu data structure. The pull-down menu is processed until the user exits it.

Create the PULLDOWN.C source file, type the following statements, and save the file.

```
/*********************************************************************/
/*                                                                   */
/* File : PULLDOWN.C                                                 */
/*                                                                   */
/* Purpose : This 'C' source file initializes, displays and processes */
/*           a pull-down menu.                                       */
/*                                                                   */
/* Include Files : \graphics\COLORS.H - This include file contains   */
/*           the color definitions used by the Menu Library functions.*/
/*                                                                   */
/*           MENU.H - This include file contains the data structure  */
/*           definitions that define a pull-down menu.               */
/*                                                                   */
/*           DEFINES.H - This include file contains the defined data */
/*           definitions used by the Menu Library functions.         */
/*                                                                   */
```

```
/*            KEYBOARD.H - This include file contains the defined data */
/*            definitions used to determine keyboard input.            */
/*                                                                     */
/* Functions : ProcessPullDownMenu () - This functions initializes,    */
/*            displays, and processes a pull-down menu.                */
/*                                                                     */
/***********************************************************************/

#include "\graphics\colors.h"
#include "menu.h"
#include "defines.h"
#include "keyboard.h"

extern int Number_ActionBar_Menus;
extern int ActionBar_Hot_Keys[10];
```

Create the PULLDOWN.C Function — ProcessPullDownMenu ( )

The ProcessPullDownMenu ( ) function is called whenever a pull-down menu needs to be displayed and processed. This function is passed a pointer to the pull-down menu data structure to process.

The pull-down menu is initialized on the screen by first saving the screen data information of where the pull-down menu is to be displayed. The pull-down menu is displayed on the screen and waits for user input to select an item from the pull-down menu list. If an item is selected, the application specific function to perform for that selection is called. When the user exits the pull-down menu, the original screen data, i.e., the way the screen looked before the pull-down menu was displayed, is restored.

Edit the PULLDOWN.C source file, type the following statements, and save the file.

```
/*=====================================================================*/
/* Function : ProcessPullDownMenu (pd);                                */
/*                                                                     */
/* Purpose : This function initializes, displays, and processes a      */
/*            pull-down menu.                                          */
/*                                                                     */
/* Entry Parameters : MENU_FORM *md - A pointer to the pull-down menu  */
/*            structure to process.                                    */
/*                                                                     */
/* Include Files : <malloc.h> - This include file is part of the       */
/*            standard 'C' memory allocation functions.                */
/*                                                                     */
/* Local Data Definitions : int i - This variable is used as a         */
/*            temporary variable for loops.                            */
/*                                                                     */
/*            int menu_width - This variable is used to calculate how  */
/*            wide the menu is in bytes.                               */
/*                                                                     */
```

```
/*          int item_width - This variable is used to calculate the   */
/*          width of the largest selection from the pull-down menu.    */
/*                                                                     */
/*          int header_width - This variable is used to hold the       */
/*          width of the header string.                                */
/*                                                                     */
/*          int temp_width - This variable is used as a temporary      */
/*          width of the largest width found.                          */
/*                                                                     */
/*          int row - This variable is used to hold the row value of   */
/*          the display.                                               */
/*                                                                     */
/*          int current_row - This variable is used to hold the        */
/*          location of the current row.                               */
/*                                                                     */
/*          int index - This variable is used to contain the value     */
/*          of the active selection.                                   */
/*                                                                     */
/*          int current_index - This variable contains the current     */
/*          selection.                                                 */
/*                                                                     */
/*          int key - This variable contains the keyboard input from   */
/*          the user.                                                  */
/*                                                                     */
/*          char *menu_buffer - This buffer is used to contain the     */
/*          screen information over which the pull-down menu will       */
/*          display.                                                   */
/*                                                                     */
/* Functions Called : malloc () - This standard 'C' function allocates*/
/*          memory and returns a pointer to the memory allocated.      */
/*                                                                     */
/*          DisplayToBuffer () - This function copies screen data to   */
/*          a buffer.                                                  */
/*                                                                     */
/*          DrawBox () - This function displays a box on the screen.   */
/*                                                                     */
/*          ClearWindow () - This function clears a window on the      */
/*          screen in a given color.                                   */
/*                                                                     */
/*          DisplayString () - This function displays a string on      */
/*          the screen.                                                */
/*                                                                     */
/*          GetKey () - This function returns a keystroke from the     */
/*          keyboard.                                                  */
/*                                                                     */
/*          BufferToDisplay () - This function restores screen data    */
/*          that had been saved to a buffer.                           */
/*                                                                     */
/*          free () - This standard 'C' function frees up memory       */
/*          that was allocated by the malloc () function.              */
/*                                                                     */
/* Logic Flow : The ProcessPullDownMenu () function is called with     */
/*          a pointer to the pull-down menu to process.  The variable*/
```

```
/*              int header_width is calculated to be the width of the    */
/*              header string.  The variable menu_width is set to the    */
/*              length of the header string.  To be able to save the     */
/*              correct screen data, the width of the menu selections and*/
/*              the header need to be calculated. Each selection from     */
/*              pull-down menu is checked to determine what is the        */
/*              maximum width of the menu.  The variable char             */
/*              *menu_buffer is set to the return code from the function */
/*              malloc ().  This function is called with the width of     */
/*              the screen size in bytes to save, which is the menu       */
/*              width divided by four dots to the byte, multiplied by     */
/*              the number of pull-down menu selections plus one,         */
/*              multiplied by the height of a character icon, plus one    */
/*              half of the height of the icon.  The function             */
/*              DisplayToBuffer () is called to save the screen data      */
/*              that will be overwritten by the pull-down menu.  The      */
/*              DrawBox () function is called to draw a box around the    */
/*              pull-down menu selection that is currently active.  This  */
/*              function is called again to draw a box big enough to      */
/*              contain the selections from the pull-down menu.  The      */
/*              function ClearWindow () is called to clear the window     */
/*              where the selections are displayed.  Each selection in    */
/*              the pull-down menu is then displayed on the screen.  The  */
/*              variable index is set to the current selection in the     */
/*              pull-down menu.  The variable row is set to the row       */
/*              where the current selection is to be displayed.  The      */
/*              current selection is displayed on the screen in reverse   */
/*              video and the exit variable is cleared.  While the exit   */
/*              variable has not been changed, do the following.  Set     */
/*              the variable current_index to be equal to index. Set the  */
/*              variable current_row to be equal to row.  The variable    */
/*              key is set to the return code from the function           */
/*              GetKey ().  If key is equal to an UP_ARROW, then the      */
/*              current index is moved up one selection.  If the index    */
/*              is already at the top of the selection list, then the     */
/*              last selection is used.  If key is equal to a DOWN_ARROW,*/
/*              then the current index is moved down one selection. If    */
/*              the index is already at the last selection, then the      */
/*              first selection is used.  If key is the ENTER key, then   */
/*              the selection from the pull-down menu has been selected   */
/*              and the application specific function declared for this   */
/*              selection is called.  If key is equal to ESC, LEFT_ARROW,*/
/*              or RIGHT_ARROW, then the exit flag is set and the pull-   */
/*              down menu is finished.  If the current index changes,     */
/*              then the old selection is dehighlighted, and the new      */
/*              current index is highlighted.  When the pull-down menu    */
/*              is finished, the function BufferToDisplay () is called    */
/*              to restore the screen data to the screen and the memory   */
/*              used is freed.                                            */
/*                                                                        */
/* Exit : The pull-down menu is initialized, displayed, and processed.*/
/*                                                                        */
/*======================================================================*/
```

```
ProcessPullDownMenu (pd)
PULL_DOWN *pd;
{
   #include <malloc.h>

   int  i, menu_width, item_width, header_width, temp_width;
   int  row, current_row, index, current_index, key;
   char *menu_buffer;

   header_width = (strlen (pd->str) * FONTWIDTH) + (FONTWIDTH / 2) + 1;
   menu_width = header_width;
   item_width = 0;
   for (i = 0; i < pd->num_items; i++)
   {
      temp_width = (strlen (pd->item_list[i]) * FONTWIDTH) +
                   (FONTWIDTH / 2) + 1;
      if (temp_width > menu_width) menu_width = temp_width;
      if (temp_width > item_width) item_width = temp_width;
   }
   menu_buffer = malloc (((menu_width / 4) + 2) *
                          (((pd->num_items + 1) * FONTHEIGHT) +
                          (FONTHEIGHT / 2) + 3));
   DisplayToBuffer (pd->r - 1, pd->c - 1, menu_width,
                    ((pd->num_items + 1) * FONTHEIGHT) +
                    (FONTHEIGHT / 2) + 2, menu_buffer);
   DrawBox (pd->r - 1, pd->c - 1, header_width, FONTHEIGHT + 3,
            BLACKDOT);
   DrawBox (pd->r + FONTHEIGHT + 1, pd->c - 1, item_width,
            (pd->num_items * FONTHEIGHT) + (FONTHEIGHT / 2) - 1,
            BLACKDOT);
   ClearWindow (pd->r + FONTHEIGHT + 2, pd->c, item_width - 2,
                (pd->num_items * FONTHEIGHT) + (FONTHEIGHT / 2) - 3,
                WHITE);
   for (i = 0; i < pd->num_items; i++)
      DisplayString (pd->r + (FONTHEIGHT * (i + 1)) + 3, pd->c,
                     pd->item_list[i], BLACK, WHITE);
   index  = pd->start;
   row    = pd->r + (FONTHEIGHT * (index + 1)) + 3;
   DisplayString (row, pd->c + 1, pd->item_list[index], WHITE, BLACK);
   pd->exit = 0;
   do
   {
      current_index = index;
      current_row = row;
      key = GetKey ();
      switch (key)
      {
         case UP_ARROW:
            if (index > 0)
            {
               index--;
               row -= FONTHEIGHT;
            }
```

```
        else
        {
            index = pd->num_items - 1;
            row   = pd->r + (FONTHEIGHT * (index + 1)) + 3;
        }
        break;

    case DOWN_ARROW:
        if (index < (pd->num_items - 1))
        {
            ++index;
            row += FONTHEIGHT;
        }
        else
        {
            index = 0;
            row   = pd->r + FONTHEIGHT + 3;
        }
        break;

    case ENTER:
        pd->start = index;
        (*pd->function) (pd);
        pd->exit = ESC;
        break;

    case ESC:
    case LEFT_ARROW:
    case RIGHT_ARROW:
        pd->exit = key;
        break;

    default:
        for (i = 0; i <= Number_ActionBar_Menus; i++)
            if (key == ActionBar_Hot_Keys[i])
                pd->exit = key;
        break;
    }
    if (index != current_index)
    {
        DisplayString (current_row, pd->c + 1,
                       pd->item_list[current_index], BLACK, WHITE);
        DisplayString (row, pd->c + 1, pd->item_list[index], WHITE,
                       BLACK);
    }
} while (!pd->exit);
pd->start = index;
BufferToDisplay (pd->r - 1, pd->c - 1, menu_width,
                 ((pd->num_items + 1) * FONTHEIGHT) +
                 (FONTHEIGHT / 2) + 1, menu_buffer);
free (menu_buffer);
}
```

The PULLDOWN.C source file contains the function ProcessPullDownMenu ( ). This function is called by ProcessActionBar ( ) to process a pull-down menu associated with the current action bar menu. If the user selects one of the items from the pull-down menu, then an application specific function is called to process this selection. Usually, the application uses a dialog box to do the processing.

SUMMARY

The Menu Library is made up of several different 'C' source files. These source files use include files to define the data structures needed to initialize, display, and process the different types of menus needed. The Menu Library makes extensive use of the CGA Graphics Library functions to draw the menus on the screen.

The overall purpose for creating the Menu Library is to separate the Menu specific functions from the rest of the application. By doing this, the programmer can more easily work on the Menu Library and use it in other applications. This ability alone greatly increases the productivity of the application programmer.

This chapter dealt with the 'C' source files, MENU.C, KEYBOARD.C, ACTION.C, and PULLDOWN.C. These source files contain the functions needed to process and display a primary menu, the action bar, and pull-down menus.

In the next chapter we create the functions that are needed to initialize, display, and process a dialog box. Dialog boxes can be part of a primary menu or they can stand alone. They are used to display and receive information from the user.

Chapter 11

THE MENU LIBRARY 'C' SOURCE FILES FOR DIALOG BOXES

INTRODUCTION

In this chapter we create the source files that process the dialog boxes. Dialog boxes are pop-up menus that display and receive information from the user using push buttons, entry fields, list boxes, check boxes, and radio buttons. The source files DIALOG.C, PUSHBUTN.C, ENTRY.C, GROUPS.C, LISTBOX.C, and MESSAGE.C contain the functions needed to do the processing of the dialog boxes.

Create the DIALOG.C Source File

The DIALOG.C source file contains the functions needed to initialize, display, and process a dialog box. These functions are called by the application whenever it needs to get information from the user.

Create the DIALOG.C source file, type the following statements, and save the file.

```
/*********************************************************************/
/* File : DIALOG.C                                                 */
/*                                                                 */
/* Purpose : This 'C' source file contains the functions needed to */
/*           initialize, display, and process a dialog box.        */
/*                                                                 */
/* Include Files : \graphics\COLORS.H - This include file contains */
/*           the color definitions used by the Menu Library.       */
/*                                                                 */
/*           DIALOG.H - This include file contains the data structure */
/*           definitions that define a dialog box.                 */
/*                                                                 */
/*           DEFINES.H - This include file contains the defined data */
/*           definitions used by the Menu Library functions.       */
/*                                                                 */
```

```
/*          KEYBOARD.H - This include file contains the defined data */
/*          definitions used to determine keyboard input.            */
/*                                                                   */
/* Static Data Definitions : int Field_Num - This variable is used to */
/*          contain the current field number active on the dialog    */
/*          box.                                                      */
/*                                                                    */
/*          int Field_type - This variable is used to contain the    */
/*          current field type that is active.                        */
/*                                                                    */
/*          int Group_Number - This variable is used to determine    */
/*          which group of radio buttons or check boxes are used.     */
/*                                                                    */
/* Functions : InitializeDialogBox () - This function initializes and */
/*          displays a dialog box on the screen.                      */
/*                                                                    */
/*          ProcessDialogBox () - This function processes a dialog    */
/*          box that has been initialized and displayed on the        */
/*          screen.                                                   */
/*                                                                    */
/*          SearchNextField () - This function is called to search    */
/*          for the next logical field in the dialog box.             */
/*                                                                    */
/*          SearchEntryFields () - This function is called to search  */
/*          the entry fields for the next logical field.              */
/*                                                                    */
/*          SearchPushButtons () - This function is called to search  */
/*          the push buttons for the next logical field.              */
/*                                                                    */
/*          SearchGroups () - This function is called to search the   */
/*          groups of radio buttons and check boxes for the next      */
/*          logical field.                                            */
/*                                                                    */
/*          SearchRadioButtons () - This function is called to        */
/*          search a group of radio buttons for the next logical      */
/*          field.                                                    */
/*                                                                    */
/*          SearchCheckBoxes () - This function is called to search   */
/*          a group of check boxes for the next logical field.        */
/*                                                                    */
/********************************************************************/

#include "\graphics\colors.h"
#include "dialog.h"
#include "defines.h"
#include "keyboard.h"

static int Field_Num, Field_Type, Group_Number;
```

Create the DIALOG.C Function — InitializeDialogBox ( )

The InitializeDialogBox ( ) function is called by the application whenever a dialog box needs to be initialized and displayed on the screen. This function saves the screen memory used by the dialog box, initializes, and displays the dialog box. Then control is passed to an application specific function. When control returns, the screen is restored back to its original state.

Edit the DIALOG.C source file, type the following statements, and save the file.

```
/*========================================================================*/
/*                                                                        */
/* Function : InitializeDialogBox (db);                                   */
/*                                                                        */
/* Purpose : This function initializes and displays a dialog box.         */
/*                                                                        */
/* Entry Parameters : DIALOG_BOX *db - A pointer to the dialog box        */
/*          structure to initialize and display.                          */
/*                                                                        */
/* Include Files : <malloc.h> - This standard 'C' include file is         */
/*          used by the memory functions.                                 */
/*                                                                        */
/* Local Data Definitions : char *dialogbox_buffer - This variable is     */
/*          used as a pointer to the screen memory buffer that is         */
/*          saved before displaying the dialog box.                       */
/*                                                                        */
/*          int i - This variable is used to calculate the display        */
/*          location of the header string.                                */
/*                                                                        */
/* Functions Called : malloc () - This standard 'C' function allocates    */
/*          memory and returns a pointer to that memory.                  */
/*                                                                        */
/*          DisplayToBuffer () - This function saves the screen           */
/*          data to a buffer to be restored later.                        */
/*                                                                        */
/*          DrawMenuOutline () - This function displays the menu          */
/*          outline for the dialog box. Note - This function also         */
/*          displays the outline for a primary menu.                      */
/*                                                                        */
/*          DisplayString () - This function displays a string of         */
/*          characters on the screen at a given location and color.       */
/*                                                                        */
/*          ClearWindow () - This function clears a window on the         */
/*          screen in a given color.                                      */
/*                                                                        */
/*          InitializeWorkGroups () - This function initializes           */
/*          the dialog box's work groups of check boxes and/or            */
/*          radio buttons.                                                */
/*                                                                        */
/*          InitializePushButtons () - This function initializes          */
/*          the dialog box's push buttons.                                */
/*                                                                        */
```

```
/*              InitializeEntryFields () - This function initializes    */
/*              the dialog box's entry fields.                          */
/*                                                                      */
/*              InitializeListBox () - This function initializes the    */
/*              dialog box's list boxes.                                */
/*                                                                      */
/*              BufferToDisplay () - This function restores screen data */
/*              that was saved in the given buffer.                     */
/*                                                                      */
/*              free () - This standard 'C' function frees up the       */
/*              memory allocated by malloc ().                          */
/*                                                                      */
/* Logic Flow : The InitializeDialogBox () function is called with a    */
/*              pointer to the dialog box to initialize and display.    */
/*              The standard 'C' function malloc () is called to get    */
/*              the memory needed to save the screen data that will be  */
/*              over-written by the dialog box.  The function call      */
/*              DisplayToBuffer () saves the screen data into the       */
/*              buffer.  The function DrawMenuOutline () is called to    */
/*              draw the border around the dialog box.  The variable    */
/*              int i is calculated to determine the display location   */
/*              of the header string.  The function DisplayString () is */
/*              called to display the header string.  The function      */
/*              ClearWindow () is called to clear the dialog box        */
/*              window area.  If the dialog box contains work groups,   */
/*              then the function InitializeWorkGroups () is called to  */
/*              initialize and display the work groups.  If the dialog  */
/*              box contains push buttons, then the function            */
/*              InitializePushButtons () is called to initialize and    */
/*              display the push buttons.  If the dialog box contains   */
/*              entry fields, then the function InitializeEntryFields ()*/
/*              is called to initialize and display the entry fields.   */
/*              If the dialog box contains list boxes, then the function*/
/*              InitializeListBox () is called to initialize the list   */
/*              box.  At this point, an application specific function    */
/*              is called to take control of the dialog box.  When      */
/*              control is returned, then the function BufferToDisplay()*/
/*              is called to restore the screen data. The standard 'C'  */
/*              function free () is called to free the memory allocated */
/*              by malloc ().                                           */
/*                                                                      */
/* Exit : The dialog box has been initialized, displayed, and exited.   */
/*                                                                      */
/*======================================================================*/

InitializeDialogBox (db)
DIALOG_BOX *db;
{
   #include <malloc.h>

   char    *dialogbox_buffer;
   int i;
```

```
    dialogbox_buffer = malloc (((db->w / 4) + 2) * db->h);
    DisplayToBuffer (db->r, db->c, db->w, db->h, dialogbox_buffer);
    DrawMenuOutline (db->r, db->c, db->w, db->h);
    i = ((db->w - 3) / 2) - ((strlen (db->hdr) * FONTWIDTH) / 2);
    DisplayString (db->r + 4, db->c + i, db->hdr, WHITE, BLACK);
    ClearWindow (db->r + FONTHEIGHT + (FONTHEIGHT / 2) + 1,
                 db->c + (FONTWIDTH / 2) + 1,
                 db->w - (FONTWIDTH + 2),
                 db->h - ((FONTHEIGHT * 2) - 1), WHITE);
    if (db->workarea[0].group_num )
        InitializeWorkGroups (&db->workarea[0]);
    if (db->workarea[0].button_num)
        InitializePushButtons (&db->workarea[0]);
    if (db->workarea[0].entry_num)
        InitializeEntryFields (&db->workarea[0]);
    if (db->workarea[0].box_num)
        InitializeListBox (&db->workarea[0].listbox[0]);
    (*db->function) (db);
    BufferToDisplay (db->r, db->c, db->w, db->h, dialogbox_buffer);
    free (dialogbox_buffer);
}
```

Create the DIALOG.C Function — ProcessDialogBox ( )

The ProcessDialogBox ( ) function is called by the application after the InitializeDialogBox ( ) function has been called. This function controls the dialogue of the dialog box.

Generally, the application first makes a call to the function InitializeDialogBox ( ). When InitializeDialogBox ( ) calls the function that was specified by the application, the application can make changes to the screen or to the data structures before calling the function ProcessDialogBox ( ). In this way the application can gain control of the dialog box after it has been initialized and displayed and before the dialog box has actually been processed. The dialog box also does not get erased from the screen without giving the application a chance to verify the data in the dialog box.

Edit the DIALOG.C source file, type the following statements, and save the file.

```
/*========================================================================*/
/*                                                                        */
/* Function : ProcessDialogBox (db);                                      */
/*                                                                        */
/* Purpose : This function processes a dialog box that has already        */
/*           been initialized and displayed.                             */
/*                                                                        */
/* Entry Parameters : DIALOG_BOX *db - A pointer to the dialog box        */
/*           structure to process.                                       */
/*                                                                        */
/* Local Data Definitions : int number - This variable is used to        */
```

```
/*              contain the current field number being processed.      */
/*                                                                     */
/*              int return_code - This variable is used to contain the */
/*              return code from ProcessEntryField ().                 */
/*                                                                     */
/* Functions Called : SearchNextField () - This function is called     */
/*              to search through the dialog box fields for a given     */
/*              field number.                                          */
/*                                                                     */
/*              ProcessEntryField () - This function is called to      */
/*              process a given entry field.                           */
/*                                                                     */
/*              ProcessPushButton () - This function is called to      */
/*              process the push buttons.                              */
/*                                                                     */
/*              ProcessRadioButtons () - This function is called to    */
/*              process the radio buttons.                             */
/*                                                                     */
/*              ProcessCheckBoxes () - This function is called to      */
/*              process the check boxes.                               */
/*                                                                     */
/* Logic Flow : The ProcessDialogBox () function is called with a      */
/*              pointer to the dialog box to process.  The first field */
/*              that is active is field number 1.  Until the dialog    */
/*              box is exited, the function SearchNextField () is       */
/*              called to locate the field number and type of field    */
/*              to process.  If the field type is ENTRY, then the      */
/*              function ProcessEntryField () is called to process     */
/*              this entry field.  If the return code from this function*/
/*              is ENTER or ESC, then the dialog box is completed.     */
/*              If the return code is CTRL_RIGHT_ARROW or              */
/*              CTRL_DOWN_ARROW, then the field number is incremented   */
/*              to the next field.  If the return code is              */
/*              CTRL_LEFT_ARROW or CTRL_UP_ARROW, then the field number */
/*              is decremented.  If the field type is BUTTONS, then the */
/*              function ProcessPushButtons () is called.              */
/*                                                                     */
/* Exit : The dialog box has been processed.                           */
/*                                                                     */
/*====================================================================*/

ProcessDialogBox (db)
DIALOG_BOX *db;
{
   int    number, return_code;

   number = 1;
   for (;;)
   {
      SearchNextField (db, number);
      switch (Field_Type)
      {
         case ENTRY:
```

```
       return_code = ProcessEntryField (&db->workarea[0],
                                         Field_Num);
    switch (return_code)
    {
       case ENTER:
       case ESC:
          return (return_code);

       case CTRL_RIGHT_ARROW:
       case CTRL_DOWN_ARROW:
       case TAB:
          number++;
          break;

       case CTRL_LEFT_ARROW:
       case CTRL_UP_ARROW:
       case SHIFT_TAB:
          if (number > 0) number--;
          break;
    }
    break;

case BUTTONS:
    return (ProcessPushButton (&db->workarea[0]));

case RADIOS:
    return_code = ProcessRadioButtons (
                     &db->workarea[0].groups[Group_Number],
                     Field_Num);
    switch (return_code)
    {
       case ESC:
          return (return_code);

       case CTRL_RIGHT_ARROW:
       case CTRL_DOWN_ARROW:
       case TAB:
       case RIGHT_ARROW:
       case DOWN_ARROW:
          number++;
          break;

       case CTRL_LEFT_ARROW:
       case CTRL_UP_ARROW:
       case SHIFT_TAB:
       case LEFT_ARROW:
       case UP_ARROW:
          if (number > 0) number--;
          break;
    }
    break;

case BOXES:
```

```
           return_code = ProcessCheckBoxes (
                           &db->workarea[0].groups[Group_Number],
                           Field_Num);
           switch (return_code)
           {
              case ESC:
                 return (return_code);

              case CTRL_RIGHT_ARROW:
              case CTRL_DOWN_ARROW:
              case TAB:
              case RIGHT_ARROW:
              case DOWN_ARROW:
                 number++;
                 break;

              case CTRL_LEFT_ARROW:
              case CTRL_UP_ARROW:
              case SHIFT_TAB:
              case LEFT_ARROW:
              case UP_ARROW:
                 if (number > 0) number--;
                 break;
           }
           break;
      }
   }
}
```

Create the DIALOG.C Function — SearchNextField ( )

The SearchNextField ( ) function is called by the ProcessDialogBox ( ) function to search for a given field number inside of a dialog box.

Edit the DIALOG.C source file, type the following statements, and save the file.

```
/*=======================================================================*/
/*                                                                       */
/* Function : SearchNextField (db, number);                             */
/*                                                                       */
/* Purpose  : This function searches the given dialog box for a given */
/*            field number.                                              */
/*                                                                       */
/* Entry Parameters : DIALOG_BOX *db - A pointer to the dialog box      */
/*            structure to search.                                       */
/*                                                                       */
/*            int number - The field number to search for.              */
/*                                                                       */
/* Local Data Definitions : int i - This variable is used to contain   */
/*            the field number if found.                                 */
/*                                                                       */
/* Functions Called : SearchEntryFields () - This function is called   */
```

```
/*              to search the entry fields for the given field number.  */
/*                                                                       */
/*              SearchPushButtons () - This function is called to search*/
/*              the push buttons for the given field number.            */
/*                                                                       */
/*              SearchGroups () - This function is called to search the  */
/*              work groups of check boxes and radio buttons for the     */
/*              given field number.                                      */
/*                                                                       */
/* Logic Flow : The SearchNextField () function is called with a         */
/*              pointer to the dialog box to search and the field        */
/*              number to search for.  The function SearchEntryFields ()*/
/*              is called to search the entry fields for the given       */
/*              field number.  If the field number is found, then        */
/*              the field type is set to ENTRY, and the field number     */
/*              is saved.  If the field number is not found, then the    */
/*              function SearchPushButtons () is called to search the    */
/*              push buttons for the given field number.  If the field   */
/*              number is not found, then the function SearchGroups ()   */
/*              is called to search the groups of radio buttons and      */
/*              check boxes for the given field number.                  */
/*                                                                       */
/* Exit : The dialog box has been searched for a given field number.     */
/*                                                                       */
/*=====================================================================*/

SearchNextField (db, number)
DIALOG_BOX *db;
int number;
{
   int    i,j,k;

   i = SearchEntryFields (db, number);
   if (i > -1)
   {
      Field_Type = ENTRY;
      Field_Num = i;
      return;
   }
   i = SearchPushButtons (db, number);
   if (i > -1)
   {
      Field_Type = BUTTONS;
      Field_Num = i;
      return;
   }
   i = SearchGroups (db, number);
   if (i > -1)
   {
      Field_Num = i;
      return;
   }
}
```

Create the DIALOG.C Function SearchEntryFields ( )

The SearchEntryFields ( ) function is called to search a dialog box's entry fields for a given field number. If the field number is found, then the field number of the entry field is returned. If it is not found, then a negative one is returned.

Edit the DIALOG.C source file, type the following statements, and save the file.

```
/*====================================================================*/
/*                                                                    */
/* Function : SearchEntryFields (db, number);                         */
/*                                                                    */
/* Purpose  : This function searches a dialog box's entry fields for  */
/*            a given field number.                                   */
/*                                                                    */
/* Entry Parameters : DIALOG_BOX *db - A pointer to the dialog box    */
/*            structure to search.                                    */
/*                                                                    */
/*            int number - The field number for which to search.      */
/*                                                                    */
/* Local Data Definitions : int i - This variable is used as a        */
/*            counter for the number of entry fields.                 */
/*                                                                    */
/* Logic Flow : The SearchEntryFields () function is called with a    */
/*            pointer to the dialog box to search and the field       */
/*            number for which to search.  Check each entry field in  */
/*            the dialog box; if its field number is equal to the     */
/*            one we are looking for, then return its location. If    */
/*            no field is found, then return a negative one.          */
/*                                                                    */
/* Exit : return > -1 : The field was found.                          */
/*        return = -1 : The field was not found.                      */
/*                                                                    */
/*====================================================================*/

SearchEntryFields (db, number)
DIALOG_BOX *db;
int number;
{
   int i;

   for (i = 0; i < db->workarea[0].entry_num; i++)
      if (db->workarea[0].entry[i].field_num == number) return (i);
   return (-1);
}
```

Create the DIALOG.C Function — SearchPushButtons ( )

The SearchPushButtons ( ) function searches a dialog box's push buttons for a given field number. If the field number is found, then its location is returned. If there is no match, then a negative one is returned.

Edit the DIALOG.C source file, type the following statements, and save the file.

```
/*========================================================================*/
/*                                                                        */
/* Routine   : SearchPushButtons (db, number);                            */
/*                                                                        */
/* Purpose : This function searches a dialog box's push buttons for a     */
/*           given field number.                                          */
/*                                                                        */
/* Entry Parameters : DIALOG_BOX *db - A pointer to the dialog box        */
/*           structure to search.                                         */
/*                                                                        */
/*           int number - The field number for which to search.          */
/*                                                                        */
/* Local Data Definitions : int i - This variable is used as a           */
/*           counter for the number of push buttons.                      */
/*                                                                        */
/* Logic Flow : The SearchPushButtons () function is called with a        */
/*           pointer to the dialog box to search and the field            */
/*           number for which to search.  Each push button is             */
/*           checked in the dialog box; if its field number is equal      */
/*           to the one we are looking for, then return its location.     */
/*           If no field is found, then return a negative one.            */
/*                                                                        */
/* Exit : return > -1 : The field was found.                              */
/*        return = -1 : The field was not found.                          */
/*                                                                        */
/*========================================================================*/

SearchPushButtons (db, number)
DIALOG_BOX *db;
int number;
{
    int i;

    for (i = 0; i < db->workarea[0].button_num; i++)
      if (db->workarea[0].buttons[i].field_num == number) return (i);
    return (-1);
}
```

Create the DIALOG.C Function — SearchGroups ( )

The SearchGroups ( ) function is called to search a dialog box's work groups of radio buttons and check boxes. If the field number is found, then its location is returned. If it is not found, then a negative one is returned.

Edit the DIALOG.C source file, type the following statements, and save the file.

```
/*========================================================================*/
/*                                                                        */
/* Function : SearchGroups (db, number);                                  */
/*                                                                        */
```

```
/* Purpose   : This function searches a dialog box's work groups for a */
/*             given field number.                                      */
/*                                                                      */
/* Entry Parameters : DIALOG_BOX *db - A pointer to the dialog box     */
/*             structure to search.                                     */
/*                                                                      */
/*             int number - The field number for which to search.     */
/*                                                                      */
/* Local Data Definitions : int i - This variable is used as a         */
/*             return code from the SearchRadioButtons () function and */
/*             the SearchCheckBoxes () function.                        */
/*                                                                      */
/* Logic Flow : The SearchGroups () function is called with a pointer  */
/*             to the dialog box to search and the field number for    */
/*             which to search.  If the return code from the function  */
/*             SearchRadioButtons () returns a value greater than       */
/*             negative one, then a radio button was found.  If the    */
/*             function SearchCheckBoxes () returns a value greater     */
/*             than negative one, then a check box was found.          */
/*                                                                      */
/* Exit : return > -1 : The field was found.                           */
/*        return = -1 : The field was not found.                       */
/*                                                                      */
/*====================================================================*/

SearchGroups (db, number)
DIALOG_BOX *db;
int number;
{
   int i;

   i = SearchRadioButtons (&db->workarea[0], number);
   if (i > -1)
   {
      Field_Type = RADIOS;
      return (i);
   }
   i = SearchCheckBoxes (&db->workarea[0], number);
   if (i > -1)
   {
      Field_Type = BOXES;
      return (i);
   }
   return (-1);
}
```

Create the DIALOG.C Function — SearchRadioButtons ( )

The SearchRadioButtons ( ) function is called to search a dialog box's work group of radio buttons for a given field number. If the field number was found, then its location is returned. If it was not found, then a negative one is returned.

Edit the DIALOG.C source file, type the following statements, and save the file.

```
/*========================================================================*/
/*                                                                        */
/* Function : SearchRadioButtons (db, number);                            */
/*                                                                        */
/* Purpose  : This function searches a dialog box's radio buttons for     */
/*            a given field number.                                       */
/*                                                                        */
/* Entry Parameters : DIALOG_BOX *db - A pointer to the dialog box        */
/*            structure to search.                                        */
/*                                                                        */
/*            int number - The field number for which to search.         */
/*                                                                        */
/* Local Data Definitions : int i - This variable is used as a           */
/*            counter for the number of radio buttons.                    */
/*                                                                        */
/* Logic Flow : The SearchRadioButtons () function is called to          */
/*            search a dialog box's radio buttons for a given field       */
/*            number.  Each work group is checked to see if it is         */
/*            the radio button type.  If it is, then each radio           */
/*            button in the group is checked to see if it is the          */
/*            field number we are searching for.  If the field number     */
/*            is found, then its location is returned.  If the field      */
/*            number is not found, then a negative one is returned.       */
/*                                                                        */
/* Exit : return > -1 : The field was found.                             */
/*            return = -1 : The field was not found.                      */
/*                                                                        */
/*========================================================================*/

SearchRadioButtons (wa, number)
WORK_AREA *wa;
int number;
{
   int i, j;

   for (i = 0; i < wa->group_num; i++)
   {
      if (wa->groups[i].type == RADIO_BUTTON)
      {
         for (j = 0; j < wa->groups[i].number; j++)
         {
            if (wa->groups[i].fields[j].field_num == number)
            {
               Group_Number = i;
               return (j);
            }
         }
      }
   }
   return (-1);
}
```

Create the DIALOG.C Function — SearchCheckBoxes ( )

The SearchCheckBoxes ( ) function is called to search a dialog box's work group of check boxes for a given field number. If the field number is found, then its location is returned. If it is not found, then a negative one is returned.

Edit the DIALOG.C source file, type the following statements, and save the file.

```
/*===================================================================*/
/*                                                                   */
/* Function : SearchCheckBoxes (db, number);                         */
/*                                                                   */
/* Purpose  : This function searches a dialog box's check boxes for a */
/*            given field number.                                    */
/*                                                                   */
/* Entry Parameters : DIALOG_BOX *db - A pointer to the dialog box   */
/*            structure to search.                                   */
/*                                                                   */
/* Local Data Definitions : int i - This variable is used as a       */
/*            counter for the number of entry fields.                */
/*                                                                   */
/* Logic Flow : The SearchCheckBoxes () function is called to search */
/*            a dialog box's check boxes for a given field number.   */
/*            Each work group is checked to see it is the check box  */
/*            type.  Each group of check boxes is checked to see if  */
/*            it is the field number we are searching for.  If the   */
/*            field number is found, then its location is returned.  */
/*            If the field number is not found, then a negative one  */
/*            is returned.                                           */
/*                                                                   */
/* Exit : return > -1 : The field was found.                         */
/*        return = -1 : The field was not found.                     */
/*                                                                   */
/*===================================================================*/

SearchCheckBoxes (wa, number)
WORK_AREA *wa;
int number;
{
   int i, j;

   for (i = 0; i < wa->group_num; i++)
   {
      if (wa->groups[i].type == CHECK_BOX)
      {
         for (j = 0; j < wa->groups[i].number; j++)
         {
            if (wa->groups[i].fields[j].field_num == number)
            {
               Group_Number = i;
               return (j);
```

```
                }
              }
            }
          }
      return (-1);
}
```

Create the PUSHBUTN.C Source File

The PUSHBUTN.C source file contains the functions needed to initialize, display, and process the push buttons. Push buttons are large buttons that appear in a dialog box. They will usually allow the user to accept or cancel a particular dialog box, but can also contain other information.

Create the PUSHBUTN.C source file, type the following statements, and save the file.

```
/*********************************************************************/
/* File    : PUSHBUTN.C                                           */
/*                                                                */
/* Purpose : This 'C' source file contains the functions needed to */
/*           initialize, display, and process push buttons.       */
/*                                                                */
/* Include Files : \graphics\COLORS.H - This include file contains */
/*           the color definitions used by the Menu Library       */
/*           functions.                                           */
/*                                                                */
/*           DIALOG.H - This include file contains the data structure */
/*           definitions that define a dialog box.                */
/*                                                                */
/*           DEFINES.H - This include file contains the defined data */
/*           definitions used by the Menu Library functions.      */
/*                                                                */
/*           KEYBOARD.H - This include file contains the defined data */
/*           definitions used to determine keyboard input.        */
/*                                                                */
/* Functions : InitializePushButtons () - This function initializes */
/*           and displays a group of push buttons on the screen.  */
/*                                                                */
/*           DisplayPushButton () - This function is called to     */
/*           display a given push button on the screen.           */
/*                                                                */
/*           ButtonOutline () - This function is called to draw the */
/*           outline around a push button.                        */
/*                                                                */
/*           ProcessPushButton () - This function is called to     */
/*           process a group of push buttons.                     */
/*                                                                */
/*********************************************************************/
```

```
#include "\graphics\colors.h"
#include "dialog.h"
#include "defines.h"
#include "keyboard.h"
```

Create the PUSHBUTN.C Function — InitializePushButtons ( )

The InitializePushButtons ( ) function is passed a pointer to the dialog box's work area. Each push button in the work area is displayed on the screen. This function is called by the Menu ( ) function or the InitializeDialogBox ( ) function to initialize and display a given set of push buttons.

Edit the PUSHBUTN.C source file, type the following statements, and save the file.

```
/*===================================================================*/
/*                                                                   */
/* Function : InitializePushButtons (wa)                             */
/*                                                                   */
/* Purpose  : This function initializes and displays a group of push */
/*            buttons on the screen.                                 */
/*                                                                   */
/* Entry Parameters : WORK_AREA *wa - A pointer to the dialog box's  */
/*            work area structure.                                   */
/*                                                                   */
/* Local Data Definitions : int i - This variable is used as a       */
/*            counter for the number of push buttons.                */
/*                                                                   */
/* Functions Called : DisplayPushButton () - This function is called */
/*            to display a given push button on the screen.          */
/*                                                                   */
/* Logic Flow : The InitializePushButtons () function is called with */
/*            a pointer to the dialog box's work area.  Each push     */
/*            button in the dialog box is displayed on the screen.    */
/*                                                                   */
/* Exit : The dialog box's push buttons are initialized and displayed */
/*        on the screen.                                             */
/*                                                                   */
/*===================================================================*/

InitializePushButtons (wa)
WORK_AREA *wa;
{
   int   i;

   for (i = 0; i < wa->button_num; i++) DisplayPushButton (wa, i);
}
```

Create the PUSHBUTN.C Function — DisplayPushButton ( )

The DisplayPushButton ( ) function is called to display a given push button on the screen. If the push button is the active push button, then it is displayed with a double line around it instead of a single line.

Edit the PUSHBUTN.C source file, type the following statements, and save the file.

```
/*========================================================================*/
/*                                                                        */
/* Function : DisplayPushButtons (wa, index)                              */
/*                                                                        */
/* Purpose  : This function displays a given push button on the           */
/*                screen.                                                  */
/*                                                                        */
/* Entry Parameters : WORK_AREA *wa - A pointer to the dialog box's        */
/*                work area structure.                                    */
/*                                                                        */
/*                int index - The push button number to display.           */
/*                                                                        */
/* Local Data Definitions : int r - This variable is used as the row      */
/*                coordinate at which to display the push button.          */
/*                                                                        */
/*                int c - This variable is used as the column coordinate  */
/*                at which to display the push button.                    */
/*                                                                        */
/*                int w - This variable is used as the width of the push  */
/*                button to display.                                       */
/*                                                                        */
/*                int h - This variable is used as the height of the       */
/*                push button to display.                                  */
/*                                                                        */
/*                char *str - This variable is used to contain the string */
/*                to display inside of the push button.                    */
/*                                                                        */
/* Functions Called : ClearWindow () - This function is called to          */
/*                clear a window large enough to display the push button. */
/*                                                                        */
/*                ButtonOutline () - This function draws an outline of     */
/*                a push button on the screen.                             */
/*                                                                        */
/*                DisplayString () - This function displays the push       */
/*                button string on the screen.                            */
/*                                                                        */
/*                DisplayCursor () - This function displays an underline   */
/*                under the first character of the active push button.     */
/*                                                                        */
/* Logic Flow : The DisplayPushButton() function is called with a         */
/*                pointer to the dialog box's work area and the push       */
/*                button number to display.  The variables int r, int c,  */
/*                and int h, are set to the push button's upper left-hand  */
/*                row and column coordinates and the height of the push    */
/*                button.  The variable char *str is assigned to the       */
```

```
/*                push button string to display.  The variable int w is  */
/*                set to the width of the push button.  The function     */
/*                ClearWindow () is called to clear a window on the       */
/*                screen for the push button.  If the push button is      */
/*                the active push button, then the function               */
/*                ButtonOutline () is called to display a double outline  */
/*                around the push button, else, it is called to display   */
/*                only a single outline.  The function DisplayString ()   */
/*                is called to display the push button string inside of   */
/*                the push button outline.  If the push button is the     */
/*                active push button, then the function DisplayCursor ()   */
/*                is called to display an underline underneath the first  */
/*                character of the push button.                           */
/*                                                                        */
/* Exit : The Dialog Box's Push Button is displayed on the screen.        */
/*                                                                        */
/*======================================================================*/

DisplayPushButton (wa, index)
WORK_AREA *wa;
int index;
{
    int    r,c,w,h;
    char *str;

    r = wa->buttons[index].r;
    c = wa->buttons[index].c;
    h = FONTHEIGHT + 3;
    str = wa->buttons[index].label;
    w = (strlen (str) * FONTWIDTH) + 8;
    ClearWindow (r - 1, c - 1, w + 3, h + 3, WHITE);
    if (wa->current_button == index) ButtonOutline (r, c, w, h, 1);
    else ButtonOutline (r, c, w, h, 0);
    DisplayString (r + 2, c + 5,  str, BLACK, WHITE);
    if (wa->current_button == index)
        DisplayCursor ( r + 2, c + 5, *str, BLACK, WHITE);
}
```

Create the PUSHBUTN.C Function — ButtonOutline ( )

The ButtonOutline ( ) function is called to display a push button's outline on the screen. There are two types of push button outlines: a single line around it, or a double line around it. The double line indicates that the push button is the active button, i.e., if Enter is pressed, then this button is the one that was selected.

Edit the PUSHBUTN.C source file, type the following statements, and save the file.

```
/*======================================================================*/
/*                                                                        */
/* Function : ButtonOutline (r, c, w, h, t)                               */
/*                                                                        */
```

```
/* Purpose  : This function displays a push button outline at the    */
/*            given location and type.                               */
/*                                                                   */
/* Entry Parameters : int r - The upper left-hand row coordinate of  */
/*            the push button outline.                               */
/*                                                                   */
/*            int c - The upper left-hand column coordinate of the   */
/*            push button outline.                                   */
/*                                                                   */
/*            int w - The width of the push button outline.          */
/*                                                                   */
/*            int h - The height of the push button outline.         */
/*                                                                   */
/*            int t - The type of push button outline to draw.       */
/*                                                                   */
/* Functions Called : HLine () - This function is called to display  */
/*            a horizontal line on the screen.                       */
/*                                                                   */
/*            DisplayDot () - This function is called to display a   */
/*            dot on the screen.                                     */
/*                                                                   */
/*            VLine () - This function is called to display a        */
/*            vertical line on the screen.                           */
/*                                                                   */
/* Logic Flow : The ButtonOutline () function is called with the     */
/*            upper left-hand row and column coordinates, the width  */
/*            and height, and the type of push button outline to     */
/*            display.  The HLine (), DisplayDot (), and VLine ()    */
/*            functions are called to display a single line outline  */
/*            on the screen.  If the type of button outline is one,  */
/*            then another push button outline is drawn indicating   */
/*            that this push button is the active push button.       */
/*                                                                   */
/* Exit : The dialog box's push button outline is displayed.         */
/*                                                                   */
/*=================================================================*/

ButtonOutline (r, c, w, h, t)
int   r, c, w, h, t;
{
   HLine (r, c + 2, w - 3, BLACK);
   DisplayDot (r + 1, c + 1, BLACKDOT);
   DisplayDot (r + 1, c + w - 1, BLACKDOT);
   VLine (r + 2, c, h - 3, BLACK);
   VLine (r + 2, c + w, h - 3, BLACK);
   DisplayDot (r + h - 1, c + 1, BLACKDOT);
   DisplayDot (r + h - 1, c + w - 1, BLACKDOT);
   HLine (r + h, c + 2, w - 3, BLACK);
   if (t == 1)
   {
      r--;
      c--;
      w += 2;
```

```
        h += 2;
        HLine (r, c + 2, w - 3, BLACK);
        DisplayDot (r + 1, c + 1, BLACKDOT);
        DisplayDot (r + 1, c + w - 1, BLACKDOT);
        VLine (r + 2, c, h - 3, BLACK);
        VLine (r + 2, c + w, h - 3, BLACK);
        DisplayDot (r + h - 1, c + 1, BLACKDOT);
        DisplayDot (r + h - 1, c + w - 1, BLACKDOT);
        HLine (r + h, c + 2, w - 3, BLACK);
    }
}
```

Create the PUSHBUTN.C Function — ProcessPushButton ( )

The ProcessPushButton ( ) function is called to process a group of push buttons in a dialog box. Basically, all that this means is that the active push button can be changed at this time, or one of the push buttons can be selected.

Edit the PUSHBUTN.C source file, type the following statements, and save the file.

```
/*======================================================================*/
/*                                                                      */
/* Function : ProcessPushButton (wa)                                    */
/*                                                                      */
/* Purpose  : This function processes a group of push buttons in a      */
/*            dialog box.                                               */
/*                                                                      */
/* Entry Parameters : WORK_AREA *wa - A pointer to the dialog box's     */
/*            work area containing the push buttons.                    */
/*                                                                      */
/* Local Data Definitions : int cur_button - This variable is used to   */
/*            indicate which push button is currently active.           */
/*                                                                      */
/*            int key - The variable contains the keystroke value       */
/*            from the keyboard.                                        */
/*                                                                      */
/* Functions Called : GetKey () - This function is called to return     */
/*            a keystroke from the keyboard.                            */
/*                                                                      */
/*            DisplayPushButton () - This function is called to         */
/*            display a push button on the screen.                      */
/*                                                                      */
/* Logic Flow : The ProcessPushButton () function is called with a      */
/*            pointer to the dialog box's work area containing the      */
/*            push buttons to process. The variable int cur_button      */
/*            is set to the current push button.  Then, while the       */
/*            key returned from the function GetKey () is not equal      */
/*            to Enter or Esc, do the following.  If the key is a        */
/*            LEFT_ARROW, then the current push button is turned off     */
/*            and redisplayed.  Then the current push button is moved    */
/*            to the left.  If there are no more push buttons to the     */
/*            left, then the rightmost push button is set to the        */
```

```
/*              currently active push button.  The current push button  */
/*              is then displayed.  If the key returned is a            */
/*              RIGHT_ARROW, then the same procedure is performed,       */
/*              except that the current push button is moved to the     */
/*              right.                                                   */
/*                                                                      */
/* Exit : Return - The Enter or the Esc key depending on which one      */
/*        was pressed.                                                  */
/*                                                                      */
/*====================================================================*/

ProcessPushButton (wa)
WORK_AREA *wa;
{
   int   cur_button;
   int   key;

   cur_button = wa->current_button;
   do
   {
      switch ((key = getkey ()))
      {
         case LEFT_ARROW:
         case CTRL_LEFT_ARROW:
         case SHIFT_TAB:
            wa->current_button = -1;
            DisplayPushButton (wa, cur_button);
            cur_button--;
            if (cur_button < 0) cur_button = wa->button_num - 1;
            wa->current_button = cur_button;
            DisplayPushButton (wa, cur_button);
            break;

         case RIGHT_ARROW:
         case CTRL_RIGHT_ARROW:
         case TAB:
            wa->current_button = -1;
            DisplayPushButton (wa, cur_button);
            cur_button++;
            if (cur_button == wa->button_num) cur_button = 0;
            wa->current_button = cur_button;
            DisplayPushButton (wa, cur_button);
            break;
      }
   } while (key != ENTER && key != ESC);
   return (key);
}
```

Create the ENTRY.C Source File

The ENTRY.C source file contains the functions needed to initialize, display, and process an entry field. An entry field is a type of dialog box field that allows the user to input strings of data.

Create the ENTRY.C source file, type the following statements, and save the file.

```
/******************************************************************/
/*                                                                */
/* File : ENTRY.C                                                 */
/*                                                                */
/* Purpose : This 'C' source file contains the function needed to */
/*           initialize, display, and process entry fields.       */
/*                                                                */
/* Include Files : \graphics\COLORS.H - This include file contains */
/*           the color definitions used by the Menu Library functions.*/
/*                                                                */
/*           DIALOG.H - This include file contains the data structure */
/*           definitions that define a dialog box.                */
/*                                                                */
/*           DEFINES.H - This include file contains the defined data */
/*           definitions used by the Menu Library functions.      */
/*                                                                */
/*           KEYBOARD.H - This include file contains the defined data */
/*           definitions used to determine keyboard input.        */
/*                                                                */
/* Functions : InitializeEntryFields () - This function initializes */
/*           a dialog box's entry fields.                         */
/*                                                                */
/*           DisplayEntryField () - This function displays an entry */
/*           field on the screen.                                 */
/*                                                                */
/*           ProcessEntryField () - This function processes a given */
/*           entry field.                                         */
/*                                                                */
/******************************************************************/

#include "\graphics\colors.h"
#include "dialog.h"
#include "defines.h"
#include "keyboard.h"
```

Create the ENTRY.C Function — InitializeEntryFields ( )

The InitializeEntryFields ( ) function initializes and displays a group of entry fields from a given dialog box on the screen. The function is called from the Menu ( ) function and the InitializeDialogBox ( ) function to initialize and display a given entry field on the screen.

Edit the ENTRY.C source file, type the following statements, and save the file.

```
/*=====================================================================*/
/*                                                                     */
/* Function : InitializeEntryFields (wa);                              */
/*                                                                     */
/* Purpose  : This function initializes and displays a group of        */
/*            entry fields on the screen.                              */
/*                                                                     */
/* Entry Parameters : WORK_AREA *wa - A pointer to the dialog box's    */
/*            work area containing the entry fields.                   */
/*                                                                     */
/* Local Data Definitions : int i - This variable is used as a         */
/*            counter for the number of entry fields.                  */
/*                                                                     */
/* Functions Called : DisplayEntryField () - This function is called   */
/*            to display a given entry field.                          */
/*                                                                     */
/* Logic Flow : The InitializeEntryFields () function is called with   */
/*            a pointer to the work area of the dialog box containing  */
/*            the entry fields to initialize and display.  Each entry  */
/*            field is displayed by calling the DisplayEntryField ()   */
/*            function.                                                 */
/*                                                                     */
/* Exit : The entry fields are initialized and displayed.              */
/*                                                                     */
/*=====================================================================*/

InitializeEntryFields (wa)
WORK_AREA *wa;
{
   int i;

   for (i = 0; i < wa->entry_num; i++) DisplayEntryField (wa, i, 0);
}
```

Create the ENTRY.C Function — DisplayEntryField ( )

The DisplayEntryField ( ) function is called to display a given entry field from the dialog box on the screen. This function is called with a pointer to the work area containing the entry field, the entry field's location, and the type of line to draw around the entry field box.

Edit the ENTRY.C source file, type the following statements, and save the file.

```
/*=====================================================================*/
/*                                                                     */
/* Function : DisplayEntryField (wa, number, type);                    */
/*                                                                     */
/* Purpose  : This function displays a given entry field on the        */
/*            screen.                                                  */
/*                                                                     */
/* Entry Parameters : WORK_AREA *wa - A pointer to the dialog box's    */
```

```
/*           work area containing the entry fields.                 */
/*                                                                  */
/*           int num - The entry field number to display.           */
/*                                                                  */
/*           int type - The type of entry field to display,         */
/*           highlighted or not highlighted.                        */
/*                                                                  */
/* Functions Called : DisplayString () - This function is called to */
/*           display the entry field label on the screen.           */
/*                                                                  */
/*           ClearWindow () - This function is called to clear the   */
/*           entry field window area on the screen.                 */
/*                                                                  */
/*           DrawBox () - This function is called to draw a box      */
/*           around the entry field input window.                   */
/*                                                                  */
/*           DisplayStrNum () - This function is called to display   */
/*           the entry field data buffer.                           */
/*                                                                  */
/* Logic Flow : The DisplayEntryField () function is called with a   */
/*           pointer to the work area of the dialog box containing   */
/*           the entry field to display.  It is also passed the      */
/*           entry field number to display, along with the type of   */
/*           display to use.  The function DisplayString () is called*/
/*           to display the label associated with the entry field.   */
/*           The function ClearWindow () is called to clear the      */
/*           window area of the entry field.  The function DrawBox ()*/
/*           is called to draw a box around the entry field buffer   */
/*           area.  If the entry field is to be highlighted, then    */
/*           another box is drawn to indicate that this entry field  */
/*           is the one currently being edited.  If the entry field  */
/*           buffer contains data, then the function DisplayStrNum ()*/
/*           is called to display the entry field buffer.            */
/*                                                                  */
/* Exit : The entry field is displayed on the screen.               */
/*                                                                  */
/*================================================================*/

DisplayEntryField (wa, num, type)
WORK_AREA *wa;
int num, type;
{
   DisplayString (wa->entry[num].label_row, wa->entry[num].label_col,
                  wa->entry[num].label, BLACK, WHITE);
   ClearWindow (wa->entry[num].box_row, wa->entry[num].box_col,
                wa->entry[num].box_width, wa->entry[num].box_height,
                WHITE);
   DrawBox (wa->entry[num].box_row, wa->entry[num].box_col,
            wa->entry[num].box_width, wa->entry[num].box_height, BLACK);
   if (type == HIGHLIGHT)
   {
      DrawBox (wa->entry[num].box_row + 1, wa->entry[num].box_col + 1,
               wa->entry[num].box_width - 2,
```

```
                   wa->entry[num].box_height - 2, BLACK);
   }
   if(wa->entry[num].buffer != 0)
      DisplayStrNum (wa->entry[num].box_row + 2,
                     wa->entry[num].box_col + 3,
                     wa->entry[num].buffer, wa- >entry[num].line_length,
                     BLACK, WHITE);
}
```

Create the ENTRY.C Function — ProcessEntryField ( )

The ProcessEntryField ( ) function is called to process a given entry field. This function accepts keyboard input and places it into the entry field buffer data stream.

Edit the ENTRY.C source file, type the following statements, and save the file.

```
/*======================================================================*/
/*                                                                      */
/* Function : ProcessEntryField (wa, number);                          */
/*                                                                      */
/* Purpose  : This function processes a given entry field.             */
/*                                                                      */
/* Entry Parameters : WORK_AREA *wa - A pointer to the dialog box's    */
/*           work area containing the entry fields.                    */
/*                                                                      */
/*           int number - The entry field number to process.          */
/*                                                                      */
/* Include Files : <stdio.h> - This standard 'C' include file contains*/
/*           the 'C' standard input/output functions.                  */
/*                                                                      */
/*           <string.h> - This standard 'C' include file contains     */
/*           the 'C' standard string functions.                        */
/*                                                                      */
/*           <malloc.h> - This standard 'C' include file contains      */
/*           the memory allocation functions.                          */
/*                                                                      */
/* Local Data Definitions : int i - This variable is used as a         */
/*           temporary variable.                                        */
/*                                                                      */
/*           char *buffer - This variable is used as a pointer to      */
/*           the entry field buffer to process.                        */
/*                                                                      */
/*           char *tmp_buf - This variable is used to contain the      */
/*           starting entry field buffer data.                         */
/*                                                                      */
/*           int row - The current row coordinate of the entry         */
/*           field buffer display.                                     */
/*                                                                      */
/*           int column - This variable is used to contain the         */
/*           current column coordinate of the entry field buffer       */
/*           character the cursor is currently on.                     */
/*                                                                      */
```

```
/*              int length - This variable contains the maximum length  */
/*              of the entry field buffer.                              */
/*                                                                      */
/*              int foreground - This variable contains the current     */
/*              foreground color of the entry field buffer.             */
/*                                                                      */
/*              int background - This variable contains the current     */
/*              background color of the entry field buffer.             */
/*                                                                      */
/*              int key - This variable contains the keystroke returned */
/*              from the keyboard.                                      */
/*                                                                      */
/*              int index - This variable contains the current index    */
/*              into the entry field data buffer.                       */
/*                                                                      */
/*              int insert_flag - This variable is set to toggle from   */
/*              inserting data or overwriting the data into the entry   */
/*              field data buffer.                                      */
/*                                                                      */
/*              int break_flag - This variable is used to determine     */
/*              when the ProcessEntryField () function is finished.     */
/*                                                                      */
/*              int display_start - This variable is used to contain    */
/*              the starting index of the entry field buffer display.   */
/*                                                                      */
/*              int display_end - This variable is used to contain the  */
/*              ending index into the entry field buffer display.       */
/*                                                                      */
/*              int loc - This variable is used to determine the        */
/*              current location of the cursor in the display box.      */
/*                                                                      */
/* Functions Called : DisplayEntryField () - This function is called    */
/*              to display an entry field on the screen.                */
/*                                                                      */
/*              malloc () - This function is called to allocate memory  */
/*              for the temporary buffer used to process an entry field.*/
/*                                                                      */
/*              strcpy () - This function is called to copy the entry   */
/*              field buffer into the temporary buffer.                 */
/*                                                                      */
/*              DisplayStrNum () - This function is called to display    */
/*              the part of the entry field buffer that can currently   */
/*              be seen on the screen.                                  */
/*                                                                      */
/*              DisplayCursor () - This function is called to display    */
/*              an underline underneath the current character in the    */
/*              entry field buffer.                                     */
/*                                                                      */
/*              GetKey () - This function is called to return a         */
/*              keystroke from the keyboard.                            */
/*                                                                      */
/*              DisplayChar () - This function is called to display     */
/*              an individual character on the screen.                  */
```

```
/*                                                              */
/*            strlen () - This function is called to determine the   */
/*            length of a given string.                         */
/*                                                              */
/*            free () - This function is called to free the memory   */
/*            allocated for the temporary buffer.               */
/*                                                              */
/* Logic Flow : The ProcessEntryField () function is called with a   */
/*            pointer to the work area of a dialog box containing the */
/*            entry field to process along with the entry field */
/*            number to process.  The variables int insert_flag,     */
/*            int loc, int index, int break_flag, and int       */
/*            display_start are set to zero.  The variable int   */
/*            display_end is set to the number of characters that are */
/*            displayable on the screen at one time.  The variable   */
/*            char *buffer is set to point at the entry field data   */
/*            buffer to process.  The variables int row and int column*/
/*            are set to the starting row and column of the entry    */
/*            field data buffer display.  The variable length is set */
/*            to the maximum number of characters allowed in the     */
/*            buffer.  The current foreground and background colors   */
/*            are set to WHITE and BLACK.  The DisplayEntryField ()   */
/*            function is called to display this entry field as the  */
/*            active entry field.  The function malloc () is called  */
/*            to allocate memory to place a copy of the entry field  */
/*            buffer before editing it.  The function strcpy () is    */
/*            called to copy the entry field buffer into the buffer  */
/*            just allocated.  The DisplayStrNum () function is       */
/*            called to display the entry field buffer data.  The    */
/*            function DisplayCursor () is called to underline the   */
/*            current character in the display, i.e., the character  */
/*            that will be overwritten by the next keystroke or where */
/*            the next character will be added.  While the break_flag */
/*            is equal to zero, do the following.  Call the GetKey () */
/*            function to return a keystroke from the keyboard. If    */
/*            the key is Esc, then copy the original entry field      */
/*            data buffer from the temporary buffer back into the    */
/*            entry field data buffer and set the break_flag to exit. */
/*            If the key is either a BACKSPACE or a LEFT_ARROW and if */
/*            the index is not already at the beginning of the buffer,*/
/*            do the following.  If the cursor is already at the      */
/*            first displayable character on the screen, then move    */
/*            to the left one character and display the string on     */
/*            the screen.  If the cursor is not on the first          */
/*            displayable character, then move the cursor over one    */
/*            character on the screen.  If the key is a RIGHT_ARROW   */
/*            and the cursor is not already at the end of the string, */
/*            then do the following.  If the cursor is at the right-  */
/*            most displayable character on the screen, then advance  */
/*            one character to the right and display the string.      */
/*            If the cursor is not on the rightmost displayable       */
/*            character, then move the cursor over one character to   */
/*            the right.  If the key is either HOME, PGUP, CTRL_HOME, */
```

```
/*           or CTRL_PGUP, then move the cursor to the beginning of    */
/*           the entry field display buffer.  If the key is either     */
/*           ENTER, CTRL_UP_ARROW, CTRL_DOWN_ARROW, CTRL_LEFT_ARROW,    */
/*           or CTRL_RIGHT_ARROW, then set the break_flag to exit.      */
/*           If the key is either END, PGDN, CTRL_END, or CTRL_PGDN,    */
/*           then move the cursor to the end of the Entry Field         */
/*           display buffer.  If the key is INSERT, then toggle the     */
/*           insert_flag On or Off.  If the key is DELETE and the       */
/*           entry field buffer is not empty, then delete the current*/
/*           character from the data buffer and display the string.     */
/*           If the key is none of the above and the key is             */
/*           displayable and the buffer is not full, then do the        */
/*           following.  If the insert_flag is on, insert the           */
/*           character into the data buffer.  If the insert_flag is     */
/*           off, overwrite this character over the current             */
/*           character.  When the break_flag is set, the function       */
/*           free () is called to free the memory allocated for the     */
/*           temporary buffer.  The function DisplayEntryField ()       */
/*           is called to dehighlight the entry field in the            */
/*           dialog box.  The function then returns to the caller the*/
/*           key that caused the exit from the ProcessEntryField ()     */
/*           function.                                                  */
/*                                                                      */
/* Exit : The given entry field is processed.                          */
/*                                                                      */
/*====================================================================*/

ProcessEntryField (wa, number)
WORK_AREA *wa;
int number;
{
    #include   <stdio.h>
    #include   <string.h>
    #include   <malloc.h>

    int    i;
    char   *buffer, *tmp_buf;
    int    row, column, length, foreground, background;
    int    key, index, insert_flag;
    int    break_flag;
    int    display_start, display_end, loc;

    insert_flag = 0;
    loc = 0;
    index = 0;
    break_flag = 0;
    display_start = 0;
    display_end = wa->entry[number].line_length;
    buffer = wa->entry[number].buffer,
    row = wa->entry[number].box_row + 2;
    column = wa->entry[number].box_col + 3;
    length = wa->entry[number].buffer_length;
    foreground = BLACK;
```

```
background = WHITE;
DisplayEntryField (wa, number, HIGHLIGHT);
tmp_buf = malloc (length + 1);
strcpy (tmp_buf, buffer);
DisplayStrNum (row, column, buffer + display_start,
                display_end - display_start, foreground, background);
DisplayCursor (row, column, *buffer, foreground, background);
do
{
    key = getkey ();
    switch (key)
    {
        case ESC:
            strcpy (buffer, tmp_buf);
            break_flag = 1;
            break;

        case BACKSPACE:
        case LEFT_ARROW:
            if (index)
            {
                if (display_start)
                {
                    --display_start;
                    --display_end;
                    DisplayStrNum (row, column, buffer + display_start,
                                    display_end-display_start,
                                    foreground, background);
                }
                else
                {
                    if (*(buffer + index) == 0)
                        DisplayChar (row, (loc * FONTWIDTH) + column, ' ',
                                    foreground, background);
                    else
                        DisplayChar (row, (loc * FONTWIDTH) + column,
                                    *(buffer + index), foreground,
                                    background);
                    --loc;
                }
                --index;
                DisplayCursor (row, (loc * FONTWIDTH) + column,
                                *(buffer + index), foreground, background);
            }
            break;

        case RIGHT_ARROW:
            if (index < length && *(buffer + index) != 0)
            {
                if (index == (display_end - 1))
                {
                    ++display_start;
                    ++display_end;
```

```
                    DisplayStrNum (row, column, buffer + display_start,
                                   display_end-display_start,
                                   foreground, background);
               }
               else
               {
                    DisplayChar (row, (loc * FONTWIDTH) + column,
                                 *(buffer + index), foreground,
                                 background);
                    ++loc;
               }
               ++index;
               if (*(buffer + index) == 0)
                    DisplayCursor (row, (loc * FONTWIDTH) + column, ' ',
                                   foreground, background);
               else DisplayCursor (row, (loc * FONTWIDTH) + column,
                                   *(buffer + index), foreground,
                                   background);
          }
          break;

     case HOME:
     case PGUP:
     case CTRL_HOME:
     case CTRL_PGUP:
          index = 0;
          DisplayCursor (row, column, *(buffer + index),
                         foreground, background);
          break;

     case ENTER:
     case CTRL_UP_ARROW:
     case CTRL_DOWN_ARROW:
     case CTRL_LEFT_ARROW:
     case CTRL_RIGHT_ARROW:
     case TAB:
     case SHIFT_TAB:
          break_flag = 1;
          break;

     case END:
     case PGDN:
     case CTRL_END:
     case CTRL_PGDN:
          index = strlen (buffer);
          DisplayCursor (row, column + (loc * FONTWIDTH),
                         *(buffer + index),
                         foreground, background);
          break;

     case INSERT:
          insert_flag = !insert_flag;
          break;
```

```
case DELETE:
   if (index < strlen (buffer))
   {
      strcpy (buffer + index, buffer + index + 1);
      if (loc < (display_end - 1))
         DisplayStrNum (row, column, buffer + display_start,
                        display_end - display_start,
                        foreground, background);
      if (strlen(buffer) < display_end)
         DisplayChar (row,
                      column + (strlen (buffer) * FONTWIDTH),
                      ' ', foreground, background);
      if (*(buffer + index) == 0)
         DisplayCursor (row, (loc * FONTWIDTH) + column, ' ',
                        foreground, background);
      else DisplayCursor (row, (loc * FONTWIDTH) + column,
                          *(buffer + index), foreground,
                          background);
   }
   break;

default:
   if (key > 0x1F && key < 0x7F && index < length)
   {
      if (insert_flag)
      {
         if (index < length)
         {
            buffer[length - 1] = 0;
            i = strlen (buffer + index) + 1;
            while (i--)
               (buffer + index)[i + 1] = (buffer + index)[i];
            *(buffer + index) = ' ';
            if (loc < (display_end - 1))
               DisplayStrNum (row, column,
                              buffer + display_start,
                              display_end - display_start,
                              foreground, background);
            DisplayCursor (row, column + (loc * FONTWIDTH),
                           *(buffer + index), foreground,
                           background);
         }
      }
      if (buffer[index] == 0) buffer[index + 1] = 0;
      buffer[index] = key;
      if (index == (display_end - 1))
      {
         ++display_start;
         ++display_end;
         DisplayStrNum (row, column, buffer + display_start,
                        display_end - display_start,
                        foreground, background);
```

```
                }
                else
                {
                    DisplayChar (row, (loc * FONTWIDTH) + column, key,
                                foreground, background);
                    ++loc;
                }
                ++index;
                if (*(buffer + index) == 0)
                    DisplayCursor (row, (loc * FONTWIDTH) + column, ' ',
                                foreground, background);
                else DisplayCursor (row, (loc * FONTWIDTH) + column,
                                    *(buffer + index), foreground,
                                    background);
            }
            break;
        }
    } while (break_flag == 0);
    free (tmp_buf);
    DisplayEntryField (wa, number, NO_HIGHLIGHT);
    return (key);
}
```

Create the GROUPS.C Source File

The GROUPS.C source file contains the functions needed to initialize, display, and process groups of check boxes and radio buttons.

Check boxes are groups of similar items that can be selected. A check box can be either OFF or ON. Groups of check boxes can have any combination of OFF or ON check boxes.

Radio buttons are groups of related items that can be selected, but only ONE item can be ON at any one time.

Create the GROUPS.C source file, type the following statements, and save the file.

```
/**********************************************************************/
/* File : GROUPS.C                                                    */
/*                                                                    */
/* Purpose : This 'C' source file contains the functions needed to    */
/*           initialize, display, and process groups of check boxes   */
/*           and radio buttons.                                       */
/*                                                                    */
/* Include Files : \graphics\COLORS.H - This include file contains     */
/*           the color definitions used by the Menu Library           */
/*           functions.                                               */
/*                                                                    */
/*           DIALOG.H - This include file contains the data structure */
/*           definitions that define a dialog box.                    */
/*                                                                    */
```

```
/*              DEFINES.H - This include file contains the defined data  */
/*              definitions used by the Menu Library functions.          */
/*                                                                        */
/*              KEYBOARD.H - This include file contains the defined data */
/*              definitions used to determine keyboard input.            */
/*                                                                        */
/*              CHECKBOX.H - This include file contains the icon array   */
/*              descriptions for displaying the check boxes.             */
/*                                                                        */
/*              RADIO.H - This include file contains the icon array      */
/*              descriptions for displaying the radio buttons.           */
/*                                                                        */
/* Functions : InitializeWorkGroups () - This function initializes       */
/*              a dialog box's work groups.                              */
/*                                                                        */
/*              DisplayRadioButtons () - This function displays a work   */
/*              group of radio buttons on the screen.                    */
/*                                                                        */
/*              DisplayCheckBoxes () - This function displays a work     */
/*              group of check boxes on the screen.                      */
/*                                                                        */
/*              ProcessRadioButtons () - This function is called to      */
/*              process the radio buttons.                               */
/*                                                                        */
/*              ProcessCheckBoxes () - This function is called to        */
/*              process the check boxes.                                 */
/*                                                                        */
/***********************************************************************/

#include "\graphics\colors.h"
#include "defines.h"
#include "dialog.h"
#include "keyboard.h"
#include "checkbox.h"
#include "radio.h"
```

Create the GROUPS.C Function — InitializeWorkGroups ( )

The InitializeWorkGroups ( ) function is called to display a dialog box's work group
fields. There are two different types of work group fields: check boxes and radio
buttons.

Edit the GROUPS.C source file, type the following statements, and save the file.

```
/*=====================================================================*/
/*                                                                      */
/* Function : InitializeWorkGroups (wa);                                */
/*                                                                      */
/* Purpose  : This function initializes and displays the work groups    */
/*            of a given dialog box.                                    */
/*                                                                      */
/* Entry Parameters : WORK_AREA *wa - A pointer to the dialog box       */
```

```
/*           work area containing the work groups.              */
/*                                                              */
/* Local Data Definitions : int i - This variable is used as a  */
/*           temporary variable to count the work groups.       */
/*                                                              */
/* Functions Called : DrawBox () - This function is called to draw */
/*           a box around the work group being initialized.     */
/*                                                              */
/*           DisplayString () - This function is called to display */
/*           the work group label string.                       */
/*                                                              */
/*           DisplayRadioButtons () - This function is called to */
/*           display a group of radio buttons.                  */
/*                                                              */
/*           DisplayCheckBoxes () - This function is called to  */
/*           display a group of check boxes.                    */
/*                                                              */
/* Logic Flow : The InitializeWorkGroups () function is called with a */
/*           pointer to the dialog box work area containing the */
/*           work groups to initialize.  For each work group in the */
/*           dialog box, a box is drawn around the work group area. */
/*           The work group label string is displayed.  If the work */
/*           group type is a radio button, then the function    */
/*           DisplayRadioButtons () is called to display the radio */
/*           buttons on the screen.  If the work group is a check */
/*           box, then the function DisplayCheckBoxes () is called */
/*           to display the check boxes on the screen.          */
/*                                                              */
/* Exit : The dialog box work groups are displayed on the screen. */
/*                                                              */
/*==============================================================*/

InitializeWorkGroups (wa)
WORK_AREA *wa;
{
   int   i;

   for (i = 0; i < wa->group_num; i++)
   {
      DrawBox (wa->groups[i].r + 5, wa->groups[i].c,
               wa->groups[i].w, wa->groups[i].h,
               BLACKDOT);
      DisplayString (wa->groups[i].r, wa->groups[i].c + FONTWIDTH,
                     wa->groups[i].group_str, BLACK, WHITE);
      if (wa->groups[i].type == RADIO_BUTTON)
         DisplayRadioButtons (wa, i);
      else DisplayCheckBoxes (wa, i);
   }
}
```

Create the GROUPS.C Function — DisplayRadioButtons ( )

The DisplayRadioButtons ( ) function is called to display a group of radio buttons on the screen. The icon arrays On_Radio_Button and Off_Radio_Button are used to display the current status of the radio button on the screen.

Edit the GROUPS.C source file, type the following statements, and save the file.

```
/*=======================================================================*/
/*                                                                       */
/* Function : DisplayRadioButtons (wa, i)                                */
/*                                                                       */
/* Purpose  : This function displays a group of radio buttons.           */
/*                                                                       */
/* Entry Parameters : WORK_AREA *wa - A pointer to the dialog box        */
/*            work area containing the radio buttons to display.         */
/*                                                                       */
/*            int i - The work group number containing the radio         */
/*            buttons to display.                                        */
/*                                                                       */
/* Local Data Definitions : int j - This variable is used as a           */
/*            counter for the number of radio buttons displayed.         */
/*                                                                       */
/*            int row - This variable is used to calculate the row       */
/*            coordinate of the radio button.                            */
/*                                                                       */
/*            int column - This variable is used to calculate the        */
/*            column coordinate of the radio button.                     */
/*                                                                       */
/* Functions Called : DisplayIcon () - This function is called to        */
/*            display a radio button icon on the screen.                 */
/*                                                                       */
/*            DisplayString () - This function is called to display      */
/*            the radio button field description string.                 */
/*                                                                       */
/* Logic Flow : The DisplayRadioButtons () function is called with a     */
/*            pointer to the dialog box work area containing the         */
/*            group of radio buttons to display and the work group       */
/*            number to display.  For each radio button in the work      */
/*            group, do the following.  The variables int row and        */
/*            int column are set to the radio button row and column      */
/*            coordinates.  If the radio button status if ON, then       */
/*            the function DisplayIcon () is called to display a         */
/*            radio button that is ON, else, the function is called      */
/*            to display a radio button that is OFF.  The function       */
/*            DisplayString () is called to display the radio button     */
/*            field description.                                         */
/*                                                                       */
/* Exit : The work group radio buttons are displayed.                    */
/*                                                                       */
/*=======================================================================*/

DisplayRadioButtons (wa, i)
```

```
WORK_AREA *wa;
int i;
{
   int   j, row, column;

   for (j = 0; j < wa->groups[i].number; j++)
   {
      row = wa->groups[i].fields[j].r;
      column = wa->groups[i].fields[j].c;
      if (wa->groups[i].fields[j].status == ON)
         DisplayIcon (On_Radio_Button[0], row, column, 8, 8);
      else DisplayIcon (Off_Radio_Button[0], row, column, 8, 8);
      DisplayString (row, column + (FONTWIDTH * 2),
                     wa->groups[i].fields[j].label,
                     BLACK, WHITE);
   }
}
```

Create the GROUPS.C Function — DisplayCheckBoxes ( )

The DisplayCheckBoxes ( ) function is designed to display a group of check boxes on the screen. There are two different kinds of check boxes that can be displayed and they are defined by the icon arrays On_Check_Box and Off_Check_Box.

Edit the GROUPS.C source file, type the following statements, and save the file.

```
/*========================================================================*/
/*                                                                        */
/* Function : DisplayCheckBoxes (wa, i);                                  */
/*                                                                        */
/* Purpose  : This function displays a group of check boxes.              */
/*                                                                        */
/* Entry Parameters : WORK_AREA *wa - A pointer to the dialog box         */
/*            work area containing the check boxes to display.            */
/*                                                                        */
/*            int i - The work group number to display.                   */
/*                                                                        */
/* Local Data Definitions : int j - This variable is used as a            */
/*            counter for the number of check boxes displayed.            */
/*                                                                        */
/*            int row - This variable is used to calculate the row        */
/*            coordinate of the check box.                                */
/*                                                                        */
/*            int column - This variable is used to calculate the         */
/*            column coordinate of the check box.                         */
/*                                                                        */
/* Functions Called : DisplayIcon () - This function is called to         */
/*            display a check box icon on the screen.                     */
/*                                                                        */
/*            DisplayString () - This function is called to display       */
/*            the check box field description string.                     */
/*                                                                        */
```

```
/* Logic Flow : The DisplayCheckBoxes () function is called with a   */
/*              pointer to the dialog box work area containing the    */
/*              group of check boxes to display and the work group    */
/*              number to display.  For each check box in the work    */
/*              group, do the following.  The variables int row and   */
/*              int column are set to the check box row and column    */
/*              coordinates.  If the check box status if ON, then     */
/*              the function DisplayIcon () is called to display a     */
/*              check box that is ON, else, the function is called     */
/*              to display a check box that is OFF.  The function      */
/*              DisplayString () is called to display the check box    */
/*              field description.                                     */
/*                                                                     */
/* Exit : The work groups check boxes are displayed.                  */
/*                                                                     */
/*===================================================================*/

DisplayCheckBoxes (wa, i)
WORK_AREA *wa;
int i;
{
    int    j, row, column;

    for (j = 0; j < wa->groups[i].number; j++)
    {
        row = wa->groups[i].fields[j].r;
        column = wa->groups[i].fields[j].c;
        if (wa->groups[i].fields[j].status == ON)
            DisplayIcon (On_Check_Box[0], row, column, 8, 8);
        else DisplayIcon (Off_Check_Box[0], row, column, 8, 8);
        DisplayString (row, column + 10, wa->groups[i].fields[j].label,
                    BLACK, WHITE);
    }
}
```

Create the GROUPS.C Function — ProcessRadioButtons ( )

The ProcessRadioButtons ( ) function is called to process a group of radio buttons. A pointer to the work group is passed along with the work group number. This function accepts keyboard input and changes the status of the radio button.

Edit the GROUPS.C source file, type the following statements, and save the file.

```
/*===================================================================*/
/*                                                                     */
/* Function : ProcessRadioButtons (wg, i);                             */
/*                                                                     */
/* Purpose  : This processes a group of radio buttons.                 */
/*                                                                     */
/* Entry Parameters : WORK_GROUP *wg - A pointer to the dialog box     */
/*              work group containing the check boxes to process.      */
/*                                                                     */
```

```
/*              int i - The work group number to process.          */
/*                                                                 */
/* Local Data Definitions : int j - This variable is used as a     */
/*              counter for the number of radio buttons displayed. */
/*                                                                 */
/*              int row - This variable is used to calculate the row */
/*              coordinate of the radio button.                    */
/*                                                                 */
/*              int column - This variable is used to calculate the */
/*              column coordinate of the radio button.             */
/*                                                                 */
/* Functions Called : DisplayIcon () - This function is called to  */
/*              display a radio button icon on the screen.         */
/*                                                                 */
/*              DisplayString () - This function is called to display */
/*              the radio button field description string.         */
/*                                                                 */
/* Logic Flow : The ProcessRadioButtons () function is called with a */
/*              pointer to the dialog box work group containing the */
/*              group of radio buttons to display and the work group */
/*              number to display.  For each radio button in the work */
/*              group, do the following.  The variables int row and */
/*              int column are set to the radio button row and column */
/*              coordinates.  If the radio button status if ON, then */
/*              the function DisplayIcon () is called to display a  */
/*              radio button that is ON, else, the function is called */
/*              to display a radio button that is OFF.  The function */
/*              DisplayString () is called to display the radio button */
/*              field description.                                 */
/*                                                                 */
/* Exit : The work groups radio buttons are processed.             */
/*                                                                 */
/*===============================================================*/

ProcessRadioButtons (wg, index)
WORK_GROUP *wg;
int index;
{
   int   j, row, column, width, key;

   row = wg->fields[index].r - 2;
   column = wg->fields[index].c - 3;
   width = (strlen (wg->fields[index].label) + 3) * FONTWIDTH;
   DrawBox (row, column, width, 14, BLACKDOT);
   key = GetKey ();
   switch (key)
   {
      case ENTER:
         if (wg->fields[index].status == OFF)
         {
            for (j = 0; j < wg->number; j++)
            {
               if (wg->fields[j].status == ON)
```

```
                {
                    DisplayIcon (Off_Radio_Button[0],
                                 wg->fields[j].r,
                                 wg->fields[j].c, 8, 8);
                    wg->fields[j].status = OFF;
                }
            }
            wg->fields[index].status = ON;
            DisplayIcon (On_Radio_Button[0], row + 2, column + 3, 8, 8);
        }
        break;

    case LEFT_ARROW:
    case UP_ARROW:
    case CTRL_LEFT_ARROW:
    case CTRL_UP_ARROW:
    case SHIFT_TAB:
    case RIGHT_ARROW:
    case DOWN_ARROW:
    case CTRL_DOWN_ARROW:
    case CTRL_RIGHT_ARROW:
    case TAB:
    case ESC:
        DrawBox (row, column, width, 14, WHITEDOT);
        return (key);
    }
}
```

Create the GROUPS.C Function — ProcessCheckBoxes ( )

The ProcessCheckBoxes ( ) function is called to process a group of check boxes. A pointer to the work group is passed along with the work group number. This function accepts keyboard input and changes the status of the check boxes.

Edit the GROUPS.C source file, type the following statements, and save the file.

```
/*=======================================================================*/
/*                                                                       */
/* Function : ProcessCheckBoxes (wg, i);                                 */
/*                                                                       */
/* Purpose  : This function displays a group of check boxes.             */
/*                                                                       */
/* Entry Parameters : WORK_GROUP *wg - A pointer to the dialog box       */
/*            work group containing the check boxes to process.          */
/*                                                                       */
/*            int i - The Work Group number to process.                  */
/*                                                                       */
/* Local Data Definitions : int j - This variable is used as a          */
/*            counter for the number of check boxes processed.           */
/*                                                                       */
/*            int row - This variable is used to calculate the row       */
/*            coordinate of the check box.                               */
```

```
/*                                                                    */
/*          int column - This variable is used to calculate the       */
/*          column coordinate of the check box.                       */
/*                                                                    */
/* Functions Called : DisplayIcon () - This function is called to     */
/*          display a check box icon on the screen.                   */
/*                                                                    */
/*          DisplayString () - This function is called to display     */
/*          the check box field description string.                   */
/*                                                                    */
/* Logic Flow : The ProcessCheckBoxes () function is called with a    */
/*          pointer to the dialog box work group containing the       */
/*          group of check boxes to display and the work group        */
/*          number to display.  For each check box in the work        */
/*          group, do the following.  The variables int row and       */
/*          int column are set to the check box row and column        */
/*          coordinates.  If the check box status if ON, then         */
/*          the function DisplayIcon () is called to display a        */
/*          check box that is ON, else, the function is called        */
/*          to display a check box that is OFF.  The function         */
/*          DisplayString () is called to display the check box       */
/*          field description.                                        */
/*                                                                    */
/* Exit : The work groups check boxes are processed.                  */
/*                                                                    */
/*==================================================================*/

ProcessCheckBoxes (wg, index)
WORK_GROUP *wg;
int index;
{
    int   row, column, width, key;

    row = wg->fields[index].r - 2;
    column = wg->fields[index].c - 3;
    width = (strlen (wg->fields[index].label) + 3) * FONTWIDTH;
    DrawBox (row, column, width, 14, BLACKDOT);
    key = GetKey ();
    switch (key)
    {
      case ENTER:
        if (wg->fields[index].status == OFF)
        {
            DisplayIcon (On_Check_Box[0], row + 2, column + 3, 8, 8);
            wg->fields[index].status = ON;
        }
        else
        {
            DisplayIcon (Off_Check_Box[0], row + 2, column + 3, 8, 8);
            wg->fields[index].status = OFF;
        }
        break;
```

```
        case LEFT_ARROW:
        case UP_ARROW:
        case CTRL_LEFT_ARROW:
        case CTRL_UP_ARROW:
        case SHIFT_TAB:
        case RIGHT_ARROW:
        case DOWN_ARROW:
        case CTRL_DOWN_ARROW:
        case CTRL_RIGHT_ARROW:
        case TAB:
        case ESC:
            DrawBox (row, column, width, 14, WHITEDOT);
            return (key);
    }
}
```

Create the LISTBOX.C Source File

The LISTBOX.C source file contains the functions needed to initialize, display, and process a list box. List boxes are windows of data that can be scrolled up, down, left or right.

Create the LISTBOX.C source file, type the following statements, and save the file.

```
/*******************************************************************/
/*                                                                 */
/* File : LISTBOX.C                                                */
/*                                                                 */
/* Purpose : This 'C' source contains the functions needed to      */
/*           initialize, display, and process a dialog box list    */
/*           box.                                                   */
/*                                                                 */
/* Include Files : \graphics\COLORS.H - This include file contains */
/*           the color definitions used by the Menu Library functions.*/
/*                                                                 */
/*           MENU.H - This include file contains the data structure */
/*           definitions that define a list box.                   */
/*                                                                 */
/*           DEFINES.H - This include file contains the defined data */
/*           definitions used by the Menu Library functions.       */
/*                                                                 */
/*           KEYBOARD.H - This include file contains the defined data */
/*           definitions used to determine keyboard input.         */
/*                                                                 */
/*           ARROWS.H - This include file contains the icon array  */
/*           descriptions for displaying the scroll bar arrows.    */
/*                                                                 */
/* External Data Definitions : int Current_Record - This variable  */
/*           contains the current record number of the file used   */
/*           in the application.                                   */
/*                                                                 */
/*           int Number_Of_Records - This variable contains the    */
```

```
/*           number of records in the application data file.      */
/*                                                                */
/*           int Listbox_Start_Str - This variable contains the   */
/*           string number of the starting string displayed in the */
/*           list box.                                            */
/*                                                                */
/*           int Listbox_End_Str - This variable contains the string */
/*           number of the last string displayed in the list box. */
/*                                                                */
/*           int Listbox_Start_Col - This variable contains the   */
/*           column number of the first character displayed in the */
/*           strings in the list box.                             */
/*                                                                */
/*           int Listbox_End_Col - This variable contains the column */
/*           number of the last character displayed in the string in */
/*           the list box.                                        */
/*                                                                */
/*           int H_Max_Len - This variable contains the maximum   */
/*           length of the horizontal scroll bar in characters.   */
/*                                                                */
/*           int V_Max_Len - This variable contains the maximum   */
/*           length of the vertical scroll bar in characters.     */
/*                                                                */
/* Functions : InitializeListBox () - This function initializes and */
/*           displays a list box on the screen.                   */
/*                                                                */
/*           ProcessListBox () - This function processes a given  */
/*           list box.                                            */
/*                                                                */
/*           UpdateListBox () - This function updates the list box */
/*           whenever it needs to scroll up, down, left, or right. */
/*                                                                */
/*           DisplayListBoxColumn () - This function displays the  */
/*           list box strings for a given column.                 */
/*                                                                */
/*           DisplayListBoxItem () - This function displays a given */
/*           list box string on the screen.                       */
/*                                                                */
/*           UpdateVerticalScrollBar () - This function updates the */
/*           list box vertical scroll bars on the screen.         */
/*                                                                */
/*           UpdateHorizontalScrollBar () - This function updates the */
/*           list box horizontal scroll bars on the screen.       */
/*                                                                */
/******************************************************************/

#include "\graphics\colors.h"
#include "keyboard.h"
#include "defines.h"
#include "menu.h"
#include "arrows.h"

extern int Current_Record;
```

```
extern int Number_Of_Records;
extern int Listbox_Start_Str;
extern int Listbox_End_Str;
extern int Listbox_Start_Col;
extern int Listbox_End_Col;
extern int Number_ActionBar_Menus;
extern int ActionBar_Hot_Keys[10];
extern int H_Max_Len;
extern int V_Max_Len;
```

Create the LISTBOX.C Function — InitializeListBox ( )

The InitializeListBox ( ) function initializes and displays a dialog box list box. The list box scroll bars are displayed on the screen. An application specific function initializes the list box strings, then the list box display strings are displayed.

Edit the LISTBOX.C source file, type the following statements, and save the file.

```
/*=====================================================================*/
/*                                                                     */
/* Function : InitializeListBox (lb);                                  */
/*                                                                     */
/* Purpose : This function initializes and displays a given list box.  */
/*                                                                     */
/* Entry Parameters : LIST_BOX *lb - A pointer to the list box to      */
/*           initialize and display.                                   */
/*                                                                     */
/* Local Data Definitions : int i - This variable is used as a         */
/*           counter for the number of list box strings there are      */
/*           to be displayed.                                          */
/*                                                                     */
/*           int row - This variable is used to calculate the row      */
/*           coordinates needed to display the scroll bars and list    */
/*           box strings.                                              */
/*                                                                     */
/*           int column - This variable is used to calculate the       */
/*           column coordinates needed to display the scroll bars and  */
/*           list box strings.                                         */
/*                                                                     */
/*           int width - This variable is used to calculate the width  */
/*           of the scroll bars and list box.                          */
/*                                                                     */
/*           int height - This variable is used to calculate the       */
/*           height of the scroll bars and list box.                   */
/*                                                                     */
/*           int return_code - This variable is used to contain the    */
/*           return code from the application specific function that   */
/*           initializes the list box strings.                         */
/*                                                                     */
/* Functions Called : DrawBox () - This function is called to draw     */
/*           boxes on the screen for the scroll bars and list box.     */
/*                                                                     */
```

```
/*          ClearWindow () - This function is called to clear a     */
/*          window on the screen for the scroll bars and list box.  */
/*                                                                  */
/*          DisplayIcon () - This function is called to display the */
/*          scroll bar arrow icons on the screen.                   */
/*                                                                  */
/*          HLine () - This function is called to display horizontal */
/*          lines on the screen for the scroll bars.                */
/*                                                                  */
/*          DisplayListBoxItem () - This function is called to      */
/*          display the list box strings.                          */
/*                                                                  */
/* Logic Flow : The InitializeListBox () function is called with a  */
/*          pointer to list box to initialize.  The variables int   */
/*          row, int column, and int height are set to be equal to  */
/*          the list box vertical scroll bar coordinates.  The      */
/*          DrawBox () function is called to draw a box representing */
/*          the vertical scroll bar.  The top of the scroll bar is  */
/*          then cleared and the icon array Up_Arrow_Icon is        */
/*          displayed by calling the DisplayIcon () function.  The  */
/*          scroll bar area is then cleared in BLUE and the icon    */
/*          array Down_Arrow_Icon is displayed.  The location box   */
/*          representing the relative location of the current list  */
/*          box string to the rest of the strings in the list box   */
/*          is displayed.  The variables, int row, int column, and  */
/*          int height are reassigned for the horizontal scroll bar. */
/*          The horizontal scroll bar is displayed.  An application */
/*          specific function is called to initialize the list box  */
/*          strings that are to be displayed.  If the application   */
/*          function returns a successful return code, then each    */
/*          displayable string in the list box is displayed by the  */
/*          DisplayListBoxItem () function.  The return code from   */
/*          the application specific function is returned to the    */
/*          calling function.                                       */
/*                                                                  */
/* Exit : The list box is initialized and displayed.                */
/*                                                                  */
/*================================================================*/


InitializeListBox (lb)
LIST_BOX *lb;
{
   int i, row, column, width, height, return_code;

   row = lb->v_scroll_bar[0].r;
   column = lb->v_scroll_bar[0].c;
   height = lb->v_scroll_bar[0].l;
   DrawBox (row, column, 11, height, BLACKDOT);
   ClearWindow (row + 1, column + 1, 9, 9, WHITE);
   DisplayIcon (Up_Arrow_Icon[0], row + 2, column + 2, 8, 8);
   HLine (row + 11, column + 1, 9, BLACKDOT);
   ClearWindow (row + 12, column + 1, 9, height - 24, BLUE);
   HLine (row + height - 12, column + 1, 9, BLACKDOT);
```

```
      ClearWindow (row + height - 11, column + 1, 9, 9, WHITE);
      DisplayIcon (Down_Arrow_Icon[0], row + height - 10, column + 2,
                8, 8);
      DrawBox (row + lb->v_scroll_bar[0].bl + 11, column, 11, 11,
             BLACKDOT);
      ClearWindow (row + lb->v_scroll_bar[0].bl + 12, column + 1, 9, 9,
                WHITE);
      row = lb->h_scroll_bar[0].r;
      column = lb->h_scroll_bar[0].c;
      width = lb->h_scroll_bar[0].l;
      DrawBox (row, column, width, 11, BLACKDOT);
      ClearWindow (row + 1, column + 1, 9, 9, WHITE);
      DisplayIcon (Left_Arrow_Icon[0], row + 2, column + 2, 8, 8);
      VLine (row + 1, column + 11, 9, BLACKDOT);
      ClearWindow (row + 1, column + 12, width - 24, 9, BLUE);
      VLine (row + 1, column + width - 12, 9, BLACKDOT);
      ClearWindow (row + 1, column + width - 11, 9, 9, WHITE);
      DisplayIcon (Right_Arrow_Icon[0], row + 2, column + width - 10,
                8, 8);
      DrawBox (row, column + lb->h_scroll_bar[0].bl + 11, 11, 11,
             BLACKDOT);
      ClearWindow (row + 1, column + lb->h_scroll_bar[0].bl + 12, 9, 9,
                WHITE);
      return_code = (*lb->initialize_function) (lb);
      if (return_code == 0)
         for (i = 0; i < lb->num_items; i++)
            DisplayListBoxItem (lb, i);
      return (return_code);
   }
```

Create the LISTBOX.C Function — ProcessListBox ( )

The ProcessListBox ( ) function processes a dialog box list box. By using the arrow keys the user can scroll the list box up, down, left, or right. When the display string data needs to be updated, the function calls an application specific function in the list box data structure to update the display string data.

Edit the LISTBOX.C source file, type the following statements, and save the file.

```
/*====================================================================*/
/*                                                                    */
/* Function : ProcessListBox (lb)                                     */
/*                                                                    */
/* Purpose  : This function processes a dialog box list box.          */
/*                                                                    */
/* Entry Parameters : LIST_BOX *lb - A pointer to the list box        */
/*            structure to process.                                   */
/*                                                                    */
/* Local Data Definitions : int key - This variable is used to        */
/*            contain the keystroke returned from the GetKey ()       */
/*            function.                                               */
```

```
/*                                                                      */
/* Functions Called : GetKey () - This function is called to return     */
/*            a keystroke from the keyboard.                             */
/*                                                                       */
/*            UpdateListBox () - This function is called to update       */
/*            the list box whenever the user presses a key that causes   */
/*            the list box display to change.                            */
/*                                                                       */
/*            UpdateVerticalScrollBar () - This function is called       */
/*            when the vertical scroll bar of the list box needs to      */
/*            be updated.                                                */
/*                                                                       */
/*            UpdateHorizontalScrollBar () - This function is called     */
/*            when the horizontal scroll bar of the list box needs to    */
/*            be updated.                                                */
/*                                                                       */
/* Logic Flow : The ProcessListBox () function is called with a          */
/*            pointer to the list box structure to process.  Until       */
/*            a key is pressed that exits the list box, do the           */
/*            following.  Call the function GetKey () to get a           */
/*            keystroke from the keyboard.  If the key is an UP_ARROW,    */
/*            then scroll the list box up, update the vertical scroll     */
/*            bar, and call an application specific function if needed.   */
/*            If the key is a DOWN_ARROW, then scroll the list box        */
/*            down, update the vertical scroll bar, and call the         */
/*            application specific function that updates the list box     */
/*            display strings.  If the key is a LEFT_ARROW, then          */
/*            scroll the list box to the left and update the horizontal   */
/*            scroll bar.  If the key is RIGHT_ARROW, then scroll         */
/*            the list box to the right and update the horizontal         */
/*            scroll bar.  If the key is either an Enter, Home, or        */
/*            Esc key, then return the key to the calling program.        */
/*                                                                       */
/* Exit : The dialog box list box is processed.                          */
/*         Returns when one of the following keys are pressed:           */
/*         Enter, Esc, Home                                              */
/*                                                                       */
/*=====================================================================*/

ProcessListbox (lb)
LIST_BOX *lb;
{
   int    key, i;

   for (;;)
   {
      key = GetKey ();
      switch (key)
      {
        case UP_ARROW:
           if (Listbox_Start_Str < Current_Record)
           {
              UpdateListbox (lb, UPARROW);
```

```
            Current_Record--;
            UpdateVerticalScrollBar (&lb->v_scroll_bar[0],
                                Current_Record);
      }
      else if (Listbox_Start_Str > 0)
      {
         lb->index = 0;
         Current_Record = Listbox_Start_Str;
         Current_Record--;
         Listbox_Start_Str--;
         Listbox_End_Str--;
         (*lb->update_function) (lb, SCROLL_DOWN);
         UpdateListbox  (lb, SCROLL_DOWN);
         UpdateVerticalScrollBar (&lb->v_scroll_bar[0],
                                Current_Record);
      }
      else return (-2);
      break;

case DOWN_ARROW:
      if (Listbox_End_Str > Current_Record)
      {
         UpdateListbox (lb, DOWNARROW);
         Current_Record++;
         UpdateVerticalScrollBar (&lb->v_scroll_bar[0],
                               Current_Record);
      }
      else if (Listbox_End_Str < (Number_Of_Records - 1))
      {
         lb->index = lb->num_items - 1;
         Current_Record = Listbox_End_Str;
         Current_Record++;
         Listbox_Start_Str++;
         Listbox_End_Str++;
         (*lb->update_function) (lb, SCROLL_UP);
         UpdateListbox  (lb, SCROLL_UP);
         UpdateVerticalScrollBar (&lb->v_scroll_bar[0],
                               Current_Record);
      }
      else return (-1);
      break;

case LEFT_ARROW:
      if (Listbox_Start_Col > 0)
      {
         (*lb->update_function) (lb, SCROLL_RIGHT);
         UpdateListbox  (lb, SCROLL_RIGHT);
         Listbox_Start_Col--;
         Listbox_End_Col--;
         UpdateHorizontalScrollBar (&lb->h_scroll_bar[0],
                                 Listbox_Start_Col);
      }
      break;
```

```
        case RIGHT_ARROW:
            if (lb->items[lb->index][Listbox_End_Col -
              Listbox_Start_Col] != 0)
            {
                (*lb->update_function) (lb, SCROLL_LEFT);
                UpdateListbox  (lb, SCROLL_LEFT);
                Listbox_Start_Col++;
                Listbox_End_Col++;
                UpdateHorizontalScrollBar (&lb->h_scroll_bar[0],
                                           Listbox_End_Col);
            }
            break;

        case ENTER:
        case F10:
        case ESC:
            return(key);

        default:
            for (i = 0; i <= Number_ActionBar_Menus; i++)
              if (key == ActionBar_Hot_Keys[i])
                 return (key);
            break;
    }
  }
}
```

Create the LISTBOX.C Function — UpdateListBox ()

The UpdateListBox ( ) function is called to update the list box strings on the screen. The function either scrolls the list box strings up, down, left, or right.

Edit the LISTBOX.C source file, type the following statements, and save the file.

```
/*=========================================================================*/
/*                                                                         */
/* Function : UpdateListBox (lb, function);                                */
/*                                                                         */
/* Purpose : Updates the given list box according to the given            */
/*           function request.                                             */
/*                                                                         */
/* Entry Parameters : LIST_BOX *lb - A pointer to the list box to         */
/*           update                                                        */
/*                                                                         */
/*             int function - The update list box function request.       */
/*                                                                         */
/* Local Data Definitions : int i - This variable is used as a            */
/*           temporary variable to update the list box.                    */
/*                                                                         */
/* Functions Called : ScrollWindow () - This function is called to        */
/*           scroll a window of screen data up, down, left, or right.*/
```

```
/*                                                                    */
/*          DisplayListBoxColumn () - This function is called to      */
/*          display a given column of the list box strings.           */
/*                                                                    */
/*          DisplayListBoxItem () - This function is called to        */
/*          display a given list box string.                          */
/*                                                                    */
/* Logic Flow : The UpdateListBox () function is called with a        */
/*          pointer to the list box to update and a function          */
/*          request.  If the function request is SCROLL_RIGHT, then   */
/*          the function ScrollWindow () is called to scroll the      */
/*          list box to the right one character.  The leftmost        */
/*          characters of the list box strings are then updated       */
/*          on the screen by the DisplayListBoxColumn () function.    */
/*          If the function request is SCROLL_LEFT, then the          */
/*          list box is scrolled to the left and the rightmost        */
/*          character of the list box strings is displayed. If the    */
/*          function request is SCROLL_UP, then the list box          */
/*          is scrolled up one line and the DisplayListBoxItem ()     */
/*          function is called to highlight the new current record.   */
/*          If the function request is SCROLL_DOWN, then the list      */
/*          box is scrolled down one line and the new current record  */
/*          is highlighted.  If the function request is UPARROW,      */
/*          then the current record is moved up one record. If the    */
/*          function request is DOWNARROW, then the current           */
/*          record is moved down one record.                          */
/*                                                                    */
/* Exit : The dialog box list box is updated.                         */
/*                                                                    */
/*==================================================================*/

UpdateListbox (lb, function)
LIST_BOX *lb;
int function;
{
    int   i;

    switch (function)
    {
    case REFRESH:
        for (i = 0; i < lb->num_items; i++)
            DisplayListBoxItem (lb, i);
        break;

    case SCROLL_RIGHT:
        ScrollWindow (lb->r + 3,
                     lb->c + 1 + (lb->length * FONTWIDTH),
                     lb->r + 3,
                     lb->c + 1 + ((lb->length - 1) * FONTWIDTH),
                     ((lb->length - 1) * FONTWIDTH) + 1,
                     lb->num_items * FONTHEIGHT,  SCROLL_RIGHT);
        DisplayListBoxColumn (lb, 0);
        break;
```

223

```
case SCROLL_LEFT:
    ScrollWindow (lb->r + 3, lb->c + 1, lb->r + 3,
                  lb->c + 1 + FONTWIDTH,
                  ((lb->length - 1) * FONTWIDTH) + 1,
                  lb->num_items * FONTHEIGHT,
                  SCROLL_LEFT);
    DisplayListBoxColumn (lb, lb->length - 1);
    break;

case SCROLL_UP:
    ScrollWindow (lb->r + 3,
                  lb->c + 1,
                  lb->r + FONTHEIGHT + 3,
                  lb->c + 1, (lb->length * FONTWIDTH) + 1,
                  (lb->num_items - 1) * FONTHEIGHT,
                  SCROLL_UP);
    i = lb->index;
    i--;
    DisplayListBoxItem (lb, i);
    DisplayListBoxItem (lb, lb->index);
    break;

case SCROLL_DOWN:
    ScrollWindow (lb->r + 3 + (FONTHEIGHT * lb->num_items),
                  lb->c + 1,
                  lb->r + 3 + (FONTHEIGHT * (lb->num_items - 1)),
                  lb->c + 1, (lb->length * FONTWIDTH) + 1,
                  ((lb->num_items - 1) * FONTHEIGHT) - 1,
                  SCROLL_DOWN);
    i = lb->index;
    i++;
    DisplayListBoxItem (lb, i);
    DisplayListBoxItem (lb, lb->index);
    break;

case UPARROW:
    i = lb->index;
    lb->index--;
    DisplayListBoxItem (lb, i);
    DisplayListBoxItem (lb, lb->index);
    break;

case DOWNARROW:
    i = lb->index;
    lb->index++;
    DisplayListBoxItem (lb, i);
    DisplayListBoxItem (lb, lb->index);
    break;
    }
}
```

Create the LISTBOX.C Function — DisplayListBoxColumn ( )

The DisplayListBoxColumn ( ) function is called to display a given column of the list box display strings on the screen.

Edit the LISTBOX.C source file, type the following statements, and save the file.

```
/*=====================================================================*/
/*                                                                     */
/* Function : DisplayListBoxColumn (lb, offset);                       */
/*                                                                     */
/* Purpose : Updates a given column of list box display strings.       */
/*                                                                     */
/* Entry Parameters : LIST_BOX *lb - A pointer to the list box         */
/*          to update.                                                 */
/*                                                                     */
/*          int offset - The list box column to update.                */
/*                                                                     */
/* Local Data Definitions : int i - This variable is used as a         */
/*          counter for the number of list box strings to update.      */
/*                                                                     */
/*          int foreground - This variable contains the current        */
/*          foreground color of the list box string to update.         */
/*                                                                     */
/*          int background - This variable contains the current        */
/*          background color of the list box string to update.         */
/*                                                                     */
/* Functions Called : DisplayChar () - This function is called to      */
/*          to display the list box strings column character.          */
/*                                                                     */
/* Logic Flow : The DisplayListBoxColumn () function is called with    */
/*          a pointer to the list box to update and the column         */
/*          number to update.  For each list box string to update,     */
/*          do the following.  Set the foreground and background        */
/*          colors.  If the current record is the record being         */
/*          updated, then display it in reverse video.  Call the       */
/*          DisplayChar () function to display the list box string      */
/*          character.                                                 */
/*                                                                     */
/* Exit : The list box string columns are updated                      */
/*                                                                     */
/*=====================================================================*/

DisplayListBoxColumn (lb, offset)
LIST_BOX *lb;
int offset;
{
    int  i, foreground, background;

    for (i = 0; i < lb->num_items; i++)
    {
        foreground  = BLACK;
        background = WHITE;
```

```
        if (lb->index == i)
        {
           foreground  = WHITE;
           background = BLACK;
        }
        DisplayChar (lb->r + 3 + (FONTHEIGHT * i),
                     lb->c + 1 + (offset * FONTWIDTH),
                     *(lb->items[i] + offset), foreground, background);
    }
}
```

Create the LISTBOX.C Function — DisplayListBoxItem ( )

The DisplayListBoxItem ( ) function is called to display a given list box string on the screen. If the current record is the string being displayed, then display it in reverse video.

Edit the LISTBOX.C source file, type the following statements, and save the file.

```
/*========================================================================*/
/*                                                                        */
/* Function : DisplayListBoxItem (lb, item);                              */
/*                                                                        */
/* Purpose : This function displays a given string from a list box.       */
/*                                                                        */
/* Entry Parameters : LIST_BOX *lb - A pointer to the list box            */
/*           structure to update.                                         */
/*                                                                        */
/*           int item - The list box string number to display.            */
/*                                                                        */
/* Local Data Definitions : int foreground - This variable is used as     */
/*           the foreground color of the list box string to display.      */
/*                                                                        */
/*           int background - This variable is used as the background      */
/*           color of the list box string to display.                     */
/*                                                                        */
/* Functions Called : DisplayStrNum () - This function is called to        */
/*           display the list box string on the screen.                   */
/*                                                                        */
/* Logic Flow : The DisplayListBoxItem () function is called with a        */
/*           pointer to the list box structure and the string number       */
/*           to display.  If the current record is the string being        */
/*           displayed, then string is displayed in reverse video.        */
/*           The function DisplayStrNum () is called to display the        */
/*           the list box string on the screen.                           */
/*                                                                        */
/* Exit : The list box string is displayed on the screen.                 */
/*                                                                        */
/*========================================================================*/

DisplayListBoxItem (lb, item)
LIST_BOX *lb;
```

```
int item;
{
    int    foreground, background;

    foreground = BLACK;
    background = WHITE;
    if (lb->index == item)
    {
        foreground  = WHITE;
        background  = BLACK;
    }
    DisplayStrNum (lb->r + 3 + (FONTHEIGHT * item), lb->c + 1,
                   lb->items[item], lb->length, foreground, background);
}
```

Create the LISTBOX.C Function — UpdateVerticalScrollBar ( )

The UpdateVerticalScrollBar ( ) function is called to update the vertical scroll bar of a list box. The function is passed an index that is used to determine where to display the location box within the scroll bar.

Edit the LISTBOX.C source file, type the following statements, and save the file.

```
/*=======================================================================*/
/*                                                                       */
/* Function : UpdateVerticalScrollBar (sb, index);                       */
/*                                                                       */
/* Purpose : Updates the given vertical scroll bar on the screen.        */
/*                                                                       */
/* Entry Parameters : SCROLL_BAR *sb - A pointer to the vertical         */
/*          scroll bar to update.                                        */
/*                                                                       */
/*          int index - The index of the vertical scroll bar             */
/*          location box.                                                */
/*                                                                       */
/* Local Data Definitions : int row - This variable is used to           */
/*          calculate the row coordinates for the scroll bar.            */
/*                                                                       */
/*          int height - This variable is used to calculate the          */
/*          height of the scroll bar.                                    */
/*                                                                       */
/* Functions Called :  ClearWindow () - This function is called to       */
/*          clear the old scroll bar location box and display the        */
/*          location box.                                                */
/*                                                                       */
/*          DrawBox () - This function is called to draw the scroll      */
/*          bar location box.                                            */
/*                                                                       */
/* Logic Flow : The UpdateVerticalScrollBar () function is called        */
/*          with a pointer to the vertical scroll bar to update and      */
/*          the index of the location box.  The variables int row        */
/*          and int height are set to the row coordinate and height      */
```

```
/*          of the old location box.  The function ClearWindow ()   */
/*          is called to clear the old location box from the screen. */
/*          The variable index is used to calculate the coordinates  */
/*          for the new location box.  The new location box is        */
/*          displayed on the screen.                                  */
/*                                                                    */
/* Exit : The vertical scroll bar is updated.                        */
/*                                                                    */
/*==================================================================*/

UpdateVerticalScrollBar (sb, index)
SCROLL_BAR *sb;
int index;
{
   int row, height;
   float j;

   row = sb->r + 12;
   j = (float) ((float) (sb->l - 28) / (float) V_Max_Len);
   if (sb->bl != 0)
   {
      row += sb->bl - 1;
      height = 11;
      if (index == (V_Max_Len - 2) &&
          sb->bl > ((float) index * j)) height--;
   }
   else height = 10;
   ClearWindow (row, sb->c + 1, 9, height, BLUE);
   if (index == 0) sb->bl = index;
   else sb->bl = ((float) index * j);
   DrawBox (sb->r + sb->bl + 11, sb->c, 11, 11, BLACKDOT);
   ClearWindow (sb->r + sb->bl + 12, sb->c + 1, 9, 9, WHITE);
}
```

Create the LISTBOX.C Function — UpdateHorizontalScrollBar ( )

The UpdateHorizontalScrollBar ( ) function is called to update a list box horizontal scroll bar. The function is called with an index to use as the location to display the scroll bar location box.

Edit the LISTBOX.C source file, type the following statements, and save the file.

```
/*==================================================================*/
/*                                                                    */
/* Function : UpdateHorizontalScrollBar (sb, index);                 */
/*                                                                    */
/* Purpose : Updates the given horizontal scroll bar on the screen.  */
/*                                                                    */
/* Entry Parameters : SCROLL_BAR *sb - A pointer to the horizontal   */
/*          scroll bar to update.                                    */
/*                                                                    */
/*          int index - The index of the horizontal scroll bar       */
```

```
/*            location box.                                        */
/*                                                                 */
/* Local Data Definitions : int row - This variable is used to     */
/*            calculate the row coordinates for the scroll bar.     */
/*                                                                 */
/*            int height - This variable is used to calculate the   */
/*            height of the scroll bar.                             */
/*                                                                 */
/* Functions Called :  ClearWindow () - This function is called to */
/*            clear the old scroll bar location box and display the */
/*            location box.                                        */
/*                                                                 */
/*            DrawBox () - This function is called to draw the scroll */
/*            bar location box.                                    */
/*                                                                 */
/* Logic Flow : The UpdateHorizontalScrollBar () function is called */
/*            with a pointer to the vertical scroll bar to update and */
/*            the index of the location box.  The variables int row  */
/*            and int height are set to the row coordinate and height */
/*            of the old location box.  The function ClearWindow ()  */
/*            is called to clear the old location box from the screen. */
/*            The variable index is used to calculate the coordinates */
/*            for the new location box.  The new location box is      */
/*            displayed on the screen.                              */
/*                                                                 */
/* Exit : The horizontal scroll bar is updated.                     */
/*                                                                 */
/*=================================================================*/

UpdateHorizontalScrollBar (sb, index)
SCROLL_BAR *sb;
int index;
{
    int column, width;
    int i;
    float j;

    column = sb->c + 12;
    width = 10;
    if (sb->bl != 0)
    {
        column += sb->bl - 1;
        if (sb->bl < sb->l - 34) width++;
    }
    ClearWindow (sb->r + 1, column, width, 9, BLUE);
    if (index == 0) sb->bl = index;
    else
    {
        j = (float) ((float) (sb->l - 33) / (float) H_Max_Len);
        sb->bl = ((float) index * j) + 1;
        if (sb->bl > (sb->l - 34))
            sb->bl = sb->l - 33;
    }
```

```
    DrawBox (sb->r, sb->c + sb->bl + 11, 11, 11, BLACKDOT);
    ClearWindow (sb->r + 1, sb->c + sb->bl + 12, 9, 9, WHITE);
}
```

Create the MESSAGE.C Source File

The MESSAGE.C source file contains the functions needed to initialize, display, and process a message box. A message box is a type of dialog box but is limited in interaction to only the push buttons.

Create the MESSAGE.C source file, type the following statements, and save the file.

```
/**********************************************************************/
/*                                                                    */
/* File    : MESSAGE.C                                                */
/*                                                                    */
/* Purpose : This 'C' source file initializes, displays, and          */
/*           processes a message box.                                 */
/*                                                                    */
/* Include Files : \graphics\COLORS.H - This include file contains    */
/*           the color definitions needed to display the message box. */
/*                                                                    */
/*           DEFINES.H - This include file contains the data          */
/*           definitions needed to display the message box.           */
/*                                                                    */
/*           MESSAGE.H - This include file contains the data structure*/
/*           definitions needed to define a message box.              */
/*                                                                    */
/* Functions : Message () - This function initializes, displays, and  */
/*           processes a Message Box.                                 */
/*                                                                    */
/**********************************************************************/

#include "\graphics\colors.h"
#include "defines.h"
#include "message.h"
```

Create the MESSAGE.C Function — Message ( )

The Message ( ) function is called to initialize, display, and process a message box. A message box notifies the user that something special has happened, such as a 'File Not Found' error message.

Edit the MESSAGE.C source file, type the following statements, and save the file.

```
/*====================================================================*/
/*                                                                    */
/* Function : Message (db);                                           */
/*                                                                    */
/* Purpose : This function initializes, displays, and processes a     */
/*           message box.                                             */
```

```
/*                                                               */
/* Entry Parameters : MESSAGE_BOX *mb - A pointer to the message box */
/*          data structure to process.                           */
/*                                                               */
/* Include Files : <malloc.h> - This standard 'C' include file is */
/*          used for the memory allocation functions.            */
/*                                                               */
/* Local Data Definitions : char *message_buffer - This variable is */
/*          used to contain the screen information that will be   */
/*          overwritten by the message box.                      */
/*                                                               */
/*          int i - This variable is used as a temporary variable. */
/*                                                               */
/*          int return_code - This variable is used to contain the */
/*          return code from the ProcessPushButtons () function.  */
/*                                                               */
/* Functions Called : malloc () - This function is called to allocate */
/*          memory into which to save the screen data.           */
/*                                                               */
/*          DisplayToBuffer () - This function is called to save the */
/*          screen display data into the buffer that was allocated. */
/*                                                               */
/*          DrawBox () - This function is called to draw a box on */
/*          the screen for the message box outline.              */
/*                                                               */
/*          VLine () - This function is called to draw vertical   */
/*          lines on the screen.                                 */
/*                                                               */
/*          HLine () - This function is called to draw horizontal */
/*          lines on the screen.                                 */
/*                                                               */
/*          ClearWindow () - This function is called to clear a   */
/*          window on the screen in a given color.               */
/*                                                               */
/*          DisplayString () - This function is called to display */
/*          strings on the screen.                               */
/*                                                               */
/*          InitializePushButtons () - This function is called to */
/*          initialize the push buttons for the message box.      */
/*                                                               */
/*          ProcessPushButtons () - This function is called to    */
/*          process the message box push buttons.                */
/*                                                               */
/*          BufferToDisplay () - This function is called to restore */
/*          the saved screen buffer to the screen.               */
/*                                                               */
/*          free () - This standard 'C' function is called to free */
/*          the memory that was allocated by the malloc () function. */
/*                                                               */
/* Logic Flow : The Message () function is called with a pointer to */
/*          the message box to initialize, display, and process.  */
/*          The function malloc () is called to allocate enough   */
/*          memory to save the screen data that will be overwritten */
```

```
/*          by the Message Box.  The DisplayToBuffer () function is  */
/*          called to save the screen data into the buffer just      */
/*          allocated.  The functions DrawBox (), VLine (), HLine (),*/
/*          and ClearWindow () are called to display the message     */
/*          box on the screen.  The DisplayString () function is      */
/*          called to display the message box header string and the  */
/*          message to be displayed in the message box. The function */
/*          InitializePushButtons () is called to initialize and     */
/*          display the push buttons on the screen.  The function     */
/*          ProcessPushButtons () is called to process the message   */
/*          box push buttons.  The BufferToDisplay () function is     */
/*          called to restore the screen data to the screen that was */
/*          saved earlier.  The standard 'C' function free () is      */
/*          called to free the screen buffer memory. The return      */
/*          code from ProcessPushButtons () is returned to the       */
/*          calling function.                                         */
/*                                                                    */
/* Exit : The message box is initialized, displayed, and processed.  */
/*                                                                    */
/*==================================================================*/


Message (mb)
MESSAGE_BOX *mb;
{
    #include <malloc.h>

    char    *message_buffer;
    int i, return_code;
    int count;

    message_buffer = malloc (((mb->w / 4) + 2) * mb->h);
    DisplayToBuffer (mb->r, mb->c, mb->w, mb->h, message_buffer);
    DrawBox (mb->r, mb->c, mb->w, mb->h, BLACKDOT);
    VLine   (mb->r, mb->c + 1, mb->h, BLACKDOT);
    VLine   (mb->r, mb->c + mb->w - 2, mb->h, BLACKDOT);
    DrawBox (mb->r + 1, mb->c + 2, mb->w - 4, mb->h - 2, WHITEDOT);
    DrawBox (mb->r + 2, mb->c + 3, mb->w - 6, mb->h - 4, BLACKDOT);
    ClearWindow (mb->r + 3, mb->c + 4, mb->w - 8, FONTHEIGHT + 2, RED);
    HLine   (mb->r + 5 + FONTHEIGHT, mb->c + 4, mb->w - 8, BLACK);
    i = ( (mb->w - 3) / 2) - ((strlen (mb->hdr) * FONTWIDTH) / 2);
    DisplayString (mb->r +  4, mb->c + i, mb->hdr,  WHITE, BLACK);
    ClearWindow    (mb->r + 16, mb->c + 4, mb->w - 8, mb->h - 19, WHITE);
    for (count = 0; count < mb->msgarea[0].strs_num; count++)
    {
        i = strlen(mb->msgarea[0].strs[count]) * FONTWIDTH;
        i = ((mb->w - i) / 2) + 1;
        DisplayString (mb->r + 22 + (FONTHEIGHT * count), mb->c + i,
                    mb->msgarea[0].strs[count], BLACK, WHITE);
    }
    if (mb->msgarea[0].button_num)
        InitializePushButtons (&mb->msgarea[0]);
    return_code = ProcessPushButton (&mb->msgarea[0]);
```

```
    BufferToDisplay (mb->r, mb->c, mb->w, mb->h, message_buffer);
    free (message_buffer);
    return (return_code);
}
```

SUMMARY

This chapter has dealt with the source files needed to initialize, display, and process dialog boxes. The source files DIALOG.C, PUSHBUTN.C, ENTRY.C, GROUPS.C, LISTBOX.C, and MESSAGE.C contain the functions needed to perform these functions for the Menu Library.

There are many different types of menus that can be created using the CGA Graphics Library screen functions. The kinds created in this book are primary menus, dialog boxes, and message boxes. These menus make use of five different types of user interface devices: push buttons, entry fields, list boxes, check boxes, and radio buttons to convey and retrieve information to the user.

While these functions are fully operational, they are by no means completed. They are written open ended so that the programmer can adjust and change these functions to suit their own particular needs. For example, the foreground and background colors are often defined inside of the menu itself. The code could be modified to expect the foreground and background colors to be passed to it, or the data structure definitions could be modified to contain these as extra parameters.

There are several places where memory problems could occur. These could be tied off using an interrupt service that displays this type of information to the user.

The menu functions written here are designed to give the reader the overall understanding of menu structures, not to write a complete windows driver package. Although these menus do not do everything the application programmer might desire, they do provide him with a very solid base from which to work.

Chapter 12

THE FILER LIBRARY

INTRODUCTION

The Filer Library is designed to perform the functions needed by the application to do file input and output. All of the functions in the Filer Library are written in 'C.' This Library is used exclusively by the application and contains only the minimum functions needed for the mail list application. The programmer should modify this Library whenever he needs to add more functionality to his file input and output.

The mail list application modifies a list of customer records. Each record describes an individual entry into the mail list. Two different array definitions are needed to maintain the list of customer records. The first is the index array and the second is the data array. The index array is used to maintain the sorted locations of the customer records on disk. The data array holds the actual customer records. These two arrays are explained in more detail in the following chapters.

The Filer Library maintains these two arrays and stores the information permanently to two disk files. The names of these files depend upon the name of the mail list customer filename. For example, the sample customer file used in this book is called SAMPLE. There are two files used to maintain this customer's database, SAMPLE.IDX and SAMPLE.DAT.

The file SAMPLE.IDX contains the information needed to create a sorted index into the SAMPLE.DAT file. The SAMPLE.DAT file contains the actual information about the customer, i.e., the customer name, address, and so on. With this background information, let's begin programming the Filer Library.

First, a decision must be made on the functions that are needed in the Filer Library. The following list is only the bare minimum of functions needed to perform the file input of the mail list application. The reader should add new functions, such as a delete file to the Filer Library.

THE FILER LIBRARY FUNCTIONS

- InitDataFile ( ) - This function initializes the index array and the data array for the mail list application.
- ReadIndex ( ) - This function reads in the index used to read the customer data file.
- ReadRecords ( ) - This function reads in the records from the customer data file.
- CreateNewFile ( ) - This function is called to create a new customer data file.
- InitRecords ( ) - This function is called to initialize the Record and Index data arrays.
- WriteRecords ( ) - This function is called to write the customer data records to disk.

I have not included all of the functions needed to perform the file input and output, because most of them go outside of the intent of this book. This book is intended to give the programmer a good understanding behind user interface design using menus, not to write a file indexing scheme. So the basic purpose of this book's Filer Library is to provide the mail list application with information needed to display a list box on the screen. The reader, if he wishes to make the mail list application truly functional, should add to the Filer Library those functions needed by his application, like DeleteFile ( ). Another alternative is a packaged database system.

In either case, it is important for the reader to understand that the file maintenance of the application is just as important as the menu driven graphical user interface. The program can look very pretty on the screen and have a very logical and easy-to-use user interaction through the use of menus, but if it can't maintain information for the user to a permanent storage devise, then its usability is greatly limited. Also, if it can't maintain several files, or a large number of records, or it is very slow, then its usability is greatly reduced. The programmer must take all of these things into account before choosing and/or designing a file input and output system.

The Filer Library is made up of one include source file and two 'C' source files.

- RECORD.H - This include source file contains the data structure definition of a customer record.
- RECORD.C - This 'C' source file contains the functions needed to initialize a customer data file and the read records from the customer data file.

- INDEX.C - This 'C' source file contains the functions needed to read in a customer data file index.

CREATE THE FILER LIBRARY FILES

The Filer Library batch files are designed in the same manner as the CGA Graphics Library and the Menu Library batch files except that these manage the Filer Library.

Creating the Batch File — BUILD.BAT

The BUILD.BAT file is very similar to the previous BUILD.BAT files made for the other Libraries. First, at the DOS command prompt:

Type **CD \FILER** and press **Return**.

This will change directories to the Filer Library directory created earlier.

NOTE
Since the BUILD.BAT file was created earlier in other directories, the programmer must make sure he is in the right directory before creating the file.

Create the BUILD.BAT file, type the following statements, and save the file.

```
copy FILER.LIB FILER.BAK
del FILER.LIB
make MAKEFILE.FIL
```

Now when the programmer wants to recompile the Filer Library, he needs only to complete the following while in the filer subdirectory.

Type **BUILD** and press **Return**.

Of course, typing this statement at this time will generate errors because the rest of the required files have not been created.

Creating the Make-File Utility File — MAKEFILE.FIL

The Make-File Utility uses the file MAKEFILE.FIL to create the Filer Library file FILER.LIB. Create the MAKEFILE.FIL file, type the following statements, and save the file.

```
record.obj: record.c record.h
   msc record;

index.obj: index.c record.h
   msc index;

filer.lib: index.obj record.obj
```

```
lib @filer.lnk
```

The MAKEFILE.FIL directs the Make-File Utility to compile the files RECORD.C and INDEX.C whenever changes have been made to one of them or changes were made to the include file RECORD.H. The file FILER.LIB is created using the file FILER.LNK.

Creating the Filer Library Linker File — FILER.LNK

The FILER.LNK file contains the information needed by the 'C' Run Time Library Utility to create the FILER.LIB file. Create the FILER.LNK file, type the following statements, and save the file.

```
filer
Y
+index+record
filer.map
```

After the build process is complete, the programmer will have a new Filer Library called FILER.LIB in the subdirectory FILER. This library is linked in with the application when the application is linked into its executable form.

CREATING THE FILER LIBRARY INCLUDE AND 'C' SOURCE FILES

The Filer Library is made up of one include source file and two 'C' source files. The include file RECORD.H contains the data structure definition needed to define a customer record. The RECORD.C source file contains the functions needed to initialize the customer data file and to read in the records from the disk. The INDEX.C source file contains the functions needed to read in the index from the disk.

Create the RECORD.H Include Source File

The RECORD.H include source file contains the data structure definition RECORD_FORM. The structure is used to contain the customer data information, such as the customer's name and address.

Create the RECORD.H file, type the following statements, and save the file.

```
/*======================================================================*/
/*                                                                      */
/* File : RECORD.H                                                      */
/*                                                                      */
/* Purpose : This include file contains the data structure             */
/*           definitions needed to define a customer record.           */
/*                                                                      */
/* Data Structures : typedef struct RECORD_FORM defines a structure    */
/*           that is used to define a customer record.  The customer    */
```

```
/*              record is made up of the following fields:        */
/*              char title[5] - The title of the customer, Mr., Ms., Dr. */
/*              char fname[20] - The customer's first name        */
/*              char mname[20] - The customer's middle name       */
/*              char lname[20] - The customer's last name         */
/*              char affil[25] - The customer's affiliation       */
/*              char address[25] - The customer's address         */
/*              char city[25] - The customer's city               */
/*              char state[3] - The customer's state              */
/*              char zipcode[10] - The customer's zip code        */
/*              char phone[13] - The customer's phone number      */
/*              char comment[60] - A personal comment about the customer */
/*                                                                */
/*================================================================*/

typedef struct
{
    char title[5];
    char fname[20];
    char mname[20];
    char lname[20];
    char affil[25];
    char address[25];
    char city[25];
    char state[3];
    char zipcode[10];
    char phone[13];
    char comment[60];
} RECORD_FORM;
```

Create the Filer Library Source File — RECORD.C

The RECORD.C source file contains the functions needed to initialize the records from the customer's disk data file into the record data array Record. The global variable Record is defined by the application and is used by the ReadRecords ( ) function. It is hard coded to have thirty customers because the functions needed to update the data file have not been written and must be implemented by the programmer.

Create the RECORD.C source file, type the following statements, and save the file.

```
/*================================================================*/
/*                                                                */
/* File : RECORD.C                                                */
/*                                                                */
/* Purpose : This 'C' source file contains the functions needed to */
/*           initialize and read in the customer data file.       */
/*                                                                */
/* Standard Include Files : <fcntl.h>, <sys\types.h>, <sys\stat.h> */
/*           These include files are standard 'C' include files that */
/*           contain the DOS file input and output defines.       */
```

```
/*                                                                      */
/* Include Files : "record.h" - This include file contains the data     */
/*          structure definitions that define a customer record.        */
/*                                                                      */
/* External Data Definitions : RECORD_FORM Record[30] - The data        */
/*          variable Record is defined to be of the type RECORD_FORM.    */
/*          This variable is originally defined by the application.      */
/*          The array Record is used to contain the actual customer     */
/*          data, such as name, for each customer.                      */
/*                                                                      */
/*          long Index[30] - The data variable array Index is used      */
/*          to contain pointers to where the next sorted customer       */
/*          record is on disk.                                          */
/*                                                                      */
/*          int Number_Of_Records - This variable is used to contain    */
/*          the actual number of records in the customer data file.     */
/*                                                                      */
/* Functions : InitDataFile () - This function is called by the         */
/*          application whenever it wishes to initialize a new          */
/*          customer data file into memory.                             */
/*                                                                      */
/*          ReadRecords () - This function is called by the             */
/*          InitDataFile () function to read the customer data into      */
/*          the Record [] array.                                        */
/*                                                                      */
/*          CreateNewFile () - This function is called to create a      */
/*          new customer data file.                                     */
/*                                                                      */
/*          InitRecords () - This function is called to initialize      */
/*          the Record and Index data arrays.                           */
/*                                                                      */
/*          WriteRecords () - This function is called to write the      */
/*          customer data records to disk.                              */
/*                                                                      */
/*======================================================================*/

#include    <fcntl.h>
#include    <sys\types.h>
#include    <sys\stat.h>
#include    "record.h"

extern RECORD_FORM Record[30];
extern long Index[30];
extern int Number_Of_Records;
```

Create the RECORD.C Function — InitDataFile ( )

The InitDataFile ( ) function is called by the application whenever it needs to initialize a new data file. The InitDataFile ( ) function is very limited; it first tries to read in the customer data file index and then reads in the customer data records. If there are any file errors, then these are returned. This function should be modified by the programmer to more extensively test the error conditions that are possible, such as a corrupted index or data file.

Edit the RECORD.C source file, type the following statements, and save the file.

```
/*========================================================================*/
/*                                                                        */
/* Function : InitDataFile (filename);                                    */
/*                                                                        */
/* Purpose : This function initializes a new customer data file.          */
/*                                                                        */
/* Entry Parameters : char *filename - The variable filename is a         */
/*             pointer to the customer file to initialize.                */
/*                                                                        */
/* Local Data Definitions - int return_code - This variable is used       */
/*             to contain the return code from ReadIndex ().              */
/*                                                                        */
/* Functions Called : ReadIndex () - This function is called to read      */
/*             the customer file index.                                   */
/*                                                                        */
/*             ReadRecords () - This function is called to read the       */
/*             customer data into the Record [] array.                    */
/*                                                                        */
/* Logic Flow : The InitDataFile () function is called with a pointer     */
/*             to the customer file to initialize.  The function          */
/*             ReadIndex () is called to read in the customer file        */
/*             index.  If an error occurred while trying to read in the*/
/*             index, then the error code is returned.  The function      */
/*             ReadRecords () is then called to read in the customer      */
/*             records into memory.                                       */
/*                                                                        */
/* Exit : The return code from ReadRecords () is returned.                */
/*          return <= 0 - An error  occurred                              */
/*          return > 0  - No errors occurred                              */
/*                                                                        */
/*========================================================================*/

InitDatafile (filename)
char *filename;
{
    int return_code;

    if ((return_code = ReadIndex (filename)) <= 0)
        return (return_code);
    return (ReadRecords (filename));
}
```

Create the RECORD.C Function — ReadRecords ( )

The ReadRecords ( ) function is called to read the customer data records from disk. The array Index[] is used to locate the next sorted record in the file. This function is limited and should be modified by the programmer to handle more error conditions.

Edit the RECORD.C source file, type the following statements, and save the file.

```
/*=======================================================================*/
/*                                                                       */
/* Function : ReadRecords (filename);                                    */
/*                                                                       */
/* Purpose : This function initializes a new customer data file.         */
/*                                                                       */
/* Entry Parameters : char *filename - The variable filename is a        */
/*          pointer to the customer file to initialize.                  */
/*                                                                       */
/* Local Data Definitions - int handle - This variable is used as the    */
/*          file handle for the customer data file.                      */
/*                                                                       */
/*          int i - This variable is used as a counter for each          */
/*          customer record read in.                                     */
/*                                                                       */
/*          long loc - This variable is used as a record pointer         */
/*          to the place on disk where the customer record is.           */
/*                                                                       */
/* Functions Called : sprintf () - This function is called to add        */
/*          on the extension, 'dat' to the filename passed to be         */
/*          able to open the customer data file.                         */
/*                                                                       */
/*          open () - This function is called to open the customer       */
/*          data file.                                                   */
/*                                                                       */
/*          lseek () - This function is called to move the disk          */
/*          file's current pointer to the next customer record.          */
/*                                                                       */
/*          read () - This function is called to read in the customer*/
/*          data record into the array Record [].                        */
/*                                                                       */
/*          close () - This function is called to close the customer     */
/*          record data file.                                            */
/*                                                                       */
/* Logic Flow : The ReadRecords () function is called with a pointer     */
/*          to the customer filename to use.  The extension 'dat'        */
/*          is added to the filename.  The function open () is           */
/*          called to open the file. If an invalid file handle is        */
/*          returned, then the error is returned to the calling          */
/*          function. Read in customer records until all of them         */
/*          have been read in.  Use the location provided by the         */
/*          Index [] array and add the size of one int to it to get      */
/*          the actual location of the customer data record. When        */
/*          all of the records have been read in, then call the          */
/*          function close () to close the customer data file.           */
```

```
/*                                                                    */
/* Exit : The customer data file records have been read into memory.  */
/*         return <= 0 - An error  occurred                           */
/*         return > 0  - No errors occurred                           */
/*                                                                    */
/*==================================================================*/

ReadRecords (filename)
char *filename;
{
    int handle;
    int i;
    long loc;

    sprintf (filename + strlen(filename) - 3, "dat");
    handle = open (filename, O_RDWR | O_BINARY, S_IREAD | S_IWRITE);
    if (handle < 1) return (handle);
    loc = 0;
    for (i = 0; i < Number_Of_Records; i++)
    {
        loc = Index[i] + sizeof(int);
        lseek (handle, loc, 0);
        read  (handle, &Record[i], sizeof (RECORD_FORM));
    }
    close (handle);
    return (handle);
}
```

Create the RECORD.C Function — CreateNewFile ( )

The CreateNewFile ( ) function is designed to create a new customer data file for the reader. The mail list application opens the file SAMPLE.IDX to read in the file index. This function is used as a seed to the customer data files needed by the application.

Edit the RECORD.C source file, type the following statements, and save the file.

```
/*==================================================================*/
/*                                                                    */
/* Function : CreateNewFile (filename);                               */
/*                                                                    */
/* Purpose : This function creates a new customer data file.          */
/*                                                                    */
/* Entry Parameters : char *filename - The variable filename is a     */
/*          pointer to the customer file to create.                   */
/*                                                                    */
/* Local Data Definitions - int return_code - This variable is used   */
/*          as the return code from CreateIndex ().                   */
/*                                                                    */
/* Functions Called : InitRecords () - This function is called to     */
/*          initialize the Record data array with string data and     */
```

```
/*           to initialize the Index data array.                  */
/*                                                                */
/*           CreateIndex () - This function is called to create the  */
/*           index for the new customer file.                     */
/*                                                                */
/*           WriteRecords () - This function is called to create the */
/*           data records for the new customer data file          */
/*                                                                */
/* Logic Flow : The InitRecords () function is called to initialize  */
/*           the Record data array with temporary data.  The function */
/*           CreateIndex () is called to create the new customer   */
/*           data file.  The WriteRecords () function is called to */
/*           create the new customer record data file.            */
/*                                                                */
/* Exit : The new customer data file has been created.            */
/*           return <= 0 - An error  occurred                     */
/*           return > 0  - No errors occurred                     */
/*                                                                */
/*================================================================*/

CreateNewFile (filename)
char *filename;
{
   int return_code;

   InitRecords ();
   if ((return_code = CreateIndex (filename)) <= 0)
      return (return_code);
   return (WriteRecords (filename));
}
```

Create the RECORD.C Function — InitRecords ( )

This function is also used to seed the sample customer data files. It initializes 25 records and 25 indexes to be used as sample data by the application.

Edit the RECORD.C source file, type the following statements, and save the file.

```
/*================================================================*/
/*                                                                */
/* Function : InitRecords ();                                     */
/*                                                                */
/* Purpose : This function creates a new customer data file.      */
/*                                                                */
/* External Data Definitions : int Number_Of_Records - This variable */
/*           is used to contain the actual number of records in the  */
/*           customer data file.                                  */
/*                                                                */
/* Local Data Definitions - int i - This variable is used as a    */
/*           counter for each customer record initialized.        */
/*                                                                */
/*           char str[11] - This string variable is used to       */
```

```
/*          initialize the Record data strings.                  */
/*                                                               */
/* Functions Called : strcpy () - This function is called to     */
/*          initialize the str variable with string data.        */
/*                                                               */
/*          strset () - This function is called to set the str   */
/*          variable for each record being initialized.          */
/*                                                               */
/*          strncpy () - This function is called to copy the str */
/*          variable into Record data array.                     */
/*                                                               */
/*          sizeof () - This function is called to copy calculate*/
/*          the size of a Record data array.                     */
/*                                                               */
/* Logic Flow : The str variable is initialized with 'a's.  The  */
/*          Number_Of_Records variable is initialized with 25.  The */
/*          str variable is changed according to the record number */
/*          being initialized.  Each field in the Record data array */
/*          is initialized.  The Index array is initialized to the */
/*          address of where the Record will be stored on disk.  */
/*                                                               */
/* Exit : The new customer data file has been initialized.       */
/*                                                               */
/*=============================================================*/

InitRecords ()
{
    int i;
    char str[11];

    strcpy (str, "aaaaaaaaaa");
    Number_Of_Records = 25;
    for (i = 0; i < Number_Of_Records; i++)
    {
        strset (str, i + 'a');
        strncpy (Record[i].title,   str, 3);
        strncpy (Record[i].fname,   str, 5);
        strncpy (Record[i].mname,   str, 3);
        strncpy (Record[i].lname,   str, 6);
        strncpy (Record[i].affil,   str, 8);
        strncpy (Record[i].address, str, 6);
        strncpy (Record[i].city,    str, 4);
        strncpy (Record[i].state,   str, 2);
        strncpy (Record[i].zipcode, str, 5);
        strncpy (Record[i].phone,   str, 6);
        strncpy (Record[i].comment, str, 4);
        Index[i] = i * sizeof (RECORD_FORM);
    }
}
```

Create the RECORD.C Function — WriteRecords ( )

This function is also used to seed the sample customer data files. It write the arrays initialized by the InitRecords ( ) function.

Edit the RECORD.C source file, type the following statements, and save the file.

```
/*======================================================================*/
/*                                                                      */
/* Function : WriteRecords (filename);                                  */
/*                                                                      */
/* Purpose : This function creates a new customer data file.            */
/*                                                                      */
/* Entry Parameters : char *filename - The variable filename is a       */
/*           pointer to the customer file to create.                    */
/*                                                                      */
/* Local Data Definitions - int handle - This variable is used as the   */
/*           file handle for the customer data file.                    */
/*                                                                      */
/*           int i - This variable is used as a counter for each        */
/*           customer record read in.                                   */
/*                                                                      */
/*           int j - This variable is used as a marker for the Index.   */
/*                                                                      */
/*           long loc - This variable is used as a record pointer       */
/*           to the place on disk where the customer record is.         */
/*                                                                      */
/* Functions Called : sprintf () - This function is called to add       */
/*           on the extension 'dat' to the filename passed to be        */
/*           able to open the customer data file.                       */
/*                                                                      */
/*           open () - This function is called to open the customer     */
/*           data file.                                                 */
/*                                                                      */
/*           lseek () - This function is called to move the disk        */
/*           file's current pointer to the next customer record.        */
/*                                                                      */
/*           write () - This function is called to write the customer   */
/*           data record to the disk.                                   */
/*                                                                      */
/*           close () - This function is called to close the customer   */
/*           record data file.                                          */
/*                                                                      */
/* Logic Flow : The WriteRecords () function is called with a pointer   */
/*           to the customer filename to use.  The extension 'dat'      */
/*           is added to the filename.  The function open () is         */
/*           called to open the file. If an invalid file handle is      */
/*           returned, then the error is returned to the calling        */
/*           function. Write the customer records until all of them     */
/*           have been written.  Use the location provided by the       */
/*           Index [] array and add the size of one int to it to get    */
/*           the actual location of the customer data record. When      */
/*           all of the records have been written, then call the        */
```

```
/*             function close () to close the customer data file.     */
/*                                                                    */
/* Exit : The customer data file records have been written to disk.   */
/*        return <= 0 - An error  occurred                            */
/*        return > 0  - No errors occurred                            */
/*                                                                    */
/*====================================================================*/

WriteRecords (filename)
char *filename;
{
    int handle;
    int i,j;
    long loc;

    sprintf (filename + strlen(filename) - 3, "dat");
    handle = open (filename,
                   O_WRONLY | O_TRUNC | O_CREAT | O_BINARY,
                   S_IREAD | S_IWRITE);
    if (handle < 1) return (handle);
    loc = 0;
    j = 1;
    for (i = 0; i < Number_Of_Records; i++)
    {
        loc = Index[i];
        lseek (handle, loc, 0);
        write (handle, &j, sizeof (int));
        loc = Index[i] + sizeof (int);
        write (handle, &Record[i], sizeof (RECORD_FORM));
    }
    close (handle);
    return (handle);
}
```

Create the Filer Library Source File — INDEX.C

The INDEX.C source file contains the ReadIndex ( ) function and is designed to read in the index of a given customer filename. It also contains the CreateIndex ( ) function which is designed to create a new index file. The programmer should note that these functions are only two of the many functions that would have to be written to be able to maintain a real indexed database. Functions such as WriteIndex ( ) and UpdateIndex ( ) will have to be written. This book will not show you how to write these functions, but the reader should be aware that these functions need to be written.

Create the INDEX.C source file, type the following statements and save the file.

```
/*====================================================================*/
/*                                                                    */
/* File : INDEX.C                                                     */
```

```
/*                                                                      */
/* Purpose : This 'C' source file contains the function  needed to      */
/*           read in the customer data file index.                      */
/*                                                                      */
/* Standard Include Files : <fcntl.h>, <sys\types.h>, <sys\stat.h>      */
/*           These include files are standard 'C' include files that    */
/*           contain the DOS file input and output defines.             */
/*                                                                      */
/* Include Files : "record.h" - This include file contains the data     */
/*           structure definitions that define a customer record.       */
/*                                                                      */
/* External Data Definitions : long Index[30] - The data variable       */
/*           array Index is used to contain pointers to the location     */
/*           of the next sorted customer record on disk.                */
/*                                                                      */
/*           int Number_Of_Records - This variable is used to contain   */
/*           the actual number of records in the customer data file.    */
/*                                                                      */
/* Functions : ReadIndex () - This function is called to read in the    */
/*           customer data file index.                                  */
/*                                                                      */
/*           CreateIndex () - This function is called to create a       */
/*           new customer data file index.                              */
/*                                                                      */
/*====================================================================*/

#include    <fcntl.h>
#include    <sys\types.h>
#include    <sys\stat.h>
#include "record.h"

extern long Index[30];
extern int Number_Of_Records;
```

Create the INDEX.C Function — ReadIndex ( )

The ReadIndex ( ) function is called to read the index to the customer data file. Each Index entry points to the beginning of the next sorted customer in the data file. The locations inside of Index [] array are used when reading or writing the customer record data.

Edit the INDEX.C source file, type the following statements, and save the file.

```
/*====================================================================*/
/*                                                                      */
/* Function : ReadIndex (filename);                                     */
/*                                                                      */
/* Purpose : This function reads in the index of a customer data file.*/
/*                                                                      */
/* Entry Parameters : char *filename - The variable filename is a       */
/*           pointer to the customer file to initialize.                */
```

```
/*                                                                    */
/* Local Data Definitions - int handle - This variable is used as the */
/*          file handle for the customer data file.                   */
/*                                                                    */
/*          int i - This variable is used as a counter for each       */
/*          customer record read.                                     */
/*                                                                    */
/*          long loc - This variable is used as a record pointer      */
/*          to the place on disk where the customer record is.        */
/*                                                                    */
/* Functions Called : sprintf () - This function is called to add     */
/*          on the extension 'idx' to the filename passed to be       */
/*          able to open the customer data file.                      */
/*                                                                    */
/*          open () - This function is called to open the customer    */
/*          data file.                                                */
/*                                                                    */
/*          lseek () - This function is called to move the disk       */
/*          file's current pointer to the next customer record.       */
/*                                                                    */
/*          read () - This function is called to read in the customer*/
/*          data record into the array Record [].                     */
/*                                                                    */
/*          close () - This function is called to close the customer  */
/*          record data file.                                         */
/*                                                                    */
/* Logic Flow : The ReadIndex () function is called with a pointer    */
/*          to the customer filename to use.  The extension 'idx'     */
/*          is added to the filename.  The function open () is        */
/*          called to open the file. If an invalid file handle is     */
/*          returned, then the error is returned to the calling       */
/*          function.  Call the function lseek () to move to the      */
/*          beginning of the file.  Read in the Number_Of_Records.    */
/*          For each record there is, read in its Index location.     */
/*          Call the function close () to close the file after it     */
/*          has been opened.                                          */
/*                                                                    */
/* Exit : The customer data file index has been read into memory.     */
/*          return <= 0 - An error   occurred                         */
/*          return > 0  - No errors occurred                          */
/*                                                                    */
/*==================================================================*/

ReadIndex (filename)
char *filename;
{
   int  handle;
   int  i;
   long loc;

   sprintf (filename + strlen (filename) - 3, "idx");
   handle = open (filename, O_RDWR | O_BINARY, S_IREAD | S_IWRITE);
   if (handle > 0)
```

```
    {
        loc = 0;
        lseek (handle, loc, 0);
        read (handle, &Number_Of_Records, sizeof (int));
        loc += sizeof (int);
        for (i = 0; i < Number_Of_Records; i++)
        {
            lseek (handle, loc, 0);
            read (handle, &Index[i], sizeof (long));
            loc += sizeof (long);
        }
        close (handle);
    }
    return (handle);
}
```

Create the INDEX.C Function — CreateIndex ( )

The CreateIndex ( ) function is called to create the index to the customer data file.
This function is also used to seed the application data files.

Edit the INDEX.C source file, type the following statements, and save the file.

```
/*======================================================================*/
/*                                                                      */
/* Function : CreateIndex (filename);                                   */
/*                                                                      */
/* Purpose : This function creates the index of a customer data file.   */
/*                                                                      */
/* Entry Parameters : char *filename - The variable filename is a       */
/*          pointer to the customer file to create.                     */
/*                                                                      */
/* Local Data Definitions - int handle - This variable is used as the   */
/*          file handle for the customer data file.                     */
/*                                                                      */
/*          int i - This variable is used as a counter for each         */
/*          customer record written.                                    */
/*                                                                      */
/*          long loc - This variable is used as a record pointer        */
/*          to the place on disk where the customer record is.          */
/*                                                                      */
/* Functions Called : sprintf () - This function is called to add       */
/*          on the extension 'idx' to the filename passed to be         */
/*          able to open the customer data file.                        */
/*                                                                      */
/*          open () - This function is called to open the customer      */
/*          data file.                                                  */
/*                                                                      */
/*          lseek () - This function is called to move the disk         */
/*          file's current pointer to the next customer record.         */
/*                                                                      */
/*          write () - This function is called to write the customer */
```

```
/*              data record into the array Index [].                  */
/*                                                                    */
/*              close () - This function is called to close the customer */
/*              record data file.                                     */
/*                                                                    */
/* Logic Flow : The CreateIndex () function is called with a pointer  */
/*              to the customer filename to use.  The extension 'idx' */
/*              is added to the filename.  The function open () is     */
/*              called to open the file. If an invalid file handle is  */
/*              returned, then the error is returned to the calling    */
/*              function.  Call the function lseek () to move to the   */
/*              beginning of the file.  Write the Number_Of_Records.   */
/*              For each record there is, write its Index location.    */
/*              Call the function close () to close the file after it  */
/*              has been opened.                                      */
/*                                                                    */
/* Exit : The customer data file index has been written to disk.      */
/*        return <= 0 - An error  occurred                            */
/*        return > 0  - No errors occurred                            */
/*                                                                    */
/*==================================================================*/

CreateIndex (filename)
char *filename;
{
    int   handle;
    int   i;
    long loc;

    sprintf (filename + strlen(filename) - 3, "idx");
    handle = open (filename,
                     O_WRONLY | O_TRUNC | O_CREAT | O_BINARY,
                     S_IREAD | S_IWRITE);
    if (handle > 0)
    {
        loc = 0;
        lseek (handle, loc, 0);
        write (handle, &Number_Of_Records, sizeof (int));
        loc += sizeof(int);
        for (i = 0; i < Number_Of_Records; i++)
        {
            lseek (handle, loc, 0);
            write (handle, &Index[i], sizeof (long));
            loc += sizeof (long);
        }
        close (handle);
    }
    return (handle);
}
```

SUMMARY

The Filer Library is designed exclusively for the mail list application and contains only those functions that are needed for the mail list application to display sample customer records on the screen using a list box. Several new functions can be added by the programmer that increase the functionality of the Filer Library. The programmer can use other file maintenance systems already on the market, such as dBASE, but he will always have to write some sort of interface to use that system.

The primary purpose for creating the Filer Library is to allow the programmer to create and maintain the functions needed to maintain the application's saved data. This maintenance of data is the one of the primary purposes for writing applications on the computer in the first place. By separating the file input and output routines into its own library the programmer can use these library systems between applications or use a different file maintenance system without changing the graphical menu driven user interface.

The final chapters of this book show the user how to create a sample application using the functions that have been written for the CGA Graphics Library, the Menu Library, and the Filer Library.

Chapter 13

THE MAIL LIST APPLICATION

INTRODUCTION

The mail list application is a sample application. The programmer should study this application to understand the basic techniques behind application programming. The mail list application is designed to only give the reader a general understanding of how to write graphical menu driven applications using a consistent user interface design. It is not by any means completed; that is for you to do. It does however do the following things:

- Teaches the overall design structure behind writing applications.
- Teaches the design, implementation, and program control flow of primary menus, dialog boxes, and message boxes.
- Teaches the design and implementation of push buttons, entry fields, list boxes, check boxes, and radio buttons.
- Teaches a basic understanding of manipulating data that is stored to disk.

From there, the programmer can understand the basic concepts behind graphical menu driven applications and can begin writing his own applications using very similar techniques.

DESIGNING THE MAIL LIST APPLICATION

To begin programming any application, the programmer must decide what he wants the application to do. For the purposes of this book I have chosen a mail list application. It does not really matter what the application is; these techniques can be used by any application.

Every application needs to have a primary menu. A primary menu is a menu that must contain the following things:

- The upper left-hand row and column coordinates of the primary menu.
- The width and height of the primary menu.
- A header string describing the primary menu, such as 'Mail List.'
- An action bar containing a list of options that the user can select to perform operations on the application, such as 'File.'
- A Work Area that contains the description of the primary menu, such as a list box or push buttons.
- An application specific function that the Menu ( ) function calls after the primary menu has been displayed on the screen.

The application primary menu is the menu that controls the program flow of the application. The application issues a call to the Menu ( ) function to begin processing of the primary menu; from then on, the application specific functions are called when certain application defined events occur.

The mail list application makes use of the CGA Graphics Library, Menu Library, and the Filer Library to perform the nonapplication specific functions. The functions that are specific to the application are defined in the following source files.

- DEFINES.H - This include file contains the defined data definitions that are specific to the application.
- MAIL.C - This 'C' source file contains the standard 'C' function main ( ) and is the main controlling thread of the application.
- MAINMENU.C - This 'C' source file contains the definition of the application's primary menu, Main_Menu.
- MAILLIST.C - This 'C' source file contains the functions that are needed to process the primary menu.
- FILE.C - This 'C' source file contains the functions that are needed to process the action bar menu File.
- EDIT.C - This 'C' source file contains the functions that are needed to process the action bar menu Edit.
- OPTIONS.C - This 'C' source file contains the functions that are needed to process the action bar menu Options.
- HELP.C - This 'C' source file contains the functions that are needed to process the action bar menu Help.
- ERRORS.C - This 'C' source file contains the functions that are needed to process the error messages.

CREATING THE APPLICATION FILES

Before we go any further into the discussion about Primary Menus and applications in general, let's go ahead and create our batch files to manage our source files for use. First, change directories to the subdirectory MAILLIST.

> Type **CD \MAILLIST** and press **Return**.

Now that you are in the application subdirectory, create the BUILD.BAT file. This batch file is very similar to the previous ones created except that it will manage the application source files.

Create the BUILD.BAT file, type the following statement, and save the file.

MAKE MAKEFILE.APP

The statement MAKE MAKEFILE.APP invokes the Make File Utility using the makefile MAKEFILE.APP. Next, create the MAKEFILE.APP file to contain the information to be able to compile and link the application.

Create the MAKEFILE.APP file, type the following statements, and save the file.

```
mail.obj: mail.c defines.h
 msc mail;

mainmenu.obj: mainmenu.c \menu\menu.h \menu\keyboard.h defines.h
 msc mainmenu;

maillist.obj: maillist.c \graphics\colors.h \menu\menu.h \filer\record.h
 msc maillist;

file.obj: file.c \menu\menu.h \menu\keyboard.h defines.h
 msc file;

edit.obj: edit.c \menu\menu.h \menu\keyboard.h \filer\record.h defines.h
 msc edit;

options.obj: options.c \menu\menu.h \menu\keyboard.h defines.h
 msc options;

help.obj: help.c \menu\message.h
 msc help;

errors.obj: errors.c \menu\message.h \menu\keyboard.h defines.h
 msc errors;

mail.exe: mail.obj mainmenu.obj maillist.obj \
          file.obj edit.obj options.obj help.obj errors.obj\
          \graphics\cgagraph.lib \menu\menu.lib \
          \filer\filer.lib
  link @appl.lnk
```

The MAKEFILE.APP file contains the information needed to direct the Make File Utility into creating a new executable. This makefile is different than the ones needed to build the Libraries because instead of calling the Library Linker, the Object Linker was called. The Object Linker creates an executable, where the Library Linker creates only a library that the Object Linker uses to create an executable.

Next create the APPL.LNK file. This file directs the Object Linker to create the executable file MAIL.EXE.

Create the APPL.LNK file, type the following statements, and save the file.

```
mail+file+options+mainmenu+help+edit+maillist+errors,,,
\graphics\cgagraph+\menu\menu+\filer\filer;
```

The APPL.LNK directs the Object Linker to use the eight object files that make up the application specific functions, and to use the CGAGRAPH.LIB, the MENU.LIB, and the FILER.LIB library files to create the executable MAIL.EXE.

Creating the Mail List Application Source Include File — DEFINES.H

Just as the Libraries needed certain defined data, the application also must use defined data. These defined data are kept in the DEFINES.H source include file.

Create the DEFINES.H source include file, type the following statements, and save the file.

```
/*=======================================================================*/
/*                                                                       */
/* File : DEFINES.H                                                      */
/*                                                                       */
/* Purpose : This include file contains the defined data definitions     */
/*           used by the mail list application.                          */
/*                                                                       */
/* Data Defined : CGA 4 - Defines the value for the color graphics       */
/*           adapter.                                                    */
/*                                                                       */
/*           FONTWIDTH 6 - Defines the width of a character icon.        */
/*                                                                       */
/*           FONTHEIGHT 10 - Defines the height of a character icon.     */
/*                                                                       */
/*           RADIO_BUTTON 0 - Defines a radio button identifier.         */
/*                                                                       */
/*           CHECK_BOX 1 - Defines a check box identifier.               */
/*                                                                       */
/*           OFF 0 - Defines an Off state.                               */
/*                                                                       */
/*           ON 1 - Defines an ON state.                                 */
/*                                                                       */
```

```
/*              FILEIO_ERROR - Defines a general file input / output    */
/*              error.                                                   */
/*                                                                      */
/*              CREATE_RECORD_ERROR 2 - Defines a record creation error. */
/*                                                                      */
/*              EDIT_RECORD_ERROR 3 - Defines an edit record error.     */
/*                                                                      */
/*              DELETE_RECORD_ERROR 4 - Defines a delete record error.  */
/*                                                                      */
/*              HELP_ERROR 5 - Defines an error for help.               */
/*                                                                      */
/*              CREATE_FILE_ERROR 6 - Defines an error creating a file. */
/*                                                                      */
/*              SAVE_FILE_ERROR 7 - Defines an error saving the file.   */
/*                                                                      */
/*              LOAD_FILE_ERROR 8 - Defines an error loading a file.    */
/*                                                                      */
/*              DELETE_FILE_ERROR 9 - Defines an error deleting a file. */
/*                                                                      */
/*              FONTHEIGHT 10 - Defines the variable FONTHEIGHT to be   */
/*              10, which is the height of a character icon.            */
/*                                                                      */
/*              RADIO_BUTTON 0 - Defines the variable RADIO_BUTTON to be */
/*              0, which is used to define a group type in a dialog box. */
/*                                                                      */
/*              CHECK_BOX 1 - Defines the variable CHECK_BOX to be 1,   */
/*              which is used to define a group type in a dialog box.   */
/*                                                                      */
/*              OFF 0 - Defines the variable OFF to be 0; it is used to */
/*              define a radio button or a check box to be off.         */
/*                                                                      */
/*              ON 1 - Defines the variable ON to be 0; it is used to   */
/*              define a radio button or a check box to be on.          */
/*                                                                      */
/*              ENTRY 1 - Define the variable ENTRY to be 1, which is   */
/*              used by the dialog box function to indicate that the    */
/*              Entry fields are being processed.                       */
/*                                                                      */
/*              BUTTONS 2 - Defines the variable BUTTONS to be 2, which */
/*              is used by the dialog box function to indicate that the */
/*              radio buttons are being processed.                      */
/*                                                                      */
/*              NO_HIGHLIGHT 0 - Defines the variable NO_HIGHLIGHT to   */
/*              be 0, which is used to indicate a listbox box string as */
/*              being not highlighted.                                  */
/*                                                                      */
/*              HIGHLIGHT 1 - Defines the variable HIGHLIGHT to be 1,   */
/*              which is used to indicate a list box string as being    */
/*              highlighted                                             */
/*                                                                      */
/*              SCROLL_UP 0 - Defines SCROLL_UP to be 0, which is used  */
/*              by the list box functions to scroll the list box UP.    */
/*                                                                      */
```

```
/*              SCROLL_DOWN 1 - Defines the SCROLL_DOWN variable to be 1,*/
/*              which is used by the list box functions to scroll the    */
/*              list box DOWN.                                            */
/*                                                                       */
/*              SCROLL_LEFT 2 - Defines the SCROLL_LEFT variable to be 2,*/
/*              which is used by the list box functions to scroll the    */
/*              list box to the LEFT.                                     */
/*                                                                       */
/*              SCROLL_RIGHT 3 - Defines the SCROLL_RIGHT variable to be */
/*              3, which is used by the list box function to scroll the  */
/*              list box to the RIGHT.                                    */
/*                                                                       */
/*              UPARROW 4 - Defines the UPARROW variable to be 4, which  */
/*              is used by the list box function to move the highlight   */
/*              one line up.                                              */
/*                                                                       */
/*              DOWNARROW 5 - Defines the DOWNARROW variable to be 5,    */
/*              which is used by the list box function to move the       */
/*              highlight down one line.                                 */
/*                                                                       */
/*              REFRESH 6 - Defines REFRESH to be 6; it is used by the   */
/*              list box functions to refresh to scroll box window.      */
/*                                                                       */
/*====================================================================*/

#define CGA                  4
#define FONTWIDTH            6
#define FONTHEIGHT          10
#define RADIO_BUTTON         0
#define CHECK_BOX            1
#define OFF                  0
#define ON                   1
#define FILEIO_ERROR         1
#define CREATE_RECORD_ERROR  2
#define EDIT_RECORD_ERROR    3
#define DELETE_RECORD_ERROR  4
#define HELP_ERROR           5
#define CREATE_FILE_ERROR    6
#define SAVE_FILE_ERROR      7
#define LOAD_FILE_ERROR      8
#define DELETE_FILE_ERROR    9
#define SCROLL_UP       0
#define SCROLL_DOWN     1
#define SCROLL_LEFT     2
#define SCROLL_RIGHT    3
#define UPARROW         4
#define DOWNARROW       5
#define REFRESH         6
```

The DEFINES.H source include file is the only include file used by the mail list application and it defines all of the defined data types that are specific to this application. The programmer can and should create more include files that contain other application specific data. Several defined data types are defined above and each one will be dealt with when the times comes in the application.

SUMMARY

The mail list application is a sample application that teaches the reader the fundamentals behind Graphical Menu Driven Applications. It is composed of one source include file and eight 'C' source files. The application implements a primary menu and the action bar menus associated with it. In the following chapters, each one of the 'C' source files is explained in detail.

Chapter 14

THE MAIL LIST APPLICATION 'C' SOURCE FILES

INTRODUCTION

The mail list application is a sample application that is made up of eight 'C' source files. These source files are divided into their application specific functions. Three of these source files, MAIL.C, MAINMENU.C, and MAILLIST.C, are discussed in this chapter.

These source files define and process the mail list application's primary menu and list box. They also define all global data variables and functions used to process the mail list application's primary menu.

Create the MAIL.C Source File

The MAIL.C source file contains the 'C' required function main ( ). Every application written in 'C' must have this function because it is the function that is called first upon entry into your application. The MAIL.C source file also defines all global data definitions used by the application or Libraries. This is done so that the programmer can find the original definition of the data variable without looking in the other 'C' source files.

Create the MAIL.C source file, type the following statements, and save the file.

```
/*===================================================================*/
/*                                                                   */
/* File : MAIL.C                                                     */
/*                                                                   */
/* Purpose : This 'C' source file contains the standard 'C' function */
/*           main () and is the main controlling thread of the mail  */
/*           list application.                                       */
```

```
/*                                                               */
/* Include Files : "\graphics\colors" - This include contains the */
/*          color definitions used by the mail list application.  */
/*                                                               */
/*          "\filer\record.h" - This include file contains the data */
/*          structure definitions needed to define a customer record.*/
/*                                                               */
/*          "defines.h" - This include file contains the defined */
/*          data definitions used by the mail list application.   */
/*                                                               */
/* Global Data Definitions : char Filename_Buffer[20] - This data */
/*          is used to contain the name of the customer file that */
/*          is currently being edited.                           */
/*                                                               */
/*          RECORD_FORM Record[30] - The data array Record[] is used */
/*          to keep track of the customer data in memory.  It is */
/*          defined to be of the structure type RECORD.          */
/*                                                               */
/*          long Index[30] - The data array Index[] is used to   */
/*          contain the location of each customer data record in */
/*          the customer data file.                              */
/*                                                               */
/*          int Number_Of_Records - This data variable is used to */
/*          contain the actual number of records in the data file. */
/*                                                               */
/*          int Current_Record - This data variable is used to keep */
/*          track of the customer record currently active.       */
/*                                                               */
/*          int Number_ActionBar_Menus - This data variable is used */
/*          to count the number of action bar menus there are on the */
/*          mail list primary menu.                              */
/*                                                               */
/*          int ActionBar_Hot_Keys[10] - This data array is used to */
/*          contain the hot keys, such as Alt+F, for each action bar */
/*          menu option.                                         */
/*                                                               */
/*          char Recs[14][350] - This data array is used by the list */
/*          box processor to display the customer records in the way */
/*          that they will appear on the screen.                 */
/*                                                               */
/*          int Listbox_Start_Str - This data variable is used to */
/*          maintain the topmost record to be displayed inside of */
/*          the list box.                                        */
/*                                                               */
/*          int Listbox_End_Str - This data variable is used to  */
/*          maintain the bottommost record to be displayed inside */
/*          of the list box.                                     */
/*                                                               */
/*          int Listbox_Start_Col - This data variable is used to */
/*          maintain the first displayable character of the records */
/*          displayed in the list box.                           */
/*                                                               */
/*          int Listbox_End_Col - This data variable is used to  */
```

```
/*          maintain the last displayable character of the records  */
/*          displayed in the list box.                              */
/*                                                                  */
/*          int H_Max_Len - This data variable is used by the scroll */
/*          bar to determine the maximum length of a horizontal     */
/*          scroll bar.                                             */
/*                                                                  */
/*          int V_Max_Len - This data variable is used by the scroll */
/*          bar to determine the maximum length of a vertical       */
/*          scroll bar.                                             */
/*                                                                  */
/* Functions : main () - This standard 'C' function is the first    */
/*          function that is called when the application begins.    */
/*                                                                  */
/*==================================================================*/

#include "\graphics\colors.h"
#include "\filer\record.h"
#include "defines.h"

char Filename_Buffer[20] = "sample.dat";

RECORD_FORM Record[30];

long Index[30];

int Number_Of_Records;
int Current_Record;
int Number_ActionBar_Menus;
int ActionBar_Hot_Keys[10];

char Recs[14][350];

int Listbox_Start_Str;
int Listbox_End_Str;
int Listbox_Start_Col;
int Listbox_End_Col;

int H_Max_Len = 63;
int V_Max_Len = 25;
```

The above code sets up the environment for the application. First, the CGA Graphics Library include file COLORS.H is needed to be able to call colors by a name, such as BLUE instead of a number. The Filer Library include file RECORD.H defines a customer record structure and is needed to define the customer data array Record[]. The DEFINES.H include file contains the defined data used by the application, such as CGA, to define the CGA Graphics Adapter Card.

Several global variables are defined, some dealing with the customer data file, and others dealing with the list box information. Each one of these data variables will be dealt with when they are actually used in the application. They are defined here so that they can all be kept in one place.

Next, the function main ( ) is added to the MAIL.C source file. Edit the MAIL.C source file, type the following statements, and save the file.

```
/*======================================================================*/
/*                                                                      */
/* Function : main (argc, argv);                                        */
/*                                                                      */
/* Purpose : This function is the first function that is called when    */
/*           the mail list application begins.  It saves the current    */
/*           screen mode, clears the screen, and transfers control to   */
/*           the MainMenu ().  When control is returned from the        */
/*           MainMenu (), then the application is finished.             */
/*                                                                      */
/* Entry Parameters : int argc - This variable is used to contain the  */
/*           number of parameters that are passed on to the mail list  */
/*           application from the DOS command line.                     */
/*                                                                      */
/*           char **argv - This variable is a group of pointers to     */
/*           strings that were passed on the command line.             */
/*                                                                      */
/* Local Data Definitions - int mode - This variable is used to        */
/*           contain the screen mode that is currently set when the    */
/*           mail list application begins.                             */
/*                                                                      */
/* Functions Called : sprintf () - This standard 'C' function is       */
/*           called whenever the user passes a filename to the mail    */
/*           list application.                                         */
/*                                                                      */
/*           GetCrtMode () - This function is called to return the     */
/*           current screen CRT mode so that it can be restored when   */
/*           the program is ended.                                     */
/*                                                                      */
/*           SelectDisplayPage () - This function is called to         */
/*           activate display page zero.                               */
/*                                                                      */
/*           SetCrtMode () - This function is called to select the     */
/*           CGA graphics mode as the current display mode.            */
/*                                                                      */
/*           ClearScreen () - This function is called to clear the     */
/*           screen in blue to begin the mail list application.        */
/*                                                                      */
/*           MainMenu () - This function is called to begin the        */
/*           processing of the mail list main menu.                    */
/*                                                                      */
/* Logic Flow : The standard 'C' function main () is required by all   */
/*           'C' programs and it is always the first function that is  */
/*           called when the application begins execution.  The        */
/*           variable int argc is checked to see if the user passed    */
/*           a filename to the mail list application. If this          */
/*           variable is greater than one, then a customer filename    */
```

```
/*            is assumed to be passed and it is copied into the       */
/*            global variable Filename_Buffer.  The variable int      */
/*            mode is set to the return code from the GetCrtMode ()   */
/*            function and it is used later to restore the screen     */
/*            back to this value when the mail list application is    */
/*            finished.  The SelectDisplayPage () function is called  */
/*            to activate display page zero. Next, the function       */
/*            SetCrtMode () is called to select the CGA display mode. */
/*            The screen is then cleared in blue using the            */
/*            ClearScreen () function.  Control is now passed to the   */
/*            function MainMenu ().  This function will process the    */
/*            the mail list applications primary menu.  When control   */
/*            is returned, the function SetCrtMode () is called to     */
/*            restore the original screen CRT mode.                    */
/*                                                                     */
/* Exit : The mail list application has finished processing.           */
/*                                                                     */
/*=====================================================================*/

main (argc, argv)
int argc;
char **argv;
{
    int    mode;

    if (argc > 1) sprintf (Filename_Buffer, "%s", argv[1]);
    mode = GetCrtMode ();
    SelectDisplayPage (0);
    SetCrtMode (CGA);
    ClearScreen (BLUE);
    MainMenu ();
    SetCrtMode (mode);
}
```

The function main ( ) is required of all 'C' applications. This is the first function called, and when the function has finished the application ends. First, any application can be passed extra parameters on the command line, such as the statement:

MAIL SAMPLE.DAT

The first part of the statement, MAIL, issues the command to start executing the MAIL.EXE file. The second part, SAMPLE.DAT, is passed to the application and it will be used as a filename.

The variables argc and argv are standard 'C' variables for determining whether or not the application was passed extra information on the command line. The variable argc is used as a counter to the number of arguments passed. The application is always passed the name of the application, such as MAIL. If argc is greater than one, then something else was passed and its location is pointed at the variable argv[]. The mail list application assumes this to be a user-defined customer filename and copies this into the Filename_Buffer. The programmer should note that validation of the information passed should be done, i.e., is this a valid filename.

The next statement calls the CGA Graphics Library function GetCrtMode ( ). Every application should make this one of the first things to do, especially when they are using graphics, because the application needs to restore the original screen mode. For example, if the original screen mode was 80 x 25 color text, and the application using graphics runs and does not restore the screen mode, then when it finishes processing, the user will be left in graphics mode. This is not a very user friendly thing to do. So a call is made to save the current screen mode, so that it can be restored upon exit of the application back to DOS.

Next, the application must set up its own environment using the Color Graphics Adapter. The function SelectDisplayPage ( ) is called to activate page 0 of video memory. This book does not make use of the other video display pages, but the reader should make note that there are more than one and that certain techniques can be used to switch back and forth between them. The function SetCrtMode (CGA) sets the CRT mode to the Color Graphics Adapter. After these two calls have been made, then the application is in graphics mode.

The next function call, ClearScreen (BLUE), is a CGA Graphics Library function that clears the screen in the color passed. Usually, the application will want to do this because it gives the application a better look and feel.

Next, the most important part of the main ( ) function is done. The function MainMenu ( ), found in MAINMENU.C, is called to begin the processing of the mail list application's primary menu. After the primary menu has finished processing, the original screen's CRT mode is restored and the application exits to DOS.

Create the Mail List Application Source File — MAINMENU.C

The MAINMENU.C source file defines the application's primary menu, Main_Menu. It is this menu that begins, controls, and ends the mail list application. When the primary menu has finished processing, the application is finished. The primary purpose of the Main_Menu is to teach the reader how to create a primary menu. As stated earlier, a primary menu must contain the following things:

- The upper left-hand row and column coordinates of the primary menu.
- The width and height of the primary menu.
- A header string describing the primary menu, such as 'Mail List.'
- An action bar containing a list of options that the user can select to perform operations on the application, such as 'File.'

- A work area containing the description of the primary menu, such as a list box or push buttons.
- An application specific function that the Menu ( ) function calls after the primary menu has been displayed on the screen.

The primary menu, Main_Menu, has a work area that defines only a list box; examples of push buttons and other things are dealt with later in the book.

Create the MAINMENU.C source file, type the following statements, and save the file.

```
/*=====================================================================*/
/*                                                                     */
/* File : MAINMENU.C                                                   */
/*                                                                     */
/* Purpose : This 'C' source file processes the mail list             */
/*           application's primary menu Main_Menu.                     */
/*                                                                     */
/* Include Files : "\menu\menu.h" - This include file contains the     */
/*           structure definitions needed to define a primary menu.    */
/*                                                                     */
/*           "\menu\keyboard.h" - This include file contains the       */
/*           keyboard definitions needed by the mail list primary      */
/*           menu.                                                     */
/*                                                                     */
/* External Function Declarations : int File () - This function is     */
/*           defined to be the function called whenever the action     */
/*           bar selection 'File' has been selected.                   */
/*                                                                     */
/*           int Edit () - This function is called whenever the action */
/*           bar selection 'Edit' has been selected.                   */
/*                                                                     */
/*           int Options () - This function is called whenever the     */
/*           action bar selection 'Options' has been selected.         */
/*                                                                     */
/*           int Help () - This function is called whenever the action */
/*           bar selection 'Help' has been selected.                   */
/*                                                                     */
/*           int MailList () - This function is called after the       */
/*           primary menu Main_Menu has been initialized on the screen.*/
/*                                                                     */
/*           int InitializeMailListBox () - This function is called to */
/*           initialize the primary menu Main_Menu list box.           */
/*                                                                     */
/*           int UpdateMailListBox () - This function is called        */
/*           whenever the primary menu Main_Menu list box needs to be  */
/*           updated.                                                  */
/*                                                                     */
/* Primary Menu Definitions - The mail list primary menu Main_Menu     */
/*           is defined by the following data definitions.             */
/*                                                                     */
```

```
/*          ITEM_PTR File_List[] - The array File_List[] is defined    */
/*          to contain the list of selections that are available to    */
/*          the user whenever the action bar menu 'File' is to be       */
/*          displayed and processed.                                    */
/*                                                                      */
/*          ITEM_PTR Edit_List[] - The array Edit_List[] is defined     */
/*          to contain the list of selections that are available to     */
/*          the user whenever the action bar menu 'Edit' is to be       */
/*          displayed and processed.                                    */
/*                                                                      */
/*          ITEM_PTR Option_List[] - The array Options_List[] is        */
/*          defined to contain the list of selections that are          */
/*          available to the user whenever the action bar menu          */
/*          'Options' is to be displayed and processed.                 */
/*                                                                      */
/*          ITEM_PTR Help_List[] - The array Help_List[] is defined     */
/*          to contain the list of selections that are available to     */
/*          the user whenever the action bar menu 'Help' is to be       */
/*          displayed and processed.                                    */
/*                                                                      */
/*          ACTION_BAR Action_Bar_List[] - The action bar menus are     */
/*          defined by the Action_Bar_List array.  This array contains*/
/*          the data definitions needed to define each of the action    */
/*          bar menus for the Mail List application.                     */
/*                                                                      */
/*          char *Mail_Listbox_Strings[14] - This array contains a      */
/*          list of pointers to the strings to be displayed in the      */
/*          mail list primary menu's list box.                          */
/*                                                                      */
/*          SCROLL_BAR Mail_Vertical_Scrollbars[] - This array defines*/
/*          the vertical scroll bar used by the mail list list box.     */
/*                                                                      */
/*          SCROLL_BAR Mail_Horizontal_Scrollbars[] - This array        */
/*          defines the horizontal scroll bar used by the mail list     */
/*          list box.                                                    */
/*                                                                      */
/*          LIST_BOX Mail_Listbox[] - The array Mail_Listbox[] defines*/
/*          the listbox that is used by the maillist application's      */
/*          primary menu Main_Menu.                                      */
/*                                                                      */
/*          WORK_AREA Mail_Workarea[] - The array Mail_Workarea []      */
/*          defines the mail list primary menu Main_Menu work area.      */
/*                                                                      */
/*          MENU_FORM Main_Menu - The array Main_Menu defines the       */
/*          mail list application's primary menu.                        */
/*                                                                      */
/* Functions : MainMenu () - This function is called to process the     */
/*           primary menu of the mail list application, Main_Menu.      */
/*                                                                      */
/*==================================================================*/

#include "\menu\menu.h"
#include "\menu\keyboard.h"
```

```
extern int File ();
extern int Edit ();
extern int Options ();
extern int Help ();
extern int MailList ();
extern int InitializeMailListBox ();
extern int UpdateMailListBox ();

ITEM_PTR File_List[] =
{
    " Create ", " Load   ", " Save   ", " Delete ", 0
};

ITEM_PTR Edit_List[] =
{
    " Insert ", " Edit   ", " Delete ", 0
};

ITEM_PTR Option_List[] =
{
    " Display ", " Sort    ", " Print   ", 0
};

ITEM_PTR Help_List[] =
{
    " Help ", 0
};

ACTION_BAR Action_Bar_List[] =
{
    {0, 0, " File ",    ALT_F, 1, File_List  , 4, File   , 0, 0 },
    {0, 0, " Edit ",    ALT_E, 1, Edit_List  , 3, Edit   , 0, 0 },
    {0, 0, " Options ", ALT_O, 1, Option_List, 3, Options, 0, 0 },
    {0, 0, " Help ",    ALT_H, 1, Help_List  , 1, Help   , 0, 0 },
    0
};

char *Mail_Listbox_Strings[14];

SCROLL_BAR Mail_Vertical_Scrollbars[] =
{
    {VERT_SCROLL, 32, 302, 145, 0 },
    0
};

SCROLL_BAR Mail_Horizontal_Scrollbars[] =
{
    {HORZ_SCROLL, 176, 8, 295, 0},
    0
};

LIST_BOX Mail_Listbox[] =
```

```
{
   {31, 10, 48, 0, Mail_Listbox_Strings, 14,
    Mail_Vertical_Scrollbars, Mail_Horizontal_Scrollbars,
    InitializeMailListBox, UpdateMailListBox},
    0
};

WORK_AREA Mail_Workarea[] =
{
   { 0, 0, 0, 0, 0, 0, 0, Mail_Listbox, 1 },
   0
};

MENU_FORM Main_Menu =
{
   5, 5, 311, 184, " Mail List ", Action_Bar_List, Mail_Workarea, MailList
};
```

The MAINMENU.C source file uses the Menu Library include files MENU.H and KEYBOARD.H to define a menu structure and keyboard definitions.

Several external functions are declared at the beginning of the file to tell the 'C' compiler that these are functions and that pointers to these functions have been declared. For example, the function File ( ) is called whenever the user selects one of the action bar menu file options.

To be able to define a primary menu several things must be done first. The 'C' compiler cannot resolve certain expressions inside of structures without first having known about them. For example, I cannot use the File ( ) function inside of a structure until I have first declared it.

The primary menu requires a list of action bar menus. The action bar is the list of options available to the user at a given point in time. The mail list application defines four different action bar menus, File, Edit, Options, and Help. Each one of these menus contains a list of options, such as Create, Load, Save, Delete, that will be displayed whenever the user is in this action bar menu.

The statement ACTION_BAR Action_Bar_List defines the action bar menus used by the mail list application. The upper left-hand corner of the action bar list strings, such as 'File,' is left blank and it is filled in by the InitializeActionBar ( ) function. Next comes the string to display on the primary menu action bar, such as 'File,' is defined. Next is the hot key that allows the user to automatically get to the action bar menu, such as Alt_F. Next, the character number to underline on the action bar for this menu, such as the 'F' in 'File' is defined. Next, a pointer to a list of strings to display when the user is selecting an option from this menu, such as 'Create,' 'Load,' 'Save,' and 'Delete.' Next, the number of strings in the list, such as in the case above, where there are four strings. Next, a pointer to the function to call whenever the user selects one of the options in the action bar menu, such as File ( ). Next, the starting string number to display, i.e., which one of the selections is the one that is highlighted. Last, the exit value from the action bar menu is defined.

By defining the action bar menus the programmer can now control the program flow much more easily. Whenever the user needs to perform a function, he selects one of the options from the action bar, and the application specific functions defined for that menu are called to process the request.

The next important thing that a primary menu contains is a work area. A work area is made up of one or more of the following things:

- Push Buttons - A group of push buttons that are used to terminate a dialog box.
- Entry Fields - A way of displaying and/or retrieving data to the user, such as a customer name.
- List Boxes - A way of displaying information to the user that cannot all be displayed on the screen at one time.
- Check Boxes - A way of allowing the user to choose one or more selections from a group of related items.
- Radio Buttons - A way of allowing the user to select only one item from a group of related items.

The primary menu, Main_Menu, defines a work area containing only a list box. A list box is the most difficult type of work area to manipulate because it requires a lot of data management.

The statement LIST_BOX Mail_Listbox[] defines a list box for the primary menu, Main_Menu. A List Box must contain the following information:

- The upper left-hand row and column coordinates of the list box.
- The number of characters that are displayable on one line.
- The string number that is the string that will be highlighted.
- A pointer to the strings that are displayed in the list box.
- The number of strings that can be displayed in the list box.
- A pointer to the vertical scroll bar definitions.
- A pointer to the horizontal scroll bar definitions.
- A function to initialize the data in the list box display strings.
- A function to update the data in the list box display strings.

The list box definition Mail_Listbox defines a list box that has an upper left-hand corner at row 31, column 10. The list box has 48 displayable characters per line and the first string in the list box is highlighted, i.e., the current string in the list box. The

Mail_Listbox_Strings are defined to be the pointers to the list box display strings. There are 14 displayable strings in the list box. The Mail_Vertical_Scrollbars are defined to contain the vertical scroll bar definitions, and the Mail_Horizontal_ Scrollbars are defined to contain the horizontal scroll bar definitions. The function InitializeMailListBox ( ) is defined to be that function that InitializeListBox ( ) calls to initialize the data in the list box display strings. For example, the customer data records need to be read into memory before they can be displayed in the list box. The function UpdateMailListBox ( ) is defined to be the function that UpdateListBox ( ) calls whenever the ProcessListBox ( ) function determines that the list box display strings need to be updated. For example, the user has pressed the Down Arrow and has reached the end of the display; the list box display strings need to be updated to show the customer records below and they need to be displayed on the screen.

The mail list application primary menu, Main_Menu, is defined by the statement MENU_FORM Main_Menu. It defines a primary menu that has an upper left-hand corner at row 5, column 5. The width of the primary menu is 311 and it has a height of 184. The header string is defined to be 'Mail List.' The action bar menus are defined by the Action_Bar_List. The primary menu's work area is defined by Mail_Workarea. The primary menu's controlling function, i.e., the function that the Menu ( ) function calls after the primary menu has been initialized and displayed on the screen, is defined to be MailList ( ).

The reader is encouraged to change the variables defined by the primary menu so that he may better understand how the primary menu structure is designed. The following code actually issues the call to the Menu ( ) function. The Menu ( ) function is passed a pointer to the primary menu, Main_Menu. When control returns from the Menu ( ) function, the mail list application has finished processing.

Edit the MAINMENU.C source file, type the following statements, and save the file.

```
/*=======================================================================*/
/*                                                                       */
/* Function : MainMenu ();                                               */
/*                                                                       */
/* Purpose : This function processes the mail list application's         */
/*           primary menu, Main_Menu.                                    */
/*                                                                       */
/* Functions Called : Menu () - This function is called to process       */
/*           the mail list application's primary menu, Main_Menu.        */
/*                                                                       */
/* Logic Flow : The function MainMenu () is called to begin processing*/
/*           the mail list application's primary menu, Main_Menu.        */
/*           The primary menu was defined by the menu definitions        */
/*           described above.  The function Menu () is called with a     */
/*           pointer to the primary menu structure to process.  When     */
```

```
/*          control is returned, then the primary menu has been     */
/*          processed.  The function Menu () will call the function  */
/*          MailList () after the primary menu has been displayed    */
/*          on the screen.  The MailList () function controls the    */
/*          processing until the user terminates the Main_Menu.      */
/*                                                                   */
/* Exit : The mail list application primary menu, Main_Menu, has     */
/*          finished processing.                                     */
/*                                                                   */
/*=================================================================*/


MainMenu ()
{
    Menu (&Main_Menu);
}
```

Creating the Mail List Application Source File — MAILLIST.C

The MAILLIST.C source file contains the functions that control the mail list application after the primary menu, Main_Menu, has been initialized and displayed. It contains the function MailList ( ). This function was defined in the primary menu, Main_Menu, to be the function that Menu ( ) calls after the primary menu has been initialized and displayed.

This source file also contains the functions that initialize and update the mail list application's list box. The function InitializeMailListBox ( ) was called by the InitializeListBox ( ) function when the primary menu, Main_Menu, was initialized.

The logic flow of a primary menu is as follows:

1. The Menu ( ) function is passed a pointer to the primary menu to process. In this application, this was done in MAINMENU.C by the statement Menu (&Main_Menu).

2. The Menu ( ) function draws the menu outline and clears out the window area used by the primary menu. In this application, the upper left-hand corner of the window is at row 5, column 5. The width of the window is 311 and the height is 184 dots.

3. Then, the Menu ( ) function displays the header string. In this application, the string 'Mail List' is displayed centered at the top of the window.

4. Then, the Menu ( ) function calls the InitializeActionBar ( ) function to initialize and display the primary menu action bar. In this application, the action bar is defined as Action_Bar_List. Each one of the action bar menus in the Action_Bar_List are initialized, and its header string is displayed.

5.   Then, the Menu ( ) function will call the InitializeWorkGroups ( ) function if there are any groups of radio buttons or check boxes in the primary menu work area. If there are, then each group is initialized and displayed on the screen. In this application, there are no radio buttons or check boxes in the primary menu.

6.   Then, the Menu ( ) function will call the InitializePushButtons ( ) function if there are any push buttons in the primary menu work area. If there are, then each push button is initialized and displayed on the screen. In this application there are no push buttons in the primary menu.

7.   Then, the Menu ( ) function will call the InitializeEntryFields ( ) function if there are any entry fields in the primary menu work area. If there are, then each entry field is initialized and displayed on the screen. In this application, there are no entry fields in the primary menu.

8.   Then, the Menu ( ) function will call the InitializeListBox ( ) function if there are any list boxes in the primary menu work area. If there are, then the list box is initialized and displayed on the screen. In this application, there is one list box and it is defined by Mail_Listbox. The InitializeListBox ( ) function calls a function defined in the list box definition to initialize the list box strings. In this application, that function is defined to be InitializeMailListBox ( ).

9.   Finally, the Menu ( ) function calls the function that was defined in the primary menu to be the function that is called after the primary menu has been initialized and displayed. In this application, that function is defined to be MailList ( ).

The following piece of code defines all of the data structures, defines, and global data used in the MAILLIST.C source file.

Create the MAILLIST.C source file, type the following statements, and save the file.

```
/*========================================================================*/
/*                                                                        */
/* File : MAILLIST.C                                                      */
/*                                                                        */
/* Purpose : This 'C' source file processes the mail list application */
/*           primary menu Main_Menu.                                      */
/*                                                                        */
/* Include Files : "\graphics\colors.h" - This include contains the      */
/*           color definitions used by the mail list application.         */
/*                                                                        */
/*           "\menu\menu.h" - This include file contains the data         */
/*           structure definitions needed to define a primary menu.       */
/*                                                                        */
/*           "\menu\keyboard.h" - This include file contains the          */
/*           keyboard definitions.                                        */
/*                                                                        */
```

```
/*          "\filer\record.h" - This include file contains the data  */
/*          structure definitions needed to define a customer record.*/
/*                                                                    */
/*          "defines.h" - This include file contains the defined      */
/*          data definitions used by the mail list application.       */
/*                                                                    */
/* Global Data Definitions : char Filename_Buffer[20] - This data     */
/*          is used to contain the name of the customer file that      */
/*          is currently being edited.                                 */
/*                                                                    */
/*          RECORD_FORM Record[30] - The data array Record[] is used   */
/*          to keep track of the customer data in memory.  It is       */
/*          defined to be of the structure type RECORD.                */
/*                                                                    */
/*          long Index[30] - The data array Index[] is used to         */
/*          contain the location of each customer data record in       */
/*          the customer data file.                                    */
/*                                                                    */
/*          int Number_Of_Records - This data variable is used to      */
/*          contain the actual number of records in the data file.     */
/*                                                                    */
/*          int Current_Record - This data variable is used to keep    */
/*          track of the customer record currently active.             */
/*                                                                    */
/*          int Number_ActionBar_Menus - This data variable is used    */
/*          to count the number of action bar menus that are on the    */
/*          mail list primary menu.                                    */
/*                                                                    */
/*          int ActionBar_Hot_Keys[10] - This data array is used to    */
/*          contain the hot keys, such as Alt+F, for each action bar   */
/*          menu option.                                               */
/*                                                                    */
/*          char Recs[14][350] - This data array is used by the list   */
/*          box processor to display the customer records in the way   */
/*          that they will appear on the screen.                       */
/*                                                                    */
/*          int Listbox_Start_Str - This data variable is used to      */
/*          maintain the topmost record to be displayed inside of      */
/*          the list box.                                              */
/*                                                                    */
/*          int Listbox_End_Str - This data variable is used to        */
/*          maintain the bottommost record to be displayed inside      */
/*          of the list box.                                           */
/*                                                                    */
/*          int Listbox_Start_Col - This data variable is used to      */
/*          maintain the first displayable character of the records    */
/*          displayed in the list box.                                 */
/*                                                                    */
/*          int Listbox_End_Col - This data variable is used to        */
/*          maintain the last displayable character of the records     */
/*          displayed in the list box.                                 */
/*                                                                    */
/* Functions : MailList () - This function is called by the Menu ()    */
```

```
/*          function after it has initialized and displayed the    */
/*          primary menu Main_Menu.                                 */
/*                                                                  */
/*          InitializeMailListBox () - This function is called by   */
/*          the InitializeListBox () function to initialize the     */
/*          display strings for the list box.                       */
/*                                                                  */
/*          UpdateMailListBox () - This function is called whenever */
/*          the List Box needs its display strings to be updated.   */
/*                                                                  */
/*          CopyMailListRecord () - This function is called to      */
/*          copy a customer record into a list box display string.  */
/*                                                                  */
/*==================================================================*/

#include "\graphics\colors.h"
#include "\menu\menu.h"
#include "\menu\keyboard.h"
#include "\filer\record.h"
#include "defines.h"

extern char Filename_Buffer[20];

extern RECORD_FORM Record[30];

extern long Index[30];

extern int Number_Of_Records;
extern int Current_Record;
extern int Number_ActionBar_Menus;
extern int ActionBar_Hot_Keys[10];

extern char Recs[14][350];

extern int Listbox_Start_Str;
extern int Listbox_End_Str;
extern int Listbox_Start_Col;
extern int Listbox_End_Col;
```

Create the MAILLIST.C Source File Function — MailList ()

As stated earlier, the MailList ( ) function was defined to be the function that is called by Menu ( ) to take control after the primary menu has been initialized and displayed. Every primary menu must have a function assigned to it. In this way, the application passes control back and forth to the Menu Library.

The MailList ( ) function is passed a pointer to the primary menu being processed. In this application the pointer is to the primary menu, Main_Menu. The MailList ( ) function's purpose is to control the logic flow of the primary menu, Main_Menu.

The primary menu, Main_Menu, is designed to have an action bar and a list box. The user is automatically defaulted to the list box by the ProcessListBox ( ) function call. If the user presses a key that the ProcessListBox ( ) function does not recognize, such as an Alt_F, then this key is passed to the MailList ( ) function.

The MailList ( ) function then decides on what to do about the key. The only other thing, besides exiting the application, that the user can do, is to access the primary menu action bar. The F10 key and the Home key are common ways to get to the action bar. If either one of these keys are pressed, then the ProcessActionBar ( ) function is called to process the current action bar menu. If a key was pressed that matches one of the action bar hot keys defined for quick access of the action bar menu, then that particular action bar menu is processed.

If the user pressed the Esc key, then the MailList ( ) function returns to its calling function, Menu ( ). The Menu ( ) function then returns to its calling function, MainMenu ( ), which in turn returns to the function main ( ). Then the application returns to DOS.

The programmer should not let a real application terminate like this. Special checks should be made to determine if anything needs to be saved to disk. Also, a dialog box or message box is recommended to display this information to the user.

The MailList ( ) function controls the primary menu by calling a Menu Library function, such as ProcessListBox ( ), to take control of the application. When the Menu Library function returns, the return code is acted upon. Each Menu Library function returns different kinds of return codes. The ProcessListBox ( ) function returns a keystroke, whereas the ProcessActionBar ( ) function returns the current action bar menu.

The reader is encouraged to experiment with the primary menu and the functions that control it.

Edit the MAILLIST.C source file, type the following statements, and save the file.

```
/*=====================================================================*/
/*                                                                     */
/* Function : MailList (md);                                           */
/*                                                                     */
/* Purpose : This function is defined in the primary menu, Main_Menu,  */
/*           to be the function that is called by Menu ().  It is      */
/*           called after the primary menu has been initialized and    */
/*           displayed on the screen.  It processes user keyboard      */
/*           input until the user is finished with the application.    */
/*                                                                     */
/* Entry Parameters : MENU_FORM *md - The MailList () function is      */
/*           passed a pointer to the primary menu being processed.     */
/*                                                                     */
/* Local Data Definitions - int action_index - This variable is used  */
```

```
/*              to keep track of which action bar menu is current.     */
/*                                                                     */
/*              int key - This data variable is used to contain the    */
/*              keystroke and/or return code from the ProcessListBox () */
/*              function.                                               */
/*                                                                     */
/*              int i - This data variable is used as a temporary      */
/*              counter for the number of action bar menus.            */
/*                                                                     */
/* Functions Called : ProcessListBox () - This function is called to   */
/*              process the primary menu list box.                     */
/*                                                                     */
/*              ProcessActionBar () - This function is called to process */
/*              an action bar menu request.                            */
/*                                                                     */
/* Logic Flow : The MailList () function is passed a pointer to the    */
/*              primary menu Main_Menu.  The variable, int action_index, */
/*              is initialized to zero.  Until the Esc key is pressed,  */
/*              do the following things.  Call the ProcessListBox ()    */
/*              function with a pointer to the list box to process.     */
/*              The data variable int key is assigned to the return     */
/*              code from ProcessListBox ().  A switch is made on this  */
/*              return code.  If the key is Esc, then return to the     */
/*              calling function.  If the key is F10 or Home key, then  */
/*              call the ProcessActionBar () function with a pointer to */
/*              the primary menu and the current action_index.  If the  */
/*              key is anything else, then check to see if it is one    */
/*              of the action bar menu hot keys.  If it is, then call   */
/*              ProcessActionBar () with the correct action_index.      */
/*              The function returns control to Menu ()after the Esc    */
/*              key has been pressed.                                   */
/*                                                                     */
/* Exit : The mail list application has finished processing.            */
/*                                                                     */
/*=====================================================================*/

MailList (md)
MENU_FORM *md;
{
    int action_index, key, i;

    action_index = 0;
    for (;;)
    {
        switch (key = ProcessListbox (&md- >workarea[0].listbox[0]))
        {
            case ESC:
                return (key);

            case F10:
            case HOME:
                action_index = ProcessActionBar (md, action_index);
                break;
```

```
        default:
            for (i = 0; i <= Number_ActionBar_Menus; i++)
                if (key == ActionBar_Hot_Keys[i])
                    action_index = ProcessActionBar (md, i);
            break;
        }
    }
}
```

Create the MAILLIST.C Source File Function — InitializeMailListBox ( )

The InitializeMailListBox ( ) function is defined by the primary menu list box as the function that InitializeListBox ( ) calls before displaying the list box strings on the screen.

The logic flow of the List Box function goes like this:

- The InitializeListBox ( ) function is called to initialize and display a list box on the screen.
- The InitializeListBox ( ) function displays the vertical and horizontal scroll bars defined in the list box structure. In this application, the vertical scroll bars are defined by SCROLL_BAR Mail_Vertical_Scrollbars and the horizontal scroll bars are defined by SCROLL_BAR Mail_Horizontal_Scrollbars.
- The InitializeListBox ( ) function then calls the function defined in the list box structure to initialize the list box display strings. In this application, the InitailizeMailListBox ( ) function was defined to be that function.
- The InitializeListBox ( ) function then displays the list box display strings on the screen.

The InitializeMailListBox ( ) function is designed to initialize the list box display strings. The first thing that needs to be done is to execute a Filer Library call that initializes the customer data records into memory. After the data has been read in successfully, then the list box global variables need to be initialized. Then, the first customer records, up until the last displayable one on the screen, are initialized into the list box display strings Recs[].

The InitializeListBox ( ) function uses the display strings contained in Recs[] as the data to display inside of the list box.

Edit the MAILLIST.C source file, type the following statements, and save the file.

```
/*===================================================================*/
/*                                                                   */
/* Function : InitializeMailListBox (lb);                            */
/*                                                                   */
```

```
/* Purpose  : This function is defined in the primary menu, Main_Menu,*/
/*            to be the function that InitializeListBox () calls        */
/*            to initialize the list box display strings.               */
/*                                                                       */
/* Entry Parameters : LIST_BOX *lb - The InitializeMailListBox ()       */
/*            is called with a pointer to the list box to initialize.    */
/*                                                                       */
/* Local Data Definitions - int i, j - These data variables are used    */
/*            as temporary variables.                                    */
/*                                                                       */
/* Functions Called : InitDataFile () - This function is called to       */
/*            initialize the customer data file into memory.             */
/*                                                                       */
/*            CreateNewFile () - This function creates a new file to     */
/*            use if the one given is not found.                         */
/*                                                                       */
/*            Error () - This function is called to display an error     */
/*            message on the screen.                                     */
/*                                                                       */
/*            CopyMailListRecord () - This function is called to copy    */
/*            a customer record into the list box display string.        */
/*                                                                       */
/* Logic Flow : The InitializeMailListBox () function is called with     */
/*            a pointer to the list box to initialize. First, the        */
/*            function InitDataFile () is called with a pointer to       */
/*            the customer filename to use.  If InitDataFile () had      */
/*            any errors, then the function Error () is called. The      */
/*            global variables Listbox_Start_Str, Listbox_End_Str,      */
/*            Listbox_Start_Col, and Listbox_End_col are initialized.   */
/*            The current record is initialized to zero and the          */
/*            first part of the customer records are copied into the     */
/*            display records.                                           */
/*                                                                       */
/* Exit : The list box has been initialized with the customer data.     */
/*                                                                       */
/*=====================================================================*/

InitializeMailListBox (lb)
LIST_BOX *lb;
{
   int i,j;

   j = 1;
   do
   {
     if ((i = InitDataFile (Filename_Buffer)) <= 0)
        if ((i = CreateNewFile (Filename_Buffer)) <= 0)
           if ((j = Error (FILEIO_ERROR, Filename_Buffer)) != -1)
           return(-1);
   } while (j != 1);

   Listbox_Start_Str = 0;
   Listbox_End_Str = (lb->num_items - 1);
```

```
   Listbox_Start_Col = 0;
   Listbox_End_Col = lb->length;
   Current_Record = 0;
   for (i = 0; i < lb->num_items; i++)
   {
       CopyMailListRecord (Recs[i], i);
       lb->items[i] = Recs[i];
   }
   return (0);
}
```

Create the MAILLIST Source File Function — UpdateMailListBox ( )

The UpdateMailListBox ( ) function is defined in the primary menu, Main_Menu, to be the function that ProcessListBox ( ) calls whenever the display string data inside of the list box needs to be updated. An example of this is when the user reaches the bottom of the list box and needs to see the next customer record.

The ProcessListBox ( ) function was called by the MailList ( ) function to take control of the application by processing the given list box. The ProcessListBox ( ) function handles keyboard input from the user, such as a Left Arrow, and acts accordingly. The logic flow of the ProcessListBox ( ) function is as follows:

- The ProcessListBox ( ) function is called to process the keyboard input from the user in a given list box.
- If the user presses the UP_ARROW key, then the current display string, the string that is displayed in reverse video, is decremented by one. If the current display string is the topmost display string, then the application defined function that updates the list box strings is called. In this application, the UpdateMailListBox ( ) function is called with the command SCROLL_ DOWN. The UpdateMailList ( ) function will then update the list box display strings and return to the ProcessListBox ( ) function. The updated display string data is then displayed.
- If other list box specific keys are pressed, then similar actions are taken.
- If a key other than a list box specific key is pressed, then the key is returned to the calling function. In this application, the key is returned to MailList ( ).

The UpdateMailList ( ) function is a very important function to the mail list application because without it, the ProcessListBox ( ) function could not update the list box display strings properly.

It is important for the reader to remember that a list box must have two application specific functions defined to process a list box. One is the function that the InitializeListBox ( ) function calls to initialize the list box display strings. The other is the function that the ProcessListBox ( ) function calls to update the list box display strings.

The UpdateMailListBox ( ) function is called with a pointer to the list box to update and a command to take action on the list box display string data. Each command, like SCROLL_UP, causes the UpdateMailListBox ( ) function to act differently.

The SCROLL_UP command tells the UpdateMailListBox ( ) that the user has pressed a key that has caused the list box display strings to have to be scrolled up one line in the list box. Each list box display string pointer is then scrolled up one, and the next customer data record is copied into the list box display string.

Each command acts a little differently, but each is designed to change to list box display strings. The programmer can modify this function to include such commands as PAGE_UP and so on.

Edit the MAILLIST.C source file, type the following statements, and save the file.

```
/*========================================================================*/
/*                                                                        */
/* Function : UpdateMailListBox (lb, command);                            */
/*                                                                        */
/* Purpose : This function is defined in the primary menu, Main_Menu,*/
/*           to be the function that ProcessListBox () calls to           */
/*           update the list box display strings.                         */
/*                                                                        */
/* Entry Parameters : LIST_BOX *lb - The UpdateMailListBox () function*/
/*           is called with a pointer to the list box to update.          */
/*                                                                        */
/*           int command - The command to direct the function on what */
/*           to do - SCROLL_UP, SCROLL_DOWN, SCROLL_RIGHT, SCROLL_LEFT*/
/*                                                                        */
/* Local Data Definitions - int i - This data variable is used as a    */
/*           temporary counter.                                           */
/*                                                                        */
/*           char *tmp - This variable is used as a temporary pointer.*/
/*                                                                        */
/* Functions Called : CopyMailListRecord () - This function is called */
/*           to copy a customer record into the list box display          */
/*           string.                                                      */
/*                                                                        */
/* Logic Flow : The UpdateMailListBox () function is called with a     */
/*           pointer to the list box to update and the command by         */
/*           which to update the list box.  This function is called       */
/*           by the ProcessListBox () function whenever the display       */
/*           strings in the list box need to be updated.  If the          */
/*           command is SCROLL_UP, then the pointer char *tmp is          */
/*           assigned to point at the first item in the list box          */
/*           display list.  Each display string is moved up one; the      */
/*           function CopyMailListRecord () is called to copy the new     */
/*           current record into the display string list.  If the         */
```

```
/*              command is SCROLL_DOWN, then a similar process is done    */
/*              except that everything is moved down.  If the command is  */
/*              SCROLL_LEFT, then the pointers to the strings are moved    */
/*              over one character to the left.  If the command is        */
/*              SCROLL_RIGHT, then they are moved to the right one         */
/*              character.                                                 */
/*                                                                         */
/* Exit : The list box has been updated.                                  */
/*                                                                         */
/*=======================================================================*/

UpdateMailListBox (lb, command)
LIST_BOX *lb;
int command;
{
    int    i;
    char *tmp;

    switch (command)
    {
      case SCROLL_UP:
          tmp = lb->items[0];
          for (i = 0; i < (lb->num_items - 1); i++)
             lb->items[i] = lb->items[i + 1];
          lb->items[i] = tmp;
          CopyMailListRecord (tmp - Listbox_Start_Col, Current_Record);
          break;

      case SCROLL_DOWN:
          tmp = lb->items[lb->num_items - 1];
          for (i = (lb->num_items - 1); i > 0; i--)
             lb->items[i] = lb->items[i - 1];
          lb->items[i] = tmp;
          CopyMailListRecord (tmp - Listbox_Start_Col, Current_Record);
          break;

      case SCROLL_LEFT:
          for (i = 0; i < lb->num_items; i++) lb->items[i]++;
          break;

      case SCROLL_RIGHT:
          for (i = 0; i < lb->num_items; i++) lb->items[i]--;
          break;
    }
}
```

Create the MAILLIST.C Source File Function — CopyMailListRecord ( )

The CopyMailListRecord ( ) function is called by the InitializeMailListBox ( ) function and the UpdateMailListBox ( ) function to copy a given customer record into the given list box display string. The function is called with a pointer to the string to copy the customer record into and the customer record number.

Each field in the customer record is copied into the string for the mail list application. The programmer can modify this function to display only parts of the customer record, and in any order that he wishes.

Edit the MAILLIST.C source file, type the following statements, and save the file.

```
/*=========================================================================*/
/*                                                                         */
/* Function : CopyMailListRecord (string, number);                         */
/*                                                                         */
/* Purpose : This function is called to copy a customer record into        */
/*           the list box display strings.                                 */
/*                                                                         */
/* Entry Parameters : char *string - A pointer to the string where         */
/*           the customer record will be copied into.                      */
/*                                                                         */
/*           int number - The customer record number to copy.              */
/*                                                                         */
/* Logic Flow : The CopyMailListRecord () function is called with a        */
/*           pointer to the string into which to copy the customer         */
/*           record.  It is also called with the customer record           */
/*           number to copy.  The standard 'C' functions sprintf ()        */
/*           and strlen() are called to copy the customer record into      */
/*           the list box display string.                                  */
/*                                                                         */
/* Exit : The given customer record has been copied into the list box      */
/*        display string.                                                  */
/*                                                                         */
/*=========================================================================*/

CopyMailListRecord (string, number)
char *string;
int number;
{
    sprintf (string                 , "%s ", Record[number].title);
    sprintf (string + strlen(string), "%s ", Record[number].fname);
    sprintf (string + strlen(string), "%s ", Record[number].mname);
    sprintf (string + strlen(string), "%s ", Record[number].lname);
    sprintf (string + strlen(string), "%s ", Record[number].affil);
    sprintf (string + strlen(string), "%s ", Record[number].address);
    sprintf (string + strlen(string), "%s ", Record[number].city);
    sprintf (string + strlen(string), "%s ", Record[number].state);
    sprintf (string + strlen(string), "%s ", Record[number].zipcode);
```

```
        sprintf (string + strlen(string), "%s ", Record[number].phone);
        sprintf (string + strlen(string), "%s ", Record[number].comment);
}
```

SUMMARY

This chapter has dealt with the files MAIL.C, MAINMENU.C, and MAILLIST.C. The program logic flow has gone from the function main ( ) in MAIL.C, to the MainMenu ( ) function in MAINMENU.C, to the MAILLIST.C function MailList ( ). The primary menu, Main_Menu, was defined in the file MAINMENU.C and it defined the primary menu action bar and list box.

The MAIL.C source file is the source file that contains the required 'C' function main ( ). It also defines all global data requirements of the application. By isolating the global variables into one 'C' file, the programmer can easily find the original data definition if needed. By having the MAIL.C source file contain only one function, main ( ), the programmer can be assured that at least this source file does not contain any other functions that are used by the application.

The MAINMENU.C source file defines the mail list application's primary menu, Main_Menu. It also issues the call to the Menu Library function Menu ( ). By defining the primary menu and isolating the call to the Menu ( ) function in one source file, the programmer can easily trace the logic flow.

The MAILLIST.C source file contains the functions needed to process the primary menu, Main_Menu. It also contains the functions that are needed to initialize and update the primary menu list box. The MailList ( ) function takes control of the primary menu after it has been initialized and displayed on the screen. It calls the ProcessListBox ( ) function to process the primary menu list box. It also calls the ProcessActionBar ( ) function to process an action bar request from the user.

In the following chapter, the functions that were assigned to the action bar menus are written. These functions were defined in the primary menu action bar to be the functions that the ProcessActionBar ( ) function would call whenever one of the selections from the action bar is selected.

Chapter 15

THE APPLICATION ACTION BAR MENU 'C' SOURCE FILES

INTRODUCTION

The last chapter defined the mail list application's primary menu, Main_Menu. The primary menu contained an action bar and a list box. The primary menu and list box functions were defined in that chapter; this chapter deals with the functions that were defined to process the action bar menus.

These functions were defined as File ( ), Edit ( ), Options ( ), and Help ( ). The functions have been divided into separate 'C' files to allow the programmer to manage them better. They are FILE.C, EDIT.C, OPTIONS.C, and HELP.C, respectively. The HELP.C source file is discussed in the next chapter.

An action bar is a group of action bar menus. Each action bar menu has a list of options associated with it and is defined to contain the following things:

- The upper left-hand row and column coordinates to display the action bar header string, such as 'File.' These coordinates are initialized by the Initialize ActionBar ( ) function.

- The header string to display for the given action bar menu. Each action bar menu contains a header string that is displayed on the primary menu action bar line, such as 'File.'

- Each action bar menu has a hot key assigned to it. A hot key is usually a combination of keystrokes held down at the same time, such as Alt_F, which is the Alt key and the 'F' key pressed at the same time. A hot key causes the MailList ( ) function to display that particular action bar menu.

- Each action bar menu has an underline beneath the character that represents the hot key assigned to that action bar menu, such as the 'F' in the header string 'File.' The character number, starting at zero, is given, such as one.

- Each action bar menu has a list of selections that are displayed whenever the action bar menu is being processed, such as the ITEM_PTR File_List declaration made in MAINMENU.C that defines the strings 'Create,' 'Load,' 'Save,' 'Delete.' These strings are displayed by the ProcessPullDown Menu ( ) function that was called by ProcessActionBar ( ) to process the action bar menu.

- The number of strings in the action bar menu selections is defined, such as in the example above.

- Each action bar menu must have a function assigned that is called whenever a selection is made from the list of selections, such as the user selected 'Create,' from the action bar menu File. The function File ( ) would be called.

- Each action bar menu has a default selection assigned to it. This default is the selection that is the current selection from the action bar menu, i.e., when Enter is pressed, this is the selection chosen.

- Each action bar menu has an exit condition that is set by the ProcessActionBar ( ) function to determine the canceling of a function.

Each one the action bar menus was defined in the MAINMENU.C source file. The MailList ( ) function in MAILLIST.C calls the function ProcessActionBar ( ) whenever a keystroke is made to cause an action bar menu to be processed, such as a hot key.

The ProcessActionBar ( ) function calls the ProcessPullDownMenu ( ) function to process the given action bar menu. The selections for the action bar menu are displayed on the screen and the keyboard input from the user is processed. If the user presses the Up or Down Arrows, then the action bar menu selection is changed. If the user presses the Left or Right Arrows, then the action bar menu to the left or right is displayed and processed.

If the user presses the Enter key, then the selection which is currently highlighted is selected and the function assigned to the action bar menu being processed is called. So in this way the application is able to gain control back from the ProcessActionBar ( ) function to be able to handle this user request.

CREATE THE MAIL LIST APPLICATION SOURCE FILE — FILE.C

The mail list application source file FILE.C contains the functions that process a request from the action bar menu File. The File ( ) function was defined in the primary menu, Main_Menu, to be the function that is called whenever a selection was made from this action bar. The action bar section defined in the source file MAINMENU.C defined four different action bar menus, each one having a different function assigned to it.

So far, only primary menus have been discussed. This chapter deals with the creation of dialog boxes. Dialog boxes are used to display and retrieve information to the user. Usually, after a selection has been made from a pull-down menu, a dialog box is processed. A dialog box is like a primary menu except that it does not have an action bar.

A dialog box contains the following things:

- The upper left-hand row and column coordinates of the dialog box.
- The width and the height of the dialog box.
- The header string of the dialog box.
- A pointer to the dialog box work area.
- A function to call after the dialog box has been initialized

The FILE.C source file defines four different dialog boxes. Each one of these dialog boxes is associated with a given selection from the action bar menu File. The specific dialog box that is displayed is based upon the selection made. The following is a list of the dialog boxes defined in the FILE.C source file.

- DIALOG BOX Create_File_Menu - This dialog box is processed whenever the user selects the 'Create' option from the action bar menu File.
- DIALOG BOX Load_File_Menu - This dialog box is processed whenever the user selects the 'Load' option from the action bar menu File.
- DIALOG BOX Save_File_Menu - This dialog box is processed whenever the user selects the 'Save' option from the action bar menu File.
- DIALOG BOX Delete_File_Menu - This dialog box is processed whenever the user selects the 'Delete' option from the action bar menu File.

Every dialog box must have a work area. A work area of a dialog box is just like the work area of a primary menu. The work area defines the dialog box to contain certain things such as push buttons, entry fields, radio buttons, check boxes, and list boxes. The dialog boxes defined in the FILE.C source file define only push buttons and entry fields.

To define entry fields in a dialog box they must contain the following information:

- The field number assigned to this entry field. The ProcessDialogBox ( ) function needs to have field numbers assigned to each data field in a dialog box so that it can determine which field to go to next.
- The upper left-hand row and column coordinates of where to display the entry field label, such as 'Filename.'
- The upper left-hand row and column coordinates of the box that is displayed around the entry field.
- The width and the height of the entry field box.
- The number of characters that are displayable inside of the entry field box.
- The maximum number of characters that the entry field can contain.
- The string that contains the entry field information.

When the InitializeDialogBox ( ) function is called, it checks to see if there are any entry fields in the dialog box. If there are, then the InitializeEntryFields ( ) function is called to initialize and display them on the screen.

Each one of the dialog boxes defined in FILE.C contain one entry field. This entry field is used to contain the name of the customer data file. Each one of the dialog boxes also contains three push buttons. The definition of a push button contains the following:

- The field number assigned to the push button.
- The string to display inside of the push button.
- The upper left-hand row and column coordinates of the push button.

If the InitializeDialogBox ( ) function determines that the dialog box contains push buttons, then the function InitializePushButtons ( ) is called to initialize and display the push buttons.

Create the FILE.C source file, type the following statements, and save the file.

```
/*=======================================================================*/
/*                                                                       */
/* File : FILE.C                                                         */
/*                                                                       */
/* Purpose : This 'C' source file processes the action bar menu for      */
/*           the File selections.  This function is called by the        */
/*           ProcessPullDownMenu () function whenever one of the         */
/*           File options has been selected.                             */
/*                                                                       */
/* Include Files : "\menu\menu.h" - This include file contains the       */
/*           data structure definitions needed to define a dialog box.   */
/*                                                                       */
```

```
/*          "\menu\keyboard.h" - This include file contains the        */
/*          keyboard definitions.                                      */
/*                                                                     */
/*          "defines.h" - This include file contains the defined       */
/*          data definitions used by the mail list application.        */
/*                                                                     */
/* External Function Declarations : int CreateFile () - This function  */
/*          is called whenever the user has selected the File option   */
/*          'Create' to create a new customer data file.               */
/*                                                                     */
/*          int LoadFile () - This function is called whenever the     */
/*          user has selected the File option 'Load' to load in a      */
/*          customer data file.                                        */
/*                                                                     */
/*          int SaveFile () - This function is called whenever the     */
/*          user has selected the File option 'Save' to save the       */
/*          customer file to disk.                                     */
/*                                                                     */
/*          int DeleteFile () - This function is called whenever the   */
/*          user has selected the File option 'Delete' to delete a     */
/*          customer file from the disk.                               */
/*                                                                     */
/* External Data Definitions : char Filename_Buffer[20] - This string  */
/*          contains the name of the current customer data file.       */
/*                                                                     */
/* Dialog boxes Defined : DIALOG_BOX Create_File_Menu - This dialog    */
/*          box will be displayed whenever the user has selected       */
/*          from the action bar menu File the Create option.  Its      */
/*          upper left-hand corner is at row 80 and column 50. It      */
/*          has a width of 200 and a height of 65. The header string   */
/*          is 'Create File.'  Its work area is File_Workarea and      */
/*          the function to call after initializing and displaying     */
/*          the dialog box is CreateFile ().  The work area contains   */
/*          1 entry field defined by ENTRY_FIELD File_Entry.  It       */
/*          also contains 3 push buttons defined by PUSH_BUTTON        */
/*          File_Buttons.  The ENTRY_FIELD File_Entry defines 1        */
/*          entry field that displays the string 'Filename' at row     */
/*          105 and column 58.  It defines the screen area to          */
/*          display the filename at row 103, column 108.  The width    */
/*          and height of the entry field box is defined next.         */
/*          The display length and the maximum length of the string    */
/*          are defined to be 20.  The buffer that contains the name   */
/*          of the customer file is located in Filename_Buffer.  The   */
/*          PUSH_BUTTON File_Buttons define 3 push buttons, Accept,    */
/*          Cancel, and Help.  They are assigned the work area field   */
/*          numbers and their locations on the screen.                 */
/*                                                                     */
/*          DIALOG_BOX Load_File_Menu - This dialog box is displayed   */
/*          whenever the user selects 'Load' from the action bar       */
/*          menu File.  This dialog box is similar to the              */
/*          Create_File_Menu dialog box, except that the header        */
/*          string is 'Load File.'                                     */
/*                                                                     */
```

```
/*          DIALOG_BOX Save_File_Menu - This dialog box is displayed */
/*          whenever the user selects 'Save' from the action bar     */
/*          menu File.  This dialog box is similar to the            */
/*          Create_File_Menu dialog box, except that the header      */
/*          string is 'Save File.'                                   */
/*                                                                   */
/*          DIALOG_BOX Delete_File_Menu - This dialog box is         */
/*          displayed whenever the user selects 'Delete' from the    */
/*          action bar menu File.  This dialog box is similar to the */
/*          Create_File_Menu dialog box, except that the header      */
/*          string is 'Delete File.'                                 */
/*                                                                   */
/* Functions : File () - This function was defined by the primary    */
/*          menu, Main_Menu, to be called whenever the user has      */
/*          selected an option from the action bar menu File. It     */
/*          processes the selection and displays the appropriate     */
/*          dialog box.                                              */
/*                                                                   */
/*          CreateFile () - This function is called by the           */
/*          InitializeDialogBox () function after the dialog box     */
/*          Create_File_Menu has been initialized and displayed.     */
/*                                                                   */
/*          LoadFile () - This function is called by the             */
/*          InitializeDialogBox () function after the dialog box     */
/*          Load_File_Menu has been initialized and displayed.       */
/*                                                                   */
/*          SaveFile () - This function is called by the             */
/*          InitializeDialogBox () function after the dialog box     */
/*          Save_File_Menu has been initialized and displayed.       */
/*                                                                   */
/*          DeleteFile () - This function is called by the           */
/*          InitializeDialogBox () function after the dialog box     */
/*          Delete_File_Menu has been initialized and displayed.     */
/*                                                                   */
/*==================================================================*/

#include "\menu\menu.h"
#include "\menu\keyboard.h"
#include "defines.h"

extern int CreateFile ();
extern int LoadFile ();
extern int SaveFile ();
extern int DeleteFile ();
extern char Filename_Buffer[20];

ENTRY_FIELD File_Entry[] =
{
   {1, 105, 58, "Filename", 103, 108, FONTWIDTH  * 22,
    FONTHEIGHT + 4, 20, 20, Filename_Buffer},
    0
};
```

```
PUSH_BUTTON File_Buttons[] =
{
    {2, "Accept", 123,  59},
    {3, "Cancel", 123, 130},
    {4, "Help"  , 123, 206},
    0
};

WORK_AREA File_Workarea[] =
{
    {File_Entry, 1, File_Buttons, 3, 0, 0, 0, 0, 0},
    0
};

DIALOG_BOX Create_File_Menu =
{
    80, 50, 200, 65, " Create File ", File_Workarea, CreateFile
};

DIALOG_BOX Save_File_Menu =
{
    80, 50, 200, 65, " Save File "  , File_Workarea, SaveFile
};

DIALOG_BOX Load_File_Menu =
{
    80, 50, 200, 65, " Load File "  , File_Workarea, LoadFile
};

DIALOG_BOX Delete_File_Menu =
{
    80, 50, 200, 65, " Delete File ", File_Workarea, DeleteFile
};
```

Create the FILE.C Source File Function — File ( )

The File ( ) function determines which dialog box is processed based upon the action bar variable, start. This variable is set by the ProcessPullDownMenu ( ) to indicate which one of the selections was made, counting from selection 0. The first selection defined for the action bar menu File is 'Create,' the second, 'Load,' and so on.

The function InitializeDialogBox ( ) is called to initialize and display the given dialog box. Each dialog box has a function assigned to it that is called to take control after the dialog box has been initialized and displayed. In the above example, the function CreateFile ( ) is defined to be the function that the InitializeDialogBox ( ) function calls after it has initialized and displayed the Create_File_Menu dialog box.

The File ( ) function is designed only to display and process the dialog boxes associated with the action bar menu File. It does not take any action after the dialog boxes have been displayed. The programmer can modify this function or the following functions to implement the File ( ) function more completely.

Edit the FILE.C source file, type the following statements, and save the file.

```
/*======================================================================*/
/*                                                                      */
/* Function : File (ab);                                                */
/*                                                                      */
/* Purpose : This function is defined in the primary menu, Main_Menu,  */
/*           to be the function that is called whenever the user        */
/*           selects an option from the action bar menu File.           */
/*                                                                      */
/* Entry Parameters : ACTION_BAR *ab - A pointer to the action bar of  */
/*           primary menu to process.                                   */
/*                                                                      */
/* Functions Called : InitializeDialogBox () - This function is         */
/*           called to initialize and display a dialog box on the       */
/*           screen.                                                     */
/*                                                                      */
/* Logic Flow : The File () function is passed a pointer to the         */
/*           action bar menu structure to process.  It is called        */
/*           whenever the user has selected one of the action bar       */
/*           menu File options.  The action bar variable start is       */
/*           used to determine which one of the File options has        */
/*           been selected.  If the user selected the option 'Create,'*/
/*           then the function InitializeDialogBox () is called with     */
/*           a pointer to the Create_File_Menu dialog box.  If the       */
/*           user selected 'Load,' then the InitializeDialogBox ()      */
/*           function is called with a pointer to the Load_File_Menu     */
/*           dialog box.  If the user selected 'Save,' then the         */
/*           InitializeDialogBox () function is called with a pointer    */
/*           to the Save_File_Menu dialog box.  If the user selected     */
/*           'Delete,' then the InitializeDialogBox () function is       */
/*           called with a pointer to the Delete_File_Menu.             */
/*                                                                      */
/* Exit : The selection from the action bar menu File has been          */
/*        processed.                                                    */
/*                                                                      */
/*======================================================================*/

File (ab)
ACTION_BAR *ab;
{
   switch (ab->start)
   {
      case 0:
         InitializeDialogBox (&Create_File_Menu);
         break;

      case 1:
         InitializeDialogBox (&Load_File_Menu);
         break;
```

```
    case 2:
       InitializeDialogBox (&Save_File_Menu);
       break;

    case 3:
       InitializeDialogBox (&Delete_File_Menu);
       break;
   }
}
```

Create the FILE.C Source File Function — CreateFile ( )

The CreateFile ( ) was defined in the Create_File_Menu dialog box to be the function that InitializeDialogBox ( ) calls after it has initialized and displayed the Create_File_Menu dialog box.

The ProcessDialogBox ( ) function is called to do the actual processing of the dialog box. When control is returned from the ProcessDialogBox ( ) function the Create_File_Menu has been processed and the dialog box's current push button is checked to see how the user terminated the dialog Box.

The first push button defined in the Create_File_Menu dialog box is 'Accept.' If the current push button is determined to be 0, then the user has accepted the input from the dialog box. In the mail list application, I have chosen to display an error message when this happens because the managing of the customer data files is beyond the scope of this book.

If the programmer wishes to write the code to open a new customer data file, he should take into consideration at least the following things:

- Does the current customer file need to be saved?
- Is the filename typed in by the user a file that already exits?
- Is there enough room on the disk to create a new file?

The CreateFile ( ) function also displays a message box whenever the Help push button is selected because there is no Help available in this application for this dialog box. The reader should look at the examples in the HELP.C source file to create these message boxes.

Edit the FILE.C source file, type the following statements, and save the file.

```
/*=====================================================================*/
/*                                                                     */
/* Function : CreateFile (db);                                         */
/*                                                                     */
/* Purpose : This function is defined in the Create_File_Menu dialog   */
```

```
/*            box to be the function that InitializeDialogBox () calls */
/*            after the dialog box has been initialized and displayed. */
/*                                                                      */
/* Entry Parameters : DIALOG_BOX *db - A pointer to the dialog box to   */
/*            process.                                                   */
/*                                                                      */
/* Local Data Definitions : int return_code - This variable is used     */
/*            to contain the return code from the ProcessDialogBox ()    */
/*            function.                                                  */
/*                                                                      */
/* Functions Called : ProcessDialogBox () - This function is called     */
/*            to process the Create_File_Menu dialog box.                */
/*                                                                      */
/*            Error () - This function is called if there was an         */
/*            error processing the dialog box.                           */
/*                                                                      */
/* Logic Flow : The CreateFile () function is passed a pointer to the   */
/*            Create_File_Menu Dialog box.  The ProcessDialogBox ()      */
/*            is called with the pointer to the dialog box.  The         */
/*            variable return_code is assigned to the return code from   */
/*            ProcessDialogBox ().  If the return_code is the Esc key,    */
/*            then no further action is taken.  The dialog box's          */
/*            current push button is then checked.  If the current        */
/*            button is Accept, then the function Error () is called to   */
/*            display the Create File Error Message. If the current       */
/*            button is 'Cancel,' then no further action is taken.        */
/*            If the current button is 'Help,' then the function          */
/*            Error () is called to display the Create Help Error         */
/*            Message box.                                               */
/*                                                                      */
/* Exit : The Create_File_Menu dialog box has been processed.            */
/*                                                                      */
/*======================================================================*/

CreateFile (db)
DIALOG_BOX *db;
{
   int    return_code;

   return_code = ProcessDialogBox (db);
   if (return_code == ESC) return (-1);
   switch (db->workarea[0].current_button)
   {
      case 0:
         Error (CREATE_FILE_ERROR, 0);
         return (db->workarea[0].current_button);

      case 1:
         return (db->workarea[0].current_button);
```

```
        case 2:
            Error (HELP_ERROR, 0);
            return (db->workarea[0].current_button);
    }
}
```

Create the FILE.C Source File Function — LoadFile ( )

The LoadFile ( ) function is similar to the CreateFile ( ) function except that this function was defined by the Load_File_Menu dialog box to be the function called after the Load_File_Menu dialog box has been initialized and displayed. The ProcessDialogBox ( ) function is called to process the Load_File_Menu dialog box. When control is returned, the user has terminated the dialog box.

Message boxes are displayed based upon the current push button returned from ProcessDialogBox ( ). The programmer should add code to load in a customer data file and should take care of any error conditions that can occur.

Edit the FILE.C source file, type the following statements, and save the file.

```
/*======================================================================*/
/*                                                                      */
/* Function : LoadFile (db);                                            */
/*                                                                      */
/* Purpose : This function is defined in the Load_File_Menu dialog      */
/*           box to be the function that InitializeDialogBox () calls   */
/*           after the dialog box has been initialized and              */
/*           displayed.                                                 */
/*                                                                      */
/* Entry Parameters : DIALOG_BOX *db - A pointer to the dialog box to   */
/*           process.                                                   */
/*                                                                      */
/* Local Data Definitions : int return_code - This variable is used     */
/*           to contain the return code from the ProcessDialogBox ()    */
/*           function.                                                  */
/*                                                                      */
/* Functions Called : ProcessDialogBox () - This function is called     */
/*           to process the Load_File_Menu dialog box.                  */
/*                                                                      */
/*           Error () - This function is called if there was an         */
/*           error processing the dialog box.                           */
/*                                                                      */
/* Logic Flow : The LoadFile () function is passed a pointer to the     */
/*           Load_File_Menu dialog box.  The ProcessDialogBox ()        */
/*           is called with the pointer to the dialog box.  The         */
/*           variable return_code is assigned to the return code from   */
/*           ProcessDialogBox ().  If the return_code is the Esc key,   */
/*           then no further action is taken.  The dialog box's         */
/*           current push button is then checked.  If the current       */
/*           button is Accept, then the function Error () is called to  */
/*           display the Load File Error Message box. If the current    */
```

```
/*              button is 'Cancel,' then no further action is taken.     */
/*              If the current button is 'Help,' then the function       */
/*              Error () is called to display the Load Help Error        */
/*              message box.                                             */
/*                                                                       */
/* Exit : The Load_File_Menu dialog box has been processed.             */
/*                                                                       */
/*=====================================================================*/

LoadFile (db)
DIALOG_BOX *db;
{
   int    return_code;

   return_code = ProcessDialogBox (db);
   if (return_code == ESC) return (-1);
   switch (db->workarea[0].current_button)
   {
      case 0:
          Error (LOAD_FILE_ERROR, 0);
          return (db->workarea[0].current_button);

      case 1:
          return (db->workarea[0].current_button);

      case 2:
          Error (HELP_ERROR, 0);
          return (db->workarea[0].current_button);
   }
}
```

Create the FILE.C Source File Function — SaveFile ( )

The SaveFile ( ) function is similar to the previous two functions except that it is called after the Save_File_Menu dialog box has been initialized and displayed by the InitializeDialogBox ( ) function. The ProcessDialogBox ( ) function is called to process the Save_File_Menu dialog box. When control is returned, the dialog box has finished processing.

Actions are taken based upon the current push button of the Save_File_Menu dialog box. The programmer should add code that handles these push buttons, the Saving of the file, the canceling of the request, and the displaying of help.

Edit the FILE.C source file, type the following statements, and save the file.

```
/*=====================================================================*/
/*                                                                       */
/* Function : SaveFile (db);                                             */
/*                                                                       */
/* Purpose : This function is defined in the Save_File_Menu dialog      */
/*           box to be the function that InitializeDialogBox () calls   */
```

```
/*          after the dialog box has been initialized and       */
/*          displayed.                                           */
/*                                                               */
/* Entry Parameters : DIALOG_BOX *db - A pointer to the dialog box to */
/*          process.                                             */
/*                                                               */
/* Local Data Definitions : int return_code - This variable is used  */
/*          to contain the return code from the ProcessDialogBox ()  */
/*          function.                                            */
/*                                                               */
/* Functions Called : ProcessDialogBox () - This function is called  */
/*          to process the Save_File_Menu dialog box.            */
/*                                                               */
/*          Error () - This function is called if there was an   */
/*          error processing the dialog box.                     */
/*                                                               */
/* Logic Flow : The SaveFile () function is passed a pointer to the  */
/*          Save_File_Menu dialog box.  The ProcessDialogBox ()  */
/*          is called with the pointer to the dialog box.  The   */
/*          variable return_code is assigned to the return code from */
/*          ProcessDialogBox ().  If the return_code is the Esc key, */
/*          then no further action is taken.  The dialog box's   */
/*          current push button is then checked.  If the current */
/*          button is Accept, then the function Error () is called to*/
/*          display the Save File Error Message box. If the current  */
/*          button is 'Cancel,' then no further action is taken.  */
/*          If the current button is 'Help,' then the function   */
/*          Error () is called to display the Save Help Error     */
/*          message box.                                         */
/*                                                               */
/* Exit : The Save_File_Menu dialog box has been processed.      */
/*                                                               */
/*=============================================================*/

SaveFile (db)
DIALOG_BOX *db;
{
    int    return_code;

    return_code = ProcessDialogBox (db);
    if (return_code == ESC) return (-1);
    switch (db->workarea[0].current_button)
    {
        case 0:
            Error (SAVE_FILE_ERROR, 0);
            return (db->workarea[0].current_button);

        case 1:
            return (db->workarea[0].current_button);
```

```
        case 2:
            Error (HELP_ERROR, 0);
            return (db->workarea[0].current_button);
    }
}
```

Create the FILE.C Source File Function — DeleteFile ( )

The DeleteFile ( ) function is similar to the previous functions except that it is called after the Delete_File_Menu dialog box has been initialized and displayed. The ProcessDialogBox ( ) function is called to process the dialog box. When control is returned, actions are taken on the current push button of the Delete_File_Menu dialog box.

The programmer should add code that handles these requests from the user taking into account the possible error conditions that can occur.

Edit the FILE.C source file, type the following statements, and save the file.

```
/*========================================================================*/
/*                                                                        */
/* Function : DeleteFile (db);                                            */
/*                                                                        */
/* Purpose : This function is defined in the Delete_File_Menu dialog      */
/*           box to be the function that InitializeDialogBox () calls     */
/*           after the dialog box has been initialized and                */
/*           displayed.                                                   */
/*                                                                        */
/* Entry Parameters : DIALOG_BOX *db - A pointer to the dialog box to     */
/*           process.                                                     */
/*                                                                        */
/* Local Data Definitions : int return_code - This variable is used      */
/*           to contain the return code from the ProcessDialogBox ()      */
/*           function.                                                    */
/*                                                                        */
/* Functions Called : ProcessDialogBox () - This function is called      */
/*           to process the Delete_File_Menu dialog box.                  */
/*                                                                        */
/*           Error () - This function is called if there was an           */
/*           error processing the dialog box.                             */
/*                                                                        */
/* Logic Flow : The DeleteFile () function is passed a pointer to the     */
/*           Delete_File_Menu dialog box.  The ProcessDialogBox ()        */
/*           is called with the pointer to the dialog box.  The           */
/*           variable return_code is assigned to the return code from     */
/*           ProcessDialogBox ().  If the return_code is the Esc key,     */
/*           then no further action is taken.  The dialog box's           */
/*           current push button is then checked.  If the current         */
/*           button is Accept, then the function Error () is called to     */
/*           display the Delete File Error Message box. If the current     */
/*           button is 'Cancel,' then no further action is taken.         */
```

```
/*              If the current button is 'Help,' then the function     */
/*              Error () is called to display the Delete Help Error     */
/*              message box.                                            */
/*                                                                      */
/* Exit : The Delete_File_Menu dialog box has been processed.           */
/*                                                                      */
/*====================================================================*/

DeleteFile (db)
DIALOG_BOX *db;
{
    int    return_code;

    return_code = ProcessDialogBox (db);
    if (return_code == ESC) return (-1);
    switch (db->workarea[0].current_button)
    {
       case 0:
          Error (DELETE_FILE_ERROR, 0);
          return (db->workarea[0].current_button);

       case 1:
          return (db->workarea[0].current_button);

       case 2:
          Error (HELP_ERROR, 0);
          return (db->workarea[0].current_button);
    }
}
```

Create the Mail List Application Source File — EDIT.C

The FILE.C source file handles the action bar menu File selection requests. It defines dialog boxes that contain push buttons and one entry field. The EDIT.C source file handles the action bar menu Edit selection requests that actually edit a customer record. The dialog boxes defined in EDIT.C contain push buttons — almost all dialog boxes contain push buttons — and it also contains a work area of eleven entry fields.

Create the EDIT.C source file, type the following statements, and save the file.

```
/*====================================================================*/
/*                                                                      */
/* File : EDIT.C                                                        */
/*                                                                      */
/* Purpose : This 'C' source file processes the action bar menu for     */
/*           the Edit selections.  This function is called by the       */
/*           ProcessPullDownMenu () function whenever one of the        */
/*           Edit options has been selected.                            */
/*                                                                      */
```

```
/* Include Files : "\graphics\colors.h" - This include contains the    */
/*          color definitions used by the mail list application.        */
/*                                                                      */
/*          "\menu\menu.h" - This include file contains the data        */
/*          structure definitions needed to define a primary menu.      */
/*                                                                      */
/*          "\menu\keyboard.h" - This include file contains the         */
/*          keyboard definitions.                                       */
/*                                                                      */
/*          "\filer\record.h" - This include file contains the data     */
/*          structure definitions needed to define a customer record.*/
/*                                                                      */
/*          "defines.h" - This include file contains the defined        */
/*          data definitions used by the mail list application.         */
/*                                                                      */
/* External Function Declarations : int CreateNewRecord () - This       */
/*          function is called whenever the user has selected the       */
/*          Edit option 'Insert' to insert a new record into the        */
/*          customer data file.                                         */
/*                                                                      */
/*          int EditCurrentRecord () - This function is called          */
/*          whenever the user has selected the Edit option 'Edit'       */
/*          to edit the current customer record.                        */
/*                                                                      */
/*          int DeleteCurrentRecord () - This function is called        */
/*          whenever the user has selected the Edit option              */
/*          'Delete' to delete the current customer record.             */
/*                                                                      */
/* External Data Definitions : RECORD_FORM Record[30] - The data array*/
/*          Record[] is used to keep track of the customer data in      */
/*          memory. It is defined to be of the structure type RECORD.*/
/*                                                                      */
/*          int Current_Record - This data variable is used to keep     */
/*          track of the customer record currently active.              */
/*                                                                      */
/*          char Recs[14][350] - This data array is used by the List */
/*          box processor to display the customer records in the way */
/*          that they will appear on the screen.                       */
/*                                                                      */
/* Static Data Definitions : static RECORD_FORM Temp_Record[1] - The   */
/*          variable Temp_Record[] is used as a temporary copy of       */
/*          the current record being edited.                            */
/*                                                                      */
/* Dialog boxes Defined : DIALOG_BOX Create_Record_Menu - This         */
/*          dialog box is defined to contain the necessary entry        */
/*          fields and push buttons to be able to create a new          */
/*          customer record.  Its upper left-hand corner is defined */
/*          to be at row 10, column 50.  The width of the dialog        */
/*          box is 257 and the height is 163.  The header string is  */
/*          defined as ' Create a customer record .'  Its work area  */
/*          is defined to be the Record_Workarea. The function          */
/*          CreateNewRecord () is defined to be the function that       */
/*          the InitializeDialogBox () function calls after the         */
```

```
/*      dialog box has been initialized and displayed.  The      */
/*      dialog box Create_Record_Menu has a work area that       */
/*      defines Record_Entry to be the entry fields for the      */
/*      dialog box. There are 11 different entry fields defined.  */
/*      The push button structure Record_buttons is defined to   */
/*      be the push buttons for the dialog box. There are three   */
/*      push buttons defined.  There are no radio buttons, check  */
/*      boxes, or list boxes defined.  The entry field structure  */
/*      Record_Entry defines the Entry fields that are used by    */
/*      the dialog box.  Information for each one of the fields   */
/*      that define a customer record is defined as an entry      */
/*      field so that information can be displayed and received   */
/*      for each field, such as title or last name. The push      */
/*      button structure Record_Buttons defines the dialog box's  */
/*      push buttons.                                             */
/*                                                                */
/*      DIALOG_BOX Edit_Record_Menu - This dialog box contains    */
/*      the necessary entry fields and push buttons that are      */
/*      needed to edit a customer record.  This dialog box is     */
/*      very similar to the Create_Record_Menu except that the    */
/*      header is different and the EditCurrentRecord ()          */
/*      function is called after the dialog box has been          */
/*      initialized and displayed.                                */
/*                                                                */
/*      DIALOG_BOX Delete_Record_Menu - This dialog box is        */
/*      defined to contain the necessary entry fields and push    */
/*      buttons that are needed to delete a customer record.      */
/*      This dialog box is similar to the previous two, except    */
/*      for the header and function declarations.                 */
/*                                                                */
/* Functions : Edit () - This function was defined by the primary */
/*      menu, Main_Menu, to be called whenever the user has       */
/*      selected an option from the action bar menu Edit. It      */
/*      processes the selection and displays the appropriate      */
/*      dialog box.                                               */
/*                                                                */
/*      CreateNewRecord () - This function is called by the       */
/*      InitializeDialogBox () function after the dialog box      */
/*      Create_Record_Menu has been initialized and displayed.    */
/*                                                                */
/*      EditCurrentRecord () - This function is called by the     */
/*      InitializeDialogBox () function after the dialog box      */
/*      Edit_Record_Menu has been initialized and displayed.      */
/*                                                                */
/*      DeleteCurrentRecord () - This function is called by the   */
/*      InitializeDialogBox () function after the dialog box      */
/*      Delete_Record_Menu has been initialized and displayed.    */
/*                                                                */
/*      InitializeTempRecord () - This function is called to      */
/*      initialize the temporary record for creating a new        */
/*      customer record.                                          */
/*                                                                */
/*      CopyRecordTemp () - This function is called to copy a     */
```

```
/*          given customer record into the temporary customer record.*/
/*                                                                     */
/*=====================================================================*/

#include "\graphics\colors.h"
#include "\menu\menu.h"
#include "\menu\keyboard.h"
#include "\filer\record.h"
#include "defines.h"

int CreateNewRecord ();
int EditCurrentRecord ();
int DeleteCurrentRecord ();

extern RECORD_FORM Record[30];
extern int Current_Record;
extern char Recs[14][350];

static RECORD_FORM Temp_Record[1];

ENTRY_FIELD Record_Entry[] =
{
    { 1, 28,  58, "Title",          38,  58, FONTWIDTH *  5,
      FONTHEIGHT + 5,          4,  4, Temp_Record[0].title},

    { 2, 28,  99, "First",          38,  93, FONTWIDTH * 10,
      FONTHEIGHT + 5,          9, 19, Temp_Record[0].fname},

    { 3, 28, 164, "M",              38, 159, FONTWIDTH *  3,
      FONTHEIGHT + 5,          2, 19, Temp_Record[0].mname},

    { 4, 28, 188, "Last name",      38, 184, FONTWIDTH * 19,
      FONTHEIGHT + 5,         18, 19, Temp_Record[0].lname},

    { 5, 57,  58, "Affiliation",    55, 148, FONTWIDTH * 25,
      FONTHEIGHT + 5,         24, 24, Temp_Record[0].affil},

    { 6, 74,  58, "Street Address", 72, 148, FONTWIDTH * 25,
      FONTHEIGHT + 5,         24, 24, Temp_Record[0].address},

    { 7, 91,  58, "City,",          89, 148, FONTWIDTH * 10,
      FONTHEIGHT + 5,          9, 24, Temp_Record[0].city},

    { 8, 91,  90, "State,",         89, 214, FONTWIDTH *  3,
      FONTHEIGHT + 5,          2,  2, Temp_Record[0].state},

    { 9, 91, 126, "Zip",            89, 238, FONTWIDTH * 10,
      FONTHEIGHT + 5,          9,  9, Temp_Record[0].zipcode},

    {10,108,  58, "Phone",         106, 148, FONTWIDTH * 13,
      FONTHEIGHT + 5,         12, 12, Temp_Record[0].phone},

    {11,125,  58, "Comments",      123, 112, FONTWIDTH * 31,
```

```
         (FONTHEIGHT * 2) + 5, 30, 30, Temp_Record[0].comment},

     0
};

PUSH_BUTTON Record_Buttons[] =
{
     {12, "Accept", 152,  59 },
     {13, "Cancel", 152, 160 },
     {14, "Help"  , 152, 262 },
     0
};

WORK_AREA Record_Workarea[] =
{
     {Record_Entry, 11, Record_Buttons, 3, 0, 0, 0, 0},
     0
};

DIALOG_BOX Create_Record_Menu =
{
     10, 50, 257, 163,   " Create a customer record ", Record_Workarea,
     CreateNewRecord
};

DIALOG_BOX Edit_Record_Menu =
{
     10, 50, 257, 163,   " Edit a customer record "  , Record_Workarea,
     EditCurrentRecord
};

DIALOG_BOX Delete_Record_Menu =
{
     10, 50, 257, 163,   " Delete this customer ? "  , Record_Workarea,
     DeleteCurrentRecord
};
```

Create the EDIT.C Source File Function — Edit ( )

The EDIT.C source file function Edit ( ) is called whenever a selection is made from the action bar menu Edit. It was defined in the primary menu, Main_Menu, in the source file MAINMENU.C. The ProcessPullDownMenu ( ) function called the Edit ( ) function when Enter was pressed while processing the Edit action bar menu.

The Edit ( ) function acts very similar to the File ( ) function except that it processes an action bar menu selection from Edit, not File. The Edit ( ) function displays one of the dialog boxes defined above depending upon the option selected. If the option 'Insert' was selected from the action bar menu Edit, then the dialog box Create_Record_Menu is initialized and displayed by the InitializeDialogBox ( ) function.

One important difference between the Edit ( ) function and the File ( ) function is that the Edit ( ) function calls other functions that initialize the data in the entry fields before calling InitializeDialogBox ( ). In this way the application can update the data contained in the entry fields.

For example, if the user wanted to edit a particular customer record, then he would access the action bar menu Edit and press Enter on the 'Edit' selection. The Edit ( ) function would then be called by the ProcessPullDownMenu ( ) function to process this request. The Edit ( ) function would determine the type of request based on the action bar menu variable start. The entry fields defined by the Edit_Record_Menu dialog box need to contain the information about that customer, so the function CopyRecordTemp ( ) is called to get a copy of the customer data record.

Edit the EDIT.C source file, type the following statements, and save the file.

```
/*=======================================================================*/
/*                                                                       */
/* Function : Edit (ab);                                                 */
/*                                                                       */
/* Purpose : This function is defined in the primary menu, Main_Menu,    */
/*           to be the function that is called ProcessPullDownMenu ()    */
/*           whenever a selection has been made from the action bar      */
/*           menu Edit.                                                  */
/*                                                                       */
/* Entry Parameters : ACTION_BAR *ab - A pointer to the action bar of    */
/*           the primary menu to process.                                */
/*                                                                       */
/* Functions Called : InitializeTempRecord () - This function is         */
/*           called to initialize the temporary customer record          */
/*           Temp_Record whenever the user wants to create a new          */
/*           customer record.                                            */
/*                                                                       */
/*           InitializeDialogBox () - This function is called to         */
/*           initialize and display a dialog box on the screen.          */
/*                                                                       */
/*           CopyRecordTemp () - This function is called to copy          */
/*           the current customer record into the temporary customer     */
/*           record to either edit or delete the customer record.        */
/*                                                                       */
/* Logic Flow : The Edit () function is passed a pointer to the          */
/*           action bar menu structure to process.  It is called         */
/*           whenever the user has selected on the the action bar        */
/*           menu Edit options.  The action bar variable start is        */
/*           used to determine which of the Edit options has             */
/*           been selected.  If the user selected the option 'Insert,'   */
/*           then the function InitializeTempRecord () is called to       */
/*           initialize the temporary record used by the dialog box      */
/*           Create_Record_Menu.  The InitializeDialogBox () function    */
/*           is called with a pointer to the Create_Record_Menu.          */
/*           If the user selected the option 'Edit,' then the function    */
/*           CopyRecordTemp () is called to copy the current customer     */
```

```
/*          record into the temporary record.  The function         */
/*          InitializedialogBox () is called with a pointer to       */
/*          the dialog Box Edit_Record_Menu.  If the user selected   */
/*          the option 'Delete,' then the function CopyRecordTemp () */
/*          is called to copy the current customer record into the   */
/*          temporary record.  The function InitializeDialogBox ()   */
/*          is called with a pointer to the Delete_Record_Menu       */
/*          dialog box.                                              */
/*                                                                   */
/* Exit : The selection from the action bar menu Edit has been       */
/*        processed.                                                 */
/*                                                                   */
/*==================================================================*/

Edit (ab)
ACTION_BAR *ab;
{
   switch (ab->start)
   {
      case 0:
         InitializeTempRecord (Current_Record);
         InitializeDialogBox (&Create_Record_Menu);
         break;

      case 1:
         CopyRecordTemp (Current_Record);
         InitializeDialogBox (&Edit_Record_Menu);
         break;

      case 2:
         CopyRecordTemp (Current_Record);
         InitializeDialogBox (&Delete_Record_Menu);
         break;
   }
}
```

Create the EDIT.C Source File Function — CreateNewRecord ( )

The CreateNewRecord ( ) function is defined by the Create_Record_Menu dialog box to be the function that is called after the Create_Record_Menu dialog box has been initialized and displayed. It is very similar to the CreateFile ( ) function except that this function is designed to create a new customer record.

The ProcessDialogBox ( ) function is called to process the dialog box. When control is returned, the dialog box has finished processing. Action is taken upon the dialog box's current push button.

The programmer should add code that actually places the new customer data into the customer record data file. To do this, the programmer should take into account at least the following things:

- Is the data received from the user acceptable data? For example, does the phone number really contain a phone number?
- Is there room on the disk to save the customer data?
- Is this a duplicate of another record already in the customer data file?
- Code should be written to sort, save, and update the List box on the screen.

These functions are not written in this book, but the programmer should be aware that this would be the place to validate the customer data entry and to save it if it needs to be saved.

Edit the EDIT.C source file, type the following statements, and save the file.

```
/*=========================================================================*/
/*                                                                         */
/* Function : CreateNewRecord (db);                                        */
/*                                                                         */
/* Purpose : This function is defined in the Create_Record_Menu            */
/*           dialog box to be the function that InitializeDialogBox ()*/
/*           calls after it has been initialized and displayed.            */
/*                                                                         */
/* Entry Parameters : DIALOG_BOX *db - A pointer to the dialog box to */
/*           process.                                                      */
/*                                                                         */
/* Local Data Definitions : int return_code - This variable is used        */
/*           to contain the return code from the ProcessDialogBox ()       */
/*           function.                                                     */
/*                                                                         */
/* Functions Called : ProcessDialogBox () - This function is called        */
/*           to process the Create_Record_Menu dialog box.                 */
/*                                                                         */
/*           Error () - This function is called if there was an            */
/*           error processing the dialog box.                              */
/*                                                                         */
/* Logic Flow : The CreateNewRecord () function is passed a pointer         */
/*           to the dialog box to process.  The ProcessDialogBox ()         */
/*           function is called to process the dialog box passed, in        */
/*           this case, the Create_Record_Menu.  The local variable         */
/*           return_code is assigned to the return code from the            */
/*           ProcessDialogBox () function.  If the user pressed the          */
/*           Esc key to escape from the dialog box, then no further         */
/*           action will be taken and the dialog box has finished           */
/*           processing.  The current push button is the one that           */
/*           the user selected to determine the next action taken.          */
/*           If the user selected the 'Accept' push button, then the        */
/*           function Error () is called to display the Create Record */
/*           Error Message box and the current push button is               */
/*           returned.  If the user selected 'Cancel,' then the             */
/*           current push button is returned.  If the user selected         */
/*           'Help,' then the function Error () is called to display         */
/*           the Help Error Message () and the current push button is */
/*           returned.                                                     */
```

```
/*                                                                    */
/* Exit : The Create_Record_Menu dialog box has been processed.       */
/*                                                                    */
/*================================================================*/

CreateNewRecord (db)
DIALOG_BOX *db;
{
    int    return_code;

    return_code = ProcessDialogBox (db);
    if (return_code == ESC) return(-1);
    switch (db->workarea[0].current_button)
    {
       case 0:
          Error (CREATE_RECORD_ERROR, 0);
          return (db->workarea[0].current_button);

       case 1:
          return (db->workarea[0].current_button);

       case 2:
          Error (HELP_ERROR, 0);
          return (db->workarea[0].current_button);
    }
}
```

Create the EDIT.C Source File Function — EditCurrentRecord ( )

The EditCurrentRecord ( ) is called after the Edit_Record_Menu dialog box has been initialized and displayed. Its purpose is to allow the user to edit a customer data record. The function ProcessDialogBox ( ) is called to process the Edit_Record_ Menu dialog box. When control is returned, the dialog box has finished processing.

The EditCurrentRecord ( ) function is not complete and the programmer should add the functions necessary to implement it.

Edit the EDIT.C source file, type the following statements, and save the file.

```
/*================================================================*/
/*                                                                    */
/* Function : EditCurrentRecord (db);                                 */
/*                                                                    */
/* Purpose : This function is defined in the Edit_Record_Menu dialog  */
/*           box to be the function that InitializeDialogBox () calls */
/*           after it has been initialized and displayed.             */
/*                                                                    */
/* Entry Parameters : DIALOG_BOX *db - A pointer to the dialog box to */
/*           process.                                                 */
/*                                                                    */
/* Local Data Definitions : int return_code - This variable is used   */
```

```
/*              to contain the return code from the ProcessDialogBox ()  */
/*              function.                                                 */
/*                                                                        */
/* Functions Called : ProcessDialogBox () - This function is called      */
/*              to process the Edit_Record_Menu dialog box.              */
/*                                                                        */
/*              Error () - This function is called if there was an        */
/*              error processing the dialog box.                          */
/*                                                                        */
/* Logic Flow : The EditCurrentRecord () function is passed a pointer */
/*              to the Edit_Record_Menu dialog box.  The function        */
/*              ProcessDialogBox () is called with a pointer to this      */
/*              dialog box. The variable return_code is assigned to the   */
/*              return code from the ProcessDialogBox () function.  If    */
/*              the user pressed the Esc key to exit the dialog box, then*/
/*              no further action is taken.  The current push button is   */
/*              then checked.  If the user selected 'Accept,' then the    */
/*              function Error () is called to display the Edit Record    */
/*              message box.  If the user selected 'Help,' then the       */
/*              function Error () is called to display the Help Error     */
/*              message box.  The current push button is returned.        */
/*                                                                        */
/* Exit : The Edit_Record_Menu dialog box has been processed.            */
/*                                                                        */
/*======================================================================*/

EditCurrentRecord (db)
DIALOG_BOX *db;
{
    int    return_code;

    return_code = ProcessDialogBox (db);
    if (return_code == ESC) return(-1);
    switch (db->workarea[0].current_button)
    {
       case 0:
          Error (EDIT_RECORD_ERROR, 0);
          return (db->workarea[0].current_button);

       case 1:
          return (db->workarea[0].current_button);

       case 2:
          Error (HELP_ERROR, 0);
          return (db->workarea[0].current_button);
    }
}
```

Create the EDIT.C Source File Function — DeleteCurrentRecord ( )

The DeleteCurrentRecord ( ) function is called after the Delete_Record_Menu dialog box has been initialized and displayed. It is designed to process the 'Delete' option from the action bar menu Edit. The ProcessDialogBox ( ) function is called to process the dialog box. When control is returned, the dialog box has finished processing.

The programmer should add code to handle the requests made from this dialog box, delete the record, cancel the delete, or show help on delete record.

Edit the EDIT.C source file, type the following statements, and save the file.

```
/*====================================================================*/
/*                                                                    */
/* Function : DeleteCurrentRecord (db);                               */
/*                                                                    */
/* Purpose : This function is defined in the Delete_Record_Menu dialog*/
/*           box to be the function that InitializeDialogBox () calls */
/*           after it has been initialized and displayed.             */
/*                                                                    */
/* Entry Parameters : DIALOG_BOX *db - A pointer to the dialog box to */
/*           process.                                                 */
/*                                                                    */
/* Local Data Definitions : int return_code - This variable is used  */
/*           to contain the return code from the ProcessDialogBox ()  */
/*           function.                                                */
/*                                                                    */
/* Functions Called : ProcessDialogBox () - This function is called  */
/*           to process the Delete_Record_Menu dialog box.            */
/*                                                                    */
/*           Error () - This function is called if there was an      */
/*           error processing the dialog box.                        */
/*                                                                    */
/* Logic Flow : The DeleteCurrentRecord () function is passed a       */
/*           pointer to the Delete_Record_Menu dialog box.  The       */
/*           ProcessDialogBox () function is called with a pointer to */
/*           this dialog box.  The variable return_code is assigned   */
/*           to the return code from ProcessDialogBox ().  If the     */
/*           user pressed the Esc key to exit the dialog box, then no */
/*           further action is taken.  The current push button is then*/
/*           checked.  If the user selected 'Accept,' then the        */
/*           function Error () is called to display the Delete Record */
/*           message box.  The current push button is returned.       */
/*                                                                    */
/* Exit : The Delete_Record_Menu dialog box has been processed.       */
/*                                                                    */
/*====================================================================*/

DeleteCurrentRecord (db)
DIALOG_BOX *db;
{
```

```
    int    return_code;

    return_code = ProcessPushButton (&db->workarea[0]);
    if (return_code == ESC) return(-1);
    switch (db->workarea[0].current_button)
    {
        case 0:
            Error (DELETE_RECORD_ERROR, 0);
            break;

        case 1:
            break;

        case 2:
            Error (HELP_ERROR, 0);
            break;
    }
}
```

Create the EDIT.C Source File Function — InitializeTempRecord ( )

The InitializeTempRecord ( ) function is called by the Edit ( ) function to initialize a blank customer record in the Create_File_Menu dialog box. The Create_File_Menu dialog box is designed to allow the user to create a new customer record. To be able to do this, the old data in the entry fields must be wiped out.

Edit the EDIT.C source file, type the following statements, and save the file.

```
/*=========================================================================*/
/*                                                                         */
/* Function : InitializeTempRecord ();                                     */
/*                                                                         */
/* Purpose : This function is called to initialize the temporary          */
/*           customer record for the creating of a new customer           */
/*           record.                                                       */
/*                                                                         */
/* Functions Called : sprintf () - This function is called to             */
/*           clear out the temporary customer record.                     */
/*                                                                         */
/* Logic Flow : The InitializeTempRecord () function is called to         */
/*           initialize the temporary record for the creating of a        */
/*           new customer record. The standard 'C' function is called     */
/*           to clear each field in the temporary record.                 */
/*                                                                         */
/* Exit : The temporary customer record has been initialized to           */
/*        create a new customer record.                                   */
/*                                                                         */
/*=========================================================================*/

InitializeTempRecord ()
{
```

```
      sprintf (Temp_Record[0].title,  " ");
      sprintf (Temp_Record[0].fname,  " ");
      sprintf (Temp_Record[0].mname,   " ");
      sprintf (Temp_Record[0].lname,   " ");
      sprintf (Temp_Record[0].affil,   " ");
      sprintf (Temp_Record[0].address, " ");
      sprintf (Temp_Record[0].city,    " ");
      sprintf (Temp_Record[0].state,   " ");
      sprintf (Temp_Record[0].zipcode, " ");
      sprintf (Temp_Record[0].phone,   " ");
      sprintf (Temp_Record[0].comment, " ");
}
```

Create the EDIT.C Source File Function — CopyRecordTemp ( )

The CopyRecordTemp ( ) function is called whenever the user wants to Edit or Delete a customer record. The Edit ( ) function calls the CopyRecordTemp ( ) function with the customer record number to initialize in the entry fields assigned to the Edit_Record_Menu dialog box or the Delete_Record_Menu dialog box before the call is made to the InitializeDialogBox ( ) function.

Each part of the customer record is copied into its corresponding entry field.

Edit the EDIT.C source file, type the following statements, and save the file.

```
/*======================================================================*/
/*                                                                      */
/* Function : CopyRecordTemp (number);                                  */
/*                                                                      */
/* Purpose : This function is called to copy a customer record into     */
/*           the temporary customer record.                             */
/*                                                                      */
/* Entry Parameters : int number - The customer record number to        */
/*           copy into the temporary record.                            */
/*                                                                      */
/* Functions Called : sprintf () - This standard 'C' function is        */
/*           called to copy parts of the customer record into the       */
/*           temporary record.                                          */
/*                                                                      */
/* Logic Flow : The CopyRecordTemp () function is called to copy a      */
/*           customer record into the temporary record.  The customer   */
/*           record number to copy is passed.  The standard 'C'         */
/*           function sprintf () is called to copy the individual       */
/*           parts of the customer record into the temporary record.    */
/*                                                                      */
/* Exit : The given customer record is copied into the temporary        */
/*        customer record.                                              */
/*                                                                      */
/*======================================================================*/

CopyRecordTemp (number)
```

```
int number;
{
    sprintf (Temp_Record[0].title,    "%s", Record[number].title);
    sprintf (Temp_Record[0].fname,    "%s", Record[number].fname);
    sprintf (Temp_Record[0].mname,    "%s", Record[number].mname);
    sprintf (Temp_Record[0].lname,    "%s", Record[number].lname);
    sprintf (Temp_Record[0].affil,    "%s", Record[number].affil);
    sprintf (Temp_Record[0].address,  "%s", Record[number].address);
    sprintf (Temp_Record[0].city,     "%s", Record[number].city);
    sprintf (Temp_Record[0].state,    "%s", Record[number].state);
    sprintf (Temp_Record[0].zipcode,  "%s", Record[number].zipcode);
    sprintf (Temp_Record[0].phone,    "%s", Record[number].phone);
    sprintf (Temp_Record[0].comment,  "%s", Record[number].comment);
}
```

CREATE THE MAIL LIST APPLICATION SOURCE FILE OPTIONS.C

The OPTIONS.C source file contains the function Options ( ). This function was defined in the primary menu to be the function called if the user selected one of the options under the action bar menu Options. By now you should be getting used to this calling pattern from the Menu Library functions. The OPTIONS.C source file shows the reader how to program groups of radio buttons and check boxes.

A radio button acts just like the buttons on your car radio. Only one button is on at a time. If you press a radio button that is not on, it turns on and the one that was on, turns off. The programmer can use the radio buttons to group related objects that are exclusive.

For example, we might have an application that needs to perform operations on many different file types, but only on one at a time. These file types can be put into a group of radio buttons, where the user can see easily the possible selections and choose one of them.

A group of radio buttons are defined by the following:

- A pointer in the work area pointing to the dialog box's work group structure and the number of work groups there are. In this application, the WORK_ GROUP Display_Work_Group is defined in the WORK_AREA Display_ Workarea.

- Next the work group definition is defined. In this application, the WORK_ GROUP Display_Work_Groups is used to define one group of radio buttons. A work group must have a header string that is displayed to title the group. Next, the upper left-hand row and column coordinates, the width, and the height of the box around the group is defined. Next a pointer to the work group's group field is defined by GROUP_FIELD Display_Radio_Buttons.

The number of fields in the group is four and they are defined to be radio buttons.

- Next the group field definition GROUP_FIELD is defined to contain the actual radio button definitions. First, a field number is assigned to the radio button. Next the string to display that represents the radio button to the user is defined. Next, the upper left-hand corner of where to display the string is defined. Last, the status of the radio button is defined. The programmer should note that only one radio button should be defined to be ON.

The check box is similar to the radio buttons except that they are groups of related items that are not mutually exclusive. The group of check boxes allows the user to select none or all of the items in the check box group.

The definition of a check box is also very similar to the definition of a radio button. The only difference being in the WORK_GROUP definition the defined data variable RADIO_BUTTON should be replaced with the defined variable CHECK_BOX.

Create the OPTIONS.C source file, type the following statements, and save the file.

```
/*========================================================================*/
/*                                                                        */
/* File : OPTIONS.C                                                       */
/*                                                                        */
/* Purpose : This 'C' source file processes the action bar menu for       */
/*           the Options selections.  This function is called by the      */
/*           ProcessPullDownMenu () function whenever one of the          */
/*           Options options has been selected.                           */
/*                                                                        */
/* Include Files : "\menu\menu.h" - This include file contains the         */
/*           data structure definitions needed to define a dialog box.*/
/*                                                                        */
/*           "\menu\keyboard.h" - This include file contains the          */
/*           keyboard definitions.                                        */
/*                                                                        */
/*           "defines.h" - This include file contains the defined         */
/*           data definitions used by the mail list application.          */
/*                                                                        */
/* External Function Declarations : int DisplayOptions () - This           */
/*           function is called whenever the user has selected the        */
/*           Options option 'Display.'                                    */
/*                                                                        */
/*           int SortOptions () - This function is called whenever        */
/*           the user has selected the Options option 'Sort.'             */
/*                                                                        */
/* Dialog boxes Defined : DIALOG_BOX Options_Display_Menu - This          */
/*           dialog box is displayed whenever the user selects the        */
/*           'Display' options from the action bar menu Options.          */
/*           Its upper left-hand corner is row 50, column 55. It has      */
```

```
/*          a width of 207 and a height of 128.  Its header string   */
/*          is 'Display Options.'  Its work area is WORK AREA        */
/*          Display_Workarea and the function to call after the      */
/*          dialog box has been initialized and displayed is         */
/*          DisplayOptions ().  The WORK AREA Display_Workarea        */
/*          defines 3 push buttons that are defined by PUSH_BUTTON    */
/*          Display_Buttons.  It also defines 1 work group that is    */
/*          defined by WORK_GROUP Display_Work_Groups.  The work      */
/*          group defines a group of 4 group fields that are defined  */
/*          by GROUP_FIELD Display_Radio_Buttons.  These group fields */
/*          are defined to be radio buttons.                          */
/*                                                                    */
/*          DIALOG_BOX Options_Sort_Menu - This dialog box is         */
/*          displayed whenever the user selects the 'Sort' option     */
/*          from the action bar menu Options.  This dialog box is     */
/*          very similar to the Options_Display_Menu except that it   */
/*          defines one group of check boxes.                         */
/*                                                                    */
/* Functions : Options () - This function was defined by the primary  */
/*          menu, Main_Menu, to be the function called if one of      */
/*          the action bar menu Options selections has been chosen.   */
/*          It will display the appropriate dialog box associated     */
/*          with the selection.                                       */
/*                                                                    */
/*          DisplayOptions () - This function is called after the     */
/*          Options_Display_Menu dialog box has been initialized      */
/*          and displayed on the screen.                              */
/*                                                                    */
/*          SortOptions () - This function is called after the        */
/*          Options_Sort_Menu dialog box has been initialized and     */
/*          displayed on the screen.                                  */
/*                                                                    */
/*====================================================================*/

#include "\menu\menu.h"
#include "\menu\keyboard.h"
#include "defines.h"

extern int DisplayOptions ();
extern int SortOptions ();

PUSH_BUTTON Display_Buttons[] =
{
   {5, "Accept", 157,  69},
   {6, "Cancel", 157, 140},
   {7, "Help"  , 157, 214},
   0
};

GROUP_FIELD Display_Radio_Buttons [] =
{
   {1, "Sample Radio Button 1", 87, 90, ON},
   {2, "Sample Radio Button 2", 102, 90, OFF},
```

```
      {3, "Sample Radio Button 3", 117, 90, OFF},
      {4, "Sample Radio Button 4", 132, 90, OFF},
      0
};

WORK_GROUP Display_Work_Groups [] =
{
      {"Display Radio Buttons", 72, 80, 158, 70,
        Display_Radio_Buttons, 4, RADIO_BUTTON},
      0
};

WORK_AREA Display_Workarea[] =
{
      {0, 0, Display_Buttons, 3, 0, Display_Work_Groups, 1, 0, 0},
      0
};

DIALOG_BOX Options_Display_Menu =
{
      50, 55, 207, 128,    " Display Options ", Display_Workarea,
      DisplayOptions
};

PUSH_BUTTON Sort_Buttons[] =
{
      {5, "Accept", 157,  69},
      {6, "Cancel", 157, 140},
      {7, "Help"  , 157, 214},
      0
};

GROUP_FIELD Sort_Check_Boxes [] =
{
      {1, "Sample Check Box 1", 87, 90, ON},
      {2, "Sample Check Box 2", 102, 90, OFF},
      {3, "Sample Check Box 3", 117, 90, OFF},
      {4, "Sample Check Box 4", 132, 90, OFF},
      0
};

WORK_GROUP Sort_Work_Groups [] =
{
      {"Sort Check Boxes", 72, 80, 158, 70,
        Sort_Check_Boxes, 4, CHECK_BOX},
      0
};

WORK_AREA Sort_Workarea[] =
{
      {0, 0, Sort_Buttons, 3, 0, Sort_Work_Groups, 1, 0, 0},
      0
};
```

```
DIALOG_BOX Options_Sort_Menu =
{
   50, 55, 207, 128,    " Sort Options ", Sort_Workarea,
   SortOptions
};
```

Create the OPTIONS.C Source File Function — Options ( )

The Options ( ) function was defined in the primary menu to be the function that is called whenever one of the selections from the action bar menu Options was selected. The Options ( ) function acts in much the same way as the File ( ) and Edit ( ) functions. A pointer is passed to the primary menu action bar menu to process. Based upon which option was selected, a dialog box is displayed.

The programmer should note that these dialog boxes are only examples of how to define radio buttons and check boxes. The applications that you write should make use of these dialog box capabilities because it allows for an easy-to-understand user interface.

Edit the OPTIONS.C source file, type the following statements, and save the file.

```
/*=======================================================================*/
/*                                                                       */
/* Function : Options (ab);                                              */
/*                                                                       */
/* Purpose : This function is defined in the primary menu, Main_Menu,    */
/*           to be the function that is called whenever the user         */
/*           selects an option from the action bar menu Options.         */
/*                                                                       */
/* Entry Parameters : ACTION_BAR *ab - A pointer to the action bar of    */
/*           primary menu to process.                                    */
/*                                                                       */
/* Functions Called : InitializeDialogBox () - This function is          */
/*           called to initialize and display a dialog box on the        */
/*           screen.                                                     */
/*                                                                       */
/* Logic Flow : The Options () function is passed a pointer to the       */
/*           action bar menu structure to process.  It is called         */
/*           whenever the user has selected one of the action bar        */
/*           menu Options options.  The action bar variable start is     */
/*           used to determine which one of the Options options has      */
/*           been selected.  If the user selected the option 'Display'   */
/*           then the function InitializeDialogBox () is called with     */
/*           a pointer to the Options_Display_Menu dialog box.  If the   */
/*           user selected 'Sort,' then InitializeDialogBox () is        */
/*           called with a pointer to the Options_Sort_Menu dialog       */
/*           box.                                                        */
/*                                                                       */
/* Exit : The selection from the action bar menu Options has been        */
```

```
/*         processed.                                                  */
/*                                                                     */
/*===================================================================*/

Options (ab)
ACTION_BAR *ab;
{
    switch (ab->start)
    {
        case 0:
            InitializeDialogBox (&Options_Display_Menu);
            break;

        case 1:
            InitializeDialogBox (&Options_Sort_Menu);
            break;

        case 2:
            break;
    }
}
```

Create the OPTIONS.C Source File Function — DisplayOptions ( )

The function DisplayOptions ( ) is called by InitializeDialogBox ( ) after it has initialized and displayed the Options_Display_Menu dialog box. The ProcessDialog Box ( ) function is called to process this dialog box of radio buttons. When control is returned, the user has finished the dialog box.

The programmer should note that whenever the program flow returns from a ProcessDialogBox ( ) function call, the dialog box is still displayed on the screen. It is not until control is returned to the InitializeDialogBox ( ) function that the dialog box is cleared from the screen. This is important because if the user did make invalid choices, then the ProcessDialogBox ( ) function can be called again without returning.

Also, it is a good practice to save the original contents in the dialog box before calling the ProcessDialogBox ( ) function because the user might change some of the data, then press the Esc key or the Cancel push button.

Edit the OPTIONS.C source file, type the following statements, and save the file.

```
/*===================================================================*/
/*                                                                     */
/* Function : DisplayOptions (db);                                     */
/*                                                                     */
/* Purpose : This function is defined in the Options_Display_Menu      */
/*           dialog box to be the function that InitializeDialogBox ()*/
/*           calls after the dialog box has been initialized and       */
/*           displayed.                                                */
```

```
/*                                                                    */
/* Entry Parameters : DIALOG_BOX *db - A pointer to the dialog box to */
/*          process.                                                  */
/*                                                                    */
/* Local Data Definitions : int return_code - This variable is used  */
/*          to contain the return code from the ProcessDialogBox ()   */
/*          function.                                                 */
/*                                                                    */
/* Functions Called : ProcessDialogBox () - This function is called   */
/*          to process the Options_Display_Menu dialog box.           */
/*                                                                    */
/*          Error () - This function is called if there was an        */
/*          error processing the dialog box.                          */
/*                                                                    */
/* Logic Flow : The DisplayOptions () function is passed a pointer to */
/*          the Options_Display_Menu dialog box.  The function        */
/*          ProcessDialogBox () is called with the pointer to the     */
/*          dialog box.  The variable return_code is assigned to the  */
/*          return code from ProcessDialogBox ().  If the return_code */
/*          is the Esc key, then no further action is taken.  The     */
/*          dialog box's current push button is then checked.  If the */
/*          current button is Help, then the function Error () is      */
/*          called to display the Help Error message box.             */
/*                                                                    */
/* Exit : The Options_Display_Menu dialog box has been processed.     */
/*                                                                    */
/*==================================================================*/

DisplayOptions (db)
DIALOG_BOX *db;
{
   int    return_code;

   return_code = ProcessDialogBox (db);
   if (return_code == ESC) return(-1);
   switch (db->workarea[0].current_button)
   {
      case 0:
         return (db->workarea[0].current_button);

      case 1:
         return (db->workarea[0].current_button);

      case 2:
         Error (HELP_ERROR, 0);
            return (db->workarea[0].current_button);
   }
}
```

Create the OPTIONS.C Source File Function — SortOptions ( )

The SortOptions ( ) function is called by InitializeDialogBox ( ) after it has initialized and displayed the Options_Sort_Menu dialog box. This dialog box contains a group of Check boxes that are processed by the ProcessDialogBox ( ) function. When control is returned from this function, the user has finished the dialog box.

Here again, the programmer must validate the selections made by the user. Simple dialog boxes like the ones described in this book are relatively easy to validate. It becomes more difficult when there are more than one group of work groups.

Edit the OPTIONS.C source file, type the following statements, and save the file.

```
/*======================================================================*/
/*                                                                      */
/*                                                                      */
/* Function : SortOptions (db);                                         */
/*                                                                      */
/* Purpose : This function is defined in the Options_Sort_Menu          */
/*           dialog box to be the function that InitializeDialogBox ()*/
/*           calls after the dialog box has been initialized and        */
/*           displayed.                                                 */
/*                                                                      */
/* Entry Parameters : DIALOG_BOX *db - A pointer to the dialog box to */
/*           process.                                                   */
/*                                                                      */
/* Local Data Definitions : int return_code - This variable is used    */
/*           to contain the return code from the ProcessDialogBox ()   */
/*           function.                                                  */
/*                                                                      */
/* Functions Called : ProcessDialogBox () - This function is called    */
/*           to process the Options_Display_Menu dialog box.           */
/*                                                                      */
/*           Error () - This function is called if there was an        */
/*           error processing the dialog box.                          */
/*                                                                      */
/* Logic Flow : The SortOptions () function is passed a pointer to     */
/*           the Options_Sort_Menu dialog box.  The function           */
/*           ProcessDialogBox () is called with the pointer to the     */
/*           dialog box.  The variable return_code is assigned to the */
/*           return code from ProcessDialogBox ().  If the return_code*/
/*           is the Esc key, then no further action is taken.  The     */
/*           dialog box's current push button is then checked.  If the*/
/*           current button is Help, then the function Error () is     */
/*           called to display the Help Error message box.             */
/*                                                                      */
/* Exit : The Options_Sort_Menu dialog box has been processed.         */
/*                                                                      */
/*======================================================================*/

SortOptions (db)
DIALOG_BOX *db;
```

```
{
    int return_code;

    return_code = ProcessDialogBox (db);
    if (return_code == ESC) return(-1);
    switch (db->workarea[0].current_button)
    {
        case 0:
            return (db->workarea[0].current_button);

        case 1:
            return (db->workarea[0].current_button);

        case 2:
            Error (HELP_ERROR, 0);
                return (db->workarea[0].current_button);
    }
}
```

SUMMARY

The source files FILE.C, EDIT.C, and OPTIONS.C contain the functions needed to process the action bar menus, File, Edit, and Options. The File ( ) function, defined in FILE.C, was defined in the primary menu, Main_Menu, to be the function that is called whenever one of the selections from the action bar menu File was made. The Edit ( ) function is called whenever the action bar menu Edit selections are made. The Options ( ) function is called whenever the action bar menu Options selections are made.

Each one of these functions is called from the ProcessPullDownMenu ( ) function at the appropriate time. They are passed a pointer to the action bar menu structure that defines their action bar menu. Based upon the information saved in the action bar menu variable start, the function can determine which one of the selections has been made.

Usually, after a selection has been made from the action bar menu, a dialog box or a message box is displayed to allow the user to process the selected option. For example, in this application, if the user selected the 'Create' option from the action bar menu Edit, the Create_File_Menu dialog box is initialized, displayed, and processed.

A dialog box is made up of many different parts. The data structure definition of a dialog box can be left up to the programmer to create any kind of dialog box he chooses by changing the dialog box's work area. The primary parts of a dialog box are:

- The location, size, and header string of the dialog box.
- The dialog box work area.
- The dialog box application specific function that controls the processing of the dialog box.

The work area of a dialog box can contain any combination of entry fields, push buttons, radio buttons, check boxes, and list boxes. The programmer is free to create a dialog box that fits the needs of the application following these steps.

- Define a dialog box that defines the type of dialog box you want to process.
- Create the function that initializes the dialog box. This function can manipulate the dialog box data before it calls the InitializeDialogBox ( ) function. It can also be used to verify data after the dialog box has been processed. Another possibility is that an error message box might need to be displayed.
- Create the function that the InitializeDialogBox ( ) function calls after the dialog box has been initialized and displayed on the screen. This function could save the data in the dialog box before it calls the ProcessDialogBox ( ) function to make it easier to put it back if the user decides to cancel the dialog box. Also, validation routines should be done at this point along with the displaying of error message boxes.

By creating the dialog box and the two functions that initialize and control it, the programmer can create any kind of menu driven application. In the following chapter, I define a Message box and explain about providing help to the user.

Chapter 16

THE APPLICATION ERROR AND HELP
C SOURCE FILES

INTRODUCTION

Every application has the need to display error messages and help screens to the user. In this chapter, we create two source files, ERRORS.C and HELP.C. These source files initialize, display, and process message boxes that are used in the displaying of errors and help.

The mail list application makes use of some simple error message boxes and help message boxes. The programmer should use these examples to create new and more descriptive error and help message boxes.

CREATE THE MAIL LIST APPLICATION SOURCE FILE — ERRORS.C

The ERRORS.C source file initializes, displays, and processes an error message box. The function Error ( ) is passed an error number to process and a pointer to a string that could contain additional information, such as a filename.

A message box is very similar to a dialog box except that the message box does NOT contain entry fields, radio buttons, check boxes, or list boxes. They MUST contain at least a group of push buttons. Basically, the message box takes a group of strings and displays them on the screen waiting for the user to press one of the push buttons.

The programmer should note that these message boxes do not have a function that is called after the message box is initialized and displayed, because the Message ( ) function will automatically process the message box push buttons. If the programmer wanted the message box to call another function before returning, then a function can be given to call.

Each one of the message boxes displays a given message about error conditions in the application.

Create the ERRORS.C source file, type the following statements, and save the file.

```
/*========================================================================*/
/*                                                                        */
/* File : ERRORS.C                                                        */
/*                                                                        */
/* Purpose : This 'C' source file processes the error message boxes       */
/*           for the mail list application.                               */
/*                                                                        */
/* Include Files : "\menu\message.h" - This include file contains the     */
/*           data structure definitions needed to define a message        */
/*           box.                                                         */
/*                                                                        */
/*           "\menu\keyboard.h" - This include file contains the          */
/*           keyboard definitions.                                        */
/*                                                                        */
/*           "defines.h" - This include file contains the defined         */
/*           data definitions used by the mail list application.          */
/*                                                                        */
/* Message boxes Defined : MESSAGE_BOX - Fileio_Menu - This message       */
/*           is defined to Display a General File Input / Output           */
/*           Error message.  Its upper left-hand corner is at row 80,     */
/*           column 50.  It has a width of 200 and a height of 60.        */
/*           The header string is ' General File Error .'  Its Work       */
/*           Area is WORK_AREA Fileio_Workarea and it does not call       */
/*           a function after it has been initialized and displayed.      */
/*                                                                        */
/*           MESSAGE_BOX Create_Record_Error_Menu - This message box      */
/*           is displayed whenever there is an error in the creating      */
/*           of a new customer record.                                    */
/*                                                                        */
/*           MESSAGE_BOX Edit_Record_Error_Menu - This message box is     */
/*           displayed whenever there is an error in the editing of       */
/*           a customer record.                                           */
/*                                                                        */
/*           MESSAGE_BOX Delete_Record_Error_Menu - This message box      */
/*           is displayed whenever there is an error in the deleting      */
/*           of a customer record.                                        */
/*                                                                        */
/*           MESSAGE_BOX Help_Error_Menu - This message box is            */
/*           displayed whenever there is an error in displaying help.     */
/*                                                                        */
/*           MESSAGE_BOX Create_File_Error_Menu - This message box is     */
/*           displayed whenever there is an error in the creating of      */
/*           a new customer data file.                                    */
/*                                                                        */
/*           MESSAGE_BOX Load_File_Error_Menu - This message box is       */
/*           displayed whenever there is an error in the loading of       */
/*           a customer data file.                                        */
/*                                                                        */
```

```
/*          MESSAGE_BOX Save_File_Error_Menu - This message box is   */
/*          displayed whenever there is an error in the saving of    */
/*          a customer data file.                                    */
/*                                                                   */
/*          MESSAGE_BOX Delete_File_Error_Menu - This message box is */
/*          displayed whenever there is an error in the deleting of  */
/*          a customer data file.                                    */
/*                                                                   */
/* Functions : Error () - This function is called whenever the mail  */
/*          list application needs to display an error message box   */
/*          on the screen.                                           */
/*                                                                   */
/*=================================================================*/

#include "\menu\message.h"
#include "\menu\keyboard.h"
#include "defines.h"

ITEM_PTR Fileio_Strings[] =
{
   "Cannot open",
   "                    ",
   0
};

PUSH_BUTTON Fileio_Buttons[] =
{
   {1, "Cancel", 119,  62},
   {2, "Retry" , 119, 133},
   {3, "Help"  , 119, 202},
   0
};

MSG_AREA Fileio_Workarea[] =
{
   {Fileio_Strings, 1, Fileio_Buttons, 3, 0},
   0
};

MESSAGE_BOX Fileio_Menu =
{
   80, 50, 200, 60, " General File Error ", Fileio_Workarea, 0
};

PUSH_BUTTON Edit_Record_Buttons[] =
{
   {1, "Cancel", 130,  32},
   {2, "Retry" , 130, 135},
   {3, "Help"  , 130, 242},
   0
};

ITEM_PTR Create_Record_Error_Strings[] =
```

```
{
   "The Create Record function is not complete.",
   "                                            ",
   "         The record was NOT created !       ",
   0
};

MSG_AREA Create_Record_Error_Workarea[] =
{
   {Create_Record_Error_Strings, 3, Edit_Record_Buttons, 3, 0},
   0
};

MESSAGE_BOX Create_Record_Error_Menu =
{
   70, 20, 270, 84, " Create Record Error ",
   Create_Record_Error_Workarea, 0
};

ITEM_PTR Edit_Record_Error_Strings[] =
{
   " The Edit Record function is not complete. ",
   "                                           ",
   "         The record was NOT updated !      ",
   0
};

MSG_AREA Edit_Record_Error_Workarea[] =
{
   {Edit_Record_Error_Strings, 3, Edit_Record_Buttons, 3, 0},
   0
};

MESSAGE_BOX Edit_Record_Error_Menu =
{
   70, 20, 270, 84, " Edit Record Error ",
   Edit_Record_Error_Workarea, 0
};

ITEM_PTR Delete_Record_Error_Strings[] =
{
   "The Delete Record function is not complete.",
   "                                           ",
   "         The record was NOT deleted !      ",
   0
};

MSG_AREA Delete_Record_Error_Workarea[] =
{
   {Delete_Record_Error_Strings, 3, Edit_Record_Buttons, 3, 0},
   0
};
```

```
MESSAGE_BOX Delete_Record_Error_Menu =
{
    70, 20, 270, 84, " Delete Record Error ",
    Delete_Record_Error_Workarea, 0
};

PUSH_BUTTON Help_Error_Buttons[] =
{
    {1, "Cancel", 110, 130},
    0
};

ITEM_PTR Help_Error_Strings[] =
{
    "Help is not available for this function !",
    0
};

MSG_AREA Help_Error_Workarea[] =
{
    {Help_Error_Strings, 1, Help_Error_Buttons, 1, 0},
    0
};

MESSAGE_BOX Help_Error_Menu =
{
    70, 20, 270, 64, " Help Error ", Help_Error_Workarea, 0
};

PUSH_BUTTON File_Error_Buttons[] =
{
    {1, "Cancel", 130,  32},
    {2, "Retry" , 130, 135},
    {3, "Help"  , 130, 242},
    0
};

ITEM_PTR Create_File_Error_Strings[] =
{
    "The Create File function is not complete !",
    "                                          ",
    "          The file is NOT created !       ",
    0
};

MSG_AREA Create_File_Error_Workarea[] =
{
    {Create_File_Error_Strings, 3, File_Error_Buttons, 3, 0},
    0
};

MESSAGE_BOX Create_File_Error_Menu =
{
```

```
   70, 20, 270, 84, " Create File Error ",
   Create_File_Error_Workarea, 0
};

ITEM_PTR Load_File_Error_Strings[] =
{
   " The Load File function is not complete ! ",
   "                                          ",
   "          The file is NOT loaded !        ",
   0
};

MSG_AREA Load_File_Error_Workarea[] =
{
   {Load_File_Error_Strings, 3, File_Error_Buttons, 3, 0},
   0
};

MESSAGE_BOX Load_File_Error_Menu =
{
   70, 20, 270, 84, " Load File Error ",
   Load_File_Error_Workarea, 0
};

ITEM_PTR Save_File_Error_Strings[] =
{
   " The Save File function is not complete ! ",
   "                                          ",
   "          The file is NOT saved !         ",
   0
};

MSG_AREA Save_File_Error_Workarea[] =
{
   {Save_File_Error_Strings, 3, File_Error_Buttons, 3, 0},
   0
};

MESSAGE_BOX Save_File_Error_Menu =
{
   70, 20, 270, 84, " Save File Error ",
   Save_File_Error_Workarea, 0

};

ITEM_PTR Delete_File_Error_Strings[] =
{
   "The Delete File function is not complete !",
   "                                          ",
   "          The file is NOT deleted !       ",
   0
};
```

```
MSG_AREA Delete_File_Error_Workarea[] =
{
   {Delete_File_Error_Strings, 3, File_Error_Buttons, 3, 0},
   0
};

MESSAGE_BOX Delete_File_Error_Menu =
{
   70, 20, 270, 84, " Delete File Error ",
   Delete_File_Error_Workarea, 0
};
```

Create the ERRORS.C Source File Function — Error ( )

The Error ( ) function is called by the application whenever it needs to display a particular error message box on the screen. It is called with an error number and a string that contains additional information about the error.

Just like a dialog box, the message box data can be changed before the call to the Message ( ) function. In this way the programmer can fill in data, such as a filename that was invalid, before the message box is displayed.

Edit the ERRORS.C source file, type the following statements, and save the file.

```
/*=====================================================================*/
/*                                                                   */
/* Function : Error (error_number, string);                          */
/*                                                                   */
/* Purpose : This function is called whenever the application needs  */
/*           to display an error message on the screen.              */
/*                                                                   */
/* Entry Parameters : int error_number - The error number to process. */
/*           The error number defines are in the "defines.h" include  */
/*           source file.                                            */
/*                                                                   */
/* Functions Called : Message () - This function is called to        */
/*           initialize, display, and process the message boxes.     */
/*                                                                   */
/* Logic Flow : The Error () function is called to process all of the */
/*           error message boxes in the application.  It is passed    */
/*           the type of error and any strings needed by the Error () */
/*           function. First a switch is performed on the error       */
/*           number passed.  If the error is FILEIO_ERROR, then the   */
/*           string passed is a filename and it is inserted into the  */
/*           message box display strings.  The function message () is  */
/*           called to process the Fileio_Menu message box. If the    */
/*           error is CREATE_RECORD_ERROR, then the Message ()        */
/*           function is called to do the Create_Record_Error_Menu.   */
/*           If the error is EDIT_RECORD_ERROR, then the Message ()   */
/*           function is called to process the Edit_Record_Error_Menu.*/
/*           If the error is DELETE_RECORD_ERROR, then the Message () */
```

```
/*              function processes the Delete_Record_Error_Menu.  If the */
/*              error is CREATE_FILE_ERROR, then the Message () function  */
/*              processes the Create_File_Error_Menu.  If the error is   */
/*              LOAD_FILE_ERROR, then the Message () function processes   */
/*              the Load_File_Error_Menu.  If the error is               */
/*              SAVE_FILE_ERROR, then the Message () function processes   */
/*              the Save_File_Error_Menu.  If the error is               */
/*              DELETE_FILE_ERROR, then the Message () function           */
/*              processes the Delete_File_Error_Menu.  If the error is   */
/*              HELP_ERROR, then the Message () function is called to     */
/*              process the Help_Error_Menu.                            */
/*                                                                      */
/* Exit : The error message box is initialized, displayed, and           */
/*        processed.                                                    */
/*                                                                      */
/*======================================================================*/

Error (error_number, string)
int error_number, string;
{
    int return_code;

    switch (error_number)
    {
      case FILEIO_ERROR:
         sprintf (Fileio_Strings[0] + strlen (Fileio_Strings[0])," ");
         sprintf (Fileio_Strings[1], "%s", string);
         Message (&Fileio_Menu);
         return (Fileio_Workarea[0].current_button);

      case CREATE_RECORD_ERROR:
         Message (&Create_Record_Error_Menu);
         return (Create_Record_Error_Workarea[0].current_button);

      case EDIT_RECORD_ERROR:
         Message (&Edit_Record_Error_Menu);
         return (Edit_Record_Error_Workarea[0].current_button);

      case DELETE_RECORD_ERROR:
         Message (&Delete_Record_Error_Menu);
         return (Delete_Record_Error_Workarea[0].current_button);

      case CREATE_FILE_ERROR:
         Message (&Create_File_Error_Menu);
         return (Create_File_Error_Workarea[0].current_button);

      case LOAD_FILE_ERROR:
         Message (&Load_File_Error_Menu);
         return (Load_File_Error_Workarea[0].current_button);

      case SAVE_FILE_ERROR:
         Message (&Save_File_Error_Menu);
         return (Save_File_Error_Workarea[0].current_button);
```

```
    case DELETE_FILE_ERROR:
       Message (&Delete_File_Error_Menu);
       return (Delete_File_Error_Workarea[0].current_button);

    case HELP_ERROR:
       Message (&Help_Error_Menu);
       return (Help_Error_Workarea[0].current_button);
   }
}
```

CREATE THE MAIL LIST APPLICATION SOURCE FILE — HELP.C

The HELP.C source file contains the function Help ( ). This function is called whenever help was selected from the action bar menu Help.

Every application should provide help to the user. Almost every dialog box should contain a push button that represents help to the user. When the user presses the Help push button a message box containing help on that particular dialog box should be displayed.

The mail list application does not define all of the help message boxes that could be defined. It only defines the main help message box from the action bar menu Help. The programmer should expand these help message boxes when he writes his own applications.

In large applications, it is generally not a good idea to store all of the help messages in memory. Instead, the Help messages should be stored on disk and read in according to a help number that is passed to the help function. In this way the programmer can save valuable memory space and can make each help message box look and feel very much the same.

Create the HELP.C source file, type the following statements, and save the file.

```
/*======================================================================*/
/*                                                                      */
/* File : HELP.C                                                        */
/*                                                                      */
/* Purpose : This 'C' source file processes the action bar menu Help    */
/*           for the mail list application.                             */
/*                                                                      */
/* Include Files : "\menu\message.h" - This include file contains the   */
/*           data structure definitions needed to define a message      */
/*           box.                                                       */
/*                                                                      */
/* Message boxes Defined : MESSAGE_BOX - Main_Help_Menu - This message  */
/*           box is defined to display a sample help message box.       */
/*                                                                      */
```

```
/* Functions : Error () - This function is called whenever the action */
/*             bar menu Help is selected.  It displays a sample Help   */
/*             message box on the screen.                              */
/*                                                                     */
/*=====================================================================*/

#include "\menu\message.h"

PUSH_BUTTON Main_Help_Buttons[] =
{
   {1, "Exit", 130, 122},
   0
};

ITEM_PTR Main_Help_Strings[] =
{
   "This is a sample Help Screen using a ",
   "                                     ",
   "  Message Box to do the displaying.  ",
   0
};

MSG_AREA Main_Help_Workarea[] =
{
   {Main_Help_Strings, 3, Main_Help_Buttons, 1, 0},
   0
};

MESSAGE_BOX Main_Help_Menu =
{
   70, 20, 270, 84, " Mail List Main Menu Help ",
   Main_Help_Workarea, 0
};

/*=====================================================================*/
/*                                                                     */
/* Function : Help ()                                                  */
/*                                                                     */
/* Purpose : This function is called whenever the user selects Help    */
/*           from the action bar menu Help.                            */
/*                                                                     */
/*                                                                     */
/* Functions Called : Message () - This function is called to          */
/*           initialize, display, and process the message boxes.       */
/*                                                                     */
/* Logic Flow : The Help () function is called to process the action   */
/*           bar menu help.  It displays a sample message box that     */
/*           can be used to display helps messages to the user.        */
/*                                                                     */
/* Exit : The action bar menu help has been processed.                 */
/*                                                                     */
/*=====================================================================*/
```

```
Help ()
{
   Message (&Main_Help_Menu);
   return (Main_Help_Workarea[0].current_button);
}
```

SUMMARY

The source files ERRORS.C and HELP.C make use of message boxes to display information to the user. The Error ( ) function is called independently by the application and is passed an error number indicating which error has occurred. The Help ( ) function is called whenever the 'Help' option is selected from the action bar menu help.

By separating these functions into their own source files, the programmer can more easily find where these message boxes are defined. Both the Error ( ) function and the Help ( ) function can be improved upon by creating a disk access system to retrieve the message box data for displaying.

Appendix A

THE SOURCE FILES BY DIRECTORY

THE CGA GRAPHICS LIBRARY

Directory - **GRAPHICS**

BUILD.BAT   This batch file contains the commands that build a new CGA Graphics Library. Whenever the programmer needs to recompile code in the CGA Graphics Library, type BUILD while in the GRAPHICS subdirectory.

MAKEFILE.CGA   This file is used by the Make-File Utility to determine which source files need to be recompiled to build a new CGA Graphics Library.

CGAGRAPH.LNK   This file is used by the Library Linker Utility to link together the correct files to make a new CGA Graphics Library.

GRAPHICS.H   This source include file contains the defined data definitions needed by the CGA Graphics Library.

COLORS.H   This source include file contains the defined color definitions used by the CGA Graphics Library.

FONTSET.H   This source include file contains the character set icon data definitions used in the CGA Graphics Library.

CGAGRAFC.C   This 'C' source file contains the CGA Graphics Library functions that are written in 'C' and use the DOS BIOS service calls.

CGAGRAFC.OBJ   This object file is the compiled version of the CGAGRAFC.C source file.

CGAGRAFA.ASM   This assembler file contains the CGA Graphics Library functions that are written in assembler and use the Direct Video Access Method.

CGAGRAFA.OBJ   This object file is the compiled version of the CGAGRAFA.ASM source file.

CGAGRAPH.LIB   This library file is the CGA Graphics Library. It is to be linked in with the application to form an executable file.

CGAGRAPH.MAP   This file is generated by the Library Linker Utility to show a mapping of the functions contained in the CGA Graphics Library.

THE MENU LIBRARY

Directory - **MENU**

BUILD.BAT   This batch file contains the commands that build a new Menu Library. Whenever the programmer needs to recompile the code in the Menu Library, type BUILD while in the MENU subdirectory.

MAKEFILE.MNU   This is used by the Make-File Utility to determine which source files to recompile to build a new Menu Library.

MENU.LNK   This file is used by the Library Linker Utility to link together the files that make up the Menu Library.

DEFINES.H   This source include file contains the most commonly used data definitions needed by the Menu Library.

KEYBOARD.H   This source include file contains the data definitions needed to interpret keystrokes from the keyboard.

MENU.H   This source include file contains the data definitions needed to define a primary menu used by the Menu Library.

DIALOG.H   This source include file contains the data definitions needed to define a dialog box used by the Menu Library.

MESSAGE.H   This source include file contains the data definitions needed to define a message box used by the Menu Library.

ARROWS.H   This source include file contains the icon data that represents the arrows that are displayed in the list box scroll bars used by the Menu Library.

RADIO.H   This source include file contains the icon data that represents the radio buttons that are displayed by the Menu Library.

CHECKBOX.H   This source include file contains the icon data that represents the check boxes that are displayed by the Menu Library.

KEYBOARD.C   This 'C' source file contains the functions that return the keystrokes from the keyboard.

KEYBOARD.OBJ   This object file is the compiled version of the KEYBOARD.C source file.

MENU.C   This 'C' source file contains the functions that are needed to process a primary menu for the Menu Library. The function Menu ( ) is called by the application when it needs to process a primary menu.

MENU.OBJ   This object file is the compiled version of the MENU.C source file.

ACTION.C   This 'C' source file contains the functions that are needed to initialize, display, and process a primary menu's action bar for the Menu Library.

ACTION.OBJ   This object file is the compiled version of the ACTION.C source file.

PULLDOWN.C   This 'C' source file contains the functions that are needed to initialize, display, and process a pull-down menu for the Menu Library.

PULLDOWN.OBJ   This object file is the compiled version of the PULLDOWN.C source file.

DIALOG.C   This 'C' source file contains the functions that are needed to initialize, display, and process a dialog box for the Menu Library.

DIALOG.OBJ   This object file is the compiled version of the DIALOG.C source file.

PUSHBUTN.C	This 'C' source file contains the functions that are needed to initialize, display, and process a dialog box's push buttons for the Menu Library.
PUSHBUTN.OBJ	This object file is the compiled version of the PUSHBUTN.C source file.
ENTRY.C	This 'C' source file contains the functions that are needed to initialize, display, and process a dialog box's push buttons for the Menu Library.
ENTRY.OBJ	This object file is the compiled version of the ENTRY.C source file.
GROUPS.C	This 'C' source file contains the functions that are needed to initialize, display, and process a dialog box's group of radio buttons or check boxes for the Menu Library.
GROUPS.OBJ	This object file is the compiled version of the GROUPS.C source file.
LISTBOX.C	This 'C' source file contains the functions that are needed to initialize, display, and process a dialog box's list box for the Menu Library.
LISTBOX.OBJ	This object file is the compiled version of the LISTBOX.C source file.
MESSAGE.C	This 'C' source file contains the functions that are needed to initialize, display, and process a message box for the Menu Library.
MESSAGE.OBJ	This object file is the compiled version of the MESSAGE.C source file.
MENU.LIB	This library file is the Menu Library. It is linked in with the application to form an executable file.
MENU.MAP	This file was created by the Library Linker Utility and is a mapping of the functions contained in the Menu Library.

THE FILER LIBRARY

Directory - **FILER**

BUILD.BAT	This batch file contains the commands needed to build a new Filer Library. When the programmer needs to build a new Filer Library, type BUILD while in the FILER subdirectory.
MAKEFILE.FIL	This file is used by the Make-File Utility to determine which source files need to be compiled to create a new Filer Library.
FILE.LNK	This file is used by the Library Linker Utility to link the files needed to create a new Filer Library.
RECORD.H	This source include file contains the data structure definitions needed to define a customer record used by the Filer Library.
RECORD.C	This 'C' source file contains the functions needed to initialize the customer data records from disk.
RECORD.OBJ	This object file is the compiled version of the RECORD.C source file.
INDEX.C	This 'C' source file contains the functions needed to initialize the customer data index used to read customer records from disk.
INDEX.OBJ	This object file is the compiled version of the INDEX.C source file.
FILER.LIB	This library file is the Filer Library. It is linked in with the application to form an executable file.
FILER.MAP	This file is created by the Library Linker Utility and it is a mapping of the functions in the Filer Library.

THE MAIL LIST APPLICATION

Directory - **MAILLIST**

BUILD.BAT	This batch file contains the commands needed to build a new executable form of the mail list application.
MAKEFILE.APP	This file is used by the Make-File Utility to determine which source files are compiled to build a new mail list application executable file.
APPL.LNK	This file is used by the Linker Utility to link together the files needed to build a new mail list application executable file.
DEFINES.H	This source file contains the defined data definitions used by the mail list application.
MAIL.C	This 'C' source file contains the 'C' required function main ( ) and defines the global variables used by the mail list application.
MAIL.OBJ	This object file is the compiled version of the MAIL.C source file.
MAINMENU.C	This 'C' source file defines the mail list application's primary menu, Main_Menu, and contains the function that issues the call to the Menu Library to begin processing of the primary menu.
MAINMENU.OBJ	This object file is the compiled version of the MAINMENU.C source file.
MAILLIST.C	This 'C' source file contains the functions needed to process the mail list application's primary menu and the functions needed to initialize and update the primary menu list box.
MAILLIST.OBJ	This object file is the compiled version of the MAILLIST.C source file.
FILE.C	This 'C' source file defines the dialog boxes and contains the functions needed to process a selection made from the action bar menu File.
FILE.OBJ	This object file is the compiled version of the FILE.C source file.

EDIT.C	This 'C' source file defines the dialog boxes and contains the functions needed to process a selection made from the action bar menu Edit.
EDIT.OBJ	This object file is the compiled version of the EDIT.C source file.
OPTIONS.C	This 'C' source file defines the dialog boxes and contains the functions needed to process a selection from the action bar menu Options.
OPTIONS.OBJ	This object file is the compiled version of the OPTIONS.C source file.
ERRORS.C	This 'C' source file defines the message boxes and contains the functions needed to display an error message box to the user.
ERRORS.OBJ	This object file is the compiled version of the ERRORS.C source file.
HELP.C	This 'C' source file defines the message boxes and contains the functions needed to display a help message box for the mail list application.
HELP.OBJ	This object file is the compiled version of the HELP.C source file.
TESTFILE.IDX	This file is used by the mail list application to contain an index to the sample customer records stored in the TESTFILE.DAT file.
TESTFILE.DAT	This file contains the data for each customer record for the mail list application.
MAIL.EXE	This executable file is the mail list application executable file.

Appendix B

THE CGA GRAPHICS LIBRARY FUNCTIONS

BufferToDisplay ( ) - This function displays a buffer of display information on the screen at the given upper left-hand row and column coordinates, the window width and height, and a pointer to the display buffer.

ClearScreen ( ) - This function clears the screen in a given color.

ClearWindow ( ) - This function clears a window on the screen, given the upper left-hand row and column coordinates, the window width and height, and the color.

DisplayChar ( ) - This function displays the given character icon on the screen starting at the given upper left-hand row and column coordinates in the given foreground and background colors.

DisplayCursor ( ) - This function displays on the screen an underline under the character passed starting at the given upper left-hand row and column coordinates in the given foreground and background colors.

DisplayDot ( ) - This function displays a dot on the screen at the given row and column coordinates and in the given color.

DisplayIcon ( ) - This function displays an icon on the screen at the given upper left-hand row and column coordinates, the icon width and height, and a pointer to the icon to display.

DisplayString ( ) - This function displays on the screen a given string of characters that are terminated with a NULL, starting at the given upper left-hand row and column coordinates in the given foreground and background colors.

DisplayStrNum ( ) - This function displays on the screen a given string of characters starting at the given upper left-hand row and column coordinates in the given foreground and background colors and the given number of characters to display from the string onto the screen.

DisplayToBuffer ( ) - This function copies a window of display information into a buffer so that the window display information can be restored back to the screen. The function is called with a pointer to the buffer, the upper left-hand row and column coordinates, and the window width and height.

DrawBox ( ) - This function draws a box on the screen starting at the given upper left-hand row and column coordinates for the given box width and box height and in the given box color.

GetCrtMode ( ) - This function returns the current screen CRT mode in use at the time the call is made.

GetFontNum ( ) - This function returns the font set number to use when displaying a character or string of characters on the screen in the given foreground and background colors.

HLine ( ) - This function draws a horizontal line on the screen at the given starting row and column coordinates, for the given line length, and in the given line color.

MapFontChar ( ) - This function returns the font set number associated with the character passed.

ScrollLeft ( ) - This function is used by the CGA Graphics Library to scroll a window of screen data to the left.

ScrollRight ( ) - This function is used by the CGA Graphics Library to scroll a window of screen data to the right.

ScrollVertical ( ) - This function is used by the CGA Graphics Library to scroll a window of screen data up or down.

ScrollWindow ( ) - This function is called by the application whenever a window of screen data needs to be scrolled up, down, left, or right. The function is called with the destination row and column coordinates, the source row and column coordinates, the window width and height, and the direction to scroll.

SelectDisplayPage ( ) - This function activates the requested video display page.

SetCrtMode ( ) - This function sets the screen CRT mode to the one that is requested.

VLine ( ) - This function draws a vertical line on the screen at the given starting row and column coordinates, for the given line length, and in the given line color.

THE MENU LIBRARY SOURCE FILE FUNCTIONS

ButtonOutline ( ) - This function is called to draw the outline around a push button.

DisplayCheckBoxes ( ) - This function display a work group of check boxes on the screen.

DisplayEntryField ( ) - This function displays an entry field on the screen.

DisplayListBoxColumn ( ) - This function displays the dialog box's list box display strings for a given column on the screen.

DisplayListBoxItem ( ) - This function displays a given dialog box's list box display string on the screen.

DisplayPushButton ( ) - This function is called to display a given push button on the screen.

DisplayRadioButtons ( ) - This function displays a work group of radio buttons on the screen.

DrawMenuOutline ( ) - This function is called by the Menu ( ) function to initialize the primary menu on the screen.

InitializeActionBar ( ) - This function is called by the Menu ( ) function to initialize the action bar of a primary menu.

InitializeDialogBox ( ) - This function initializes and displays a dialog box on the screen.

InitializeEntryFields ( ) - This function initializes a dialog box's entry fields on the screen.

InitializeListBox ( ) - This function initializes and displays a dialog box's list box on the screen.

InitializePushButtons ( ) - This function initializes and displays a dialog box's push buttons on the screen.

InitializeWorkGroups ( ) - This function initializes the dialog box work groups of radio buttons or check boxes.

GetKey ( ) - This function returns a keystroke from the keyboard.

Menu ( ) - This function is called by the application whenever a primary menu needs to be displayed on the screen.

Message ( ) - This function initializes, displays, and processes a message box.

ProcessActionBar ( ) - This function is called to process the action bar whenever the user has pressed a key that activates one of the action bar menus.

ProcessDialogBox ( ) - This function processes a dialog box that has been initialized and displayed on the screen.

ProcessEntryField ( ) - This function processes an entry field.

ProcessListBox ( ) - This function processes a given dialog box's list box.

ProcessPushButton ( ) - This function is called to process a dialog box's push buttons.

ProcessPullDownMenu ( ) - This functions initializes, displays, and processes a pull-down menu.

SearchCheckBoxes ( ) - This function is called to search the check boxes for the next logical field.

SearchEntryFields ( ) - This function is called to search the entry fields for the next logical field.

SearchGroups ( ) - This function is called to search the work groups for the next logical field.

SearchNextField ( ) - This function is called to search for the next logical field to be processed in the dialog box.

SearchPushButtons ( ) - This function is called to search the push buttons for the next logical field.

SearchRadioButtons ( ) - This function is called to search the radio buttons for the next logical field.

UpdateListBox ( ) - This function updates the dialog box's list box whenever it needs to scroll up, down, left, or right.

UpdateHorizontalScrollBar ( ) - This function updates the dialog box's list box horizontal scroll bars on the screen.

UpdateVerticalScrollBar ( ) - This function updates the dialog box's list box vertical scroll bars on the screen.

THE FILER LIBRARY SOURCE FILE FUNCTIONS

ReadIndex ( ) - This function reads the index of a customer data file.

InitDataFile ( ) - This function is called by the application to initialize a new customer data file into memory.

ReadRecords ( ) - This function is called by the InitDataFile ( ) function to read the customer data into the Record[] array.

THE MAIL LIST APPLICATION SOURCE FILE FUNCTIONS

CopyMailListRecord ( ) - This function is called to copy a customer record into a list box display string.

CopyRecordTemp ( ) - This function is called to copy a given customer record into the temporary customer record.

CreateFile ( ) - This function is called by the InitializeDialogBox ( ) function after the dialog box Create_File_Menu has been initialized and displayed.

CreateNewRecord ( ) - This function is called by the InitializeDialogBox ( ) function after the dialog box Create_Record_Menu has been initialized and displayed.

DeleteCurrentRecord ( ) - This function is called by the InitializeDialogBox ( ) function after the dialog box Delete_Record_Menu has been initialized and displayed.

DeleteFile ( ) - This function is called by the InitializeDialogBox ( ) function after the dialog box Delete_File_Menu has been initialized and displayed.

DisplayOptions ( ) - This function is called after the Options_Display_Menu dialog box has been initialized and displayed on the screen.

Edit ( ) - This function was defined by the primary menu, Main_Menu, to be called whenever the user has selected an option from the action bar menu Edit. It processes the selection and displays the appropriate dialog box.

EditCurrentRecord ( ) - This function is called by the InitializeDialogBox ( ) function after the dialog box Edit_Record_Menu has been initialized and displayed.

Error ( ) - This function is called whenever the mail list application needs to display an error message box on the screen.

InitializeMailListBox ( ) - This function is the function that the InitializeListBox ( ) function calls to initialize the display strings for the list box.

InitializeTempRecord ( ) - This function is called to initialize the temporary record for creating a new customer record.

File ( ) - This function was defined by the primary menu, Main_Menu, to be called whenever the user has selected an option from the action bar menu File. It processes the selection and displays the appropriate dialog box.

Help ( ) - This function is called whenever the action bar menu Help is selected. It displays a sample help message box on the screen.

LoadFile ( ) - This function is called by the InitializeDialogBox ( ) function after the dialog box Load_File_Menu has been initialized and displayed.

MailList ( ) - This function is the function that the Menu ( ) function calls after it has initialized and displayed the primary menu, Main_Menu.

main ( ) - This standard 'C' function is the first function that is called when the application begins.

MainMenu ( ) - This function is called to process the primary menu of the mail list application, Main_Menu.

Options ( ) - This function was defined by the primary menu, Main_Menu, to be the function that is called if one of the action bar menu Options selections have been chosen. It will display the appropriate dialog box associated with the selection.

SaveFile ( ) - This function is called by the InitializeDialogBox ( ) function after the dialog box Save_File_Menu has been initialized and displayed.

SortOptions ( ) - This function is called after the Options_Sort_Menu dialog box has been initialized and displayed on the screen.

UpdateMailListBox ( ) - This function is the function that is called whenever the list box needs its display strings to be updated.

Index